MATRIMONY IN THE TRUE CHURCH

Matrimony in the True Church

The Seventeenth-Century Quaker
Marriage Approbation Discipline

KRISTIANNA POLDER
Independent Scholar

LONDON AND NEW YORK

First published 2015 by Ashgate Publishing

Published 2016 by Routledge
2 Park Square, Milton Park, Abingdon, Oxon OX14 4RN
711 Third Avenue, New York, NY 10017, USA

Routledge is an imprint of the Taylor & Francis Group, an informa business

Copyright © 2015 Kristianna Polder

Kristianna Polder has asserted her right under the Copyright, Designs and Patents Act, 1988, to be identified as the author of this work.

All rights reserved . No part of this book may be reprinted or reproduced or utilised in any form or by any electronic, mechanical, or other means, now known or hereafter invented, including photocopying and recording, or in any information storage or retrieval system, without permission in writing from the publishers.

Notices:
Product or corporate names may be trademarks or registered trademarks, and are used only for identification and explanation without intent to infringe.

British Library Cataloguing in Publication Data
A catalogue record for this book is available from the British Library

The Library of Congress has cataloged the printed edition as follows:
Polder, Kristianna.
　　Matrimony in the True Church: The Seventeenth-Century Quaker Marriage
　　Approbation Discipline / by Kristianna Polder.
　　　　pages　cm
　　Includes bibliographical references and index.
　　1. Society of Friends – Discipline. 2. Marriage – Religious aspects – Society of Friends
　　– History of doctrines. I. Title.
BX7740.P56 2015
264'.096085 – dc23
2015009335

ISBN 9781409466888 (hbk)

Contents

Acknowledgements		vii
Introduction		**1**
	The Historical Context of the Early Quaker Movement	1
	Fox, Fell and the Early Quaker Obsession with Marriage Approbation	6
	A Survey of the Secondary Sources Concerning Fox, Fell and the Early Marriage Discipline	10
	The Range and Resources of this Work	27
1	**Approbation and 'Clearness': The Early Quaker Marriage Discipline**	**31**
	Maintenance of Morality and Order	32
	Seventeenth-Century Courtship and Marriage	38
	Margaret Fell and George Fox: Their Rejection of 'Hireling Priests' and Their Defence of the Legitimacy of Quaker Marriages	43
	Clearness and Approbation: The Early Quaker Marriage Discipline	51
	Certificates, Investigations, Contrition and Regulation: The Role of the Men's Monthly Meeting	64
	The Wedding Ceremony	85
	'According to the Order of the Gospell': The Rise of the Women's Meetings	93
	Conclusion	112
2	**The True Church Coming out of the Wilderness: The Theological and Conceptual Foundation of the Early Quaker Marriage Discipline**	**115**
	Up from the Wilderness: The Return of the True Church	119
	The Communal Rise of the True Church	123
	Individual Exodus from the Wilderness	128
	Fox's Predecessors and Influences: Eschatological Hopes and Personal Conversion	132
	Maintaining the True Church: A Return to Paradise and Purity	138

	Primitive Christianity: The True Church and Gospel Order	144
	Marriage of the Lamb: Unity and Witness in Quaker Marriages	149
	Threat to the Marriage of the Lamb: Marriage with the World	154
	Resisting Exogamy on Spiritual Grounds: The Proposal of Colonel West to Margaret Fell the Younger	155
	'As it was in the beginning': Honourable Marriages and Undefiled Beds	161
	Gospel Family-Order in Households of Faith	180
3	**The Marriage of Margaret Fell and George Fox**	**199**
	The Royal Seed and the Book of Revelation	200
	The Courtship and Marriage Approbation Process of Margaret Fell and George Fox	208
	The Marriage Approbation and Wedding Testimonies	215
	Coming up out of the Wilderness: The Lamb and the New Jerusalem	227
	'Marriage of the Lamb': Fox's Self-perception in Relation to the Divine	234
	The Undefiled Bed of George Fox and Margaret Fell	247
	The Marital Relationship of George and Margaret Fox	253
Conclusion		**267**
Bibliography		*275*
Index		*291*

Acknowledgements

There are many who have been instrumental in helping me complete this work. I would like to acknowledge and thank Dr Marie-Luise Ehrenschwendtner for her valuable feedback and guidance. I would also like to thank Dr Nicholas Thompson for his advice and encouragement, particularly during the early stages of research. I am indebted to the staff of the Queen Mother Library at the University of Aberdeen, and Jennifer Milligan, the Senior Library Assistant at the Library of the Religious Society of Friends in London, who aided me in locating important resources. I thank my family for their steadfast love and support. Finally, I dedicate this book to the memory of my grandmother, Helen, who instilled in me a love of history.

Introduction

Now after Adam and Eve had eaten, they were naked, and hid themselves in the trees of the garden. Then they heard the voice of the Lord God, in the Cool of the day: 'Adam, where art thou? While thou keptst in my image thou wert my Friend.'[1]

– George Fox

The Historical Context of the Early Quaker Movement

Following the beheading of Charles I in 1649, societal and religious upheaval reached a boiling point in England. With the loss of Charles' head, the monarchy toppled, and a new era was believed to be at hand, the dawning of which was largely understood and shaped through the lens of the biblical narrative and scripture.[2] Religious visionaries and politicians alike looked to scripture for interpretations of the tumultuous times, with little distinction between the realms of religion and politics.[3] The Fifth Monarchists expected the monarchical rule of Christ on earth, as apparently predicted in the book of Revelation; the Diggers anticipated economic equality, based on a passage from the Book of Acts; and the Levellers demanded a democratic republic, proclaiming human equality.[4] For others, this was a time for the Puritan faith to be vindicated and a godly commonwealth to be established.[5] Yet when Cromwell eventually sat as

---

[1] *George Fox's Sermon at Wheeler Street, London, at the General Meeting of 1st of 4th Month, 1680*, henceforth abbreviated to *George Fox's Sermon at Wheeler Street, 1680*. (Hugh Barbour and Arthur O. Roberts [Eds], *Early Quaker Writings: 1650–1700* [Wallington, PA: Pendle Hill Publications, 2004], 503.)

[2] The historian Christopher Hill explains that the Bible permeated arts, sciences and literature, and was as much the central authority on economics and politics as it was on religion and morals (Christopher Hill, *The English Bible and the Seventeenth-Century Revolution* [London: Penguin Books, 1993], 34, 31).

[3] Christopher Hill, *The World Turned Upside Down: Radical Ideas During the English Revolution* (London: Penguin Books, 1988), 14.

[4] Christopher Hill, 'Quakers and the English Revolution'. (Michael Mullett [Ed.], *New Light on George Fox (1624–1691): A Collection of Essays* [York: William Sessions Limited, 1991], 25.)

[5] Hugh Barbour and J. William Frost, *The Quakers* (New York, NY: Greenwood Press, 1988), 16.

Lord Protector, Puritans were no longer united, as radicals and conservatives could not agree on a God-ordained system of religious and political liberty.[6]

English men and women, who found solace as members of religious groups that challenged the status quo of the established Puritan Church, were known as dissenters. Several of these dissenters were successors of separatists who had already existed in Elizabethan England.[7] In addition to the abovementioned politically motivated separatists, a number of other emerging sects included Brownists, Independents, Baptists, Millenarians, Familists, Seekers and Ranters. The historian Keith Thomas provides a useful definition of a Civil War 'sect' as a group who believed in a pure church, made spiritual regeneration a condition of membership, and insisted upon separation from the national church which contained ungodly elements.[8] Thomas suggests these groups usually encouraged the complete self-government of individual congregations, the direct inspiration of the Holy Spirit and lay preaching, and tended to devalue any outward religious ordinances and formal education for ministry that would promote spiritual inequality of the two sexes.[9]

Of the various sects that emerged in the wake of the Civil War during the Interregnum and bore the above traits outlined by Thomas, it is estimated that the Religious Society of Friends (or pejoratively the 'Quakers' for their unusual physical trembling during worship) attracted the most followers, culminating to approximately 60,000 members by 1660.[10] Under a divided Puritan parliament, the early Quakers apparently appealed to the discontent of many dissenters. Sympathetic to Quaker spirituality, the Quaker historian Hugh Barbour asserts the early Friends essentially picked up the failed Puritan triumph, continuing and expanding 'the Lamb's War' for God's victory, *not* in and through societal structures created by humanity, but rather within human hearts.[11] The 'Lamb's War' did not rest entirely on certain changes in political entities, the toppling of the monarch or the restoration of the parliament. While political circumstances and issues were not completely moot for the early Quakers, their early primary mission was driven by a prophetic call to stir up inner repentance by turning

---

[6] Ibid, 5.

[7] Keith Thomas, 'Women and the Civil War Sects', *Past and Present*, 13 (1958): 42–62; reprinted in Trevor Aston (Ed.), *Crisis in Europe, 1560–1660* (London: Routledge & Kegan Paul, 1965), 320.

[8] Ibid.

[9] Ibid.

[10] Phyllis Mack, *Visionary Women: Ecstatic Prophecy in Seventeenth Century England* (Berkeley, CA: University of California Press, 1994), 1; Catie Gill, *Women in the Seventeenth-Century Quaker Community: A Literary Study of Political Identities, 1650–1700* (Farnham: Ashgate Publishing Limited, 2005), 12; Barry Reay, *The Quakers and the English Revolution* (New York, NY: St. Martins, 1985), 9. The term 'Quakers' was adopted by the Society.

[11] Barbour and Frost, *The Quakers*, 4.

towards the 'inward light', within the consciences of the people both in England and around the world, in order to usher in the return of the True Church of God.[12] In 1658, an early prominent Quaker leader, James Nayler, declared:

> The Lamb's War is not against creatures, they wrestle not with flesh and blood which God has made, but with spiritual wickedness exalted in the hearts of men and women, where God alone should be ... his kingdom in this world ... is in the hearts of such as have believed in him.[13]

With concern for the immediate repentance of the wayward amongst all levels of society, the early Quakers believed their prophetic mission was to 'tell magistrates, priests and people what they are, and reprove them of their transgressions, and forewarn them of the judgments to come'.[14] One of the earliest recorded self-proclaimed Quakers, Elizabeth Hooton,[15] wrote to the mayor of Derby a similar prophetic cry of doom in her rebuke: 'O friend ... mercy & true judgment & justice is cried in your streets. O take heed of the woes'.[16] The Quakers' prophetic announcement of Christ's millennial judgment and return through the inward light perpetuated their hope of God's spiritual restoration of humanity and his True Church through the dismantling of the apostate Church of England.

While it is difficult to pinpoint the exact origins of the early Quaker movement as a unique entity amongst other dissenters, most Quaker historians have generally attributed its foundation and the formation of its theology

---

[12] Pink Dandelion, *The Liturgies of Quakerism* (Farnham: Ashgate Publishing Limited, 2005), 21. 'The true Church will re-emerge victorious out of the wilderness, the wife of Christ the Lamb'. The Quaker sociologist also notes the importance of the second coming being an inward second coming through the inward light of God. He explains, 'This second coming was not an external one but an inward one. "Christ is come and is coming" is a description of inward spirituality' (Pink Dandelion, *An Introduction to Quakerism* [Cambridge: Cambridge University Press, 2007], 30).

[13] Barbour and Roberts (Eds), *Early Quaker Writings*, 108.

[14] Richard Farnsworth, *Antichrist's Man of War* (London, 1653), 16.

[15] Mack, *Visionary Women*, 381. Hooton was an outspoken messenger of the Quaker movement whose letter fragments written from prison are amongst the oldest surviving Quaker documents.

[16] Barbour and Roberts (Eds), *Early Quaker Writings*, 382. Hooton would later be thrown into prison in both York (1652) and Lincoln (1654) for aggressively attacking the 'corrupt' magistrates and clergy. Between these sentences in 1653, Hooton also wrote to Oliver Cromwell, 'You make yourselves ridiculous to all people who have sense and reason ... Your judges judge for reward, and at this York many which committed murder escaped through friends and money, and poor people for lesser facts are put to death' (Mack, *Visionary Women*, 127).

around 1646-7 with the work, visions and proclamations of George Fox.[17] The Quaker historian Rosemary Moore acknowledges that 'proto-Quaker groups' may have existed within England before the first preaching of George Fox.[18] Another historian, Barry Reay, suggests the movement's origin is more accurately found in the organic merging of a variety of groups, with common religious convictions, which already existed in the late 1640s and subsequent Interregnum.[19] For example, some Diggers and Fifth Monarchists, particularly after the restoration of the monarchy, would join the Quakers after their hopes had failed to be realised.[20] Other individuals seeking after deeper forms of spirituality throughout rural northern England, including Richard Farnworth, Richard Hubberthorne, Francis Howgill, Edward Burrough, William Dewsbury and James Nayler, were already meeting with other separatists in an informal worship style of silent meetings, fasting and prayer, all forms of worship which would later be adopted by the Friends and eventually become the trademarks of their spirituality.[21] As these various separatists began to emerge and gather, equally and independently frustrated with orthodox Puritanism, or failed political triumphs, many would eventually be united under the banner of the Society of Friends. Though other prominent figures were initially involved in the leadership of the early movement, many did not live long enough to see its fruition by 1660. As Reay suggests, Fox became the Quakers' central leader by outliving them.[22]

Fox's most influential and close partner in forming the doctrine and practice of early Quakerism was a gentry woman from Lancashire called Margaret Fell. Another prominent and influential early Quaker leader, Fell has often been described as the 'mother of Quakerism' within Quaker tradition and scholarship.[23] An early convert of Fox, Fell would become a forerunning architect of early Quaker spirituality and organisation. Fell's intellectual prowess, particularly in spiritual and theological matters, as well as through her social status as a gentry

---

[17] Rosemary Moore, *The Light in Their Consciences: Early Quakers in Britain, 1646–1666* (University Park, PA: Pennsylvania State University Press, 2000), xii; Dandelion, *An Introduction to Quakerism*, 14–22.

[18] Moore, *The Light in Their Consciences*, 5.

[19] Reay, *The Quakers and the English Revolution*, 8.

[20] Ibid, 41.

[21] Ibid. James Nayler was an early Quaker seen by some as a co-leader to Fox (Dandelion, *An Introduction to Quakerism*, 15). Nayler met an early demise in his leadership that is described in this work on p. 37 in chapter one. See also William C. Braithwaite, *The Beginnings of Quakerism to 1660* (Cambridge: Cambridge University Press, 1955), 247, 252–3.

[22] Reay, *The Quakers and the English Revolution*, 41.

[23] See Isabel Ross, *Margaret Fell: Mother of Quakerism* (York: William Sessions Book Trust, 1996). First published in 1949.

woman married to a local barrister, equipped her with both legal and theological knowledge valuable to shaping the early movement.[24] Fell was a key leader who is worthy of further study today.

Together, Fox and Fell with many of the early Quakers challenged the social and religious status quo and set upon the task of establishing themselves as the one and only True Church. Hilary Hinds, in her recent work *George Fox and Early Quaker Culture*, argues that the early Quaker belief in the inward light, i.e. the presence of that of Christ, dissolved other cultural demarcations in society. They made way for their prophetic messages to be proclaimed through any vessel chosen by God (regardless of class, gender or age); they refused to use deferential titles, such as 'your grace' or 'master'; and they refrained from tipping their cap to superiors.[25] Quakers also refused to take oaths, seeing it both as explicitly against the commands of Christ in the Sermon on the Mount, as well as an unnecessary and ineffective insurance of telling the truth or giving alliance.[26] They, like others of their fellow dissenters, regarded the Church of England as

---

[24] Sally Bruyneel, *Margaret Fell and the End of Time: The Theology of the Mother of Quakerism* (Waco, TX: Baylor University Press, 2010), 13.

[25] Richard Bauman, *Let Your Words Be Few: Symbolism of Speaking and Silence Among Seventeenth-Century Quakers* (Cambridge: Cambridge University Press, 1983), 47. Bauman explains the early Quaker rejection of such social forms: 'To call someone "your grace", when he was not in a state of grace, or "master", when he was not your master, or to greet someone with "your humble servant, sir", when you were not his servant, was to lie, and this the Quakers would not do ... Unwillingness to lie, however, was only one reason for rejecting honorific and deferential titles ... Titles, and the accompanying deferential acts of bowing, taking off the hat, or curtsying, represented forms of worldly honor, honor of men's persons and gestures of deference to their fleshly pride. The way to salvation, the Quakers held, was not to glorify the earthly self, but to suppress it' (ibid).

[26] Refusing to take an oath resulted in a number of arrests, causing them increased persecution as a group who were considered disloyal to the government and dishonest in court. The historian Christopher Hill reminds us the Anabaptists (or Familists) in the sixteenth and seventeenth centuries also refused to swear oaths in England 'since they objected to a religious ceremony being used for secular judicial purposes'; nor did they pay tithes, as they subverted the concept of a national church, and rejected infant baptism in support of voluntary adult baptism (Hill, *The World Turned Upside Down*, 26). The influence of preceding groups on Quakers with similar habits will later be addressed in more detail. In the seventeenth century, the Quakers were not the only dissenters who refused to take an oath. Levellers, Diggers and Ranters all refused the oath, causing popular accusations against the Quakers that they were Ranters (Hill, 'Quakers and the English Revolution', in Mullett [Ed.], *New Light on George Fox*, 29). After the restoration of the monarchy in 1660, the Convention Parliament was purged of sectaries who refused imposed oaths of allegiance and supremacy, which was effective since, as Christopher Hill explains, 'Refusal to swear was one of the hall-marks of sincere sectaries' (Hill, *The World Turned Upside Down*, 348). According to Pink Dandelion, in 1722 'Quakers were given permission not to have to swear an oath in

an 'apostate' den of 'hireling priests' who compelled congregants to take part in empty ceremonies, and thus refused not only to attend church but also to pay tithes. Their refusal to pay tithes was based largely on their belief that God alone was their guide and instructor, making priests, and the established ceremonies of the Church of England, unnecessary. Quaker scholar Pink Dandelion explains the early Quaker reasoning behind their separation from the Church of England and its ceremonies:

> The word of God was given freely to all, men, women, and children ... Friends refused to pay church tithes or make any contribution to the repairing of 'mashouses' (or 'steeplehouses') or the upkeep of the 'hireling ministry' when particular outward sacramentality was seen as anachronistic.[27]

As the Quakers developed their identity as a people set apart to proclaim God's truth and judgment against social conventions, magistrates who persecuted dissenters and the 'apostate' Church of England, their efforts to maintain their particular identity as the 'true church' grew more systematized and centralised.

Fox, Fell and the Early Quaker Obsession with Marriage Approbation

Over the decades of the latter half of the seventeenth century the mission of the early Quakers thus evinced two primary occupations: the promotion of Quaker identity as the one and only 'true church' and the maintenance of both their particular identity and purity through their extensive meeting system. Maintaining their collective purity, the early Quaker meetings largely consisted of silent worship during which they sat together and listened to the inward 'light of God in their consciences', waiting quietly for a word from God which they then would share with the rest of those attending if they felt led by God to do so. But the meetings were not only a place of worship. Other meetings were set up in order to maintain communal accountability towards holy behaviour through investigations, testimonies and a good deal of paperwork.[28] The

---

all but the criminal courts', but it would not be until 1832 that British Quakers were allowed to be members of parliament (Dandelion, *An Introduction to Quakerism*, 54).

[27] Dandelion, *An Introduction to Quakerism*, 26.

[28] The practice of the liturgy of silence in Quakerism is outlined by Pink Dandelion in chapter two in *The Liturgies of Quakerism*, pp. 21–33. Again utilising the book of Revelation, Fox believed 'the judgment upon the earth that are described by John with the breaking of the seven seals are known in the practice of waiting upon the Lord. Here the birth according to the flesh is silenced and judged, so that the birth according to the Spirit may be raised up ... Quaking in worship was the quaking of the earth in people's hearts so that the seed could be loosed from captivity and raised up, after Revelation 6:12–14 and the breaking of the sixth

predominating issue regarding identity and holy behaviour, which took up a great deal, if not most, of the early Quaker meeting agenda, was the approbation process of endogamous marriages within the Quaker fold.[29] Rejecting what they perceived as the 'false church', the early Quakers refused to be married by the 'hireling priests' of the Church of England, and thus devised a system of marriage approbation within their own meetings. Not being married in a recognised church, they were often popularly accused of going 'together as brute beasts' and thus began to face legal issues.[30] Before 1661, their marriages were legally considered invalid, and subsequently their children illegitimate, until a case at the assizes in Nottingham deemed Quaker marriages valid.[31] Considering these early legal concerns, particularly the legitimacy of the children of such marriages, and property concerns, the management of marriage on a practical level took some precedence. As will be discussed later, they laid out practical procedures which allowed for their marriage approbation to be documented in an effort to be above legal reproach.

Legal issues aside, due to the great deal of time spent on marriage approbation, it is clear the Quakers regarded marriage as a key component of their spirituality and identity. The early Quaker marriage approbation discipline, developed primarily by Fox and Fell, became the primary mechanism by which the Quakers ensured endogamous marriages were brought together by God alone, and would prove to be the critical vehicle through which the Quakers held together their identity as the one and only True Church. The result was a system of investigation, approbation and certification, all meticulously recorded and regulated: a peculiar and intriguing blend of bureaucracy and spirituality. While

---

seal ... This is not a new experience but one experienced by the prophets and apostles ... The revelation of Christ comes after the breakage of the seventh seal that is followed by half an hour of silence in heaven. In the silence, the old world passes away and the new is born. Those living in this encounter with Christ experience this transition out of time in the kingdom. This is not a private experience however, the personal encounter suggesting and anticipating the formation of a holy nation (1 Peter 2:9), the true church' (Dandelion, *The Liturgies of Quakerism*, 21). Cited from D. Gwyn, *Apocalypse of the Word: The Life and Message of George Fox, 1624–1691* (Richmond, IN: Friends United Press, 1986), 186-7, 189.

[29] Russell Mortimer (Ed.), *Minute Book of the Men's Meeting of the Society of Friends in Bristol 1667–1686* (Gateshead: Northumberland Press Limited, 1971), xviii. Mortimer asserts a full quarter of their meetings were consumed with marital approbation, which will be discussed at length in chapter one.

[30] George Fox, *A Journal or historical account of the life, travels, sufferings, Christian Experiences, and labour of love in the work of the ministry, of that Ancient, Eminent, and Faithful Servant of Jesus Christ. George Fox. In Two Volumes* (Leeds: Anthony Pickard, Sixth Edition, 1836), Volume Two, 5, henceforth abbreviated to *Journal*.

[31] Braithwaite, *The Beginnings of Quakerism to 1660*, 145. See also Fox, *Journal Vol. 2* (1836), 5. This case will be discussed at length in chapter one.

Fox, Fell and other early Quakers were close to virtually silent on the issue of what makes a happy marriage, the early Quaker record offers ample information on the right process of choosing a mate and how to marry that individual.[32] With such attention being paid by the early Quakers to their own marriage discipline, a gap in scholarship remains in understanding the spiritual foundation of their marriage discipline and how it informed and correlated with the early Quakers' collective identity as the True Church.

A discussion of the early Quaker marriage discipline and spirituality leads us to another relatively underrepresented topic in Quaker scholarship: the marriage of Fox and Fell in 1669. The marriage between George Fox and Margaret Fell has been considered only in passing by various historians, while a thorough analysis of their intentions, including their theological and spiritual justifications, has only been briefly touched upon. This is surprising given that it was not only a marriage between two prevailing leaders of the early Quaker movement, but was also a controversial marital union, not well received by some both within and without the Quaker fold. Various questions beg to be answered as one peruses Fox and Fell's personal reflections, as well as those of their fellow contemporary Quakers, regarding their matrimony. Did they marry only to quell rumours of their close working relationship? Did they venture into matrimony simply to unify the leadership of the early Quaker movement that suffered from internal schisms? Did they understand their marriage solely as a metaphoric tool to explain their perceptions of a restored creation, or to set a good example of a marriage approbation process done right?

Almost twenty years after Fell first met Fox, their partnership as leaders led to a partnership in marriage, an occasion which was perceived by many of their followers as a spiritually profound event. Fox's marriage to Fell, as demonstrated through both Fell's and Fox's recollections as well as various testimonies given both during their approbation process and at the wedding itself, illuminates valuable insights into their early spiritual and theological understanding of Quaker marriage on the whole. The marriage of these two key leaders was perceived as emblematic of the original intention for the union between man and woman in the Garden of Eden, as well as a living metaphor of the marriage between Christ and his church, and most importantly a sign of the return of the True Church. This idea, found throughout Fox's writings as well as other existing resources regarding their marriage, was expressed in an apocalyptic context, as early Quakers felt they were living a renewed life 'as it was in the beginning, before sin and defilement was'.[33]

---

[32] John Stephenson Rowntree, *Quakerism Past and Present: Being an Inquiry into the Causes of Its Decline in Great Britain and Ireland* (London: Smith, Elder, and Co., 1859), 152.

[33] George Fox, *The Journal of George Fox: A Revised Edition by John Nickalls* (Cambridge: Cambridge University Press, 1952), 20.

This study examines both the practical system of marriage approbation and the spiritual foundations of the early Quaker marriage approbation discipline, as put forth by the early Quaker leaders George Fox and Margaret Fell, and as evidently practised by a majority of the early Quaker meetings. As endogamous marriage was of paramount importance to the early Quakers, the spiritual implications of endogamous marriages were great. Questions arise as to why they were so concerned about the collective process of choosing the right mate, in the right manner, and how this process was directly affected by their identity as the True Church. Why did Quakers so strongly push for endogamous marriages, brought together by God alone? I intend to demonstrate and analyse the link between the early Quaker marriage discipline and their perceived identity as the one and only True Church, as understood through the Friends' inward spirituality, and maintained in their thorough marriage approbation process. The project at hand is an attempt to understand why and how the right proceedings of choosing a mate in a collective, communal setting were so critical to their perceived identity. Exploring the early Quakers' peculiar process of marriage approbation opens a window onto a whole spectrum of early Quaker convictions. Through this window we can look into their spiritual psyche which illumined their practical processes. The practical process of marriage approbation couched in the conceptual foundation largely put forth by Fox and Fell will be examined, culminating in the marriage of Fox and Fell, a spiritual event of great repercussions at the time.

The structure of this work is thus three-fold. In chapter one, the practical process and discipline of the early Quaker marriage approbation will be discussed at length, considering the various issues which arose as couples sought marriage approbation from the meetings. This will provide a clear overview of the practice of marriage approbation, as well as the marriage ceremony within early Quaker meetings. In the second chapter, the theological rationale behind the early marriage discipline, as expressed primarily by Fox and Fell, will be further analysed. Several important themes arise in this analysis, including the notion of 'wilderness' in early Quaker thought, a desire to return to 'primitive' Christianity and the 'good' or 'Gospel' order as demonstrated by the apostolic church, and their collective desire to maintain 'unity' as the True Church based on their understanding of the 'marriage of the Lamb'. The early Quakers' unique perception of 'the undefiled bed' and what constitutes an 'honourable marriage' in relation to sexuality will also be discussed, followed by a consideration of their concern for 'Gospel Family Order'. Finally, in chapter three, I will explore how the practical and theoretical came to fruition and were demonstrated through the marriage of Fox and Fell. This analysis will include a look at their particular marriage approbation process and ceremony, and the perceived spiritual implications of their marriage, as well as the daily life within their marital relationship as husband and wife.

A Survey of the Secondary Sources Concerning Fox, Fell and the Early Marriage Discipline

The aims of this study necessitate an evaluation of three particular areas of scholarly research: first, an examination of the existing biographies about both Fox and Fell, followed by a review of scholarship concerning their personal marriage, and finally a consideration of the existing research regarding the early Quaker marriage discipline in general.

Existing Work on George Fox and Margaret Fell

Until the last three decades, scholarship regarding early Quaker history has generally revolved around quasi-hagiographical accounts portraying George Fox as the main founder and architect of the movement. According to these accounts, one of his first converts, the gentry woman Margaret Fell, helped him organise the movement and together, they have been portrayed as the guiding centre of the 'valiant sixty', a group of esteemed Quakers comprising the 'first publishers of truth' and forming the core of the early leadership of the Quaker movement. Many historians of Quakerism have been Quakers themselves (e.g. the aforementioned Hugh Barbour) which can at times colour biographical accounts and the history of Quakerism in general. Survey histories, which are of great value, often err on the side of painting a saintly persona of Fox. These include the Quaker historians William Braithwaite and Rufus Jones. Both Braithwaite's two-volume history *The Beginnings of Quakerism to 1660* and *The Second Period of Quakerism* which appeared in the beginning of the twentieth century and Rufus Jones' *The Life and Message of George Fox* paint George Fox as not only the primary architect of the movement, but as imbued with a prophetic calling and a strong moral character.[34] In 1953, the Quaker historian Howard Brinton in his work *Friends for 300 Years* described Fox as 'the principal founder of Quakerism', 'the organizing genius of the movement', and the 'greatest public Friend'.[35]

---

[34] Rufus Jones writes, 'What he [Fox] proclaimed as truth is still a live and kindling force … He is regarded more and more with the flow of time as a major prophet. We know his flaws and weaknesses more clearly than his first followers did but at the same time we can see the true greatness of the man' (Rufus Matthew Jones, *The Life and Message of George Fox 1624–1924* [New York, NY: Macmillan, 1924], 1–2). See also Braithwaite, *The Beginnings of Quakerism to 1660* (Cambridge: Cambridge University Press, 1955) & William C. Braithwaite, *The Second Period of Quakerism* (York: William Sessions Limited, 1979).

[35] Howard Brinton, *Friends for 300 Years: Beliefs and Practice of the Society of Friends since George Fox started the Quaker Movement* (London: George Allen & Unwin Limited, 1953), 7. Brinton explains the adjective 'public' as being a title attributed to those 'who went about preaching to any who would listen in market place, farmhouse, tavern, etc.' (ibid).

Not until the last three decades has more attention been increasingly afforded to Fox and Fell in a less saintly light.[36] This may in part be due to the fact that many historians in the field of Quaker scholarship were or are Quakers themselves, Braithwaite and Jones included. It may also be due to the reality that in a great deal of scholarship, much of Fox's life has been gleaned from his *Journal*, in which Fox does present himself as an exceptionally spiritually enlightened individual. As an example, Fox recounts he was born in July 1624 at Drayton-in-the-Clay in Leicestershire to Christopher Fox, a weaver, and Mary Lago who was 'of the family of the Lagos, and of the stock of the martyrs'.[37] He further explained he had a 'gravity and stayedness of mind and spirit, not usual in children', and at eleven years old he knew 'pureness and righteousness' which was taught to him by the Lord.[38] As he approached adulthood, Fox explained how some of his relations thought he should become a priest, while others persuaded him of the contrary, and he eventually took up work for a man in the wool and cattle trade.[39] During this time, Fox asserted he 'never did wrong against any man or woman'. According to Fox, in his honest dealings he frequently used the term 'verily', earning the following reputation which did not go without some ridicule:

> It was a common saying among people who knew me, 'If George says verily, there is no altering him'. When boys and rude people would laugh at me, I let them alone, and went my way; but people had generally a love to me for my innocency and honesty.[40]

Some of Fox's self-reflections, similar to the above, have prompted a few more recent scholars to view Fox as one with an elevated sense of self. In a recent collection of articles entitled *New Light on George Fox (1624–1691)*, the Quaker historian H. Larry Ingle admits in his essay 'Unravelling George Fox: The Real Person' he does not find Fox 'especially likeable', beginning his argument by citing the aforementioned lines from Fox's *Journal*, 'When I came to eleven years of age I knew pureness and righteousness'.[41] Calling him 'a prig, a young prig at 11', Ingle argues the following about Fox's personality and behaviour:

---

[36] Richard T. Vann, *The Social Development of English Quakerism, 1655–1755* (Cambridge, MA: Harvard University Press, 1969); Reay, *The Quakers and the English Revolution*; Barbour and Frost, *The Quakers*; Dandelion, *An Introduction to Quakerism*.
[37] Fox, *Journal Vol. 1* (1836), 83.
[38] Ibid, 83–4.
[39] Ibid, 84.
[40] Ibid, 84.
[41] H. Larry Ingle, 'Unravelling George Fox: The Real Person'. (Mullett [Ed.], *New Light on George Fox*, 38.)

> Fox could never bring himself to admit that he made errors ... I know of no occasion in which he apologised for anything he ever did. He knew he was right, he insisted that others recognise it, and he wanted everyone to follow the path he blazed.[42]

Ingle further admits that while Fox was a human being 'and no doubt perceived himself as such', the problem Ingle has with Fox, based on a thorough reading of his *Journal*, is that he 'was reluctant to confess his humanness'.[43] Ingle concludes his analysis affirming that while he does not find Fox particularly agreeable because of his lack of humility, Fox's works were influential as was his strong character, making him a worthy historical figure of research:

> Fox was a man of charisma and determination, and the latter, I think, led to the former ... [he] had a word for his age; he did not fear to speak it, and it gave him tremendous appeal ... whether he is liked by a later biographer is beside the point. What is important is that we continue to explore the life and career of one who spoke a word for his age.[44]

Ingle's rather forthright criticism of the 'priggish' character of Fox lies in relatively stark contrast to the more saintly accounts of Fox's character within earlier Quaker scholarship. Likewise, the historian Richard Bailey, in his similarly titled book *New Light on George Fox and Early Quakerism: The Making and Unmaking of a God*, follows the recent endeavour of shedding 'new light' on Fox. Bailey explains the purpose of his study is 'to draw out the charismatic part of Fox's life and message' through attempting to prove 'Fox was devoted to a doctrine of the inner light that divinised the saints, and gave him exalted status among his followers'.[45] Bailey argues Fox perceived himself as not only an 'undisputed prophet', but also as touting messianic claims earlier in the movement that were subsequently embarrassing and had to be retrospectively toned down.[46] As we will see in the following chapters, some of Fox's contemporaries both within and without the Quaker fold accused Fox of being an overbearing leader in a movement that was meant to encourage equanimity in leadership and spirituality, while others regarded and esteemed him as a prophet of God.[47] While Ingle's

---

[42] Ibid.
[43] Ibid, 39. Ingle argues Fox's *Journal* was 'mistitled by its literary executors', as it more resembles 'a lengthy memoir' (ibid, 38).
[44] Ibid, 43.
[45] Richard Bailey, *New Light on George Fox and Early Quakerism: The Making and Unmaking of a God* (San Francisco, CA: Mellen Research University Press, 1992), xvii.
[46] Ibid.
[47] In the preface to Fox's *Journal Vol. 1* (1836), William Penn described Fox as 'a man that God endued with a clear and wonderful depth, a discerner of others' spirits, and very

and Bailey's assertions have some merit, as Fox did indeed believe himself to be a holy person, Fox's character and self-perception may more fairly be rooted in the role of a leader, prophesying the news of God rising up the True Church, calling others to the same lifestyle and relationship with God that he himself was enjoying.[48] How Fox viewed himself, particularly in regards to whether or not he believed himself to be Christ incarnate, will have direct bearing on how he viewed his own marriage, as will be discussed shortly.

In addition to challenging Fox's saintly persona, others have also challenged the role of Fox as the founder of Quakerism, including Winthrop S. Hudson in his 1944 journal article entitled 'A Suppressed Chapter in Quaker History'. Hudson's disputation sheds light on the question of primary sources regarding any aspect of early Quaker history and the life of Fox. Hudson suggests Fox was not at all the central leader of the movement, but rather was refashioned as such through early rigorous editing and censuring of various letters, tracts and other documents, as well as through an intentional suppression of the historical documents regarding the early history of the movement. This editing and rewriting of history was done, according to Hudson, in an effort to present a collective, cohesive movement under the direction of a God-inspired prophet. Hudson asserts, 'Religious groups, like nations, are addicted to the custom of adorning their histories with a considerable amount of mythology', and concedes that while this practice is usually 'entirely unintentional', the Quakers are an example of 'one of the most successful instances of the suppression of historical fact and the creation of a pious myth to replace it'.[49] Fox himself, as Hudson acknowledges, initially undertook editing and censoring Quaker publications, but it was too great a task for him and was eventually taken over by the Quaker Yearly Meeting in London.[50] According to Hudson, after the creation of the 'Second-Day's Morning Meeting' (SDMM) established in 1673 'as a means of censorship to which all publications had to be submitted for

---

much a master of his own ... And indeed it showed, beyond all contradiction that God had sent him ... though God had visibly clothed him with a divine preference and authority, and indeed his very presence expressed a religious majesty, yet he never abused it; but held his place in the church of God with great meekness, and a most engaging humility and moderation' (Fox, *Journal Vol. 1* [1836], xxxviii–xxxix, xliii).

[48] Fox's self-perception, as well as how others viewed him, and how these perceptions were illuminated in the context of his marriage to Fell, will be discussed at length in chapter three.

[49] Winthrop S. Hudson, 'A Suppressed Chapter in Quaker History', *The Journal of Religion*, 2 no 2 (April 1944): 108–18; p. 108.

[50] Ibid, 116. See also Braithwaite, *Beginnings of Quakerism*, 134: Thomas Aldam 'in a letter at the end of 1653 rejoices that Fox is to view all books before they are printed'.

authorisation, revision, or suppression', the myth making was heavily underway.[51] Hudson presents the Morning Meeting as a heavy hand in censorship during early Quakerism, an assertion which is fair and not wholly without merit.[52]

Hudson further points to the curious editing and revising procedure of Fox's *Great Journal*, conducted by Thomas Ellwood under the direction of the SDMM.[53] With the careful examination of the *Journal* by both Ellwood and the SDMM, it was assured in the final edition that 'nothing may be omitted fit to be inserted, nor anything inserted fit to be left out', an editing procedure which Hudson argues had reshaped the early history of Quakerism and set Fox as the sole leader of the movement.[54] With this kind of editing of the story of the life of Fox, Hudson argues Fox's *Journal* is not 'an entirely trustworthy historical source'.[55] Hudson further argues while Fox did indeed make himself the 'hero of his *Journal*' as a 'divinely selected and appointed' instrument of God, any contradictory material to Fox being the sole prophetic instrument of the Quaker fold was suppressed by the SDMM.

> By the end of the [sixteen-] eighties, and probably somewhat earlier, it had become the deliberate policy of the Morning Meeting to suppress all material that would

---

[51] Ibid, 116. The Meeting was also appointed with 'the specific task of procuring and keeping two copies of each book written by a Quaker' along with every book written against Quakers (Hudson, 'A Suppressed Chapter in Quaker History', 110). Michele Lise Tarter offers the following explanation of the Second-Day's Morning Meeting (SDMM): 'This committee of men Friends was set forth to determine every tract and book to be issued by the religious society ... The men, that is, were reinventing their identity, in hopes of dignifying the movement and restoring their reputation. Resorting to traditional dualism and patriarchal conventions, they no longer valorised the tender leadings of God pouring forth spontaneously in print' (Tarter, 'George Fox and Christian Gnosis' in Pink Dandelion [Ed.], *The Creation of Quaker Theory: Insider Perspectives* [Farnham: Ashgate Publishing Limited, 1994], 91–2). According to the historian Christine Trevett, the Meeting also had a hand in silencing the prophetic writings of English and Welsh Quaker women (Christine Trevett, '"Not Fit to be Printed": The Welsh, the Women and the Second Day's Morning Meeting', *Journal of the Friends Historical Society*, 59 [2001]: 115–44).

[52] Ibid, 110. See also Braithwaite, *The Second Period of Quakerism*, 280. According to Hudson, even Fox was subject to the authoritative censorship of the Morning Meeting, evidenced in their refusal to circulate a letter he had written (Hudson, 'A Suppressed Chapter in Quaker History', 115).

[53] Ibid, 109. This edition was published in 1694, three years after Fox's death. Fox compiled his Great Journal from 1674–6 (Hudson, 'A Suppressed Chapter in Quaker History', 110).

[54] Ibid, 110. Cited from Braithwaite, *The Second Period of Quakerism* (1919 edition), 281.

[55] Ibid.

serve to contradict the officially promulgated version of Quaker beginnings which pictured George Fox as the founder of the sect.[56]

After Hudson's journal article was published, Quaker historian Henry Cadbury wrote a responsive article entitled 'An Obscure Chapter of Quaker History', published in the same journal later in 1944. As the title suggests, Cadbury argues the beginnings of Quakerism were not intentionally suppressed as Hudson suggests, but rather were obscure due to 'the gradual character of any such birth, and to its close relation to its antecedents'.[57] Cadbury suggests contrarily:

> A certain amount of obscurity usually surrounds the beginnings of social movements ... partly because the persons contemporary with their initial stages do not always recognize promptly their future significance or start at once preserving their records.[58]

The extent of Fox's leadership may have been exaggerated in early Quakerism, and in later historical writings, Cadbury argues this is only natural due to the fact that Fox was the 'most active and most successful' of the early leaders: 'Even if Quakerism of a sort flourished before 1650, no names of other leaders from that time are preserved'.[59] Cadbury recognises the work of both Fox and Fell, who 'assiduously collected, preserved, and annotated ... narratives of the many laborers in the Quaker mission at home and abroad', as work solely done in order to preserve the historical record.[60] None of these manuscripts antedate 1650, which according to Cadbury does not automatically suggest intentional omission but rather was 'natural, since previously the movement was not so far-flung, so aggressive, or so self-conscious'.[61]

In regards to the activities of the SDMM, including the editing of Fox's *Journal* by Ellwood, Cadbury states there is 'no evidence that the Morning Meeting dealt directly with the original manuscript Journal', but rather they simply 'listened to the reading of Ellwood's draft and used their memory or judgment in criticizing it'.[62] Though the *Journal* was altered in Ellwood's edition, Cadbury argues that except for its first missing pages 'it can be compared –

---

[56] Ibid, 115–16.
[57] Henry J. Cadbury, 'An Obscure Chapter of Quaker History', *The Journal of Religion*, 24 no 3 (Jul 1944): 201–13; p. 201.
[58] Ibid.
[59] Ibid, 207. Cadbury notes, 'Elizabeth Hooton is a possible exception'.
[60] Ibid.
[61] Ibid.
[62] Ibid, 211.

some nine hundred later pages of it – with the printed version'.[63] With regard to whether or not the changes Ellwood made were in the vein of refashioning Fox as the solely inspired leader, as Hudson suggests, this change is not substantiated according to Cadbury, due to Ellwood's failure to omit a passage in reference to earlier Quaker activity in the 1640s before Fox's clear active leadership of the movement as a whole in the 1650s.[64] The other changes, Cadbury argues, were 'purely verbal or literary and do not affect the picture of Fox or of Quaker history'.[65] Changes in relation to Fox's self-importance as a leader on the contrary downplayed this aspect of his character.[66]

Michael Mullett, editor of the recently published collection of essays entitled *New Light on George Fox*, also concedes there has been an inclination in historical writing to portray George Fox as the sole creator of Quakerism, and additionally acknowledges this impulse was already present in Fox's lifetime:

> This impulse to identify 'Quakerism' with Fox was already strongly evident within Fox's own lifetime … [which] was not on the whole sympathetic to Fox … for it was a widespread practice in 17th century English polemic to brand novel religious movements with the surnames of their ostensible founders.[67]

The aforementioned suggestion by historian Barry Reay that Fox emerged and survived the original leaders, coupled with the above described tendencies to associate a movement with one dominant figure, produces Fox as a central character in the early Quaker narrative worth studying.[68] Not only were Fox's writings prolific during that time period, they were read within various Quaker meetings, his ideas were widely accepted and integrated into Quaker spirituality, and Fox today is still regarded in much of Quaker scholarship as a primary architect behind Quaker theology.[69] His legacy, works and teachings can still be seen within contemporary Quakerism, making his work in relation to the early Quaker marriage discipline, in both theory and practice, worth investigating.

Fox's partner in ministry, and eventual partner in marriage, Margaret Fell, though generally considered the mother of Quakerism in Quaker tradition, has been largely underrepresented in her own right within historical scholarship. She has gained more recent attention in broader studies of women in the early Quaker movement. The last three decades have seen a new generation of works

---

[63] Ibid.
[64] Ibid.
[65] Ibid.
[66] Ibid, 212 (Footnote 40). Fox's self-perception will be dealt with in a later discussion regarding Fox and Fell's marriage.
[67] Mullett (Ed.), *New Light on George Fox*, 1.
[68] Reay, *The Quakers and the English Revolution*, 41.
[69] Dandelion, *An Introduction to Quakerism*, 19.

by women historians including Patricia Crawford, Catie Gill, Phyllis Mack, Sara Heller Mendelson, Christine Trevett and Catherine Wilcox, all of whom acknowledge not only Fell's organisational skills within the movement, but also her important theological and intellectual contributions to the shaping of early Quaker doctrine.[70] Phyllis Mack addresses Fell in the context of seventeenth-century women's spirituality and prophecy, arguing while previous Quaker historians have been 'invariably courteous towards Margaret Fell, the reverend mother of the movement', they on the whole have emphasised 'the hysterical, self-serving, and ultimately trivial character of early Quaker women'.[71] Mack asserts women in the early Quaker movement, Fell included, embodied the archetype of the 'aggressive, male Old Testament hero', exhibiting emotive behaviour which was considered unorthodox and unfeminine at the time.[72] Fell, Mack contends, was a 'loving and judging mother' to both male and female Friends, who exercised a great deal of control over her Swarthmoor estate (which Mack asserts was also unusual for that time), as well as a strong leadership presence within the Quaker community.[73]

Trevett likewise considers Fell in the context of the striking prophetic activity amongst early Quaker women which emerged in the seventeenth century. According to Trevett, Fell was a Quaker apologist who broke from seventeenth-century social conventions and exercised public religious activity.[74] Though other Quaker women took part in this religious activity, Fell emerged as an exceptionally vociferous and established female leader of the early movement.[75] From a literary standpoint, Catie Gill explains Fell had tremendous concern for the advancement of women in the role of public prophet as early as 1656, when Fell argued women's public prophetic activity was a result of God's command

---

[70] Mack, *Visionary Women*, 145, 156, 178, 161, 203, 217–22, 229, 233, 304, 310, 319; Christine Trevett, *Quaker Women Prophets in England and Wales, 1650–1700* (Lewiston, NY: Edwin Mellen, 2000), 9, 38, 214; Christine Trevett, *Women and Quakerism in the 17th Century* (York: Sessions Book Trust, 1991), 22, 55, 106; Catherine Wilcox, *Theology and Women's Ministry in Seventeenth-Century English Quakerism: Handmaids of the Lord* (Lewiston, NY: Edwin Mellen, 1995), vi, 144–5; Sara Heller Mendelson and Patricia Crawford, *Women in Early Modern England, 1550–1720* (Oxford: Clarendon Press, 1998), 33, 181, 293; Gill, *Women in the Seventeenth-Century Quaker Community*, 13, 37, 149, 164.

[71] Mack, *Visionary Women*, 134. Mack also asserts, ' ... in William Braithwaite's classic study of the beginnings of Quakerism, no women's writings are mentioned except those of Fell, but every case of "light behavior" by a woman is described in detail' (Mack, *Visionary Women*, 134).

[72] Ibid, 134.
[73] Ibid, 40, 221.
[74] Trevett, *Quaker Women Prophets in England and Wales*, 38.
[75] Gill, *Women in the Seventeenth-Century Quaker Community*, 40.

through the inward light.[76] Ten years later, Fell wrote a formal apology in support of women's preaching through a 'rhetorical slight of hand'.[77] Fell's best-known work *Women's Speaking Justified* (1666) is a retort to the Anglicans who dissuaded women from preaching based on Pauline passages from the New Testament.[78] As Michele Osherow in her work *Biblical Women's Voices in Early Modern England* explains, Fell 'addresses Paul's injunction against women's speech, claiming that those whom Paul silenced had not had the revelation and Spirit of God poured upon them'.[79] In *Women's Speaking Justified*, Fell argued God made no distinction between male and female:

> And first, when *God created Man in his own Image, in the Image of God created he them, Male and Female; and God blessed them, and God said unto them, Be fruitful and multiply: And God said, Behold, I have given you of every Herb, &c. Gen. 1.* Here God joyns them together in his own Image, and makes no such Distinctions and Differences as Men do.[80]

As did Fox and others of her fellow Quakers, Fell suggested the apostate Church of England was essentially working with Satan in suppressing women's preaching and prophesying. These strong arguments have garnered Fell recognition as one

---

[76] Ibid, 138. See also Margaret Fell, *A testimonie of the touch-stone, for all professions, and all forms, and gathered churches (as they call them), of what sort soever to try their ground and foundation by and a trial by the Scriptures, who the false prophets are, which are in the world, which John said should be in the last times; also, some of the ranters principles answered* (London: Thomas Simmons, 1656), 2.

[77] Trevett, *Quaker Women Prophets in England and Wales*, 38.

[78] See Margaret Olofson Thickstun, 'Writing the Spirit: Margaret Fell's Feminist Critique of Pauline Theology', *Journal of the American Academy of Religion*, 63 (Summer 1995): 269–79; Mack, *Visionary Women*, 312; Christine Trevett (Ed.), *Women's Speaking Justified and Other 17th Century Quaker Writings about Women* (London: Quaker Home Service, 1989). Fell has also become recognised as the first Quaker who wrote a formal document against war, also known as a 'peace testimony'. See Bonnelyn Kunze, *Margaret Fell and the Rise of Quakerism* (Stanford, CA: Stanford University Press, 1994), 6; Mack, *Visionary Women*, 220. For further information regarding pacifism within early Quakerism, see Meredith Baldwin Weddle, *Walking in the Way of Peace: Quaker Pacifism in the Seventeenth Century* (Oxford: Oxford University Press, 2001).

[79] Michele Osherow, *Biblical Women's Voices in Early Modern England* (Farnham: Ashgate Publishing Limited, 2009), 4.

[80] Margaret Fell, *Women's speaking justified, proved and allowed of by the Scriptures all such as speak by the spirit and power of the Lord Iesus: and how women were the first that preached the tidings of the resurrection of Jesus and were snet by Christ's own command before he ascended to the Father, John 20:17* (London, 1666), 1.

of the first women who formally in an apologetic treatise supported women's preaching in the public domain.[81]

In 1994, the debate regarding what kind of 'mother' Fell was actually inspired the Quaker scholar and Fell biographer Bonnelyn Kunze in her work *Margaret Fell and the Rise of Quakerism*. Kunze's biography of Fell is the first since Isabel Ross' portrait of Fell as a saintly 'nursing mother' in *Margaret Fell: Mother of Quakerism*, published in 1949. Kunze's criticism of Ross being too hagiographical is credible, but her assessment of Fell as a dominant 'mother superior' rather than a 'nurturing mother' is not convincing.[82] In an attempt to provide the reader with a more human, sometimes petty and vindictive Fell, Kunze focuses her argument on a series of glimpses into Fell's life through four lenses: Fell's domestic life, her Quaker community involvement and economic activities, her public persona, including her relationship with William Penn, and finally a brief survey of her theological beliefs and worldview. Kunze's goal in her biographical account of Fell, to deconstruct the hagiography often espoused in Quaker literature, left little room for a thorough analysis of Fell's spirituality. In a short chapter on theology Kunze focuses primarily on Fell's millenarianism, pointing out that Fell, like many of her contemporary seventeenth-century Puritans and other non-conformists, maintained an interest in Old Testament imagery along with their eschatological hopes for a second coming of Christ.[83] Imagery from the Old Testament, particularly in identification with Israel and

---

[81] Mack, *Visionary Women*, 216–18, 220, 232–3, 290; Trevett, *Women and Quakerism in the 17th Century*, 43ff. Trevett notes other Quaker women, before Fell, wrote defences for women's preaching. See Trevett, *Women and Quakerism in the 17th Century*, 49.

[82] Kunze's portrayal of Fell as a dominant mother superior rests largely on a very thorough analysis of a long, bitter business dispute between Fell and Quaker Thomas Rawlinson over his stewardship of Fell's iron bloomery, Force Forge. Fell was able to persuade her fellow Quakers to ostracise him from the Quaker community, but the incident was eventually resolved by Fox, and Rawlinson ultimately gained ownership of the forge in 1680. Kunze asserts Fell's power of persuasion was a 'hegemonic power within the early Quaker meetings that was probably without parallel anywhere in the wider English or American Quaker community' (Kunze, *Margaret Fell and the Rise of Quakerism*, 125). Kunze further argues Fox subsequently drifted from Fell and Swarthmoor, indicating the incident may have severely strained their relationship. What is troubling about Kunze's conclusion is the lack of support from any primary sources. Kunze admits her conclusion is largely speculation. After their marriage, Fox was rarely at Swarthmoor in later years, spending a good deal of time away, particularly in London, working and preaching, but it is just as likely this was due to his commitment to work abroad for the cause of Quakerism. While her analysis of the Rawlinson dispute is thorough, and certainly deserves some attention, Kunze's effort to construct Fell as domineering, and estranged from Fox, appears to be a far-reaching conclusion, with an over emphasis on this particular legal incident.

[83] Kunze, *Margaret Fell and the Rise of Quakerism*, 201.

the prophets, we will see emerged frequently throughout the writings of both Fox and Fell.

Fell had a highly developed eschatology, sharing with others the belief that a new age was dawning both before and after the restoration of the monarchy. The historian Sally Bruyneel offers the most recent study regarding Fell's eschatology in her work *Margaret Fell and the End of Time: The Theology of the Mother of Quakerism*.[84] Bruyneel thoroughly examines Fell's contributions to the eschatological hope shared by Fox and Fell and the early Quakers. A part of this work is based on Bruyneel's doctoral thesis in which she elaborated at length on Fell's desire for the urgent conversion of the Jews.[85] Bruyneel notes when Fell was sixty-three years old she published her last theological tract entitled *The daughter of Sion awakened* (1677) which largely reflected Fell's works published ten years earlier, summarising largely 'the history of salvation, from Adam and Christ', couched in the proclamation that 'a new Day has arrived, in which the true Light of God is shining in the hearts of all people'.[86] As Bruyneel does not address the eschatological framework of Fell in relation to the early Quaker marriage discipline, or in the context of Fell's marriage to Fox, Bruyneel's research provides a springboard for further research regarding Fox and Fell's

---

[84] Bruyneel, *Margaret Fell and the End of Time*.

[85] Sally Bruyneel-Padgett, *The Eschatology of Margaret Fell (1614–1702) and Its Place in Her Theology and Ministry* (Durham: University of Durham, PhD Thesis, 2003), 95. In 1656, Fell had written an open letter to Rabbi Manasseh ben Israel, a well-known Amsterdam Jewish leader, entitled *For Manasseth Ben Israel. The Call of the Jews out of Babylon. Which is good tidings to the meek, liberty to the captives, and the opening of the prison doores*, in which she encouraged Manasseh to bring his brethren into England, thus fulfilling God's promises of the conversion of the Jews. There is no evidence however that Manasseh ever received or read her pamphlet. In 1658, Margaret Fell wrote a tract to the world's Jewish population (though initially given to Jews residing in Holland) entitled *A Loving Salutation to the Seed of Abraham among the Jews, wherever they are scattered up and down upon the Face of the Earth* (Holland, 1658). The pamphlet was translated into Hebrew most likely by the recently excommunicated Jew Baruch de Spinoza, which, if true, would make this translation Spinoza's earliest publication. Spinoza likely had met with the leader of the Quaker mission at the time in Amsterdam, William Ames, in 1657. (Richard H. Popkin and Michael A. Singer [Eds], *Spinoza's Earliest Publication? The Hebrew Translation of Margaret Fell's 'A Loving Salutation to the Seed of Abraham among the Jews, wherever they are scattered up and down upon the Face of the Earth'* [Assen/Maastricht: Van Gorcum & Co., 1987], 1, 4). For further information see also Judith Gardiner, 'Margaret Fell Fox and Feminist Literary History: A "Mother in Israel" Calls to the Jews', *Prose Studies*, 17 no 3 (1994): 42–56.

[86] Bruyneel-Padgett, *The Eschatology of Margaret Fell (1614–1702) and Its Place in Her Theology and Ministry*, 95. Cited from Margaret Fell, *A brief collection of remarkable passages and occurrences relating to the birth, education, life, conversion, travels, services, and deep sufferings of that ancient, eminent, and faithful servant of the Lord, Margaret Fell; but by her second marriage, Margaret Fox* (London: J. Sowle, 1710), 510, henceforth abbreviated to *Works*.

understanding of God's new millennium and how it applied to the early Quaker marriage discipline.

The historical record demonstrates Fell's important contributions to early Quaker thought, as Bonnelyn Kunze and Sally Bruyneel cogently argue. As Quakerism grew into a national network, a leadership hierarchy developed with Fell and Fox largely leading and organising the movement.[87] Fell consistently agreed with Fox, and vice versa, forming a solid, unified front of leadership. Though challenged at times, their writings and advice were frequently referred to within the Quaker meetings, playing a significant role in the development of both early Quaker spirituality and their meeting structure, making their collective work worth analysing.

Scholarly Interpretations of the Marriage between Fox and Fell

The lack of a thorough exploration of the marriage of Fox and Fell is surprising on two counts: first, because it was a marriage between the two proclaimed and historically accepted predominant leaders of the movement in the Quaker historical record; second, the rich material of how Fox and Fell, as well as other Quakers, understood their marriage provides valuable insight on their understanding of Quaker spirituality and the eschaton as a whole. While scholarship has frequently and rightly asserted that Fox claimed his marriage was a testimony to the True Church coming out of the wilderness, few if any scholars have taken pause to thoroughly explicate what Fox meant when he uttered these words in his *Journal*.[88] Reasons for their marriage have been suggested by various scholars with little exhaustive analysis or support. Some scholars suggest their marriage was simply a spiritual union which was likely celibate.[89] Bonnelyn Kunze believes they married for many reasons, including offsetting rumours of an illicit relationship between Fell and Fox. Kunze further suggests this may be why they spent so little time together in actual fact during their marriage.[90] Kunze concludes their marriage was one in which 'shared religious ideals and personal affinity seem the most likely reasons for the bond in this marriage of twenty-two years'.[91] While this is undoubtedly true, a more thorough discussion

---

[87] Moore, *The Light in Their Consciences*, 27.
[88] Braithwaite, *The Second Period of Quakerism*, 55.
[89] Barbour and Roberts (Eds), *Early Quaker Writings*, 39. In their introduction to *Early Quaker Writings*, editors Barbour and Roberts claim 'Fox married Margaret Fell … to show that marriage could be spiritual' with virtually no documented evidence or further discussion.
[90] Kunze, *Margaret Fell and the Rise of Quakerism*, 55. Kunze also addresses Fox's restorationist theology in her interesting discussion on whether or not the relationship was consummated, a notion which will be addressed shortly.
[91] Ibid, 57.

of the place of asceticism and apocalyptic beliefs within Fox and Fell's thinking in regards to their marriage would provide a fuller and more accurate analysis of the Fox/Fell marriage.

Others purport solely pragmatic reasons for their union, a consolidation of leadership lacking any real affection between the two.[92] In his work *First Among Friends*, the Quaker scholar H. Larry Ingle includes a chapter entitled 'More Belongs to a Marriage than Four Bare Legs in a Bed' in which he first presents a chronological account of the events of the Quaker movement during their time of marriage, and concludes Fell and Fox were not necessarily elated about their marriage.[93] He alludes to the possibility that Fox married Fell solely to support the movement, as both a practical means towards strengthening and unifying their leadership in order to assuage divisions, as well as to set an example of the marital discipline they were attempting to instil in all Society of Friends meetings. According to Ingle, no personal affections or any other personal reasons affected their decision to marry. Regarding their marital approbation, Ingle wrote:

> There certainly were no passionate feelings on either side; perhaps both were getting too old for passion. As leader of a group faced with persecution because of its peculiar ways, the forty-five-year old Fox was seldom given to emotions: displaying any now seemed less important than acting as a model for his soon-to-be recommended marriage procedures. Indeed, he approached what should have been a moving occasion, grounded in love and mutual affection, with all the excitement of someone completing a business deal.[94]

This explanation is problematic as Ingle's own expectations of what a passionate marriage should look like colour his interpretation of Fox's experience, without considering Fox's unique perception of 'passion' in light of his understanding of the renewed relationships between men and women in marriage in a restored creation. What Ingle relies on instead is an abstract idea of marriage as a metaphor for the struggles of Fox's later years in the movement, with little to no analysis of the marriage itself or Fox's theology behind it.

Fox's cryptic claim that he married 'as a testimony, that all might come up into the marriage as it was in the beginning, and as a testimony that all might come up out of the wilderness to the marriage of the Lamb' is addressed by the historian Arnold Lloyd, who devotes a short chapter to marriage in his work *Quaker Social History*.[95] However, Lloyd gives no further exploration

---

[92] Bruyneel, *Margaret Fell and the End of Time*, 13.

[93] H. Larry Ingle, *First Among Friends: George Fox and the Creation of Quakerism* (New York, NY: Oxford University Press, 1994), 225.

[94] Ibid.

[95] Arnold Lloyd, *Quaker Social History: 1669–1738* (London: Green and Co., 1950), 49, 52. See also Fox, *The Journal of George Fox: A Revised Edition by John Nickalls* (Cambridge:

of the relationship between Fell and Fox, nor does he fully explicate Fox's curious statement regarding his own marriage. Like Ingle, Lloyd also neglects to thoroughly analyse both how Fell and Fox regarded their own marriage and how the rest of the movement viewed their marriage. Likewise, details of individual marriages and approbation processes as encountered by meetings and other Friends are neglected, while the focus of much scholarship remains on the procedures and arrangements of marriages within the early Quaker tradition in the broadest sense, concentrating on the development of the certificate system, the growing role of the Women's Meetings or legal issues.

A more mystical interpretation of the marriage of Fox and Fell is presented by Jacques Tual in his article 'Sexual Equality and Conjugal Harmony'.[96] Tual asserts Fox and Fell's union provided 'the ultimate illustration of Quaker conjugal praxis: the translation of nuptial joy into celestial bliss'.[97] The marriage of Fox and Fell according to Tual was a marriage in which 'all carnal or sensuous purpose' was banished, a 'decision which was obviously taken in common'.[98] Tual argues their marriage was purely symbolic, completely celibate, devoid of procreative intent, and served purely as the 'acme of cosmic love and harmony in the movement's history' representing a 'mystical union of souls which all members are invited to emulate'.[99] The platonic standards Fox placed upon his marriage to Fell, Tual contends, were the result of the androgynous spirituality the early Quakers perpetuated, a spiritual androgyny that was the direct result of their shared Edenic perceptions of the restored creation. But while Tual recognises Fox did not promote celibacy in general, he still adheres to the notion Fox applied this ascetic practice to his own marriage. Unfortunately, Tual bases his argument for Fox's purely platonic relationship with Fell on the passage from Fox's *Journal* (used also by Bailey) in which Fox tells a Puritan minister that procreation and marriage are 'below' him.[100] Again, the assumption of celibacy within their marriage, based primarily on this sole passage, fails to take into account Fox's many other writings about marriage, procreation and the 'undefiled bed' in general.

One of the more intriguing analyses of the Fox/Fell marriage lies in a short but insightful essay entitled 'Friends Historical Testimony on the Marriage Relationship' by Quaker Caroline Whitbeck, a teacher and researcher in the field of feminist philosophy. Whitbeck does not assume their marriage

---

Cambridge University Press, 1952), 20.

[96] Jacques Tual, 'Sexual Equality and Conjugal Harmony: The Way to Celestial Bliss. A View of Early Quaker Matrimony', *Journal of the Friends Historical Society*, 55 no 6 (1988): 161–74.
[97] Ibid, 168.
[98] Ibid, 168–9.
[99] Ibid, 170.
[100] Fox, *Journal* (1952), 557.

was necessarily celibate, but rather attempts to glean from Fox's writings and marriage to Fell helpful guidance for the Society of Friends today, in regards to issues concerning sexual ethics, marriage and sexuality. Regarding Fox's marriage to Fell, Whitbeck offers an unusual interpretation of Fox's claim that he married 'as a testimony, that all might come up into the marriage as it was in the beginning'.[101] Taking an apocalyptic perspective, Whitbeck argues the above statement is evidence of both Fox and Fell coming 'to a further vision of what marriage could be' by describing their marriage as 'a figure of the marriage of the Lamb to the New Jerusalem, the Holy City'.[102] Whitbeck contrasts this image of the relationship between husband and wife with the more commonly used image of the marriage of Christ and his church amongst other contemporary Protestants. The images of Christ as the 'bridegroom' and the church as his 'bride' were prominent metaphors which ultimately originated from the Old Testament book of the Song of Solomon and were used amongst the Quakers' contemporaries, including the Puritans. Whitbeck suggests the Quakers intentionally replaced the image of the relationship between Christ and his church (which she describes as an inherently hierarchical image used by their contemporaries) with the image of the 'New Jerusalem' and 'the Lamb'. This change, Whitbeck argues, was a direct statement that all Quaker marriages were restored, and therefore no longer under the curse of a gendered hierarchy.

> Other Christian sects ... interpreted the relation between husband and wife in terms of the relation of Christ and the Church. However ... they clung to the belief that human nature was basically sinful, that 'original sin' was not eliminated by Christ's atonement. Since they interpreted the Church to be a human and sinful creature that needed to be made obedient to Christ, they derived sanction for male domination in marriage from the relation of Christ to the Church. In contrast, the New Jerusalem is the perfected city.[103]

While thought provoking, the difficulty with this interpretation is Whitbeck's lack of evidence for support. Whether her interpretation is sound deserves further research and analysis, as Whitbeck's brief discussion begs questions in need of clarification.

Unlike many scholars however, Whitbeck does briefly address an important epistle sent out by Fox a few weeks prior to his marriage (which will be discussed at length later), in which he asserted his marriage would be a 'marriage in the

---

[101] Ibid.
[102] Caroline Whitbeck, 'Friends Historical Testimony on the Marriage Relationship', *Friends Journal: Quaker Thought and Life Today*, 35 no 6 (June 1989): 13–15; p. 14.
[103] Ibid, 15.

seed before the foundation of the world'.¹⁰⁴ Unfortunately, Whitbeck simply concludes Fox presented his ideas 'tactlessly' in a 'condescending' tone, and as a result the letter was not well received.¹⁰⁵ Without further exploration of Fox's particular assertions (for which, incidentally, he never apologised or publicly recanted), nor any additional explanation of why she perceived Fox's words as tactless or condescending, Whitbeck does not give any further analysis of a rich resource. This letter will be discussed and addressed at length in this work. Finally, while Whitbeck focuses primarily on the state of marriage in general, she does not consider in depth the marriage approbation process precisely.

Secondary Literature regarding the Early Quaker Marriage Discipline

In secondary literature, the early Quaker marriage approbation discipline has been set primarily in the broader context of general Quaker history as an acknowledged component of their worship and community life. A number of historians who have studied early-modern marriages in England have acknowledged the peculiarity of the Quaker marriage discipline. In his seminal work *Birth, Marriage, and Death: Ritual, Religion, and the Life-Cycle in Tudor and Stuart England*, David Cressy notes in the wake of the social upheaval of the mid seventeenth century, the Church of England began losing its grip over the marital process as religious dissenters questioned the requirement of an Anglican priest in the marital process. Cressy does not address the Quakers at length, but notes that they, unlike other dissenters, particularly reverted to the 'medieval practice of unsolemnised marriage by common consent'.¹⁰⁶ As will be discussed further in chapter one, the peculiar Quaker marriage discipline did indeed reflect the value of common consent to a point. But more accurately, the early Quakers sought common consent *verifying* through direct divine revelation that God had indeed brought the intended betrothed together.

---

¹⁰⁴ Ibid. See George Fox, *Letter of George Fox Concerning his Marriage. Bristol, Month 8th, Day the 2nd* (1669). (Henry J. Cadbury [Ed.], *Narrative Papers of George Fox: Unpublished or Uncollected, Edited from the Manuscripts with the Introductions and Notes* [Richmond, IN: Friends United Press, 1972], 78.)

¹⁰⁵ Whitbeck, 'Friends Historical Testimony on the Marriage Relationship', 15. Fell biographer Isabel Ross and Quaker historian William Braithwaite briefly refer to this epistle but provide little explanation. Ross described it as 'steeped in mystical language too difficult to understand' (Ross, *Margaret Fell*, 219). Braithwaite acknowledged the epistle was ill regarded amongst the Quakers who received the epistle, while most copies were subsequently destroyed, but makes no further direct reference to this important epistle (Braithwaite, *The Second Period of Quakerism*, 263).

¹⁰⁶ David Cressy, *Birth, Marriage, and Death: Ritual, Religion, and the Life-Cycle in Tudor and Stuart England* (Oxford: Oxford University Press, 1997), 318, 320.

The spiritual rationale underlying the early Quaker marriage discipline has been touched upon briefly by the historian Adrian Davies in his recent work *The Quakers in English Society*.[107] Davies concedes the meetings' tight control over the marriage approbation process 'was a factor which sharply distinguished Friends' marriage procedure from that of others', but provides no further analysis of why, particularly in light of early Quaker spirituality, the early Friends exercised such control.[108] The historian Arnold Lloyd briefly notes that as Fox believed in becoming the renewed Adam, as he was before the Fall, and being in direct subjection to the Spirit of God, there was no longer any need to seek refuge from sin in marriage.[109] Yet, as will be further discussed in this work, Fox's understanding of the 'Second Adam' went beyond Adam's condition before he fell. While Lloyd concedes 'Fox's high doctrine of marriage' restricted it to those who could, in effect, claim they were no longer living in sin (basing his analysis on an exchange of letters which will also be considered in a subsequent chapter), he does not explicate exactly how Fox applied this doctrine to the marriage approbation process.[110] Though neither Davies nor Lloyd give further exposition or analysis of the connection between the early Quaker identity as the True Church and their strenuous marriage approbation discipline, their useful insights open up possibilities of additional, complementary research. I will further explore and more clearly illuminate Fox's belief that each Quaker was in effect called to the state of the second Adam, and therefore must be brought together in marriage by God alone, without a priest, just as Adam had been brought to Eve.

The lengthiest and most recent discussion of the early Quaker marriage discipline has been conducted by professor of literature, Su Fang Ng, in her work *Literature and the Politics of Family in Seventeenth-Century England*. Ng provides another foundation for further research in her consideration of the language and metaphors used by Quakers in their constructions of a familial identity and in their perception of marriage. Addresses such as 'father' in reference to Fox, and 'nursing mother' in reference to Fell, promoted their communal identity within a familial structure.[111] Ng explains, 'If Quakers are brothers and sisters, the elders of the community are viewed as fathers and mothers'.[112] According to Ng, Quakers utilised the metaphor of family in maintaining a measure of hierarchy, as Fox and Fell were seen by some as leaders of a movement, while at the same

---

[107] Adrian Davies, *The Quakers in English Society, 1655–1725* (Oxford: Clarendon Press, 2000), 96.

[108] Ibid.

[109] Lloyd, *Quaker Social History*, 49.

[110] Ibid, 50.

[111] Su Fang Ng, *Literature and the Politics of Family in Seventeenth-Century England* (Cambridge: Cambridge University Press, 2007), 200–02.

[112] Ibid, 202.

time including the involvement of all members of their family community.[113] In regards to spirituality, Ng further asserts Fox spiritualised marriage, through the metaphor of marriage as a symbol of Christ and his church, as Fox used rhetoric which spiritualised:

> [T]he mundane, turning everyday actions into symbols and living testimonies. Turning marriages into metaphor, the Quakers engage in a productive confusion of reality and trope. Because they took a concrete, recurring event – marriage – as a symbol of their faith, the 'living metaphor' inhabited the space between reality and metaphor.[114]

Ng's analysis concludes this symbolic importance led the Quakers to develop a distinctive marriage procedure, in which metaphor becomes a concrete event as well as an historical record.[115] Though this is true, Ng does not note the already present long-standing symbol of marriage as that between Christ and his church in the Christian tradition, nor how the Quakers uniquely interpreted this notion as compared to their contemporaries, including the Church of England. While Ng's analysis is largely useful and accurate, her brief chapter focuses more on a discussion of early Quaker perceptions of the metaphor of marriage and family in general, rather than the spiritual and theological concepts that lie behind the early Quaker marriage approbation process, a topic that will here be analysed at length.

The Range and Resources of this Work

The scope of this work will be primarily focused in time, and in resources, on the life and work within the Quaker movement of both George Fox and Margaret Fell. I have thus concentrated my research on the latter half of the seventeenth century, coinciding with the beginning of the activity of Fox and Fell in the early Quaker movement until the death of Fox in 1691, followed by the death of Fell in 1702. Additionally, the first fifty years of the movement, generally from 1650 to 1700, represent a period which witnessed the rise and fall of the most apocalyptic and prophetic writings and activities of the early Quaker movement. These behaviours and beliefs are generally believed to have abated after the restoration of the monarchy in 1660, and to have died down by the end of this period. This is also due largely to their decreased persecution by the end of the century – a time in Quaker history which has been perceived by most historians

---

[113] Ibid.
[114] Ibid.
[115] Ibid, 204.

as a shift from high apocalyptic language about coming judgment to an increase in concerns about appearing to the general society as a socially reputable religious group.[116] The bulk of the marriage practice in early Quaker doctrine was formed during these early years, coinciding with the early Quaker attempts in forming themselves as the True Church set apart from the fallen world around them. The early years exhibited a concentrated apocalyptic drive which defined the roots and foundation of the early marriage discipline and also provided the context of the highly apocalyptic marriage of Fell and Fox. Their identity as the one and only True Church, which was inextricably linked to their marriage approbation process, would however remain intact throughout the century.

The choice to focus on the writings of Fox and Fell rests largely on their evident influence on the formation of the theological underpinnings and practical processes of the early Quaker marriage doctrine and discipline. The aforementioned discussion of the verifiability of Fox as the main architect of Quakerism and the potential editing of early documents, letters and so on, leads us also to the question of resources when approaching any study of the early Quaker movement. As already noted, whatever editing of it has been done, whether or not existing information was suppressed or to what extent has been rewritten, certainly obscures the resources for the historian attempting research on this time period. As a result, certain conclusions regarding early Quakerism may be at the mercy of a probable incomplete historical record, or a rewritten historical account of early events. Christopher Hill helpfully reminds readers of Quaker history of the limitations encountered by historians of that period:

> Our first problem is that of sources. Quakers re-wrote their own history. They edited earlier texts, including Fox's *Journal*. Many tracts of the 1650s either were not reprinted or were reprinted only in a modified form. There is nothing wrong with this, of course; Lodowick Muggleton drastically edited writings of the chief prophet, John Reeve, when he republished them after Reeve's death. When John Toland edited the republican Edmund Ludlow's Memoirs for publication in 1698 he omitted much of Ludlow's millenarianism so as to make his antimilitarism more acceptable to late 17th century Whig opinion.[117]

---

[116] Mack, *Visionary Women*, 309. Noted Quaker scholar and sociologist Pink Dandelion breaks early Quaker history down into three distinct phases: The first Friends (1647–1666); Restoration Quakerism (1666–1689); Quietism (1690–1820s) (Dandelion, *An Introduction to Quakerism*, 13–53). This breakdown suggests after decreased persecution, the Quakers turned more towards their inward spirituality in the last decade of the century. It is this highly apocalyptic activity of the first Friends, guided largely by Fell and Fox, that occupies this study.

[117] Hill, 'Quakers and the English Revolution'. (Mullett [Ed.], *New Light on George Fox*, 22.)

Though this practice of editing and rewriting may not have been exclusive to Quakers, Hill recognises this habit 'created problems for historians who until recently relied on later reprints of pamphlets of the 1650s'.[118] Bearing in mind the above concerns in regards to early Quaker resources and literature, any apparent omissions from or rewriting of the historical record will be dealt with individually within this work.

The body of work researched for this book is largely located at the Society of Friends Library in London, including the Swarthmoor manuscripts.[119] These manuscripts are a collection of 1,400 original letters and papers dating from the latter half of the seventeenth century. The available manuscripts that pertain to the marriage of Fell and Fox in particular have been edited and transcribed by the Quaker historian Henry J. Cadbury in 1972 in his collection *Narrative Papers of George Fox: Unpublished or Uncollected, Edited from the Manuscripts with the Introductions and Notes*. Comparing Cadbury's transcription to many of the originals at the Society of Friends Library, Cadbury's work has proved a valuable resource. Elsa Glines' recently published corpus of Margaret Fell's one hundred and sixty-four known letters was also an immensely useful resource.[120]

Another valuable resource is the ample pamphlets left behind by Fox and Fell as well as other early Quakers, inclusive of original pamphlets of the 1650s.[121] Pamphlets were a valuable vehicle for Fox and others in the widespread communication of their specific beliefs and rationales behind those beliefs, both to fellow Quakers as well as to those outside the Quaker fold. These pamphlets were often defences about their particular practices, including their unique marital discipline. A majority of these pamphlets are available at the Society of Friends Library in London as well as on the internet at Early English Books Online (EEBO). I have also availed myself of the valuable resources, at both the Bibliothèque Nationale François Mitterrand in Paris, France and the Huntington Library in Pasadena, California, both of which hold seventeenth-century Quaker pamphlets in bound books and collections.

As the early Quakers were such meticulous record keepers, some original meeting minutes are available at the Society of Friends Library in London. I

---

[118] Ibid.

[119] These were likely sorted by Fox when he resided at Swarthmoor Hall. See Moore, *The Light in Their Consciences*, 233.

[120] Elsa F. Glines (Ed.), *Undaunted Zeal: The Letters of Margaret Fell* (Richmond, IN: Friends United Press, 2003).

[121] With a breakdown in censorship and the availability of the printing press and publishers willing to print dissenting views, pamphlets were a primary vehicle through which dissenters could spread their message (Hill, *The World Turned Upside Down*, 17–18). These pamphlets were largely written by Fox as well as Fell and other early leaders who took advantage of this means of spreading their message, as well instructing the large network of meetings on the right processes of marriage approbation.

primarily focused on the Bristol Meeting minutes, transcribed and edited by Russell Mortimer, as they are the most consistently intact minutes available from that time period, and from such an early date.[122] Additionally, the Bristol Meeting was the Meeting at which the marriage of Fell and Fox was approbated[123], making it a significant example of how Fox and Fell envisioned the marriage discipline and approbation process to work in practical terms. It also illumines a great variety of issues which arose in the marriage approbation process, allowing us to glimpse the practical, everyday problems and queries facing the early Quakers in regards to marriage. The Bristol Meeting members' comments regarding the publication of Fox and Fell's marriage in the minutes also shed light on a marriage that was a very important spiritual occasion for the early Quakers, which other marriages could emulate. These minutes have been compared to other minutes available from that time period which, as will be demonstrated in the first chapter, reflect quite similar quandaries as well as a similar practice of marriage approbation, indicating a rather systematic and consistent approbation process.

Locale of the early Quaker movement also plays a factor in the choice of resources. While this study focuses on the meetings and works coming largely out of England, Quakerism by the end of the century was taking hold in various parts of the world. Holland, Barbados and the Americas will be addressed in brief as evidence of the marriage discipline spreading throughout the world. However, the issue primarily at hand is how the Quaker marriage approbation discipline, as experienced by the early Quakers, and as instructed and embodied by the two main leaders, unveils the original intentions and expectations of the earliest Friends in the country where Quakerism was born.

---

[122] Mortimer (Ed.), *Minute Book of the Men's Meeting of the Society of Friends in Bristol 1667–1686*; Russell Mortimer (Ed.), *Minute Book of the Men's Meeting of the Society of Friends in Bristol 1686–1704* (Gateshead,: Northumberland Press Limited, 1977).

[123] Though the term 'approbate' is not commonly used as a verb, it was used as such by the Society of Friends in the seventeenth century, and is still in use in Scottish law terminology. Its uses included 'to approbate' a marriage, and as a noun, marriage 'approbation', both referring to the final permission of a meeting, and the Quaker community's approval of a marital union.

Chapter 1
Approbation and 'Clearness': The Early Quaker Marriage Discipline

Courtship and marriage were major preoccupation for the early Quakers, and were painstakingly regulated within early Quaker meetings, thought and practice. Endogamous marriages were a necessary component to sustain and propagate the Quaker community, God's True Church.[1] Marriage provided a catalyst for the teaching of Quaker principles and beliefs, a critically important microcosm of the larger family of Quakers in various local communities, and around the world. Marrying outside the Quaker fold was detrimental to the spiritually unified whole. The individual, the married couple, the family and the local Quaker meetings were the primary integrated units of Quaker life, all necessarily unified with one another and with God. The need for collective approbation exemplified their adherence to 'unity in the Spirit'. Their desire for the maintenance of spiritual unity amongst each other and with God and their desire for the perpetuation of Quaker ideals in the family, couched in their preoccupation with documentation, which provided proof of their reputation as a people of order 'in the light', led to a proportionately large amount of time in meetings devoted to granting permission to marry. This means of social control was commonly referred to as 'approbation'. Fox and Fell's prolific writing regarding the orderly process of the marriage approbation process warned against marriage by priests, discouraged marriage 'with the world', and encouraged marriage done in an orderly fashion through the thorough documentation of the marital process.

The entire marriage approbation process, including their version of correct courtship, was a curious mixture of spirituality and immense paperwork. Intense spiritual sensitivity to God's inward revelation, including individually and communally waiting on God to verify a command from God for a marriage to be brought together, was essential. This inward verification, often referred to as 'sensing' or 'the sense of the Meeting', was then corporately and carefully documented. Once a couple received approbation to marry, often called 'clearness', their marriage would then be 'witnessed' by a meeting and 'published' in the Book of Minutes. Finally, a certificate was drawn up and signed by the

---

[1] An endogamous marriage was a marriage between two Quakers, while an exogamous marriage was between a Quaker and a non-Quaker.

witnesses. Documentation was an occupation of highest import. It was then assured that clear evidence of a marriage having taken place in an orderly and patient fashion was documented on paper, following correct and appropriate procedure in line with Quaker doctrine and practice. The juxtaposition of a bundle of red tape and revelation from God is intriguing. Questions arise as to why the early Quakers had such a fixation on the marital approbation process, including its meticulous documentation. While various seventeenth-century religious sects were in the process of regulating marriage in the interregnum period and beyond, the Quakers were the frontrunners in meticulously questioning the couple, waiting on God for direction, and carefully following official procedure.

This chapter will begin with a discussion of the social stigmas faced by the early Quakers, including popular accusations of amoral and disorderly behaviour, which contributed in part to the more pragmatic reasons for the early Quaker development of a strict courtship and marriage approbation discipline. This will be followed by a brief introduction to marriage and courtship in seventeenth-century England, in order to compare Quakers with their contemporaries in regards to views on marriage approbation. An assessment of Fell and Fox's efforts to regulate marriage approbation will follow. Then the early Quaker approbation process will be examined in greater detail, including an examination of the extant Bristol Meeting minutes of the latter half of the seventeenth century. Finally, the early Quaker wedding ceremony will be considered, followed by concluding remarks on the gradual development of the Women's Meetings and their unique responsibilities in the marriage discipline. Within this chapter we will see how the intriguing events associated with marital approbation, throughout the history of the early Friends' marriage discipline, illuminate the great lengths at which the early Quakers attempted to conduct themselves in good order. Colourful characters and various circumstances emerge, exemplifying how difficult keeping the marriage discipline 'in unity', 'in the light' and in good order was for the early Quakers. The early efforts of Fox and Fell to maintain a strict marriage discipline would lay the groundwork and leave a legacy for future Quakers to esteem and to evolve.

Maintenance of Morality and Order

In a society reeling from a fear of chaos and disorder as a result of the Civil War and Interregnum, Fox and Fell were already well aware that a façade of discipline and order was in part essential to survival in society. Though many dissenters were distrusted, because the Quakers were the most prolific and rapidly expanding sect during the late 1650s and 1660s they were also the target of a great deal of popular ridicule, hatred and abuse. Historian Barry Reay argues convincingly the general public's fear and hostility towards the Quakers in 1659 contributed to the popular belief that the restoration of the deposed monarchy was the only means to avoid social and religious anarchy.[2] George Fox's defence against this hostility was his consistent promotion of good order, particularly in the Quakers' beliefs as well as their meetings. From their inception, Quakers had encountered accusations of being connected with other popularly criticised sectaries. One such group was the 'Ranters', a religious sect which denied sin and regarded any moral behaviour (including monogamous relationships or marriages) to be irrelevant and unnecessary in the end times. Accused of 'Ranterish' behaviours, the early Quakers were targets of ridicule and hatred, while their meetings were popularly characterised and exaggerated as 'grotesque carnivals of sexual and gluttonous excess'.[3] Rosemary Moore explains popular anxieties which existed in the seventeenth century of antinomian extreme behaviour:

> People expressed a fear that popular belief in the rule of the Spirit and divine Law would lead to immoral behaviour, which certainly happened in the case of a few Ranters, such as the notorious Lawrence Clarkson, a renegade Baptist who said there was nothing wrong in having sexual relations with many women, provided he continued to support his wife.[4]

According to a vociferous opponent of Quakerism, Richard Baxter, Quakers were 'the *Ranters* turned from horrid Prophaneness and Blasphemy, to a Life of extream Austerity on the other side' and that their 'Doctrines were mostly the same with the Ranters: They make the Light which every Man hath within him to be his sufficient Rule'.[5] After Fox's first visit to Margaret Fell's church, he was accused of being a Ranter by the Ulverston Minister, William Lampitt, who cited Fox's notions of perfectionism as similar to the Ranters' denial of sin.[6] Though the early Quakers, including Fox and Fell, had apocalyptic views of their social surroundings, and considered the end of time imminent, they also believed firmly in the inner work of God to make humanity 'pure' in the restoration, and likewise continued to value marriage, monogamy and commitment, no matter

---

[2] Barry Reay, 'Popular Hostility towards Quakers in Mid-Seventeenth Century England', Social History, 5 no 3 (October 1980): 387–407; p. 388.
[3] Kathryn Gucer, '"Not Heretofore Extant in Print": Where the Mad Ranters Are', *Journal of the History of Ideas*, 61 no 1 (Jan 2000): 75–95; p. 78.
[4] Moore, *The Light in Their Consciences*, 100–01.
[5] Richard Baxter, *Reliquiae Baxterianae, or, Mr. Richard Baxters narrative of the most memorable passages of his life and times faithfully publish'd from his own original manuscript by Matthew Sylvester* (London: T. Parkhurst, I. Robinson, I. Lawrence and I. Dunton, 1696), 77. Cited by Braithwaite, *The Beginnings of Quakerism to 1660*, 22 and Mack, *Visionary Women*, 253.
[6] Moore, *The Light in Their Consciences*, 100.

when the end of the world was coming. Their strong beliefs in God's inward presence led them to increased moral behaviour and a heightened importance regarding marriage, as will be discussed shortly. Nevertheless, popular perceptions of Quakers often remained hostile.

In much of the popular mindset, deviancy from social mores or the Church of England were equivalent to moral deviance. Severe attacks were made against the Quakers in regards to their refusal to doff the hat to superiors and to pay tithes, their peculiar way of speaking with 'thee' and 'thou'.[7] These acts were considered threats to the social order and hierarchy of English society. The perceived deviant sexual behaviours of the Quakers continued to be elaborated upon in popular culture.[8] In 1655, a disgruntled ex-Quaker from Kendal, John Gilpin accused a Quaker called Hugh Bisbrown of 'a horrid buggery committed ... with a mare'.[9] In 1673, an anti-Quaker tract from London attacked the Quaker marriage process without a priest, accompanied with accusations of immoral pre-marital sex and illegitimate children:

> He is very diligent in his Generation-worke, and may therefore have many children but no heirs; for his issue comes into the World out-law'd ... he bannes the Banes, and in this respect onely refuses License, consummating his Marriage before it is solemnized; for so soon as the Spirit begins to yield to the rebellion of the flesh, and his Bowels yearn to be multiplying, he and his willing Doxy never wait the Parsons leisure, but take each others word and so to Bed.[10]

---

[7] Reay, 'Popular Hostility towards Quakers in Mid-Seventeenth-Century England', 388–9. Reay asserts, 'Why was there so much hostility? ... There was quite simply a fear of social revolution ... Their light within was a great leveller, removing and questioning formal traditional guides, the established rules on which good order was based. Scripture, ministers, the church, the rigid hierarchical structure of society, the magistracy, the law, all were challenged. The sect's "thee" and "thou" which anticipated the radicals of the French Revolution, their refusal to doff hat to social superiors, their unwillingness even to recognize tithes – courageous stuff in the deferential world of the seventeenth century – predictably enraged the men of property'.

[8] Reay, 'Popular Hostility towards Quakers in Mid-Seventeenth-Century England', 392. Reay writes regarding much of the popular mindset regarding the Quakers: 'Although we do not have any specific evidence for the popular image of the sect, what the ordinary person thought when he or she heard the name Quaker, we can get some idea from the dehumanizing anti-Quaker literature. While they may not have entirely swallowed the image of a bloodthirsty sect, possessed of an unhealthy fondness for horses and a somewhat contradictory blend of asceticism and lasciviousness ... and threatened the stability of church and state ... some of the mud would have stuck'.

[9] John Gilpin, *The Quakers Shaken, or, a warning against quaking* (London, 1655), 1.

[10] Daniel Defoe, *D'foe's answer to the Quakers catechism: or, a dark lanthorn for a friend of the light* (London, 1706), 8–9.

Two poems distributed in 1671 added to the popular perception of Quaker marriages as a haven for debauchery. *The Quakers Wedding*, written by popular seventeenth-century poet Matthew Stevenson in October 1671, was followed by *The Quakers answer, to the Quakers wedding*, published anonymously later the same year. Both mocked the Quaker marital relationship in verse, as can be seen in the following passage from *The Quakers Wedding*:

> *That they should stumble, and pretend such Light,*
> *They Marry wrong, and call't a Marriage-Rite ...*
> *... He takes the Bride, and goes to Multiply,*
> *The Bride? I do recall what I have said,*
> *'Tis not a Bridal, but a Brothel bed ...*
> *... For having Lain together all their Life,*
> *They are, but as they met, not Man and Wife.*[11]

Later in his verse, Stephenson elaborates further on the various damning implications of not being married by a priest, including the production of illegitimate children.[12] In a similar vein to the above passage, the following verse mocks Quaker commitment, and also includes a tongue-in-cheek reference to the Quaker stress on marriage by 'Witnesses':

> *And to their Faith no longer will be Debtor,*
> *Than till they see another they like Better.*
> *I take her to my Wife till my Decease*
> *And call the World to be my Witnesses.*[13]

As late as 1707 another ex-Quaker, George Keith, who had left the Society of Friends after decades of being a prominent leader, warned of the Quakers falling into adulterous affairs through their habits of evangelism which included physical touch.[14] He gave accounts of various Quakers taking advantage of this system, leading to sexual temptations:

> They want the *Spirit of Quakerism* which they reckon is a divine Spirit, ... but [is] a natural thing, and not Divine ... This efflux and effluvium of Spirits is conveyed by the touch and feeling of the hand and Wrist, as also by Kissing and Embracing ...

---

[11] Matthew Stevenson, *The Quakers Wedding* (October 24, 1671) (London: Rowland Reynolds, 1671).

[12] Ibid.

[13] Anonymous, *The Quakers answer, to the Quakers wedding* (November, 8, 1671) (London: Printed for Dorman Newman in the Kings-Armes in the Poultry, 1671).

[14] George Keith of Aberdeen left the Society of Friends over fears they had strayed too far from Orthodox Christianity. He later became an Anglican priest.

the end of those is to feel the Life in one another, and to raise and excite the Life where it is low ... to this end and effect ... some of them also press hard the Wrist as well as the Hand, to feel the Life in the Person whom they so gripe ... Men using it to Women, and Women to Men, have thereby propagated impure and filthy Lust one to another.[15]

Though Keith conceded, 'I charitably believe that many among them abominate those vile practices', he painted a picture of Quakers as a dangerous group which did not have a firm grip on the moral behaviour of all its members.[16] While not everyone would necessarily accept or take seriously the great threats of Quakerism that popular culture and opponents to Quakerism promoted, a general societal uneasiness with Quakers would persist for at least the remainder of the century.

In addition to external criticisms, Fox encountered internal troubles which also put the moral reputation and unity of the Quakers in jeopardy. Schisms erupted early in the movement, particularly as other strong personalities gained a following and challenged Fox's authority. John Perrot, an Irish Quaker who led one of the first significant schisms from Fox, believed he had direct revelation from God that men should keep their hat on while praying, while Fox advocated removing one's hat during prayer.[17] Perrot followed this proclamation with the strict denial of all forms of formal worship, including the Quaker meeting system, causing what Fox saw as a threat to the unity of Quakerism until Perrot's death in Barbados in 1665.[18] Perrot was also highly mystical, expressing spiritual unity with sexual metaphors, apparently causing Fox further alarm.[19] Finally, after Perrot had gained some notoriety with critics of Quakerism as having a predominantly female following, Fox actually criticised some of these women as 'deceitful spirits run up and down among friends, their tongues preaching one

---

[15] George Keith, *The Magick of quakerism, or the Chief mysteries of Quakerism laid open* (London: Printed for Brabazon Aylmer senior and junior, at the Three Pigeons in Cornill, 1707), 47–8.

[16] Ibid, 48.

[17] Braithwaite, *The Beginnings of Quakerism to 1660*, 425. Removing one's hat, a practice called 'hat-honour', when meeting others was not advocated by Quakers at large, but was to be done only in prayer showing reverence to God alone. In regards to Perrot's proclamation, according to Fell biographer Isabel Ross, Perrot cited this revelation after a two-year prison sentence in Rome by the Inquisition in 1657, after which signs of mental instability began to appear (Ross, *Margaret Fell*, 212).

[18] Mack, *Visionary Women*, 271.

[19] Fox had chastised Perrot for declaring he would 'take a slut for a wife' though Perrot defended himself stating he was using it as a metaphor of Hosea. See Mack, *Visionary Women*, 278.

thing, and their lives another'.[20] Though Perrot would not prove to be a long-term threat to Fox's leadership, his reputation caused further alarm amongst Quakers for the need of damage control in regards to maintaining a moral reputation, as well as the collective purity of the group.[21]

Problems with Perrot came in the wake of another threat to unity and respectability – the James Nayler controversy. Prior to 1657, Nayler was arguably as strong a leader in the Quaker movement as Fox. Though he was in close contact with Fox, subsequent circumstances would break their relationship and result in the fall of Nayler's leadership. In 1656, Nayler and two of his close women followers staged a procession into Bristol, designed to be similar to that of Jesus' entry to Jerusalem. Nayler rode on a donkey while women followed, fanning branches and crying out 'holy, holy, holy, Lord God of Sabaoth'.[22] They were seized, arrested by the local authorities, and following a lengthy debate and trial in parliament, Nayler was whipped, his tongue bored through, and a 'B' for blasphemy was branded on his forehead.[23] The Nayler affair caused great havoc amongst the Quakers in terms of their identity, beliefs and unity, while the public was greatly disturbed by Nayler's claiming to be Christ and his having questionable relations with single women. These early Nayler and Perrot crises which damaged Quaker credibility and morality in the public eye, along with questionable and curious marriage practices, harmed the reputation of Quakerism, causing it to be seen as disorderly and ethically dubious.

Under early external persecution, in addition to internal threats to the unity and moral reputation of the Quakers, Fell and Fox countered negative accusations of disunity and immorality by promoting a marriage discipline which followed official Quaker procedure. Careful documentation provided a public and historical record of Quakers as a group who respected the Gospel, listened to God, and who were dedicated to marital fidelity. The early Quakers, particularly Fox himself, had a keen awareness of a paper trail's mark on history as well as on the public record of their respectability as a religious movement. With this in mind, Fox and Fell pressed continually for meetings to exemplify the ideals of a Quaker community committed to unity and order, above legal and social reproach. Bureaucracy in the form of regular meetings, documentation of all proceedings, written testimonies and committees set up for the insurance of 'orderly walking' of all Quakers became the means to spiritual ends, as a uniquely Quaker bureaucratic spirituality emerged.

---

[20] Mack, *Visionary Women*, 278.
[21] See also Barbour and Roberts (Eds), *Early Quaker Writings*, 605.
[22] Mack, *Visionary Women*, 199.
[23] Ibid.

Seventeenth-Century Courtship and Marriage

Marriage, one of the cornerstones of seventeenth-century English society, was irregularly regulated, particularly during the English Civil War when various religious sects practised their own brands of courtship and marriage. According to Christopher Hill, legal historical research indicates the Civil War decades were a period of 'greater freedom from moral supervision than any before or immediately after'.[24] For example, obedience to the biblical ideals of waiting for marriage before engaging in sexual activity was encouraged, yet in seventeenth-century England at least one out of every three brides was pregnant at the time of her marriage, making illegitimate births more common in England than in France.[25] With social and religious upheaval, sexuality and marriage were loosely regulated, but regulation and control of sexual activity, courtship and marriage had always been a challenge for the local authorities and the Church of England.[26]

During the Interregnum, the marital union was still considered both an important social union and a representation of order within society. Both the British government and the Church of England viewed each married couple and their family as a microcosm of the British commonwealth.[27] Social and spiritual responsibilities within marriage, procreation and family existed across classes. Economic concerns were especially apparent amongst the estate families of the wealthier gentry classes. Amongst the gentry and upper classes, parents often arranged marriages based on economic interests and property transactions, a task considered by some as 'too serious to be left in the hands of children getting married'.[28] With many marriages arranged and approved by parents, engagements were not always motivated by any particular affection between the betrothed. While it is true, as historian Christine Trevett reminds us, that 'marriage for love was not encouraged',[29] there is evidence that love could be seen as a factor in choosing a mate. William Gouge, in his popular and widely read book *Of Domesticall Duties* (1622), urged young men to choose mates based on love.[30] The historian David Cressy asserts, 'Though sometimes conceived as alliances between families, gentry marriages were not all heartlessly commercial or mere dynastic arrangements'.[31] Cressy offers a brief outline of a typical courtship procedure in the seventeenth century:

---

[24] Hill, *The World Turned Upside Down*, 313.
[25] Ibid.
[26] Cressy, *Birth, Marriage, and Death*, 333.
[27] Ng, *Literature and the Politics of Family in Seventeenth-Century England*, 2.
[28] Hill, *The World Turned Upside Down*, 307.
[29] Trevett, *Women and Quakerism in the 17th Century*, 76.
[30] Ibid. See also William Gouge, *Of Domesticall Duties: Eight Treatises* (London: Printed by John Haviland for William Bladen, 1622).
[31] Cressy, *Birth, Marriage, and Death*, 254.

The procedure included cues to minimize embarrassment and mechanisms to avoid dishonour. The young man's responsibility was to make visits, offer gifts, and to bring his prospective bride to agreement. The woman had the option of being more or less tractable ... of generally signalling her inclinations. The woman's role was passive, but not entirely powerless. Agreement and contract between the couple opened the way for legal and financial agreements between their families.[32]

Whether arranged for economic interest, or brought together by mutual interest or attraction, suitability for marriage often rested on the couple's likeness in social condition, making cross class marriages infrequent.

The attempt to define what constituted a legitimate marriage had been a challenge for the church. The medieval church had declared a marriage valid if there was a personal, verbal exchange of wedding vows, made in the present tense, between two people legally free to marry.[33] It was preferred these vows would be made publicly in the presence of witnesses and solemnised by a priest before co-habitation began.[34] The historian R.B. Outhwaite explains the church began establishing rules in an effort to ensure the publicity of marriages by 'attempting to tie weddings to certain places, certain days and times, and to certain preliminary procedures', including the requirement that couples had to announce their intention to wed through 'thrice-called banns'.[35] Though these regulations were put forth by the medieval church, marriage procedures still varied tremendously.[36]

By the sixteenth century, Protestant efforts to regulate marriage and courtship emerged through the formation of ecclesiastical courts. The first Protestant court of any kind was the marriage court in Zurich established in 1525.[37] When

---

[32] Ibid. See also Richard Adair, *Courtship, Illegitimacy and Marriage in Early Modern England* (Manchester: Manchester University Press, 1996). Adair notes courtship practices across the classes in early-modern England: 'The initiative in courtship among the social groups under consideration usually came from the children themselves ... The most important factors in choosing a partner, particularly for the propertyless, were probably general parity of age and status, and personal attraction' (Adair, *Courtship, Illegitimacy and Marriage in Early Modern England*, 134–5).

[33] R.B. Outhwaite, *Clandestine Marriage in England: 1500–1850* (Cambridge: Cambridge University Press, 1995), xiii.

[34] Ibid.

[35] Ibid. This was partly done to give time to ensure the couple was legally free to marry.

[36] Ibid, xiii–xvi. Outhwaite explains, 'The church was battling, however, against a society which had its own procedural forms of entry into matrimony. Indeed the church's marriage liturgy embodied such folk customs whilst seeking to clothe them with ritual and with religious significance' (ibid, xvi).

[37] Merry E. Wiesner-Hanks, *Christianity and Sexuality in the Early Modern World* (London: Routledge, 1999), 67.

the early courts of Protestant Europe began to deal with various moral issues, church members became susceptible to communal accountability regarding such issues as sexual promiscuity, gambling and non-attendance at church. One of the more famous of these early moral courts was founded in Geneva by John Calvin.[38] Other church courts similar to Calvin's were subsequently established throughout Protestant Europe, with the primary task of dealing with marital agreements and/or disputes. The legitimacy of marriages was a frequent issue. When one spouse wanted to reinforce a marital agreement, judges often proposed the following questions: whether there was parental consent to the marriage, if the wedding took place in a church, and if there were any witnesses.[39] By the 1630s, Protestant church courts began requiring marriage licences and subsequently fined couples who married without licences, thus creating an exponential growth in the issuing of marriage licences.[40] As licences were not cheap, they became a status symbol amongst the upper and middle classes and were virtually unattainable by the poor.[41]

Other problems in the regulation of marriage included the discrepancies which existed between the Church of England and civil law regarding what was required for a legitimate marriage. In early-modern England, according to civil law a couple could be considered married simply by a personal exchange of vows (like in the medieval church), but the Church of England insisted weddings should be conducted in public following *The Book of Common Prayer* form.[42] While many followed the Church of England ceremony, others continued to avail themselves of alternative routes to marriage.[43] At the time the Quakers appeared on the historical landscape in the late 1640s and early 1650s, according to the historian David Cressy, the Church of England 'did its best to safeguard matrimonial discipline, but the effect was uneven ... Irregular weddings in alehouses and private houses became increasingly common'.[44] Ceremonies conducted without a priest, known as 'handfast marriages' or 'spousals' were

---

[38] Ibid, 68.

[39] Ibid. Parental consent would not be required for marriage by law until 1754 in England, but it was typically pursued by the intended betrothed if the parents were still living (Adair, *Courtship, Illegitimacy and Marriage in Early Modern England*, 135).

[40] Hill, *The World Turned Upside Down*, 313.

[41] Ibid. The historian Lawrence Stone explains, 'After 1660 virtually all the middling sort and above were married by licence, but the cost put it out of reach of the lower classes' (Lawrence Stone, *Uncertain Unions: Marriage in England, 1660–1753* [Oxford: Oxford University Press, 2001], 22).

[42] David Cressy and Lori Anne Ferrell, *Religion and Society in Early Modern England: A Sourcebook* (New York, NY: Routledge, 2005), 61; see also *The Book of Common Prayer* http://justus.anglican.org/resources/bcp/1559/Marriage_1559.htm (accessed 23 March 2011).

[43] Cressy and Ferrell, *Religion and Society in Early Modern England*, 61.

[44] Cressy, *Birth, Marriage, and Death*, 333.

occurring throughout the Northwest of England and in Scotland.⁴⁵ Clandestine marriages were also a continuing concern for the Church of England.⁴⁶ Lawrence Stone defines a clandestine marriage as a ceremony which was conducted by a clergyman (or one who purported to be so) and followed the ritual prescribed by *The Book of Common Prayer*, but it was 'irregular' primarily by being done in secret rather than in public at a church parish.⁴⁷ Clandestine ceremonies not only occurred in alehouses and coffee shops but were also known to take place in prisons or brothels, causing further moral alarm.⁴⁸ This practice was additionally disliked by the Church of England because these ceremonies were done without the issue of a licence from a church official and they were not recorded in the parish records.⁴⁹

While the Church of England struggled to maintain a semblance of order with the marriage process, during Quakerism's infancy the 'Barebones Parliament' of 1653 passed a civil Marriage Act making it mandatory for a marriage ceremony to be conducted in front of a justice of the peace.⁵⁰ Yet despite this advance, on

---

45   Barbour and Roberts (Eds), *Early Quaker Writings*, 475. 'Handfast marriages' were considered a folk-ceremony, practised largely in Scotland. In the years preceding Quakerism, as Martin Ingram explains, ' … a legally binding union was not the formal solemnisation of marriage in church but a contract – called, in popular usage, "spousals", "making sure" or "handfasting" – by which a couple took each other as husband and wife … In order to be fully licit in the eyes of the church and of the society as a whole, the law prescribed that contracts should be publicised by the calling of banns and solemnised in open church; and marriage in church was undoubtedly normal practice in the late sixteenth and the seventeenth centuries. But an unsolemnised or unwitnessed union, though irregular, might nonetheless be fully binding' (Martin Ingram, *Church Courts, Sex and Marriage in England, 1570–1640* [Cambridge: Cambridge University Press, 1994], 189–90). Johanna Rickman summarises the 'spousal' process: 'English civil law only required a verbal expression of consent of both parties, spoken in the present tense (*per verba de praesenti*), in order for a marriage to be valid. For example, the medieval tradition of spousals … could be interpreted as a valid marriage … A spousal was a ceremony in which a couple pronounced their intentions to be husband and wife, usually in front of family and witnesses, and exchanged gifts, such as rings' (Johanna Rickman, *Love, Lust, and License in Early Modern England: Illicit Sex and Nobility* [Farnham: Ashgate Publishing Limited, 2008], 15–16). See also Adair, *Courtship, Illegitimacy and Marriage in Early Modern England*, 142–8.

46   Cressy and Ferrell, *Religion and Society in Early Modern England*, 61. Richard Adair notes that by the end of the seventeenth century spousals were near extinction, while clandestine marriages 'rose to a height of popularity' (Adair, *Courtship, Illegitimacy and Marriage in Early Modern England*, 143).

47   Stone, *Uncertain Unions*, 22.

48   Ibid.

49   Ibid, 22–3.

50   Kunze notes, 'In 1653 a civil marriage act was passed by Barebones Parliament that made a marriage ceremony before a justice of the peace compulsory. The contract was duly

the whole, laws remained unclear regarding official marriage proceedings, while clandestine marriages were on the rise.[51] Lawrence Stone sums up the situation succinctly:

> It is not too much to say that the marriage law as it operated in practice in England from the fourteenth to the nineteenth century was a mess. The root cause of the trouble was that there was no consensus within society at large about how a legally binding marriage should be carried out.[52]

It is from this quagmire that the Quakers developed their own particular marriage discipline. In this chapter, we will discover how early Quaker courtship and marriage approbation compared to the above-described processes. Amongst the Quakers, the road to marriage on the whole included a larger degree of verified communal involvement as compared to many of their seventeenth-century contemporaries. Clandestine marriages were similarly discouraged by Fox, Fell and the Quaker meetings for many of the same reasons, but with additional theological justifications. A marriage was expected to be a very public affair, rather than a privately pursued business between individuals. Considered a highly spiritual matter, their courtships were cautiously approached in the fear of God, with great discussion between the couple verifying if both felt God had guided them to each other. The marriages were then approbated not only by the parents and the betrothed, but also by the Quaker community, a process which could take weeks or months. These guidelines, along with an elaborate recording system of the marriage approbation process and ceremony, were largely a product of the work of both George Fox and Margaret Fell, whose writings helped shape and attempted to enforce the early Quaker marriage approbation discipline.

---

recorded by the civil registrar for the public record' (Kunze, *Margaret Fell and the Rise of Quakerism*, 158). Shannon Miller explains, 'The 1653 Act voted in by the Barebones Parliament barred any marriages but those performed by a justice of the peace; the act transformed marriage into a civil act, one requiring a representative of the state to perform it ... Church marriages were consequently banned, though many couples, entirely confused by the terms of the marriage act, would marry twice, once under the auspices of the civil practice and then marry within the church' (Shannon Miller, *Engendering the Fall: John Milton and the Seventeenth-Century Women Writers* [Philadelphia, PA: University of Pennsylvania Press, 2008], 246).

[51] Stone, *Uncertain Unions*, 31. Stone asserts, 'The explosion of the clandestine marriage business between 1660 and 1763 was inexplicable, except in terms of an endless confused conflict between deeply entrenched vested interests. The public almost always found a way to get around the law for their own purposes' (Stone, *Uncertain Unions*, 31).

[52] Ibid.

Margaret Fell and George Fox: Their Rejection of 'Hireling Priests' and Their Defence of the Legitimacy of Quaker Marriages

Like their Protestant contemporaries, early Quakers did not view marriage as a sacrament. But dissimilar to the Church of England, who encouraged marriage by clergy in a church, Quakers did not believe a priest (or any human agent) had the right to marry two individuals. Referred to as 'hireling priests', clergy being paid to conduct a wedding was an act that was abhorrent to Fox and Fell.[53] Fox repeatedly maintained that nowhere in the scriptures were there records of a priest conducting a wedding.[54] While travelling through Yorkshire in 1666, at a meeting before a Quaker wedding Fox preached, 'never from Genesis to the Revelation did ever any priests marry any, as may be read in the Scriptures'.[55] Margaret Fell argued the same in her 1667 work *A touch-stone, or, A perfect tryal by the Scriptures, of all priests, bishops, and ministers*:

> They [the priests] have no Example in the Scriptures, that the people were married with a Priest, neither in the Old-Testament not New; ye do not read that Abraham and Sarah were married with a Priest; and Isaac too Rebecca to wife, and Laban gave Jacob Leah and Rachel, but not by a Priest ... And thus they run themselves quite from the scriptures.[56]

---

[53] Trevett, *Women and Quakerism in the 17th Century*, 92. See also George Fox's *General Epistle on Property and Marriages* (1668): 'Friends ... Thou to everyone ... keep your testimony against the priests and the world's joining in marriages' (Barbour and Roberts [Eds], *Early Quaker Writings*, 493).

[54] George Fox, *Concerning Marriage: How God made them Male and Female in the Beginning, 7th Month 1659* (London: Thomas Simmons, 1661), 4–5. See also George Fox, *The true marriage declared, or, Seven testimoneys from the record of Scripture concerning the true marriages and such as are not according to the truth for Friends and all others concerned to read in the feare of the Lord* (London, 1679), 7: 'It is not our practice to marry any, and we are only witnesses to the marriage, for it's the Lords worke to Joyne them together'. Fox later wrote in 1686, 'And wee have asked the priests, justices and others where did ever God command any to marry' (George Fox, *Concerning marriage, 1686.* Swarthmoor Manuscripts, portfolio X, folio 66. The Society of Friends Library London).

[55] Fox, *Journal* (1952), 506.

[56] Margaret Fell, *A touch-stone, or, A perfect tryal by the Scriptures, of all the priests, bishops, and ministers, who have called themselves, the ministers of the Gospel whose time and day hath been in the last ages past, or rather in the night of apostacy: they are tried and weighed by the Scriptures of truth, and are found out of the life and power of the scriptures, and out of the spirit and doctrine of them that gave them forth, and quite contrary to their principle and practice, both Papists and Protestants: unto which is annexed, Womens speaking justified, &c* (London, 1667), 70.

Thus both Fox and Fell argued such practices not only countered scriptural examples but were also conducted for 'Priests' to 'get money of people'.[57]

Not desiring to be married by the local Anglican priest, the Quakers, like other dissenters such as the Baptists, searched for alternative means of marriage.[58] Before the official Quaker marriage discipline of marriage by witnesses was developed, some early Quakers went to the local magistrate or were married in the clandestine or handfast fashion.[59] It was in part these 'worldly' ceremonies of marriage by magistrate, or priest, or handfast marriages which prompted criticism within the Quaker community and perpetuated both confusion and desire for clarification on how to handle the marital process in general. Out of these early cases of confusion, we see the first signs of Quakers managing and overseeing marriages for the sake of theological purity and consistency. In 1653, the year the Marriage Act was passed, George Fox wrote a pamphlet in which he first suggested all Quaker marriages be conducted in a meeting and follow a certain prescribed procedure including communal approbation and marriage by witnesses. He referred to this pamphlet in his *Journal*:

> I had given forth a paper concerning marriages about the year 1653, when truth was but little spread over the nation; advising friends who might be concerned in that case, that they might lay it before the faithful in time, before any thing were concluded, and afterward publish it in the end of a meeting, or in a market, (as they were moved thereto). And when all things were found clear, they being free from all others and their relations being satisfied, then they might appoint a meeting on purpose for the taking of each other, kin the presences of at least twelve faithful witnesses.[60]

However, the following year in 1654, a Friend called George Taylor of Kendal complained to Margaret Fell of a couple who had married according to the world's customs and not 'in the Light':

> Agnes Ayrey and John Spooner are, as we are informed, married; it were well if it had been done in the Light; our spirits cannot relish it; only we leave it in silence for fear of giving offence; but it were well if less of that were practiced amongst Friends.[61]

---

[57] Ibid.

[58] Christopher Hill suggests the Quakers followed the example of both Familists and some Baptists by practising marriage by declaration before the congregation, with no other civil or religious ceremony. See Hill, *The World Turned Upside Down*, 312.

[59] Barbour and Roberts (Eds), *Early Quaker Writings*, 475. See also Cressy, *Birth, Marriage, and Death*, 332.

[60] Fox, *Journal* (1952), 519.

[61] Barbour and Roberts (Eds), *Early Quaker Writings*, 475.

Though Fox had begun to formulate an idea of marriage approbation, some Quakers were still availing themselves of other customs of marriage. During this time Fox and Fell began to write extensively in an effort to create a more specific Quaker marriage procedure. While it is difficult to ascertain when the earliest Quaker marriage took place by witnesses without a priest, it is likely the earliest recorded marriage amongst the Quakers was that of Thomas Holme of Kendal and Elizabeth Leavens in 1654, both active Quaker preachers.[62] Thus began the process of formulating and enacting a formal Quaker marriage approbation discipline and procedure.

The legality of the early Quaker marriages, as they were neither conducted by priest nor magistrate, immediately became a source of concern for the Quakers. As discussed earlier, if Quakers were not considered legally married they ran the risk of being seen as adulterers, and their children considered as illegitimate.[63] One of the earliest known legal cases concerning Quaker marriages involved Cuthbert Hunter, who was brought before the Newcastle assizes in 1654. Having been married by Quaker customs, he admitted to Judge Hugh Wyndham that he had not been married by either priest or magistrate, leading Wyndham to condemn Hunter for breaking the law of both God and man.[64] Hunter was accused of fornication and adultery, and given the alternative to either pay a fine or be imprisoned, of which Hunter chose prison. While the ill-fated Hunter did go to prison, subsequent Friends would fare better in the courts.

In 1661, the validity of Quaker marriages was challenged at the assizes at Nottingham, where there was a trial concerning a Quaker marriage between William Ashwell and Anne Ridge that had taken place in 1658. Two years after their marriage, William became mortally ill, leaving his estate and personal effects to his wife and then unborn child. The land was considered 'copyhold' land, and as such he sent for copyholders to surrender it, but he died before they arrived. Legal historian Craig Horle summarises the lawful status of the estate:

> Legally speaking, therefore, he had died intestate because the copyhold estate of inheritance was not settled nor disposed of in his lifetime. His wife gave birth to the child, Mary, who was presented to the manor court and accepted by the tenants as next heir in law to her father, and thus admitted by the lord of the manor as tenant, with her mother Anne as guardian.[65]

---

[62] Ibid.
[63] See introduction, p. 7.
[64] Craig Horle, *The Quakers and the English Legal System 1660–1688* (Philadelphia, PA: The University of Pennsylvania Press, 1988), 234.
[65] Ibid, 235.

Things turned complicated however when Anne Ridge married John Theaker. Theaker shared the estate with Anne, until John Ashwell, brother of William Ashwell, contested this arrangement by bringing:

> A writ of ejectment against Anne and Mary on the premise that Anne's first marriage had not been legal, and that Mary was therefore illegitimate, leaving him, John Ashwell, as the legal heir.[66]

A local Quaker, Martin Mason, who knew the important and potentially disastrous implications of this case, wrote to the two judges who were to preside over the case, John Archer and Edward Atkyns, 'Shall the want of a mere punctilio in the formality of the law deprive so many thousand innocent people of protection by the law when the body or substance of the law is so clearly answered?'[67]

Considering the importance of the case, the Quakers assigned former judge Richard Newgate to represent Anne and John Theaker. They introduced three non-Quakers who testified that Anne and William had been married in an open meeting. For further evidence, they produced the marriage certificate signed by the Quaker witnesses, proving the child had been conceived within marriage. Fox explained John Ashwell's counsel spoke 'unsavoury' words concerning Friends, 'saying they went together like brute beasts'.[68] After the counsel on both sides pleaded the case, according to Fox, Judge Archer affirmed:

> It was the consent of the parties that made a marriage ... as for the Quakers, he did not know their opinions, but he did not believe they went together like brute beasts as had been said, but as Christians. Therefore he did believe the marriage was lawful and the child lawful heir, and then brought a case to satisfy the jury. It was to this purpose: A man that was weak of body and kept his bed, and in that condition his desire was to take a woman to be his wife, and she declared that she took that man to be her husband. The marriage was called in question, all the bishops did conclude the marriage to be lawful, as the judge said. And the cause was carried against the man for the child.[69]

Judge Archer ruled the Ashwell/Ridge marriage lawful and Mary the legal heir to the estate, thereby making a strong supporting statement for the validity of Quaker marriages and setting a precedent for legal cases to come. While the path would not always be smooth for all Quaker marriages in the years ahead,

---

[66] Ibid, 236.
[67] Ibid.
[68] Fox, *Journal* (1952), 422.
[69] Ibid.

this case provided a firm foundation for the protection of Quakers' legal rights of inheritance and legitimacy.

While Quakers forbade marriages by justices, the notion of letting the local magistrate know of the marriage, in order to protect the legality of early Quaker marriages, was suggested in 1656 by Margaret Fell in her epistle *To Friends, an Epistle on marriage*.[70] During her marriage to Judge Fell, Fell frequently entertained friends in the legal profession, and had subsequent exposure to and knowledge of legal matters. It is highly likely that her awareness of legal affairs influenced this proposal. Fell instructed male Friends to sign a certificate as witnesses of a marriage and take this certificate to the justice of the peace as soon as possible afterwards. This innovation of making it mandatory for the couple to alert the magistrate of their marriage was unique to Fell, according to Bonnelyn Kunze.[71] Fell directed the newly married couple to 'carry the note to the next Justice of the peace so called, the next day, or within some convenient time'.[72] Kunze further points out the curious omission of this document from the Quakers' preserved early documents, as it was not discovered until 1950 in a private collection.[73] This finding not only confirmed Fell as the innovator of the mandate to make marriages known to the local magistrate, but also served to demonstrate her knowledge of legal practice and how to avoid problems with the law.[74] Whether or not the local magistrate was alerted of the marriage did not seem to matter to Fox, who left it up to the couple and the relevant meeting 'as they are moved, they may declare it to the Magistrate, and they will or they may not'.[75] Fell also elaborated on allowing time for problems regarding the marriage to arise during the approbation process, 'A[nd] let there bee a space after the first declaration to the meeting, that if any have any thing to object against the things, they may have time to speak'.[76] This pause for any objections, unlike the obligatory 'or forever hold your peace' moment in many wedding ceremonies of today, was taken quite seriously by the early Quakers, and as will be seen in the following section, occasionally made for interesting revelations amongst those betrothed and sometimes halted the marriage proceedings altogether.

---

[70] Margaret Fell, *To Friends, an Epistle on marriage* (1656). (Glines [Ed.], *Undaunted Zeal: The Letters of Margaret Fell*, 194.)
[71] Kunze, *Margaret Fell and the Rise of Quakerism*, 158.
[72] Fell, *To Friends, an Epistle on marriage*. (Glines [Ed.], *Undaunted Zeal*, 194.)
[73] Kunze, *Margaret Fell and the Rise of Quakerism*, 158. Historian Arnold Lloyd noted that the catalogue of Fox's papers attributes this innovation to Fox. See Lloyd, *Quaker Social History*, 50, 62.
[74] Glines (Ed.), *Undaunted Zeal*, 194.
[75] Fox, *Concerning Marriage* (1661), 5.
[76] Margaret Fell, *To Friends, an Epistle on marriage* (1656). (Glines [Ed.], *Undaunted Zeal*, 195.)

Finally, we also find in Fell's epistle one of the earliest suggestions that Friends draw up a marriage certificate. Fell advised the meetings to document the marriage, 'draw a little note, concerning the action of the day, which they were witnesses of'.[77] Stressing the importance of witnesses, she reminded the meeting procedure was to be followed 'so that nothing bee acted among friends in the dark, & so come under reproach, but that truth may be clear of all scandals, & stand over all the powers of darkness'.[78] Fox concurred, giving instructions in 1661 to draw up a 'Certificate by Friends then present may be given of the Day, Month, and Year, that it may be recorded'.[79] This innovation would have lasting consequences, as drawing up a certificate practice at a marriage is still a common practice amongst Quakers today.[80]

In 1677, at a General Meeting in Amsterdam, resolutions were drawn up adopting the ideas set forth by Fox and Fell regarding marriage approbation. A 'select meeting' of Friends met 'in which the nature of marriage, and the practice of Friends relating to it and other things, were very weightily and closely discoursed'.[81] Their resolutions included marriage by communal consent rather than a priest:

> A universal and unanimous sense of Friends, that joining in marriage is the work of the Lord only, and not of priest or magistrate. For it is God's ordinance and not man: and therefore Friends cannot consent to that they should join them together. For we marry none; it is the Lord's work, and we are but witnesses.[82]

In addition, a following resolution allowed for those who, 'through tenderness, have a desire that the magistrate should know' to record their marriage with the local justice of the peace:

---

[77] Ibid.

[78] Ibid.

[79] Fox, *Concerning Marriage* (1661), 5.

[80] The Quaker lawyer and historian Nancy Black Sagafi-Nejad explains current Quaker marriage proceedings, 'The Quaker marriage ceremony has remained essentially unchanged through the centuries, and as in earlier times, the meeting gives its approval to the marriage in advance of the wedding day ... An appointed Friend reads the marriage certificate aloud to the gathering, and the couple signs it; after the rise of the meeting, each guest also signs. A Meeting Committee is responsible for legal recordation of the marriage ... ' (Nancy Black Sagafi-Nejad, *Friends at the Bar: A Quaker View of Law, Conflict Resolution, and Legal Reform* [Albany, NY: State University of New York Press, 2011], 27).

[81] William Penn, *William Penn's Journal of his travels in Holland and Germany in 1677, in the service of the Gospel; containing several letters and addresses written while there to persons of eminence and quality* (London: Darton and Harvey, Fourth Edition, 1835), 8.

[82] Ibid, 9.

> After the marriage is performed in a public meeting of Friends and others, (according to the holy order and practice of Friends in torch throughout the world, and the manner of holy men and women of old) [they] may go and carry a copy of the certificate to the magistrate ... that if they please they may register it.[83]

Though not made mandatory, meetings internationally addressed and allowed for Fell's innovative notion of alerting the magistrate as the couple and their meeting saw fit.

As Quakerism was 'being more spread over the nation', Fox more specifically instructed Friends 'by the same power and spirit of God, that marriages should be laid before the men's monthly and quarterly meetings'.[84] As with various other aspects of Quaker life and discipline, Fox felt he was commanded by God to instil these instructions for the marital approbation process, in order to preserve innocence and purity amongst the Quakers.[85] But there were practical sides to recording marriages as well. Legal records could protect the rights of children, widows and others. Fox exhorted meetings to:

> Buy convenient Books for Registering the Births and Marriages and Burials ... that every one may be ready to give Testimony and Certificate thereof, if need requires, or any be called thereunto.[86]

As Quakers did not attend their local churches, a substitute for the registration and documentation of 'Births and Marriages and Burials' had to be instituted, providing further legal protection of Friends, as well as an organised record of their communities' rites of passage.[87]

In 1661, Fox elaborated on his vision of the correct process of being married 'in the light' in an effort to dissuade clandestine marriages amongst Quakers. Marriage in public meetings was essential to avoid rumours and criticisms, helping to keep all proceedings in the open and above external or internal reproach:

---

[83] Ibid.
[84] Fox, *Journal* (1952), 519.
[85] Ibid.
[86] George Fox, *Friends Fellowship Must Be in the Spirit* (London, 1668). Cited in Richard T. Vann and David Eversley, *Friends in Life and Death: The British and Irish Quakers in the Demographic Transition, 1650–1900* (Cambridge: Cambridge University Press, 1992), 15.
[87] Vann and Eversley assert Fox's suggestion that the holy men of God recorded marriages in books was 'erroneous ... as a piece of history' (Vann and Eversley, *Friends in Life and Death*, 16).

> And if any friends go together in the Power of the Lord, or find a necessity thereunto to joyn in marriage, that after the thing hath been made known between themselves, before any thing be concluded, it be declared to Friends who are able, in the Wisdom and Power of God to see and feel into it: & if they see the thing in the light and power to stand, it may be declared to friends in the meeting or Meetings, to which the parties do belong ... that it may be by friends felt and seen in the light, and enquirie may be made touching any other engagement, to stop scandals, and things kept sweet, so that you take time in it, and you may be clear ... if friends have any thing against it ... that then the matter be laid before friend the next General meeting ... and there to been into and ended ... and after things are all sweet and clear, and Friends have unity with it, they may, as they are moved, declare it at the end of the General Meeting.[88]

Like Fell, Fox affirmed the meeting process helped to 'stop scandals'. 'Unclean' marriages were to be avoided at all costs: people marrying outside of the Quaker fold, marriages done against the wishes of relatives or parents, marriages done in secret, and finally marriages where provisions were not provided for the children of previous marriages. Fox believed the marital discipline procedures were an insurance against these lethal threats to the unity and purity of the Friends, 'So that all things might be kept clean and pure and done in righteousness to the glory of God'.[89] According to Fox, the Quaker meetings were an effort to guarantee that all 'Unrighteousness, and Filthiness, Fornication, Whoredom, and Adultery may be shut out'.[90] Establishing blameless behaviour was paramount for Fox.

During a trip to London in 1667, Fox stayed with Friends in the city and observed their practices and state of affairs with marriages in London. He wrote regarding their marriage discipline:

> I was moved to exhort them to bring all their marriages to the men's and women's-meetings, that they might lay them before the faithful there, that so care might be taken to prevent those disorders that had been committed by some. For many had gone together in marriage contrary to their relations' minds; and some young raw people that came amongst us had mixed with the world; and widows had married and had not made provision for their children by their former husbands before their second marriage.[91]

---

[88] Fox, *Concerning Marriage* (1661), 4–5.
[89] Ibid.
[90] Ibid.
[91] Ibid.

Over a decade after Fox and Fell's first writings regarding marriage, exogamous marriages were still plaguing the Quaker fold. The marital discipline process would remain a pressing matter for the Society of Friends for decades to come.

Clearness and Approbation: The Early Quaker Marriage Discipline

As Quaker Meetings began to form and meet more regularly, the marital discipline as laid out by Fox and Fell became increasingly accepted and instituted by Friends. The meeting became the fixed touchstone for the beginning of marital relations, as a defined matrimonial course was accepted, encouraged and enforced. If there were no problems encountered by the couple, the process could take just over a month, involving a great deal of paperwork including certificates from parents, and other Quaker meetings if one of the betrothed was not from the meeting conducting the approbation. If problems did occur, the approbation process could last months. The delays could include time spent on other paperwork. For example, certificates documenting one's official contrition had to be submitted to the meeting if a prospective spouse was known amongst the Quakers as having engaged in 'disorderly walking' or 'miscarriadges'. 'Miscarriadges' was a term used by early Quakers to denote any behaviour they felt to be not indicative of a person 'walking in the light' (e.g. exogamous marriages, gossiping, drunkenness, adultery, talking negatively, etc.).[92] It could be any behaviour that might disrupt the unity and purity of the Quakers, exhibited in a person carrying themselves in a way that Quakers felt dishonoured God and their communities. Members of the meeting would then be sent out to investigate delaying the process even longer. All was expected by the early Quakers to be out in the open, with little value placed on privacy.

The path to matrimony would ideally start with both the man and the woman sensing a 'leading from God' that they should marry one another. This inner sense of leading from God was in effect essential to gain Quaker approbation, as it was necessary that God's will, rather than human will or desire, led the couple together. In 1668, Isaac Penington wrote to a couple upon marrying:

> Friends, the affectionate part will be forward in things of this nature, unless it be yoked down: and it will persuade the mind to judge such things to be right and

---

[92] 'Miscarriadges' was spelled with or without a 'd'. It has no reference to miscarriage related to pregnancy, but rather relates to one's 'carriage' in regards to holy or correct behaviour.

of the Lord when indeed they are not so. Now if it be not of the Lord, but the affectionate part, friends cannot have unity with it.[93]

Just as the light of God led one to their 'convincement', waiting and listening to the light of God speaking within the conscience, so too was the marital union to begin in this manner. According to Penington, the 'affectionate part' had to be 'yoked down' in order for the Quaker to adequately hear from God. For the early Quaker the 'leading to marry' should thus not be grounded in sexual attraction or other natural affections, but rather prompted by a leading from God alone. 'Love' was rarely mentioned as a motivating factor in choosing a mate in the early Quaker record.[94] Doing so might implicate one of following one's own will versus God's will. If the marriage was not prompted by God, but rather by other natural inclinations, Penington assured his readers:

> The power (waited upon by you) may loosen your affections in this respect. But if it be of the Lord, and be orderly brought before Friends, and their counsel and advice sought in the fear of the Lord, they will have unity with it.[95]

Francis Howgill, a friend of Fox's and a prominent early Quaker leader, wrote to his daughter Abigail a letter from his deathbed in which he offered fatherly counsel and advice, including guidance on the proper road to matrimony. Howgill encouraged Abigail to guard her affections carefully, to be cautious of those professing love, and not to seek a husband actively, but let the husband seek her:

> If thou live to be a woman of perfect years, keep thyself unspotted, and let not thy mind out after sports and pastimes, the end of all these is sorrow; neither of young men: if thou have a desire to marry, do not thou seek a husband, but let a husband seek thee; and if thou live in God's fear, and an honest life, and virtuous, they that fear God will seek unto thee; let not thy affections out unto every one that profess love, but be considerate; and above all things choose one, if thou dost marry, that loves and fears the Lord: whose conversation thou knowest, and manner and course of life well, before thou givest consent.[96]

---

[93] Isaac Penington, *To a couple upon marrying* (1668). (Barbour and Roberts [Eds], *Early Quaker Writings*, 235.)
[94] Davies, *The Quakers in English Society*, 94.
[95] Ibid.
[96] Francis Howgill, *The Unchangeable Testament, and Will, and Counsel of Francis Howgill, left to his daughter Abigail Howgill* (1666). (James Backhouse [Ed.], *Memoirs of Francis Howgill, with Extracts from his Writings* [York: W. Alexander and Son, 1828], 91–2.)

Howgill encouraged his daughter to be discreet, cautious and patient in waiting on God to bring her a husband, as well as to be familiar with his 'conversation' and 'manner and course of life' before giving her consent. Interestingly, Howgill does not expect that his daughter will marry for certain, indicating perhaps an early Quaker precedence of women being spiritually active rather than focusing on, or worrying about, marriage. Howgill believed if God wanted his daughter to marry, God would effectively be the matchmaker and bring it to pass as long as Abigail feared God and led a virtuous life.

Waiting on an inner 'leading' from God for divine direction in regards to matrimony was evident in Thomas Ellwood's courtship of a fellow Friend, Mary Ellis, in 1669. Ellwood, the son of an Oxfordshire justice, became a Quaker after a meeting with Isaac Penington in 1659 and would eventually be the editor of Fox's first published *Journal*.[97] He wrote in his personal memoirs of his first meeting Mary, an account in which Ellwood stressed that neither Mary nor he had any intention of anything other than a 'free and fair Friendship':

> I had once, a Year or two before, had an Opportunity to do her a small piece of Service which she wanted some Assistance in … without the least Thought (I am verily perswaded, on her part; well assured, on mine own) of any other or further Relation, than that of free and fair Friendship: Not did it, at that time, lead us into any closer Conversation, or more intimate Acquaintance one with the other.[98]

Having made it clear that he did not extend 'common Kindness' with the intention of gaining her affection, Ellwood stated it was not until 'some time (and that a good while) after' that he had found his 'Heart secretly drawn, and inclining towards her'.[99] Ellwood explained 'Yet I was not hasty in proposing; but waited to feel a satisfactory Settlement of Mind therein, before I made any step thereto'.[100] After some time of waiting, Ellwood approached Isaac and Mary Penington, who he explained 'stood *Parentum loco*, in place or stead of Parents to me'.[101] Seeking their advice and approval to marry Ellis, Ellwood explained 'they having solemnly weighed the Matter express their Unity therewith', an approbation which he felt was 'no small Confirmation … therin'.[102] Yet Ellwood

---

[97] Barbour and Roberts (Eds), *Early Quaker Writings*, 590.
[98] Thomas Ellwood, *The History of the life of Thomas Ellwood: written by his own hand* (London: J. Sowle, 1714), 248.
[99] Ibid.
[100] Ibid.
[101] Ibid, 249. Ellwood's father was not a Quaker, and subsequently denied Ellwood his inheritance after his son had married into the Quaker fold (Ellwood, *The History of the life of Thomas Ellwood*, 260–61).
[102] Ibid.

took further time for 'Deliberation, often Retiring in Spirit to the Lord for counsel and Guidance in this ... so important affair'.[103]

Finally, during quiet reflection, according to Ellwood he heard from God a clear answer to his lengthy deliberations.

> I felt a Word sweetly rise in me, as if I had heard a Voice, which said Go, and Prevail. And Faith springing in my Heart with the Word, I immediately rose and went; nothing doubting.[104]

Incidentally, during this time Ellwood still had yet to tell Mary of his inclination. But after he believed he had felt this inner, clear confirmation, he immediately went to Mary's lodgings to speak with her, as Ellwood explained:

> After some Conversation, feeling my Spirit weightily concerned, I solemnly opened my Mind unto her, with respect to the particular Business I came about; which I soon perceived was a great Suprisal to her. For she had taken in an Apprehension (as others also had done) that mine Eye had been fixed elsewhere and nearer home. I used not many Words to her: but I felt a Divine Power in my Breast, that (as she afterwards acknowledged to me) she could not shut it out.[105]

Perhaps not surprisingly, Mary was surprised not only due to her thoughts about his purported marriage intentions directed elsewhere (Ellwood does not tell us who the other woman was), but also due to the fact that from Ellwood's account, she had had little contact with him since their encounter a year or two earlier. The nature of Quaker courtship leading to a proposal in this account involved little one-to-one contact, but heavily rested on spiritual meditation and leadings. After Ellwood had told Mary his thoughts, he likewise explained he did not expect an answer from her immediately, but rather 'desired that she would, in the most solemn Manner, weigh the Proposal made, and in due time give me such an Answer thereunto, as the Lord should give her'.[106] Again, it was not Mary's response but the Lord's response which was sought. When he visited her again shortly after, before a two-week journey, he assured her he felt an 'Increase of Affection to her', as he further explained, 'I hoped to receive a suitable Return from her in the Lord's time; to whom, in the meantime, I committed both her myself and the Concern between us'.[107]

---

[103] Ibid.
[104] Ibid.
[105] Ibid, 249–50.
[106] Ibid, 250.
[107] Ibid, 250–51.

Believing the Lord had been 'his Advocate' in his absence, when Ellwood returned, Mary accepted his proposal. From that time on, as Ellwood explained, they 'entertained each other with Affectionate Kindness in order to Marriage', which he reiterates they 'did not hasten to, but went on deliberately'.[108] Ellwood added, during the time of their engagement he did not 'use those vulgar ways of courtship, by making frequent and rich Presents'. He explained the reason was 'Not only for that my Outward Condition would not comport with the Expence: But because I liked not to obtain by such means; but preferred unbribed Affection'.[109] They finally married in October of 1669:

> A very Solemn Meeting it was, and in a weighty frame of Spirit we were; in which we sensibly felt the Lord with us, and Joyning us: the sense whereof remained with us all our Life time; and was of good Service, and very Comfortable to us on all Occasions.[110]

A generation earlier and before the beginning of Quakerism, a similar practice of following God's direction for marriage was presented by Ellwood's representative mother, Mary Penington. It is important to bear in mind Penington wrote about her first courtship and marriage after she became a Quaker, making it possible that Penington retroactively projected her Quaker beliefs onto her recollections. Nevertheless, Penington purports she similarly believed in waiting for her betrothed to be brought to her by God. Before her first marriage, Penington was a spiritual seeker who saw her future husband as someone who would be brought to her by God, rather than by social convention or effort. She was born into a gentry family in Kent in 1623. Both of her parents died when she was a child, her father leaving her a sizable estate, which no doubt put her under pressure to marry well. She was taken into the care of a relative, Katharine Springett, and Katherine's brother Sir Edward Partridge. Penington relays a brief account of how she shunned familial and societal attempts to unite her with various men they thought fit for her in terms of 'worldly' expectations. In her recollections, her current Quaker marital values were evident:

> All their threatenings and reasonings could not keep me back ... In this time I suffered not only from these persons to whom I was by my parents committed (who both died when I was not above three years of age) but also suffered much from my companions and kindred ... I minded not those marriages propounded to me of vain persons, but having desired of the Lord that I might have one that

---

[108] Ibid, 251.

[109] Ibid. This went against the aforementioned seventeenth-century practice of gift giving during the courtship process (Cressy, *Birth, Marriage, and Death*, 263).

[110] Ibid, 257.

> feared him, I had a belief, that the Lord would provide one for me; and in this belief I went, not regarding their reproaches, that would say to me, no gentleman (but mean [socially inferior] persons) was of this way, and that I would have some mean one or other; but they were disappointed, for the Lord touched the heart of him that was afterwards my husband, and my heart cleaved to him for the Lord's sake.[111]

Though a generation before Quakerism would come, she contradicted her guardians and surrounding society who believed she should not solely consider spirituality in terms of marriage. As a woman who should have had practical social concerns, those responsible for her felt she ought to marry for class and societal stability as well as financial security. According to Penington, they believed if she was to stick with her spiritual aspirations she would likely be stuck with someone of 'mean' social standing. However, she eventually met the man she felt God had brought to her, one of Katherine's children called William. She would subsequently become 'Lady Springett'.

The Springetts remained married for only two and a half years until his death in 1644, at which time Penington was expecting a child, Gulielma, the future wife of Quaker William Penn. After William Springett's death and the birth of Gulielma, Penington continued to go through spiritual turmoil. It was during this time she met her second husband Isaac Penington:

> In this condition that I mentioned of my wearied seeking and not finding, I married my dear husband Isaac Penington. My love was drawn to him, because I found he saw the deceit of all notions, and lay as one that refused to be comforted until he came to his temple, who is truth and no lie, and in this my heart cleft to him.[112]

Isaac and Mary Penington married and eventually were convinced to Quakerism after an encounter with George Fox. The Peningtons and the Penn family would become close associates of Fox and Fell in shaping Quaker spirituality and doctrine.

The Quaker ideal of waiting on God could take months and be quite a spiritually trying affair, as it was for William Caton. Near the beginning of the movement's history in 1662, Caton, an early Quaker convert and close friend of both Fell and Fox, was the first to marry in the Quaker fashion in

---

[111] David Booy (Ed.), *Autobiographical Writings by Early Quaker Women* (Farnham: Ashgate Publishing Limited, 2004), 80–81.
[112] Ibid, 87.

the Netherlands.[113] While travelling overseas, conducting itinerant preaching throughout Germany and Holland, Caton explained in his journal how the idea of marrying a Dutch Quaker, Anneken Dirrix, had 'entered his heart'.[114] Caton stressed both the length of time spent in thoughtful consideration before their marriage and his fervent belief that the command for their marriage had come from the Lord:

> And in process of time, something came before me, and upon me, as from the Lord (which afterwards did more fully appear) concerning my taking Anneken Dirrix to Wife; unto which I took little heed at first but sought rather to totally extinguish the thought out of my mind, yet behold, by how much the more I seemed to extinguish the appearance of such a thing, by so much the more did it prevail in me.[115]

Though he felt the notion had arisen in him, Caton noted he had 'tried and discussed the thing in the Light of the Lord' in his 'own heart', and in 'due time found it to be of the Lord', yet still did not mention it to anyone for a considerable amount of time, or as Caton put it, 'I did not open my mouth of it to any for the space of many Weeks (I might say Months)'.[116] Caton's emphasis on time indicates early on Quakers were very cautious and valued lengthy deliberation periods, as well as stressing all deliberation was done 'in the Light of the Lord'.

Caton did finally share the notion of marrying Dirrix, but not before he first discussed the idea with his fellow Friends while in Germany and England.[117] Though Caton felt it was 'from the Lord' he further sought confirmation from

---

[113] Trevett, *Women and Quakerism in the 17th Century*, 95. William Caton was a companion of Margaret Fell's son George Fell when both were in their teens (Trevett, *Women and Quakerism in the 17th Century*, 106). Elsa Glines, editor of *Undaunted Zeal: The Letters of Margaret Fell*, explains 'Will Caton (1636–1665) entered the household at Swarthmoor Hall when he was about fourteen years of age to study with son George Fell, who was two years younger than Caton'. Caton then went away with George Fell to Hawkshead Grammar School, and they returned to Swarthmoor together (Glines [Ed.], *Undaunted Zeal*, 218; Ross, *Margaret Fell*, 18). One year after he first arrived at Swarthmoor, Fox first visited the Hall, and subsequently 'convinced' Caton at fifteen years of age. A few years later, not desiring to proceed to college as George Fell was planning, Margaret Fell arranged for Caton to stay at Swarthmoor where he taught her children, accompanied her on visits, and became her secretary. At seventeen or eighteen years of age he left Swarthmoor to promote Quakerism overseas (Ross, *Margaret Fell*, 18–20).

[114] William Caton, *A journal of the life of that faithful servant and minister of the Gospel of Jesus Christ William Caton* (London, 1689), 73.

[115] Ibid, 71.

[116] Ibid, 72.

[117] Ibid, 71–2. See also Trevett, *Women and Quakerism in the 17th Century*, 95 and Ross, *Margaret Fell*, 73.

his fellow Quakers, which he received in 'due time' as Caton explained, 'And after they pondered upon it, and weighed it in the Light of the Lord, they made known to me the Unity they had with the thing'.[118] When Caton approached Dirrix with the idea, he presented several concerns for her to consider, including his itinerant lifestyle and minimal estate, which was 'not like unto hers'.[119] He then asked Dirrix 'when she was free, she was to return me an Answer, thereunto which in several Weeks after she did'.[120] Her response was affirmative, but the marriage was not immediate. Caton affirmed that though she, he and others around him had 'unity' with the idea of marriage, they continued to wait:

> After we had waited long in the thing, and that several Months were expired, and that I had imparted it to several Friends in Holland by word of mouth, and did not meet with any opposition.[121]

At the end of the several months, Dirrix came to see Caton, 'and soon after was exceedingly broken, and wept as I may say, in an excessive manner'.[122] Dirrix told Caton that it was 'upon her to give up her self in the Will of the Lord' at which time she was then 'moved' to tell Caton, 'We are no more twain but one Flesh' amidst a 'flood of tears'.[123] Incredibly, after months of deliberation, at the moment of Dirrix's declarations Caton recollected:

> I confess I was moved something thereby, but did not at that instant feel the life so immediately answering to the things as I desired, upon such an extraordinary occasion, but waiting a little exceedingly steadfastly in the Light of the Lord, the life begun to rise, and the Word of the Lord testified unto me thus, saying *She is the Gift of God to thee*.[124]

---

[118] Ibid, 72.
[119] Ibid, 73.
[120] Ibid.
[121] Ibid, 75.
[122] Ibid.
[123] Ibid.
[124] Ibid. The phrases 'feel the life' and 'the life begun to rise' are similar to Fox's recollection of Fell's response when he brought the idea of marriage to her: 'I had seen from the Lord a considerable time before, that I should take Margaret Fell to be my wife; and when I first mentioned it to her, she felt the answer of life from God thereunto' (Fox, *Journal Vol. 2* [1836], 114). It carries a similar meaning to the light of God, or that of God within. Isaac Penington wrote in 1667, ' ... my dear Friends ... wait for and daily follow the sensible leadings of that measure of life, which God hath placed in you, which is one with the fulness, and into which the fulness runs daily and fills it, that it may run into you and fill you' (Isaac Penington, *To Friends of Both the Chalfonts* [1667]. Printed in Douglas Van Steere [Ed.], *Quaker Spirituality: Selected Writings* [Mahweh, NJ: Paulist Press, 1984], 153).

Not until after months of internal spiritual travail did they finally feel sure of God's command. They then had their intention published in both the meetings in Amsterdam and at Swarthmoor.[125] With the approbation of the local Men's Meeting in Amsterdam, who 'did universally subscribe their Names to a Certificate', they were wed.[126]

In some accounts, such as the one above by Mary Penington, a retrospective description of one's path to matrimony could be suspect of elaboration with the intent of demonstrating Quaker values regarding the path to marriage (i.e. deliberating intensely for long periods of time, or waiting on God to bring a husband or wife). But in the case of William Caton, his marriage approbation narrative was written almost immediately after the event, as he passed away less than three years after his marriage to Dirrix. Caton's account provides further evidence that the early Quaker marital approbation process included God's commanding the marriage, long periods of waiting in the Lord to see if anything arose to contradict the leading, and the importance of seeking communal affirmation and unity. Marriage approbation was not thus sought in a hasty manner, as it seemed to Caton. He almost resisted the idea until he knew for certain that God was behind the notion, as God had brought together Adam and Eve in paradise. It was this waiting at length on the inward light, within himself, his Quaker community and his intended betrothed, that was of utmost importance in Caton's narrative of his marriage process.

While being commanded by God to marry another was of utmost importance, curiously this commandment from God could potentially be against one's particular will or desires. In 1654, the aforementioned Thomas Holme wrote to Fell regarding his marriage to Elizabeth Leavens:

> I was immediately commanded of the Lord to take her to wife that day having before seen it clear in the light eternal and had a vision of it long before as likewise she had. So in obedience to the Command of the Lord I took her to wife contrary to my will.[127]

Whether Elizabeth felt it contrary to her will as well remains unknown. It is possible Thomas and Elizabeth were concerned marriage might deter them from their active ministries. They were well-known leaders in the early days of the movement. Elizabeth Leavens worked with Elizabeth Fletcher in carrying on some of Holme's work while he was imprisoned. Upon his release from prison,

---

[125] Trevett, *Women and Quakerism in the 17th Century*, 95.

[126] Caton, *A journal of the life of that faithful servant and minister of the Gospel of Jesus Christ William Caton*, 76.

[127] Thomas Holme to Margaret Fell, 8 mo./1654. Swarthmoor Manuscripts, 1:195; 'Letters and Documents of Early Friends', 3:803–5. Cited in J. William Frost, *The Quaker Family in Colonial America* (New York, NY: St. Martin's Press, 1973), 152.

Thomas Holme and Elizabeth Leavens married then separated geographically for a time to preach, Thomas leaving for Chester, while Elizabeth went to Oxford. The following year, in 1655, Elizabeth journeyed to South Wales to meet Thomas, where they successfully preached Quakerism throughout the Welsh communities. Thomas wrote to Fell regarding Elizabeth's ministry, 'She hath A generall meting their this day. The mighty power, presence and glory of the lord is with hir to the Astoneshing of all wher she comes'.[128]

Happily for Thomas Holme, Elizabeth agreed they were commanded by God to be married. But for others who were convinced they felt a leading from God to marry another were not so fortunate in finding their 'leadings' reciprocated. Contradicting 'leadings' led to complications within the Quaker fold in interpreting God's commandments, as well as to some resentment. In 1664, a Friend called William Smith warned George Fox about a woman Friend, Martha Plats, who was seeking betrothal to her fellow Quaker Edward Langford. Writing from Nottingham gaol, where he was a fellow prisoner of Langford, Smith knew Langford did not reciprocate the 'leading'. When Plats had informed Langford of her leading, she informed Smith as well, a prominent Quaker at the time to whom she looked up as an elder. Smith explained to Fox, after Plats informed him of this, he 'had nothing further to say unto it than to Exhort her to waite in the power and cleave unto that and see if it remain onely at times something would be stirring on her part'.[129] Over a number of years (the exact amount of time was not indicated) Plats persisted while Langford resisted, as Smith confirmed to Fox in his letter:

> I never could find that the man had any clearness in himself to answer it but rather was much Exercised that such a thing should be moved unto him by her and thus it hath been for certain Yeares.[130]

While Langford could never find an affirmative answer within, he faced the toll of fending off her consistent attention. The quandary was they both felt they were hearing correctly from God. But without the confirmation from within Langford, no marriage could take place for Martha.

Finally, when the situation came to a head, the frustrated Plats informed Smith that she was not only 'sorely judging' Langford for his persistent refusals, but also Smith 'for not dealing plainly with her as to tell her positively whether her motion was right or wronge'.[131] Plats complained both Fox and Smith had

---

[128] Mabel Brailsford, *Quaker Women, 1650–1690* (London: Duckworth, 1915), 152.
[129] William Smith, *William Smith to George Fox (April 21, 1664) From Nottingham Country Gaol*. Huntington Library Letters/Manuscripts: SHA 377.
[130] Ibid.
[131] Ibid.

encouraged her to marry Langford, causing her to persist in the matter. Angry that Smith had not told her clearly whether or not her 'leadings' were sound, Plats argued had Smith not encouraged her by telling her to wait, she would have 'not gone on in the thing'; but instead, Smith's words 'did strengthen her in it'.[132] Plats then further contended she had brought 'the thing' before Fox himself, and that Fox 'did own the motion'.[133] After warning Fox that she may approach him with this problem, he concluded his letter stating he had 'been as tender toward her' as he could in order to 'keep the truth clear from her Judgement', but that he would 'have no more to doe in that matter betwixt them'.[134] Though Plats may have hoped Smith would tell Langford that God was indeed commanding their marriage, Smith would not assent. As an elder, Smith had the delicate task of encouraging his fellow Friend to listen to God but also of dissuading her from pursuing the matter further after so many years, after Langford had decidedly confirmed he had not felt commanded by God to marry Plats.

At other times a Friend might feel a leading to marry another quite abruptly without knowing the person, an occurrence which might strike one today as a Quaker version of 'love at first sight'. Richard Davies of Southwark recorded in his journal his first encounter with his future wife:

> It was not yet manifest to me where she was, or who she was. But one time, as I was at Horselydown meeting in Southward, I heard a woman Friend open her mouth, by way of testimony against an evil ranting spirit that did oppose Friends much in those days. It came to me from the Lord that the woman was to be my wife, and to go with me to the country, and to be an helpmeet for me ... We waiting upon the Lord together, she arose, and declared before me ... that in the name and power of God she consented to be my wife, and to go along with me, whither the Lord should order us; and I said, in the fear of the Lord, I receive thee as the gift of God to me.[135]

In the case of Davies and his wife, they waited together and both consented to marriage, though not seemingly based on any gradual 'getting to know one another' but solely on God ordaining it and commanding it to be so, making it 'a gift of God'. This kind of courtship, though not necessarily universal to Quakers in its abrupt nature, does nevertheless indicate the general practice of early Friends to seek corporate agreement between the betrothed, where both

---

[132] Ibid.
[133] Ibid.
[134] Ibid.
[135] Richard C. Allen, *Quaker Communities in Early Modern Wales: From Resistance to Respectability* (Cardiff: University of Wales Press, 2007), 141.

the man and the woman's consent is required along with a mutual sense of it being ordered by the Lord.[136]

After a Quaker man and woman jointly confirmed this sense of God's leading each other to marriage, they had to gain parental consent, and subsequently show evidence of this approval to the meeting in the form of a certificate.[137] This could prove problematic, especially if the parents were not Quakers, as was the case for James Barret in 1675. Barret wanted approbation to marry but his parents, not wanting him to marry a Quaker woman, withheld their permission. In this case, the Meeting overruled the parents' objections and granted approbation to Barret, showing Quakers felt it appropriate to override parental wishes if the parents were not members of the Society of Friends.[138] When parents were deceased, guardians or sometimes employees (particularly when a servant) sufficed. Margaret Lewis, a servant, explained to the Bristol Men's Meeting 'she hath noe parent nor guardian liveing' but brought to the Meeting 'her master & mistris, Jno. & Magdelent Love'. John Love, an active member of the Bristol Meeting, and his wife acted as surrogate parents to Margaret.[139] The Meeting minutes record that the Loves had lived with Margaret 'neare 3 yeares past, was present & signified they know nothing that might be reasonable to obstruct their marriage'.[140] Subsequently, Margaret Lewis and glazier Paul Smith were married with clearness and approbation.[141]

Fox, along with a small number of other Friends, served as a guardian for a parentless young woman in London, and was thus approached by a non-Quaker called John Drakes, a 'young man of Barbados' to seek her hand in marriage. Fox explained in his *Journal* the situation with Drakes, a man who in Fox's words was 'a person of some note in the world's account, but a common swearer and a bad man':

---

[136] Fox did not often use the word 'love' (Barbour and Roberts [Eds], *Early Quaker Writings*, 29). He rather encouraged his followers to be tender-hearted to one another. The word 'tenderness' was more frequently used amongst the early Quakers in regards to loving one another or showing acts of kindness in the Quaker community and within early Quaker rhetoric.

[137] In the Marriage Act of 1653 passed during the Civil War, parental consent was expressly required for minors who wanted to be married, but this was rendered null in 1660 when the monarchy was restored (Wiesner-Hanks, *Christianity and Sexuality in the Early Modern World*, 74).

[138] Davies, *The Quakers in English Society*, 197.

[139] John Love was a grocer in Bristol who had spent time in Westgate prison for his Quaker beliefs (Mortimer [Ed.], *Minute Book of the Men's Meeting of the Society of Friends in Bristol 1686–1704*, xxxv).

[140] Mortimer (Ed.), *Minute Book of the Men's Meeting of the Society of Friends in Bristol 1667–1686*, 136.

[141] Ibid.

When in London, [Drakes] had a mind to marry a Friend's daughter, left by her mother very young and with a considerable portion, to the care and government of several Friends, wherof I was one. He made application to me, that he might have my consent to marry this young maid. I told him, 'I was one of her overseers appointed by her mother, who was a widow, to take care of her ... she committed her to us, that she might be trained up in the fear of the Lord, and therefore I should betray the trust reposed in me, if I should consent that he who was out of the fear of God, should marry her; which I would not do'.[142]

Angered by Fox's decision, Drakes returned to Barbados with 'great offence' against him, 'but without just cause' according to Fox. He then explained the course of events that occurred when Drakes heard Fox was coming to Barbados in 1671:

Afterwards, when he heard I was coming to Barbadoes, he swore desperately, and threatened, that 'if he could possibly procure it, he would have me burned to death when I came there'. Which a Friend hearing, asked him, 'what I had done to him, that he was so violent against me?' He would not answer, but said again, 'I'll have him burned'. Whereupon the Friend replied, 'Do not march on too furiously, lest thou come too soon to thy journey's end'. About ten days later, he was struck with a violent burning fever of which he died ... his body was so scorched ... 'it was black as coal'. Three days before I landed, his body was laid in the dust ... a sad example.[143]

According to Fox, when Drakes threatened his life, in this case over a decision about marriage approbation, God in the end had the last word by bringing death upon Drakes. In Fox's eyes, God protected him in part because his life was obviously threatened; but additionally, God exercised judgment against a man who sought revenge against an innocent person, who had been obedient to God in not granting consent to an exogamous marriage.

When the couple showed sufficient official proof of parental or guardian approval, they then appeared at a Quaker meeting to propose an intention of marriage.[144] This was considered a serious and sober task undertaken with the utmost care, caution and patience, as spiritual preparedness and a unified inner sense of a marriage being of God was critical to a Quaker marriage done in an orderly fashion. Sober Quaker meetings, in which members quietly 'waited' on

---

[142] Fox, *Journal Vol 1* (In Two Volumes. Leeds: Anthony Pickard, Sixth Edition, 1836), 141.

[143] Ibid, 141–2.

[144] In the early years of the movement, the intention of marriage was brought to the meetings in general, or to the Men's Meetings. Later, intentions to marry were brought exclusively to the Women's Meetings.

God for direction and marriages were conducted 'in the light' with 'nothing hidden', were considered by the Quakers as concrete evidence of a people devoted to God and orderly conduct. In 1685, Friend William Loddington wrote a document supporting the Quaker marriage discipline entitled *The Good Order of Truth Justified: wherein our womens meetings and order of marriage (by some more especially opposed) are proved agreeable to Scripture and sound reason.* Loddington praised the Quaker marriage discipline and Women's Meetings, stating they were necessary 'that all things be done Decently and in Order are left to the judgment of Christians in every Age, as the Lord shall direct them'.[145] The Quaker notion of 'liberty of conscience' was *not* to be associated with disorderly conduct, free love or bigamy but was rather to be seen as rational and scripturally sound, as the meetings represented a people devoted to harmony and orderliness. Those who were 'convinced' were God's people, set apart, whose heavy responsibility it was to wait on God's direction, witness God's work in the marriage proceedings, and document it. The Meeting Minutes thus became a public witness of Quaker respectability, calm and order.

Certificates, Investigations, Contrition and Regulation: The Role of the Men's Monthly Meeting

Initially it was in the Men's Monthly Meetings (which reported to the Quarterly Meetings) that births, deaths and marriages were discussed and recorded.[146] The following brief survey of the Bristol Men's Meetings minutes between the years 1667–1704 will provide a helpful glimpse into the practical issues and frustrations encountered in the approbation process, by both the Meetings and the intended betrothed. The predominant issue that rose time and time again were difficulties in determining whether the parties were spiritually fit for marriage. These meetings illuminate the obstructions to unions, and provide a better understanding of what it meant to be 'in the truth' and 'clear' for marriage. It was a meeting which had a large and consistent following and one that exemplified the vital importance of endogamous and 'honourable' marriages to Quakers at this time. Additionally, it represents a microcosm of the larger scope of Quaker meetings around the world. As the Quaker movement broadened beyond Great Britain, the marriage approbation process through meetings was likewise largely followed internationally. According to the historian Larry

---

[145] William Loddington, *The Good Order of Truth Justified: wherein our womens meetings and order of marriage (by some more especially opposed) are proved agreeable to Scripture and sound reason* (Shoreditch: Andrew Sowle, 1685), 5.

[146] Parallel Women's Meetings, which will be discussed shortly, were largely established by the 1670s with similar responsibilities.

Gragg, for the Quakers in Barbados marriage was 'the most important matter for monthly meetings, as Friends sought to ensure marriage within the fellowship and to forbid any unions performed by priests'.[147] As did the Bristol Quakers, the Quakers of Barbados received consistent guidance from Fox, the London Yearly Meeting and other elders on a number of doctrinal matters.[148] By the 1680s the marriage doctrine and practice were in place, as all prospective Quaker marriages had to be brought before the Monthly Meetings in Barbados, were subject to investigation of the clearness of the couple, and had to wait for clearance from the Meeting before proceeding to marriage.[149] Gragg explains:

> As in other locales, the meetings would investigate the 'clearness' from prior ties and particularly the 'conversation' of the man and woman. Only after the monthly meetings had given their blessing could the marriage take place.[150]

Gragg then provides an example of an early Quaker wedding by witnesses in Barbados: 'In October 1689, more than seventy people signed a marriage certificate at the wedding of Mary Brett of Barbados and Joseph Kirll of Pennsylvania'.[151] These practices of investigation and certification, as they were done in Bristol, were largely conducted in the same manner around the world.

A full quarter of the Bristol Men's Meeting minutes were occupied with marital concerns.[152] The men of the Meeting grappled with issues including approbation and dealing with Friends who had either married someone who was not a Quaker, or had married a Friend by a 'priest of the world'.[153] Admonition and recorded repentance was required if the offending Friend wanted to avoid excommunication from the Quaker fold. For approbation, if investigation was needed for the clearness of the couple, time was spent discussing the outcome of these investigations, assessing the information together, and finally

---

[147] Larry Dale Gragg, *The Quaker Community on Barbados: Challenging the Culture of the Planter Class* (Columbia, MO: University of Missouri Press, 2009), 83.

[148] Ibid. Gragg elaborates on the expansion of the Quaker meeting system within Barbados: 'Beyond showing little or no deference to the Anglican clergy and their planter patrons, Quakers rapidly created a separate religious establishment. By the 1680s, they were maintaining five meeting houses and several Quaker cemeteries, paying for their own poor relief, and keeping their own birth, marriage, and death records' (Gragg, *The Quaker Community on Barbados*, 5).

[149] Ibid.

[150] Ibid. Cited from Barry Levy, *Quakers and the American Family: British Settlement in the Delaware Valley* (Oxford: Oxford University Press, 1988), 132.

[151] Ibid.

[152] Mortimer (Ed.), *Minute Book of the Men's Meeting of the Society of Friends in Bristol 1667–1686*, xviii.

[153] Ibid, xxiii.

recommending either further investigation or granting a decision, whether it be negative or positive. If negative, recommendations were given on what was the reason and what was needed to amend the situation. If positive and the 'way clear', both parties having no 'miscarriadges' in their private lives and spiritual orientation, the marriage intention would be 'published', meaning simply that it was recorded in the Men's Meeting minutes, being thus officially registered. When the couple encountered no troubles with approbation, the marriage process typically took about a month.[154] But if difficulties were encountered, the process could take longer, which at times caused frustrations amongst some anxious Quakers. The lengthy process allowed for waiting on God, giving time for there to be a unified 'sense' amongst the meeting granting approbation. Marriage was considered a sober undertaking, a spiritual union, done with caution and in an orderly process that was not to be rushed.

In the Bristol Minutes, over the years a number of elaborate and detailed regulating and documentation procedures, such as certificates indicating parental consent or contrition, gradually emerged and took effect. In 1672, a few years after instigating a certificate procedure to procure parental consent and in the midst of continued efforts to instil a system of approbation, the Men's Meeting sensed that thorough and careful approbations were still lacking. They believed the problem was much due to their neglect to hold some intended betrothed responsible for their 'miscarriages',[155] as a great number of Friends were still going to the local priests to be married. This gave them grave cause for concern, as the 10 June 1672 minutes read:

> This meeting being in a weighty sence of their neglect for the tyme past in not soe effectualy reproveing the miscarriages of some that profess truth and frequent our meetings, and particularly of the greate dishonour that hath been brought upon the truth and people of god by the goeing of som to the priests to be marryed ... Wee doe now againe with one concent in the feare of the lord resolve with all the strength & wisdome that god shall give us to be more diligent for the time to come and indeavor to put a stopp to all such miscarriages by admonition, privat & publicke reproofs in long suffering and patience towards them, after which if they repent not and owne their condemnation to the cleareing of truth, it is resolved with one concent that Friends will give forth a paper publickly against

---

[154] Mortimer (Ed.), *Minute Book of the Men's Meeting of the Society of Friends in Bristol 1686–1704*, xvi.

[155] As mentioned previously on p.51, 'miscarriages' was a term used by early Quakers to denote any behaviour that was not indicative of a person 'walking in the light' such as drunkenness, adultery, talking negatively, anyting that might disrupt the unity and purity of the Quakers. Here it refers to marrying outside of the Quaker fold.

them without respect of persons, that gods name and truth and us his people may be cleare of them.[156]

Efforts to regulate and approbate marriage were a serious concern for the welfare of the community of Quakers as a whole, being inextricably linked with repentance and spiritual preparedness for marriage and ministry. With no respect to persons, all Friends were expected to be spiritually ready for marriage and would be required to show proof of parental permission as well as communal, unified support from their meeting, indicating that the couple was indeed equipped spiritually and practically to pursue marriage.

Proving whether or not a person was 'clear' for marriage was not an easy task. The Quaker seeking marriage had to demonstrate a proven holy lifestyle. If there was any doubt concerning the union either within the meeting or reported to them by other Friends, generally two men from the meeting were assigned to investigate the impasse and 'search out the truth'. Investigations were often assigned to at least two regular and respected attendees of the meeting. The following investigation could lengthen the marital proceeding for up to a few months if problems occurred. It depended largely on the extenuating circumstances specific to each couple. For some, the way to matrimony was rather smooth, as was the case for Thomas Speed, a local Quaker merchant, and Ann Sherman, a Quaker woman who was not a member of the Quaker Meeting of Bristol. The minutes of 16 June 1668 read:

> Thomas Speed haveing the last meeting day presented to Friends his intention to take Ann Sherman to wife, & his desire to proceed regularly in the way of Friends therin; & friends haveing appointed some amonst themselves to speak with her, shee being unknowne to most of them both as to her purson, & principle in relations unto Trueth; & being soe farr satisfied with the account given them of her thereupon as to suffer the thing to bee done amongst them as in the way of friends, gave their consents that hee might soe doe, as hee should think fit, haveing declared their Judgment, that they were soe satisfied with the account given of her answers to such questions as were put to her as aforesayd, that they could suffer, or let the thing to bee done amongst them.[157]

Because Ann was unknown to the Men's Meeting of Bristol, her lifestyle was in need of investigation. After a questioning session, she evidently gave the impression to her questioners that she was in right relation with the 'truth', making their marriage a suitable union. A little over a year later, she would be

---

[156] Mortimer (Ed.), *Minute Book of the Men's Meeting of the Society of Friends in Bristol 1667–1686*, 63–4.
[157] Ibid, 10.

one of the signatories on the marriage certificate of George Fox and Margaret Fell.[158]

In the Bristol minutes, marriage intentions were brought forth by Friends of all classes. Servants as well as masters and mistresses, gentry or artisan, all were subject to the same requirements and expectations for being clear for marriage and the necessary steps to follow. Less than six months after Thomas Speed's marriage, his servant Katherine Phillips and a weaver called Thomas Lewis of Bedminster made their intention of marriage known to the Meeting.[159] Venturing into the same marriage procedures and submitting to equivalent requirements, their similar approbation process reflects the Friends' efforts at consistent impartiality towards class or social status. Partiality was not to be shown to those of spiritual prominence within the Quaker circles either. All were supposed to be subject to the same expectations in spiritual readiness and clearness for marriage.

Anyone who wanted to marry a person who was not a Quaker was publicly reprimanded and reproached in the meeting, and would not gain approbation. In October 1669, news reached the Men's Meeting of an 'eminent Friend in Bristoll' who 'was maryed to one of the world & that by the approbacion of this meetinge'. Realising they might have been in effect duped, the men agreed 'that a letter bee written unto some freinds att Tewxbury to desire informacion from them who that person is'. Bristol Friends Dennis Hollister and Thomas Gouldeny were entrusted with the delivery of that letter, along with an 'enclosed ... coppy of the generall paper given forth by friends as a testimony against disorderly marriages &c'.[160] After a recorded footnote that the deed was 'Don accordingly', the minutes show it was then ordered by the Meeting that 'the generall papers given forth by friends against disorderly marriages &c. bee read in the publick meeting houses on a first day, viz. by Dennis Hollister on this side the Bridge, and William Taylor on the other side of bridge'.[161]

The problem of exogamy further prompted a more thorough certification process to be implemented. Two months after the abovementioned proclamations, the certificate requirement was cemented in the Bristol Friends' marital approbation proceedings:

> Tis agreed that the subscribed forme of CERTIFICATE for mariages bee used for the future and that all persons marryinge have recourse to Francis Rogers to give forth certificates as occasion offers ... Also that for the future, the copyes of every certificate bee entered into the booke for mariages, & that the parties

---

[158] Ibid, 216.
[159] Ibid, 13.
[160] Ibid, 22.
[161] Ibid.

> marryed, & (att least) twelve of the wittnesses present doe take care to get either Wm. Yeamans, Thomas Gouldeny, Thomas Callohill, Erasmus Dole, Francis Rogers, Jno. Love or Wm. Rogers, to bee there present to the entent that the certificate may bee recorded in the register booke without which the partyes that are to bee married are not to accomplish mariage.[162]

In this declaration, there is a clear effort to avoid any other mishaps in approbating a marriage. Accurate and timely recording of marriages, regular presentation of certificates to a person who is well acquainted with what to look for, and the presence of at least twelve witnesses were instated, to help ensure clear and endogamous marriages and hopefully prevent further debacles.

Several meeting minutes indicate some Quakers willingly married outside of the Friends' fold, knowing it was not acceptable to do so, and were subsequently reprimanded by investigators who were sent by the Men's Meeting. Exogamy, or marriage by a priest, was often discovered first through rumour. The Men's Meeting would then assign two men to 'enquire into the truth thereof and admonish'.[163] However, amidst the minutes there is no sign of these investigators encouraging anyone to annul or leave their exogamous marriages or marriages by a priest. A marriage was permanent, even if it was brought together by a 'hireling priest' or was between a member of the True Church and one who was not. A marriage could not be undone as far as the Quaker was concerned.[164] Rather, what was important in these investigations was verifying there was indeed true repentance of the Quaker who married outside the Quaker fold, or of the Quakers who were married by a priest rather than by the meeting system. Signs of genuine grief over their 'miscarriage' (or 'miscarriages') were looked for, usually

---

[162] Ibid., 26. Francis Rogers was a merchant and prominent Friend from Cork, Ireland who resided in Bristol. Rogers also played a prominent role in the Quaker Meeting of Cork in relationship to certificates. The historian Richard Greaves explains the Cork Meeting appointed Rogers to inform the bishop's registrar when Quakers were married, and to ask the registrar to record Quaker marriage certificates. See Richard L. Greaves, *God's Other Children: Protestant Nonconformists and the Emergence of Denominational Churches in Ireland, 1660–1700* (Stanford, CA: Stanford University Press, 1997), 348.

[163] Mortimer (Ed.), *Minute Book of the Men's Meeting of the Society of Friends in Bristol 1667–1686*, 22.

[164] No one was encouraged to leave his or her spouse, if one became convinced and the other did not. For example, Margaret Fell did not leave Judge Thomas Fell after her convincement. Though he never became a Quaker, she remained faithful to him and committed to their household. The Quaker demographer Richard T. Vann explains, 'Those already married before their conversion to Quakerism were not required to divorce their spouses even if these remained in the "world"' (Vann and Eversley, *Friends in Life and Death*, 84).

by the two men who visited the offender or offenders to seek out whether or not they were truly repentant of their behaviour.

Marrying outside of the Society of Friends could result in serious consequences, such as disownment by the Society, if there was no sign of true repentance or contrition of the deed done. Such was the case with Friend Elizabeth Foord, who underwent an inquiry before her marriage in September 1673, when Friends heard that the 'daughter to Katheren Handbury, doth entertaine a young man in relation to marriage that is not a Friend', and subsequently requested 'W. Roggers & Richard Sneed to vissit the young woman and her mother, and advise them to be aware in that case'.[165] A note was added later indicating 'they did, and are desired to vissit them the second tyme'.[166] The advice given twice, to beware of the consequences of marrying a person not 'in the truth', did not persuade Elizabeth to change her mind. Two months later, three men including William Rogers were sent 'as messengers from the meeting' to 'caution her concerning her inclinacion to marry a man not related to the truth', and had 'laid the weight of truth upon her and hath sufficiently counceld & warn'd her'.[167] But Elizabeth's response was not what they had hoped for, as the minutes stated:

> Notwithstanding shee inclines not to embrace the councell of friends, wee therefore judge her wayes perverse & erring from the path of truth, & so having nothing more with us to continue our visits doe desire R. Vickeris, Rich. Sneed & W. Rogers to acquaint her that they disowne her proceedings & that shee must beare her owne burthen & eat the fruit of their own doings.[168]

Elizabeth remained adamant to not heed their warnings and apparently showed no remorse or contrition for her decision to marry a non-Quaker, despite their

---

[165] Mortimer (Ed.), *Minute Book of the Men's Meeting of the Society of Friends in Bristol 1667–1686*, 78. William Rogers was the brother of the aforementioned Francis Rogers. Also a successful merchant, William Rogers is described by the Quaker historians Barbour and Roberts as a 'Bristol merchant and a weighty Friend', 'weighty' meaning influential and respected (Barbour and Roberts [Eds], *Early Quaker Writings*, 607). The Quaker historian Russell Mortimer likewise describes Richard Snead as a 'leading Bristol Friend' who married in the Quaker fashion within the Bristol Meeting in 1671 (Russell Mortimer, 'Marriage Discipline in Early Friends: A Study in Church Administration Illustrated from the Bristol Records', *Journal of the Friends Historical Society*, 48 no 4 [Autumn 1957]: 175–95; p. 176). While there is no indication in the minutes as to why specific men were chosen to do certain investigations, it is possible that 'weighty' Friends were chosen for both their stature within the Quaker community as well as their social position, perhaps giving them more likelihood of being taken seriously by those they visited.
[166] Ibid, 79.
[167] Ibid, 80.
[168] Ibid, 80–81.

repeated visits and warnings.[169] As a result, she was effectively ostracised from the Quakers for marrying out.

'Marrying out' or 'exogamous marriages' continued to be a problem for the Bristol Society of Friends, throughout the latter half of the century, despite efforts to keep them from occurring.[170] In 1687, Quaker Anne Davis was proposed to by a non-Quaker called Nathaniel Wade, a socially prominent man who had joined the Monmouth Rebellion and had received a royal pardon in 1686, and eventually became town clerk and later deputy governor.[171] When news of this reached the Meeting, she was 'cautioned from many friends particularly, as well as more generally from this our mens meeting, suspecting it as an unequall yoake'. She was warned they 'could not with clearness concent to pass or countenance it in this meeting & have soe acquainted her with that … and that wee might not open a gap for our children to joyne their affections to those who doe not profess the truth with us'.[172] Again after several visits from members of the Men's Meeting and repeated cautions and warnings, Anne married Nathaniel in an unauthorised marriage, after the Meeting had refused to sanction it.[173] Interestingly, Nathaniel Wade would eventually become a convinced Quaker, as he appears later in the minutes as an active member of the Men's Bristol Meeting.

If the men sent to seek out the truth of a problematic matter discovered an exogamous marriage had indeed occurred, but sensed that the offender was truly repentant, this was then reported to and accounted for at the meeting. The process of contrition and documentation of it varied. On some occasions, the person's contrition is simply recorded in the minutes as being apparent to the visitors. On 20 September 1669, the minutes show two separate recordings of women who were married 'by a priest, and to a man of the world'. The Meeting agreed 'Theophilus Newton & Tho. Brown beinge free to speake unto Hester West … are ordered to give an account thereof next meetinge'. A note added later indicates that she was 'admonished once' and there was 'some tenderness in her'. Similarly, a woman called Ann Payne was admonished by John Love and Nathaniell Day, and it was also later noted, 'admonished once & some tenderness in her'.[174] Following these entries, there is no further mention of either Hester or Ann in the Men's Meeting minutes, but it can be assumed they were not

---

[169] There is no indication in the Meeting minutes when Elizabeth did eventually marry, only that she was choosing to marry a non-Quaker.

[170] Mortimer, 'Marriage Discipline in Early Friends', 176.

[171] Mortimer (Ed.), *Minute Book of the Men's Meeting of the Society of Friends in Bristol 1686–1704*, 264.

[172] Ibid, 22.

[173] Ibid, xxi.

[174] Mortimer (Ed.), *Minute Book of the Men's Meeting of the Society of Friends in Bristol 1667–1686*, 20.

ostracised or disowned for marrying out as they showed genuine 'tenderness of heart', indicating contrition, and there is no mention in the minutes of an official disownment, as there was for Elizabeth Foord.

At other times, particularly if a person had married 'with the world' or was married by a priest, a more elaborate repentance procedure was required. Either a 'paper of contrition' from the couple was requested, or a 'paper of condemnation' was drawn up by the meeting and given to the offending priest, in order to teach and reprimand the 'minister of men'. In 1669, when a woman called Sarah Wilkinson was married by a priest, the Bristol Men's Meeting requested, 'David Simons and John Prickett & Tho. Salthows, Ed. Martingall beinge free to speake unto Sarah Wilkinson concerninge her mariage by a priest, are desired to give an account to next meetinge'.[175] A note added later indicates they were 'Spoaken with once. David Simons undertakes to send the originall paper of condemnacion given forth by Sarah Wilkinson & her husband to the priest'.[176] Not more than a month later, Sarah and her husband, Thomas Huxon, also presented a 'paper of contrition' to the Meeting, which they were satisfied with, and therefore cleared them to remain in the Friends.

This practice of presenting papers of condemnation and receiving papers of contrition continued throughout the Bristol minutes, as seen thirty years later in the minutes. This process became relatively common for a variety of miscarriages, pertaining or *not* pertaining to marriage approbation. In 1692, Mary Barnes, a daughter of a shoemaker, and Jacob Dogget, a cooper in Bristol, acquired approbation for marriage, followed by the publication of their marriage in the minutes the following year. However in 1701, Mary was accused of adultery, and subsequently received from the Men's Meeting a paper of condemnation and disownment for her apparently committing adultery. The paper stated to Mary:

> The holly scriptures doe positively say that those you are guilty of adulterie be shut out of the kingdom of God, nither have they any place in the holly citty, & thou being a person guilty of this greate evill in thy husbands absence, which is such a scandale that wee remember not the like to have hapened amongst us before, wee therefore disowne thee & thy wickedness and doe cast the reproach of thy crime upon thyself.[177]

That same day, the Men's Meeting made a similar formal condemnation for the sin of 'marriage by a priest' committed by Robert Gibbons, Jr. Though not using

---

[175] Ibid.
[176] Ibid.
[177] Mortimer (Ed.), *Minute Book of the Men's Meeting of the Society of Friends in Bristol 1686–1704*, 179.

the language of 'wickedness' as in the above statement regarding adultery, we still find strong words of condemnation and disownment:

> A butcher [who] did make profession of the trueth and was once married amongst Friends in this citty, but haveing buried that wife is since fallen in to the sinn of uncleanness & have nevertheless contrairie to the law is since married to another person by the priest. Wee therefore find ourselves oblidged to give out this testemony against him, for in that state of uncleanness and ungodliness he is shut out of the Kingdom of god. Therefore disowned from haveing any share with us in that fellowship that is in the blessed truth: And though wee thus testifie against him yet wee in love to his soule wish him true and unfeigned repentance & amendment of life.[178]

A copy of this statement was then presented to the Women's Meeting in Bristol, as well as 'sent to Robert Gibbons' owne hands'.[179] Though they hoped for repentance, for the time being Gibbons' unrepentant spirit made him an anathema to the Friends, resulting in the rather serious declaration that he was 'shut out of the Kingdom'.

Papers of contrition, a clear public statement of repentance, could potentially secure a person's place in the Society and also potentially clear the way to matrimony if need be. This was the case for a man called Richard Lindy whose miscarriage of frequent inebriation kept him from gaining approbation to marry Sarah Mills. His statement of repentance was documented in the minutes of 30 June 1668.

> Friends, For the satisfactions of such amongst you as are concerned, these lines are given forth as a reall acknowledgment that I have walked contrary to the wayes of Trueth in by past times particularly in drinking too much, or being overcome with drink, which sinn hath reflected upon mee as a very heavy burden, as well in mine owne particular as from any without, & the sence therof have been, & is an affliction of spirit, & a sore wounding, as well as a future warning, which I desire with you may seem sufficient, for they have been, & are my affliction haveing in myselfe deeper sence of my miswalkings, then you by evidence can lay to my chardge; which I openly confess, & that through Judgment theron I am brought in measure to a more watchfulness, & therefore let this my acknowledgment find acceptance with you, & let it render satisfaction unto such as have not been satisfied herein, for which cause, and for that the name of the Lord, & his blessed Trueth, hath been blasphemed by reason of my miscarriadges since I have been convinced, which I am willing in this way what in mee lyes to redeem, & take the

---

[178] Ibid, 178–9.
[179] Ibid, 179.

shame on myselfe for transgressing; as the judgment I have thus written; & doe hereby make publique amongst you, that others alsoe whoe by my example might have been led to the same excess may hear, & fear & doe noe more soe wickedly.[180]

This public contrition apparently succeeded, making the Meeting 'soe farr satisfied as to suffer his marriage with Sarah Mills to bee mentioned & done amongst them'.[181]

If clearness and spiritual readiness for marriage was not adequately demonstrated or well proven, couples could find themselves unable to gain approbation. In the minutes of 21 February 1669, the Meeting had grave concerns regarding the intended man's spiritual renewal, resulting in an admonishment of the couple rather than approbation:

> Thomas Morrice & Joane Howell this day manifested unto this meetinge their desires to bee joined together in marriage in the way of freinds, and in regard freinds are not satisfied that the said Thomas was so far convinced of the principle of truth as to have a reall sense of truth upon his spirit, therefore doe they admonish him, and her both to waite patiently untill the Lord in his time bringes them into the sense of that with which freinds have unity.[182]

The Meeting did not tell them that the marriage would never happen. But not having a unified positive sense regarding Morrice's spiritual state, they encouraged them to wait and see. Perhaps when evidence of his personal conversion and his 'convincement' of 'the principle of truth' was produced by Morrice, the union possibly would receive unified consent. But for the time being, unfortunately for this couple, the sense of the group went against them. Whether Thomas and Joane ever eventually gained approbation is unclear, as there is no record of the marriage ever taking place with the Quakers. But it is highly possible they were eventually married (perhaps in a church), as there is a register entry for the burial of a 'Jane Morris, wife of Thomas Morris'.[183] If they were married, their experience would be indicative of some fellow Quakers who simply waited too long and sought other avenues towards marriage. The waiting and seeing made some grow impatient and frustrated. In 1669, the Meeting became aware through rumour that a Quaker called Henry Dedicott was unwilling to have one of his daughters go through the approbation process, as it had taken too long for

---

[180] Mortimer (Ed.), *Minute Book of the Men's Meeting of the Society of Friends in Bristol 1667–1686*, 11.
[181] Ibid.
[182] Ibid, 30–31.
[183] Ibid, 210.

his other daughter who had apparently had a lengthy experience in the Quaker marriage discipline:

> William Rogers and William Yeamans are to serch out the truth of what Nathaniell Day reports, (viz.) that Ann Ganeclift informes him that Mary Didicate [Dedicott] did say to her that her husband [Henry Dedicott] fownd soe much dificalty in the bringing about the marriage of his former daughter that he was not willing this his daughter (lately maryed to Thomas Taylor) shold come amongst them, and moreoever said to this purpose she wold not make them hipocrits to perswade them to it.[184]

The entry has a footnote added about two weeks later, 'The substance of the above report by Nathaniell Day is by Ann Ganeclift confest to bee truth'.[185] Practicality and efficiency was favoured over spiritual issues for the father, who was clearly irritated with the cumbersome and lengthy process. However, his son William would go through the process in 1677 with little trouble.[186] The following year, Henry was 'free to sett in the gallery to see to prevent rudeness of boys there at meeting time', and was apparently doing this same job ten years later.[187]

Practical matters including adequate financial provision and protection for widows, or the children of widows or widowers, were an additional concern in the approbation process. In April 1672, George White and widow Mary Masters proposed their intentions of marriage. The Meeting knew Mary had two children from her previous marriage as well as a considerable estate, and found 'it expedient to inspect the estate of the said Mary, that so freinds (as much as in them lyes) may bee instrumentall that her children may, in its proper season enjoy that proportion thereof as is just and equall'. John Love was sent to investigate the situation in an effort to ensure the children would not be financially abandoned in the marriage. After John Love 'made inquiry into the outward estate & condition of Mary Masters', he reported to the next Meeting 'hee doth understand that her outward estate is very little & that also incumbered & therefore friends doe not thinke fitt to take any further notice as to that matter, & they finding no cause wherefore her marriage with Geo: White should bee obstructed they have liberty to cause the publication thereof to bee made in our publick meeting house as is usuall'.[188] When they discovered Mary's remaining estate constituted very little, and that she and her children would likely be in better financial shape marrying carpenter George White, their marriage was

---

[184] Ibid, 22.
[185] Ibid.
[186] Ibid, 114.
[187] Ibid, 127.
[188] Ibid, 61.

approbated and published later that month. During the same Meeting at which the White/Master marriage was discussed, another widow called Ann North and Benjamin James, a local merchant, requested approbation. The Meeting minutes record the following assurance Ann's children would be provided for:

> Benjamin James & Ann North widow's did this day propose their intentions of mariage according to the way and order of freinds. Enquiry hath been made conceringe the Widow Norths two children & the meeting is informed by F: & W. Rogers that a will was made & that they beleive due care wilbee taken for performance of the will.[189]

It was during this case in the meetings, the Bristol Friends more clearly instigated in their Meeting regular procedures in protecting the rights of the widow and her children (as the estate would become the property of the new husband). The Meeting also took the opportunity to instate a new regulation in the protection of orphans: 'And it's the judgement of freinds that for the future the like care be taken in the like cases relatinge to orphanes'.[190] Later that same year, a marriage intention was brought to the Meeting, but proof of the security of a widow's property was not adequately ensured or demonstrated, causing the Meeting to withhold approbation until proof of the protection of the widow was brought forth. After a second proposal of intention to marry, the Meeting recorded the following:

> Wheras on Phillip Higginbotham his second proposall of marriage with Katheren Lews there is som stop in their proceedings, by reason that there is noe provission made to secure Katheren in her estate in case she survive him the said Phillip[.] It is therefore the desire of this meeting that Thomas Gouldney, Edward Martendale, Charles Jones, John Love, & William Foord or any three of them doe consider togeather and advise with the said Phillip & Katheren, in order to find out and setle the same as they with the advice and consent of Thomas Speed shall see meete.[191]

A month later, a third attempt was made by Phillip and finally for him he was granted approbation when the 'friends being satisfied from those that were appointed that sufficient provision is made on the behalfe of said Katherine: for a subsistance in case she shall survive him; they have permitted the publication therof'.[192] This demonstrates the rather unique intervention of a religious

---

[189] Ibid.
[190] Ibid, 60.
[191] Ibid, 69–70.
[192] Ibid.

Approbation and 'Clearness': The Early Quaker Marriage Discipline   77

organisation looking into a person's private financial affairs, being indicative of both the unity Quakers believed they had, as a family in the spirit, as well as being in line with the Quakers' belief in protecting the orphan and the widow.

Clearness for marriage also included making sure an intended widow or widower did indeed have a deceased spouse and was free to marry again. Proof of death was sometimes not easily attained in the seventeenth century. Problems included limited long distance communication and the inconsistency of legal records of deaths, particularly in the American colonies. In 1670, when Joel Gilson proposed his intention to marry a widow, Jane Fletcher, there was some concern over the validity of the claim that her husband Joseph Fletcher had died for certain in Maryland. Accusations of bigamy were the last thing the Quakers needed as they fought for the right to marry in their own way outside the Church of England. The death needed to be verified. Luckily, a member of the Men's Meeting, William Canons of Bristol, had 'testified in the Men's Meeting that her late husband Joseph Fletcher dyed in Maryland, which informacion of his death hee had from a friend' of the man of the house where Fletcher was lodging when he died.[193] Further verification came from the witness of another member of the Meeting:

> The truth of said Josephs death is further verified by Edward Perrin a freind of this citty: & under his hand followeth. I do hereby certify that John Clements livinge in great Choptanke in Maryland, being a man of credit, did informe me in the tenth moneth last past (I being then in Maryland) that hee helped to put Joseph Fletcher in the grave, and that diverse other persons of creditt did also informe mee that the said Joseph was dead.[194]

Short of admitting they saw the man buried, it was difficult to gain assurance at times of a person's death, particularly if the person lived far away. Fortunately for Joel and Jane their marriage was approbated and published, but only after two fellow Friends verified Jane was indeed a widow.

Quakers also differed from their contemporaries by discouraging hasty *second* marriages after the death of a spouse, as well as expressly forbidding marriage to a first or second cousin, an act allowed by British law.[195] Fox relayed the following advice to Friends in Barbados during his visit in 1671 in regards to proper waiting time before embarking on a second marriage:

---

[193] Ibid, 34.
[194] Ibid.
[195] *Rules of Discipline of the Religious Society of Friends, with Advices: Being Extracts from the Minutes and Epistles of Their Yearly Meeting, Held in London, From its First Institution* (London: Darton and Harvey, Third Edition, 1834), 97. See also Dandelion, *An Introduction to Quakerism*, 70.

To prevent over-hasty proceedings towards second marriages, after the death of a former husband or wife; advising that a decent regard might be had in such cases, to the memory of the deceased husband or wife.[196]

Twenty years later, an extract from the 1691 Yearly Meeting in London also evinced a grave concern over marrying too hastily after the death of a spouse, fearing it would bring reproach upon their religious beliefs and Society:

This meeting strongly recommends friends to avoid and to discountenance very early proceedings in regard to marriage after the death of husband or wife; esteeming such conduct as tending to the dishonour and reproach of our Christian profession.[197]

In 1675, the Yearly Meeting in London further made the following restrictions in regards to marrying first cousins:

It is our living sense and judgment, that not only those marriages of near kindred, expressly forbidding under the law, ought not to be practiced under the gospel; but that we in our day ought not to take first cousins in marriage, being brought to that spiritual dispensation which gives dominion over the affections, and leads to those marriages which are more natural, and of better report. And though some, through weakness, have been drawn into such marriages (which being done must not be broken,) yet let not their practice be a precedent to any others amongst us for the time to come.[198]

Interestingly, the Yearly Meeting cited 'the spiritual dispensation which gives dominion over the affections' as a reason for their forbidding such an act. Marrying a first cousin was perhaps motivated by physical or economical gain, both carnal motivations which were considered not indicative of, or becoming to, restored people out of the Fall.[199]

---

[196] George Fox, *To Friends in Barbados: Swarthmoor, Lancashire, 25th of 8th Month, 1676*. Printed in Samuel Tuke, *Selections from The Epistles, &c. of George Fox* (York: Alexander and Son, 1825), 180.

[197] *Rules of Discipline of the Religious Society of Friends, with Advices*, 92. Fox himself would wait eleven years after the death of Judge Fell before asking Margaret Fell to marry him (Fox, *Journal* [1952], 554).

[198] *Rules of Discipline of the Religious Society of Friends, with Advices*, 97.

[199] Fox expressly forbade seeking a mate out of such desires. In 1659, he cited Genesis 6 as a warning to people choosing mates based on carnal desires, '... in Genesis, when the Sons of God saw the Daughters of men that they were fair, they took unto them Wives of all sorts, which was in the coveting desires that grieved the Spirit of God, so their minds was rebuked

Other issues which arose in the Bristol Men's Meetings minutes provided marriage approbation cases which were slightly more theatrical than others, particularly when involving more colourful characters. A shoemaker and widower called Henry Pritchard proved to be a bit of a thorn in the Meeting's side. Denied of the Meeting's approbation for marriage, Pritchard nevertheless went ahead and married a Quaker woman called Mary Smith in 1667.[200] The reasons for the Meeting's lack of support had apparently to do with his refusal to repent of past various miscarriages including lying, drinking and 'bad conversation'. Their less than impressed view of Pritchard's behaviour is reflected in the following minutes recording an encounter with Henry:

> Friends being met togather, & Henry Pritchard presenting himselfe amongst them; & appearing in the same unruly, & bad spirit as hee had done before; & unconvinced of his former, & later miscarriadges; did Judge it not convenient that hee should remaine among them, & therefore, haveing declared the thing to him & reasons, desired him to depart.[201]

Convinced of his *not* being convinced, by his consistent misbehaviour, his presence was deemed 'not convenient' and they requested he leave the Meeting, hoping that in waiting and discussing with him in private further, he might exhibit a more positive demeanour and contrite spirit.

A further problem existed for the Bristol Men's Meeting concerning the Pritchard marriage. Some Friends of the Meeting had attended the wedding, being apparently convinced by Henry that he was fit for marriage, a miscarriage these Friends would publicly repent of, as they felt they had disrupted unity in the Society by going against the Meeting's decision. In the minutes of November 1667, the Meeting requested these Friends attend the following Meeting:

> That those friends whoe were present at the mariage of Hen Pritchard & Mary Smith notwithstanding that friends of the Mens Meeting denied to have to doe in his marriage till he owned Judgment upon his miscarriages proved upon him at the Meeting, bee desired to bee at the next Meeting.[202]

At this next Meeting, it was agreed that 'a Paper be drawne upp against the next Meeting for the disowning of Henry Pritchards marriage'.[203] Several Friends

---

that run after all sorts, that grieved the Spirit of God, that went from God's joyning; So this was the rebukable Marriage, Gen. 6.2' (Fox, *Concerning Marriage* [1661], 1).

[200] Mortimer, 'Marriage Discipline in Early Friends', 176.

[201] Mortimer (Ed.), *Minute Book of the Men's Meeting of the Society of Friends in Bristol 1667–1686*, 5.

[202] Ibid, 4.

[203] Ibid.

who had attended the Pritchard marriage signified they were 'then willing to sign a Paper to redeem their being present at the marriage of the sayd Henry'.[204] The signed declaration of repentance and disownment of the marriage read as follows:

> Wee, whose names are subscribed doe signify that upon Henry Pritchards suggestion that noe friends were against his marriage, but only two, & our not haveing understood what wee have since that many fowle miscarriagdes were proved against him, wherupon friends, whilest hee stood unjudged by himselfe therin could doe nothing in order to his marriage, wee were present among others when hee took Mary Smith to wife; which we are sorry for; partly because wee understand that his sayd suggestion was false; & partly because our presence as witnesses to his marriage tends (as upon serious consideration wee have found) to the breach of good order among friends. And therefore wee disowne the sayd marriage, & our being therat.[205]

Friends John Packer, George Phipps, William Taylor and Andrew Gale, all who had been witnesses to the marriage, were sorry for their attendance not only because the marriage was 'false', but also because they believed it to be a breach of 'good order among friends', something early Quakers saw as crucially important as early as the 1660s.

The Pritchard affair however was not over. The following month, a paper declaring Henry's 'miscarriages' was considered by the Meeting to be read and published. But the men were not hasty or eager to do so. On 13 January, the minutes recorded that Friend Charles Jones had spoken with Henry 'in pursueance of their desire the last Meeting to speak with him in order to his miscarriadges, if soe bee hee might bee made sensible, & soe the Declaration of Friends concerning his late marriage might not goe forth'.[206] Hope for Henry's repentance evidently continued, as their desire to see those convinced stay convinced and a part of the unified Society. But Henry's contrition was never exhibited. After many 'Endeavors soe to convince him, hee remained the same man standing in opposition to friends'.[207] With his lack of repentance and unity with the Friends, the 'Declaration of friends ... against that his sayd marriage, & the evill president' was published in the minutes, and read aloud by Thomas Callowhill 'on the next Sixth Day at the publique Meeting':

---

[204] Ibid.
[205] Ibid, 5.
[206] Ibid, 6.
[207] Ibid, 7.

> Friends... finding him upon sufficient proofe, to bee not only of a bad conversation; as, too much given to drinking; breaking of his promise; lying (having denyed his owne brother) but seeking severall, besides the sayd Mary, for his wife; & some of them within the time that hee sought the sayd Mary; ... Besides diverse unkindnesses, & ill useadge to his late wife (a sober friend, with whom hee had a considerable estate as to the outward, in reference unto him) to her great discouragement & greife of heart, (as by words out of her owne mouth before her death, did appear) the sayd Mary, & himselfe being both present; with severall other miscarriadges then proved before him, toe long to mention, & which wee think fit at this time to pass over with silence ... Friends at the Meeting with one consent, not one contradicting but all joyning togather ... did declare to him, & the sayd Mary in the presence of the witnesses; That they were not satisfied with his denyalls, & answers; & for that cause could not consent to, nor approve of his marriadge as it then stood, unless hee judged himselfe & soe became sensible of his miscarriadges, bowing to that of God in him, which judged, & would judge such miscarriadges as it was waited upon ... which when it should soe appear, friends declared their readiness then to proceed further to doe in answer to his desire what to them appertayned.[208]

It comes to light that Henry's 'miscarriadges' were rather rampant and consistent, as can be seen by his apparent mistreatment of his first wife who had passed away. It is also apparent for the first time in the minutes that Henry was also pursuing many women for marriage at the same time, in addition to Mary.

Their lengthy investigation included efforts to talk with him to help him see his wayward ways, and times of waiting, in hopes that he would bow to 'that of God in him, which judged and would judge such miscarriages'. With his refusal to respond to both God in him and to the Friends around him, and with his rather colourful reputation preceding him, Henry's conduct presented problems to the Bristol Friends including miscarriages, his refusal to repent and 'evill presidents' of bad order. The Declaration concluded:

> Now forasmuch as the sayd Hen. Pritchard, notwithstanding all this friendly advice for his good, & brotherly dealing, hath got togather severall of his friends, & others, & by lyes, & false suggestions perswaded some, & enticed others into a complyance with his desires (several of whom being convinced of their surprizeall & error in that particular have subscribed their hands to a Paper acknowledging accordingly) ... These are therefore to testefy ... That wee of the Mens ... doe disowne the sayd marriadge, as not being done in the Trueth, but in, & by a lye; as alsoe the manner of the doeing of it; & the coming togather of those whoe were

---

[208] Ibid, 7–8.

present therat; as a breach of good order, & doe desire all friends of Trueth to take notice therof.[209]

Henry's many miscarriages were discovered and publicly brought to attention. Done with some reticence, the public declaration made against him by the Meeting was carried out, likely with some hope (though by now dismal), of Henry's repentance. Henry's disruption of unity and good order, and his marrying not 'in the Trueth' but in and 'by a lye', were offences the Bristol Men's Meeting could neither tolerate nor accept. Two years later, in 1669, Pritchard finally expressed sorrow and repentance for rejecting and ignoring the Meeting's advice.[210]

In September 1678, Robert Rudle and Grace Marsh 'signified their intentions of marriage' with support from the Bristol Men's Meeting, 'nothing appeareing meet to obstruct it, this Meeting concents that they cause their intentions to be published in our publick meeting', having both parents' consent duly shown in certificates, including Grace's father Richard Marsh.[211] At first appearances, it seemed all would go smoothly, until fellow Friend John Streeter made a surprising declaration to the Meeting that was about to publish the marriage. In front of the men gathered, Streeter declared 'that there hath been an engadgment betwixt him & Grace Marsh & desires this meeting to apoynt some to heare what might be said betwixt them'.[212] This was a sort of 'speak now, or forever hold your peace' moment in the approbation process, which brought the Rudle/Marsh marriage approbation to an abrupt halt.

At the following Meeting, four men were assigned to 'speake with Richard Marsh, Jno. Streeter, Grace Marsh, & Robt. Rudle touching the same, & to give an account how they find it to the next meeting'.[213] Speaking with Grace's father was crucially important, as he was seen as a critical voice in the approbation process. After the investigation into the circumstances and truth of Streeter's declaration, Quakers Richard Snead, Edward Martendale, William Foord and Charles Jones gave an update two months later, stating that on 4 November:

> They have discoured with Richard Marsh, John Streeter and Grace Marsh, & som of them with Robert Rudle, and upon the whole saw reason & did advise

---

[209] Ibid.

[210] Mortimer, 'Marriage Discipline in Early Friends', 195. Mary was a committed Friend and listed as a 'sufferer' in 1664 ('sufferer' referring to a Quaker who underwent hardship for religion). She did not go through the same contrition requirements as Henry within the Bristol Men's Meeting.

[211] Mortimer (Ed.), *Minute Book of the Men's Meeting of the Society of Friends in Bristol 1667–1686*, 128.

[212] Ibid, 129.

[213] Ibid, 131.

them the said Robert and Grace as the case stood not to prosecute their former intentions any farther at present.[214]

The Meeting's request to Robert and Grace to cease seeking marriage was successful, as the minutes read:

> John Love & Richard Snead farther testefieth that, upon the 27th of the nineth moneth last, the said Robert Rudle & Grace Marsh did under their hands mutually to each other, in the presents of them the said John & Richard as wittnesses, acquit discharge and release each other of all promises, obligations or intents relateing to marriage.[215]

Instead of approbation, there is in the above quote a documented record of their 'acquittal' of promises to each other. As it stood, according to the Quakers Grace had created a grave problem by promising to marry two men at once. Releasing all promises was the only way to make Grace right with the Friends.[216] Marriage approbation was not the only issue at stake. A Friend following through on his or her word to another Friend was absolutely necessary for maintaining and preserving good order and truth with one another. Clearness, nothing hidden or deceptive, promises communicated and regulated 'in the light' were considered essential for the unity of the Quaker community. This was the case even in the form of engagements. As Grace had given her word to both men she would marry them, this was a grave matter as one's word was taken very seriously. As she could not follow through on her word to both men, it was essential that one engagement be officially broken off, in the form of acquittal of promises, in order to maintain truth and clarity in the community. While engagement was a grave commitment through verbal agreement (i.e. one's word) it was not final.[217] A marriage was not binding until the ceremony took place and it was published in the meeting minutes.

---

[214] Ibid, 133.

[215] Ibid.

[216] Four years later, Grace Marsh married the son of one of the inquisitors, Charles Jones. She had moved to London with her father, but remained in the Society. Robert Rudle also married that year another Quaker woman, and John Streeter married a Quaker woman in Jamaica called Sarah Mino.

[217] In early-modern England, engagements and verbal agreements differentiated between meaning and importance, but usually an engagement of some form was legally binding (Adair, *Courtship, Illegitimacy and Marriage in Early Modern England*, 144). In the early meeting system, Quakers intended to eschew the complications of personal promises by bringing matrimony into the communal forum, in which personal engagements were not considered legally or officially binding. However, as seen in the case of Grace Marsh, one could not marry another if they had given his or her consent to marry another.

In addition to dealing with exogamous marriages and people who were married by a priest, the Somerset Meeting was also encountering the issue of Quakers who were living together and 'ought' to be married.[218] In 1686, the Somerset Quarterly Meeting sent out a paper against such 'disorders':

> Any touching marriages, their minds immoderately and too hastily let out one to another without good advice, too much frequenting one anothers company, liveing togeather in one house while under a concerne of marriage, manifesting to the world such neareness as if marriage were concluded, when never rightly begun.[219]

Bristol's solution to co-habitation was creating an alternative wedding procedure, which was considered a sort of 'second class' wedding. The marriage would be witnessed by a group of their relations and other Quakers outside of an official meeting for worship, where marriages typically took place, followed by the production of a marriage certificate, but not by a Quaker registration. This type of marriage was explained in the Bristol Meeting minutes of 31 August 1674:

> That if it should happen that any young people or others, that profess the truth with us, being under a contract or proposition towards marriage, and before they shall accomplish the same shall fall under the temptation of the Divel defileing themsealves to the prejudice of their owne soules and dishonouring of their intended marriage, and after being brought under a true sence and sorrow for their miscarriage doe desire the advice of friends in order to their marriage. And since the law of god … and equity requires such should marry it is enqueried how farr friends should concerne them sealves therein … It is Mutually agreed: That such a marriage being not honourable may not be approved to pass in these meetings according to our accustomed manner: nor can wee, if they be really sencable of their miscarriage and doe desire advice, wholly reject and cast them off & leave them open to the temptation of goeing to the priests.[220]

Fox directly addressed the issue of pre-marital sex and co-habitation in an epistle sent to all meetings in 1669. Though the Men's Meeting of Bristol

---

[218] The approbation process as seen in the meeting minutes of the Somerset Quarterly Meeting 1668–99 resembles the process of Bristol very closely, particularly in the amount of time spent on procedures and troubles with 'disorder'. They also had the same difficulties in getting their fellow Quakers to follow consistently and patiently the approbation process. See Stephen C. Morland (Ed.), *The Somersetshire Quarterly Meeting of the Society of Friends 1668–1699* (Somerset: Somerset Record Society, 1978).

[219] Ibid, 27.

[220] Mortimer (Ed.), *Minute Book of the Men's Meeting of the Society of Friends in Bristol 1667–1686*, 89.

did not mention this epistle, it is possible they were abreast of the following recommendation from Fox:

> If any man should defile a woman, he must marry her ... for he must fulfil the law of God, for the law of God commands it, that he must marry her, and condemn his action, and clear God's truth. But no such marriages, where the bed is defiled, we bring into our meetings; but some Friends (if such a thing happen) draw up a certificate, and they to set their hands to it, that they will live faithfully together as man and wife, and fulfil the law of God.[221]

The same situations arose in Somerset with Nathaniel Bryan in 1669 and Henry Gee in 1678 in Somerset, who seemed to have undergone the same procedures as outlined by Bristol.[222]

The Wedding Ceremony

After a marriage between two Quakers was finally given group consensus through a series of meetings, a certificate would be drawn up and read at a large common meeting, declaring the marriage official. In some cases, a couple was asked not to consummate their marriage until a particular time after its publication in the minutes. In 1669 when the Bristol Men's Meeting granted John Wats and Mary Blagdon permission 'to cause publicacion of such their intencions to bee made' of their marriage they were also instructed 'not to consummate their marriage until after the next mens meetinge after publicacion'.[223] This was perhaps done to extend even further the time that any problems or obstructions may arise to prevent the marriage.

The 'ceremony' itself was simple, with little ceremony or pomp and circumstance in fact. Rufus Jones describes a typical Quaker wedding in the American colonies, not unlike the ones conducted by fellow Friends in England:

> The parties, flanked by the parents, then stood up in meeting and took each other as man and wife. No priest or minister intervened or dictated words. No ring

---

[221] George Fox, *Epistle CCLXII: An exhortation to keep to the ancient principles of truth* (s.l., 1669). Printed in Isaac Hopper (Ed.), *The Works of George Fox: A Collection of Many Select and Christian Epistles, Letters, and Testimonies, written on sundry occasions, by that Ancient, eminent, faithful Friends, and minister of Christ Jesus, George Fox. In Two Volumes* (Philadelphia, PA: Marcus T.C. Gould, 1831), Volume One, 337–8.

[222] Morland (Ed.), *The Somersetshire Quarterly Meeting of the Society of Friends 1668–1699*, 29.

[223] Mortimer (Ed.), *Minute Book of the Men's Meeting of the Society of Friends in Bristol 1667–1686*, 28.

symbolized the union. No organ broke the quiet of the occasion. But in the hush and silence of a house full of worshippers they took each other by the hand.[224]

In 1685, a couple, referred to as A.B. and E.F. respectively, appeared together before a Meeting in London to marry in a similar fashion:

> For that end and purpose in their publick Meeting place at *Bull* and *Mouth* London, and (according to the Example of the Holy Men of God recorded in the Scriptures of Truth) in a solemn manner, he the said A.B. taking the said E.F. by the hand.[225]

The Quaker wedding was effectively a solemn, communal occasion, with no priest or organ in the simple meeting room. The marriage meeting, seen as a time of worship, was an opportunity for members to gather, to share words if they felt led, to witness and to hear the declarations of the couple to one another, and, finally, to sign the certificate.

In the Quaker meeting room, being set up roughly in circular form, the bride, groom, family members and friends stood at one end of the room and the ceremony began. In recent scholarship, Caroline Whitbeck has noted the absence of the exchange of the bride from the father to the groom (notably an absence of exchange between male hands of the female) in early Quaker weddings, an event typical within weddings of other Protestant denominations. Whitbeck argues the early Quakers intentionally did away with the custom of the father giving away the bride in an attempt to recognise the equal spiritual authority of both genders in the wedding party.[226] While it is true that the change in procedures certainly reflected the Quaker mindset of a more community oriented process of marriage, it is difficult to assert this was a direct result of egalitarian ideals, as there was no mention of this in the historical record of the seventeenth century. At most one can say that the marriage ceremony itself was a spiritual event, marked by the union of a man and woman seen as equal in spiritual terms.

The vows exchanged between husband and wife at a Quaker wedding were typically referred to as 'declarations', and often differed from other standard

---

[224] Rufus Matthew Jones, *The Quakers in the American Colonies* (London: Macmillan, 1911), 547.

[225] *A copy of a marriage-certificate of the people called Quakers. Importing the method used among them: Humbly presented to the members of Parliament, to manifest the said peoples Christian care, and righteous proceedings, not admitting clandestine or unwarrantable marriages amongst them. And therefore they humbly request that their marriages may not be rendered clandestine or illegal, not they or their children exposed to suffering on that account* (London, s.l., 1685).

[226] Whitbeck, 'Friends Historical Testimony on the Marriage Relationship', 13. See also Mack, *Visionary Women*, 226.

forms of vows shared in contemporary Protestant weddings. In his introduction to Fox's *Journal*, William Penn commented, 'the words of the usual form, as "With my body I thee worship," &c. are hardly defensible', rejecting any obvious forms of vows which indicated the worship of anyone else other than God.[227] An acceptable declaration between Friends was the new phrase 'I take this my friend', used by both genders. Returning to the Marriage Certificate from the 1685 London Meeting, we see an example of Quaker wedding declarations:

> The said A.B. taking the said E.F. by Hand, did openly declare as followeth. Friends, in the fear of the Lord, and in the presence of you his People, I take this my Friend E.F. to be my Wife, promising by the assistance of God, to be to her a faithful and loving Husband, till it please the Lord to separate us by death, [or to the same effect.] And then and there in the said Assembly, the said E.F. did in like manner declare as followeth: Friends, in the fear of the Lord, and in the presence of you his People, I take this my Friend A.B. to be my Husband, promising to be to him a faithful, obedient and loving Wife, till death separate us, [or to the same effect.][228]

At a Quaker Meeting in 1684, Friends John Pemberton and Margaret Matthews exchanged declarations of commitment to one another:

> 'Friends, you are here witnesses, in the presence of God and this assembly of His people, I take this maid, Margaret Matthews, to be my loving and lawful wife, promising to be a true and faithful husband unto her till death shall us part'. And then and there in the same assembly she, the said Margaret Matthews, did in like manner declare: 'Friends, before God and you His people, I take John Pemberton to be my husband, promising to be a loving and faithful wife until death shall us part'.[229]

Quaker wedding declarations did vary in part due to the nature of the declarations, as they were shared as the silence and the inward light moved them. Whitbeck has argued that because the early Quaker bride and groom shared and spoke their own vows, since they were personally led by the inward light in the moment, this affirmed the bride was no longer seen by Quakers as a man's possession, as had been encouraged by their contemporary Puritans and other Protestant sects.[230] However, again as there is no historical record of the early

---

[227] Fox, *Journal Vol. 1* (1836), xx.
[228] *A copy of a marriage-certificate of the people called Quakers.*
[229] Jones, *The Quakers in the American Colonies*, 547–8.
[230] Whitbeck, 'Friends Historical Testimony on the Marriage Relationship', 13. See also Mack, *Visionary Women*, 226.

seventeenth century Quakers explicitly encouraging or teaching gender equality in marriage, it is hard to concur with Whitbeck's conclusion. Moreover, there are some recorded declarations that suggest women did include the term 'obey' – as seen in the vows exchanged between A.B. and E.F. – though the use of 'obey' in Quaker wedding vows was more the exception than the rule. Additionally, the aforementioned practice of saying 'I take this my friend' does underline the Quaker emphasis on the notion of 'friend in Christ', in which case the bride and groom were considered at least spiritually equal.[231] Though early Quaker perceptions of social gender equality within marriage cannot be discussed here further, what can be affirmed is that the early Quakers believed male and female to be spiritually equal, coming together in marriage and a ministerial partnership, through their mutual obedience to the leading and guiding of 'that of Christ' within. We will see in a following chapter that Margaret Fell did not include any reference to obedience in her recorded wedding declarations with George Fox, as their marriage, in addition to other Quaker marriages, exemplified more egalitarian characteristics than many of their contemporaries. These changes in attitude, particularly amongst their marriage and wedding traditions, at the very least, reflected their shared belief that women as well as men were created in the image of God and were equal vessels of God's revelation and ministry.[232]

Rings were generally not exchanged, as forms and symbols were largely rejected by early Quakers. A ring was often considered a 'form' stemming from pagan rituals for the wedding ceremony which was never used in the scriptures, and was yet simply another sign of 'stinking popery' used amongst their contemporaries.[233] As Fox stated to a General Meeting in London:

> Marriage with a priest and with a ring, this is not an ordinance of God but of man; and when the Lord brought the children of Israel out of Egypt he gave them a charge not to follow the customs and manner of the Egyptians and Canaanites. Now that which I have suffered for ... hath been as I said before against the relics of stinking popery. So if any say we are popishly affected, I say no, we are Christ

---

[231] Rosemary Moore makes a similar point in regards to the early Quaker frequent practice of both the groom and bride taking similar vows: ' ... the Quaker marriage declaration, in which the man and woman used the same words to take each other, indicated greater equality between men and women within marriage than was usual at the time' (Moore, *The Light in Their Consciences*, 120). See also John R. Gillis, *For Better, For Worse: British Marriages, 1600 to the Present* (New York, NY: Oxford University Press, 1985), 102.

[232] Hill, *The World Turned Upside Down*, 312.

[233] Many Puritans also regarded the ring in marriage as a remnant of popery (Cressy and Ferrell, *Religion and Society in Early Modern England*, 61).

Approbation and 'Clearness': The Early Quaker Marriage Discipline

affected; we are true Protestants and follow the practice of our fore-fathers and mothers, the holy men and women, and so have the scriptures on our side.[234]

In 1679, Fox compared the use of priests and rings to the 'heathenish' practices of 'Romans Marriages':

> The man also in token of good will gave a Ring unto the woman which she was to weare on her next finger, to her little finger on the left hand because that unto that finger alone proceeds a certaine Artery or veine from the heart, and doth not the Priest put on or cause to be put on a Ring on the on the same finger now when he doth Marry them? ... And now you Priests and Teachers and others, which used to say that the Quakers thought they were wiser than their Forefathers, because they did not Joyne with you in your practice of Marrying with the Ring, But now doe not you Priests thinke yourselves wiser than your Forefathers the Romans, Foe doe not you Marry with the Ring and put it upon the same finger as the Romans did?[235]

He concluded his criticism with 'And what Scripture have you to put a Ring on a womans finger when she is married?'[236]

Margaret Fell also wrote against the use of a ring in wedding ceremonies in 1667, claiming this practice was never advocated by the apostle Paul, but was an invention of the 'Generation of Priests':

> The Apostle ... doth not say that they should be married by a Priest, or with a Ring: But it is manifested that this Generation of Priests ... have set up such Imaginations and Inventions of as these.[237]

In 1682, a Quaker called William Gibson published an epistle in London, in which he quotes Fox, describing the 'heathen' roots of using a ring in wedding ceremonies:

> In the Heathen Roman Antiquities there is something of President and Example, which take as followeth out of their Antiquities Collected by John Goodwin, viz. 'In their Contracts each did promise other to live as Man and Wife ... the man also gave in token, or good will, a Ring unto the Woman, which she was to wear upon the next Finger unto the little Finger of the left hand, because unto

---

[234] *George Fox's Sermon at Wheeler Street, 1680.* (Barbour and Roberts [Eds], *Early Quaker Writings*, 509.)
[235] Fox, *The true marriage declared*, 5–6.
[236] Ibid, 7.
[237] Margaret Fell, *A touch-stone, or A perfect trial by Scriptures*, 70.

that Finger alone proceeded a certain Artery from the Heart' ... Now whence the Papists and others had there President and Example for Marrying by a Priest, and having a Ring; and who it was that taught them upon which Finger to put it, and for what Reason, it is not hard to determine.[238]

William Penn wrote of the Quakers' 'way of marriage which is peculiar to them' including their rejection of 'heathenish' and 'vain' customs such as:

> the accustomed formality of priest and ring, &c. which ceremonies they have refused, not out of humour, but conscience reasonably grounded, inasmuch as no Scripture example tells us ... for the use of the ring, it is enough to say that it was a heathenish and vain custom, and never in practice among the people of God, Jews, or primitive Christians.[239]

Interestingly, when Mary Penington married her first husband, William Springett, in the early 1640s, Penington recalled not using the ring in her marriage: 'We being both very young were joined together in the Lord, and refused a ring and such like things then used, and not denied by any that we knew of'.[240] Though Mary Penington and William Springett were not yet Quakers (Quakerism would not come about for at least another five years), in addition to refusing to wear rings, like future Quakers they also did not partake in the Eucharist or water baptisms.

While Mary considered herself simply a spiritual seeker, with no affiliation with any particular religious group, her early practices and perceptions of marriage and courtship were similar to other sectarian and spiritual seekers of the time. Water baptism, the Eucharist and rings were all associated with the established church, and all considered dead outward signs. The use of the ring subsequently was frequently associated with the use of a priest in marriage ceremonies. It was considered an empty form with no scriptural support, and therefore was generally shunned amongst the early Quakers. Quaker theologian Robert Barclay explained these symbols and ceremonies as 'mere shadows and external manifestations of the true substance'.[241] As many Quakers emerged out of other sectarian groups, such as the Baptists (e.g. Elizabeth Hooton), or other seekers such as Fox himself, it is likely their notions of what a wedding should

---

[238] William Gibson, *A General epistle given forth in obedience to the God of peace for the preservation and increase of charity and unity* (London: Printed and sold by John Bringhurst, at the Sign of the Book in Grace-Church Street near Cornhill, 1682), 79–80.

[239] Fox, *Journal Vol. 1* (1836), xx.

[240] Booy, *Autobiographical Writings by Early Quaker Women*, 81.

[241] Robert Barclay, *An Apology for the True Christian Divinity* (London, 1678). Cited in Tual, 'Sexual Equality and Conjugal Harmony', 164.

look like were influenced by their former spiritual experiences, as well as their preceding and surrounding sectarian groups.

Once the intended betrothed made their declarations to one another, witnesses gathered to sign the marriage certificate. The aforementioned marriage certificate of A.B. and E.F., from the London Meeting of 1685, was actually presented to parliament to defend Quakers against popular accusations of engaging in clandestine or illegal marriages. The marriage certificate demonstrated the couple had adhered to 'good Order' by going through a litany of the required meetings and gaining proof of the needed approval and 'clearness', as stated in the Certificate's introduction:

> A.B ... and E.F. ... Having declared their Intentions of taking each other in Marriage before several publick Meetings of the People of God called Quakers in *London*, according to the good Order used amongst them whose Proceeding therin, after a deliberate Consideration thereof, were approved by the said Meetings, they appearing clear of all others, and having Consent of Parties and Relations concerned ... They the said A.B. and E.F. appeared in a publick Assembly of the aforesaid People, and others, met together for that end and purpose in their publick Meeting place.[242]

Like the Bristol Quakers, the London Quakers demonstrated to parliament that A.B. and E.F. were following a public and orderly procedure including a certificate with signatures of witnesses. They were likewise ready with their documented approbation paperwork to prove Quaker marriage procedures across England were legally and morally sound. Signatures were essential to the wedding certificates' legitimacy for the Society of Friends. As already discussed, the certificate was their document proving they had been wedded by the example of the 'Holy Men of God', as noted in the London certificate of A.B. and E.F., through a conducted marriage in front of witnesses.

Early Quakers were flexible when it came to certain extenuating circumstances, and found ways to deal with various quandaries, including Quakers who wanted to marry, but were in prison. At times under severe persecution, Friends conducted their Monthly Meetings while in prison if need be, as was the case in Reading after the Second Conventicle Act was passed in May 1670. The question arose whether or not it was deemed appropriate to be married while incarcerated. Perhaps one of the most peculiar of early Quaker marriages, on 7 August 1671, two Friends from Reading, William Yeet and Hannah Wrenn, were granted permission to marry in prison:

---

[242] *A copy of a marriage-certificate of the people called Quakers.*

> The parties desires Friends' advice whether it be judged meet to be married here in prison or not. It is agreed and thought convenient, seeing it cannot well be otherwise, the generality of Friends being kept close prisoners, that they finish their marriage here; and they were accordingly joined in marriage the 7th of this instant month.[243]

The Quarterly Meeting minutes of Reading in April 1675 ordered the next Quarterly Meeting be held in 'Blewbury ... but if Friends at Reading shall happen to be generally in prison at that time, then it is ordered to be here at Reading'.[244] Dealing with imprisonment was a regular occurrence for the early Quakers, one which they did not allow to disrupt their meetings, nor their marriage proceedings.

The appropriate means of celebration after the marriage was an important issue for the Society of Friends, including extravagant feasts and large quantities of money being spent, which could have gone to other means such as supporting the poor. Yearly Meetings warned of ostentatious displays of wealth at celebrations after marriages. A Quaker called Ambrose Rigge commended the modest celebrations of the early church, an example he believed his fellow Quakers should follow:

> When they were at any time invited to publick as Marriages or the like, the Prudence of the Church thought fit to lay restraints upon them, only to forbid them of light and ludicrous actions, as Leaping or Dancing, but that they should dine and modestly, as becomes Christians.[245]

Historian David Cressy describes a decadent Yorkshire wedding in 1682 during which 'the bride's grandmother, a Quaker, felt moved to warn everyone "that Satan might not get advantage by our carnal mirth"'.[246]

In Fox's early recollections of the time before he was a Quaker, he refrained from going to Christmas and marriage celebrations, already showing signs of unease with wedding feasts:

---

[243] Braithwaite, *The Second Period of Quakerism*, 569.

[244] Ibid.

[245] Ambros Rigge, *True Christianity Vindicated both in Praeceding, Present, and Succeeding Ages, And the Difference between them who are Christians indeed, and them who are falsly so called Manifested: being a collection of the several testimonies of the antient writers of the doctrine, lives and manners of the primitive Christians many ages ago, which being found coherent with the doctrine, lives and manners of the true Christians, who are nicked named Quakers at this day, are therefore made publick* (London, 1679), 23.

[246] Cressy, *Birth, Marriage, and Death*, 372.

> When the time called Christmas came, while others were feasting and sporting themselves, I looked out poor widows from house to house, and gave them some money. When I was invited to marriages, (as I sometimes was,) I went to none at all, but the next day, or soon after, I would go and visit them; and if they were poor, I gave them money; for I had wherewith both to keep myself from being chargeable to others, and to administer something to the necessities of others.[247]

Fox suggested in 1690 that the money spent on elaborate weddings should be given to the poor. In an epistle addressed to London Quakers that year, Fox recommended:

> Such among Friends, who marry, and provide great dinners, that instead thereof, it will be good savour on such occasions, that they may be put in mind at such times, to give something to the poor that be widows and fatherless, and such like ... These things I do recommend to you (though it may look a little strange).[248]

Whether the above admonitions against decadent celebrations following marriage declarations were consistently followed is hard to tell. However, sources suggest wedding celebrations amongst Friends likely varied.[249] In the American colonies, committees were formed assuring sober celebrations were 'accomplished according to order', and that entertainment following the wedding 'at the house was simple and that the entertainment were free from excessive drinking and frivolity'.[250] Fox longed for a wedding ceremony that was done in worship, not in indulgence. Though perhaps not all followed his advice in practice, modest celebrations were generally upheld by Fox as the preferred way.

'According to the Order of the Gospell': The Rise of the Women's Meetings

In the late 1660s, Fox and Fell began to vigorously advocate the establishment of separate Women's Meetings. Fox saw these Meetings as a helpful and efficient means towards accomplishing tasks that needed more time than the regular business meetings allowed. The Women's Meetings were necessary in part because of the great deal of time devoted to the marital issues in the Men's Meetings. The marital approbation process brought with it many challenges that

---

[247] Fox, *Journal Vol. 1* (1836), 88.
[248] George Fox, *Epistle CCCCXIX to London, Written the 4th day of the 4th month* (1690).
[249] Frost, *The Quaker Family in Colonial America*, 173.
[250] Jones, *The Quakers in the American Colonies*, 547.

proved quite time consuming. This was one practical reason why the Women's Meetings were bestowed with the task of sifting the 'wheat from the shaft' in the marital approbation process. Some Quakers, such as William Penn, were concerned that women were more bashful and not able to speak in front of their fellow male Friends at mixed meetings, but 'when by themselves [they] exercise their gifts of wisdom and understanding in a discreet care for their own sex'.[251] Fox voiced concerns that some issues could not be delicately dealt with in mixed company, when 'modesty in women cannot so well speak of before men as they can do among their own sex'.[252]

Women's connection with family, servants, children and the home, according to both Fox and Fell, made them more suitable to deal with the affairs of family and marriage and care for those in need, particularly the widows and fatherless.[253] Maternal responsibilities and domestic leadership were considered compelling arguments for why women were equipped to deal with various disciplinary concerns facing Friends. These affairs often included disciplinary action against those walking 'disorderly' or who married 'with the world'. Fell and the Lancashire Women's Meeting encouraged women to take an active role in making moral inquiries into their families and households:

> Dear sisters it is duely Incumbent upon us to look into our families, and to prevent our Children of running into the world for husbands, or for wives, and so to the priests ... we are much in our families, amongst our children, maids, and servants and may see more into their inclinations.[254]

Similarly, Fox agreed mothers had a unique and important role in the 'ordering' of the domestic world and women in the Quaker community, which would not involve men:

> Now mothers of families, that have the ordering of children, maids, and servants, may do a great deal of good or harm in their families, to the making or spoiling of children, maids, and servants; and many things women may do and speak of amongst women, which are not men's business.[255]

---

[251] Trevett, *Women and Quakerism in the 17th Century*, 85.

[252] George Fox, *To the Men and Womens Monthly and Quarterly Meetings*. Cited in Mack, *Visionary Women*, 286.

[253] Ibid.

[254] *From our Country Women's meeting in Lancashire to be Dispersed abroad, among the Women's meetings every where* (Milton D. Speizman and Jane C. Kronick [Eds], 'A Seventeenth-Century Quaker Women's Declaration', *Signs*, 1 no 1 [Autumn 1975]: 231–45. Chicago: University of Chicago Press.)

[255] Tuke, *Selections from The Epistles, &c. of George Fox*, 220.

Mary Penington reflected this notion by connecting it with God's created order of gendered responsibilities, 'Our place in the creation is to bring forth and nurse up, to keep things orderly, sweet and clean in a family ... the men need not grudge us this place in the body'.[256]

Separate Women's Meetis did not emerge without some controversy. In fact, the greatest internal schism and challenge to Fox's authority, led by a group who came generally to be known as 'the Separatists', stemmed largely from opposition to the Meeting structure and order set up by Fox and his followers, including the Women's Meetings having designated authority over the marriage procedure. In 1673, while in Wiltshire, Fox met with 'much opposition from some who had set themselves against Women's Meetings'.[257] Opposition was largely led by John Wilkinson and John Story, two northern Quakers who expressed, amongst other complaints, strident objections to the advent of autonomous Women's Meetings (unless set up strictly for the poor in large towns) and the development of fixed marriage procedures.[258] Others who opposed the separate Women's Meetings felt they were unscriptural and unnecessary, while some feared female rule without males present. This worry was addressed by Quaker William Loddington, who in 1685 felt it necessary to assuage these fears, 'Women Friends meeting by themselves, may without the least suspicion of usurping Authority over the Men, confer and reason together'.[259] While the historian Phyllis Mack acknowledges Quakers like Loddington regarded the Women's Meetings as a means to prevent women's authority over men, she also suggests a more optimistic opinion regarding their establishment:

> The women's meeting was not a form of seventeenth-century tokenism, for while women's jurisdiction over marriage did not belong to the sphere of public policy, it did involve the authority to instruct and discipline male relatives and neighbours. Moreover, the London Six Weeks Meeting, established by Fox as the prime meeting in the city, was attended by both men and women.[260]

The historian William Braithwaite asserts that while Women's Meetings did not have an equal share in church government with the Men's Meetings, it is evident in Fox's epistles and other writings that 'the question whether the women should be given less or more authority was not in his mind' but he was rather desirous to

---

[256] Mary Penington, *Ffor those Women yt are dissastisfied at present wth the Womens meeting distinct from the Men (Amschot, Sept. 7, 1678)*. Cited in Mack, *Visionary Women*, 321.
[257] Fox, *Journal* (1952), 131.
[258] Mack, *Visionary Women*, 293.
[259] Loddington, *The Good Order of Truth Justified*, 5.
[260] Mack, *Visionary Women*, 288.

'liberate for the service of the Church the gifts of government which lay dormant and barren in both men and women'.[261]

In his letter *An Epistle relative to the station of Women in the Church* written in 1676, Fox considered the question of whether or not women were granted too much authority as a moot point in the work of the church, in which he felt men and women had equal shares in responsibility:

> And some there have been, that would not have the women to meet without the men; and some of them say, the women must not speak in the church; but if they must not speak, what should they meet with them for? ... And some men and women there are that suggest, if women should meet by themselves, in the order of the Gospel, the power of God, they would be too high; but such men and women as so suggest, are too high already, and would be ruling over men and women's possessions, and waste their own; for if they were in the power and Spirit of God, they need not fear any one's getting over them: for the power and Spirit of God gives liberty to all; for women are heirs of life as well as men.[262]

While the question of female autonomy within early Quaker Women's Meetings continues to be debated amongst historians today, what is of main concern here is how these Meetings developed and functioned in relation to marital approbation and discipline.[263]

Later in 1680, Fox addressed those who opposed the separation of women and men believing the separation went against the 'unity' Quakers cherished:

> But there is another objection: the men being in one room and the women in another. This is a separation, say they. No; for saith the apostle, though we be absent in the body, yet we are present in the Spirit, enjoying and beholding your spiritual order. So this spiritual sight beholds the heavenly order and communion. And, saith he, 'the steadfastness of your faith', which faith was heavenly received from the heavenly man. So this is no separation, for men to be in one room and women in the other, because they are present in spirit: one man may be here, another may be at Jamaica, Scotland, or Ireland or in any nation of the world, absent in body yet present in spirit.[264]

---

[261] Braithwaite, *The Second Period of Quakerism*, 274.

[262] George Fox, *An Epistle relative to the station of Women in the Church* (1676). (Tuke, *Selections from The Epistles, &c. of George Fox*, 262–3.)

[263] Mack, *Visionary Women*, 288, 293; Braithwaite, *The Second Period of Quakerism*, 274.

[264] *George Fox's Sermon at Wheeler Street, 1680.* (Barbour and Roberts [Eds], *Early Quaker Writings*, 510.)

Though some saw this physical separation as a threat to the spiritual unity of the Friends, Fox believed the threat did not exist, as men and women, though in separate rooms, were one in the Spirit and both were still in the Spirit's presence.

Despite Fox's efforts, debates over separate Women's Meetings within the Quaker circle would outlast his lifetime. As late as 1694, three years after the death of Fox, a Quaker called William Mather published a tract in London attacking separate Women's Meetings and their involvement in marriage approbation, in which he particularly addressed married women who he felt should devote themselves wholly to their households and acquiesce themselves entirely to their husbands' authority:

> No honest Married Wife is to deal in the Affairs of the Common-Wealth, much less meddle with the making of Marriages, unless for her own Children and Servants, wherein she must also refer her self to the discretion of her Husband, lest she incur the name of a Harebrain.[265]

Mather's anger spewed largely out of an episode in which he felt a fellow Quaker, Stephen Scarborrow, had been wrongly condemned for refusing to take his request of approbation to the Women's Meeting in Huntington. Scarborrow was given the following letter from the Huntington Meeting to take to the Meeting in Bedfordshire, the Meeting of his intended betrothed:

> Friends in Bedford-shire, Here came Stephen Scarborrow, to acquaint Friends of his Intention of Marriage with Marry Samm ... in Bedfordshire; as also he did to our Quarterly Meeting about a Month ago, and Friends did tenderly advise him to acquaint our Women Friends therewith, who attend Meetings to serve the Truth ... and to enquire, and see that things be clear on all parts on so weighty a Concern as Marriage; but he refusing to follow Friend's Advice herein, I know not what the Women-Friends may have to say in this Matter: Now I being one that have had some Exercise and Concern in these our Meetings, I to testifie, That that Spirit that doth oppose the good Order in publishing Marriage in Men and Women's Meetings, is not of God, and am sorry for the Young Man, and desire he may live to see his Weakness and amend.[266]

On his way to delivering the above note to the Bedfordshire Meeting, Scarborrow stopped at Mather's home, showed him the letter while allegedly saying, 'Friends gave it to me again.'[267] Mather wrote an additional letter for

---

[265] William Mather, *A Novelty: Or, a Government of Women, Distinct from Men, Erected amongst some of the People, call'd Quakers* (London: Sarah Howkins, 1695), 1.
[266] Ibid, 2.
[267] Ibid.

Scarborrow to take to the Meeting, with the following criticism, 'Can there be greater Imposers in the World, than those that judge all People, Not to be of God, for not submitting to a Female Government in Marriage?'[268] Mather further questioned:

> Whether such Women-Judges ever did any Good, who come into the Seat of Counsel, rustling in gaudy flower'd Stuffs, or Silks, from Top to Toe, mincing with their Feet, &c. except their Gifts to the Poor.[269]

While Mather was decidedly against Women's Meetings, he posed a further question regarding the role of multiple, geographically separated Meetings in the area of marriage approbation. He suggested an alternative approbation process which he believed demonstrated the original beliefs of the 'ancient Christian Quakers':

> When a Couple shall come to your private Monthly Meeting in Huntington, to acquaint you of their Intentions of Marriage, say to them, as to the ancient *Christian Quakers*. 'Friend, Who made us Judges over you? Go, if you find freedom of Spirit, and publish your Intentions at the end of the Publick Religious Meeting for Worship, to which you belong, or nearest to your Dwelling; for they know whither or no you are clear from all other Engagements in this kind, where you may have a sufficient number of Witnesses at your Certificate.[270]

Mather argued his suggestion was the:

> Innocent Practice of our dear deceased Friends in the beginning, when God sent among us, turn our Minds to Christ's Inward and Spiritual Grace, in each Soul, to be our Guides, not man.[271]

Mather followed this with the alternative of marriage approbation which included multiple meetings, some of which 'are Most commonly Strangers' to the marriage proceedings, waiting endlessly for all Meetings to say the couple may join in marriage, 'for fear you should bring a Scandal upon the Truth, tho your Dwelling be Twenty Miles off, or more, from hence'.[272]

Mather's frustration with Women's Meetings was thus multifaceted. Though he blatantly felt that women involved in church government was for the most

---

[268] Ibid, 4.
[269] Ibid, 5.
[270] Ibid.
[271] Ibid.
[272] Ibid.

part undesirable, he also felt the multiple meeting system including Women's Meetings detracted from the core truths of inward guidance from the Spirit. Mather demonstrated a nostalgia for the past, early patterns of marriage approbation, which he envisioned (rightly or wrongly) were shorter due to in part the absence of Women's Meetings. Mather's sentiments were not wholly new, but his criticisms arising at such a late date indicate the long-lasting struggle of the early Quakers to implement Women's Meetings and their role in the marriage approbation process, from their shaky beginnings through to at least the end of the century.

While some Quakers, including the men and women followers of Wilkinson and Story already mentioned, did not agree with the separation of Women's Meetings, others were supportive of this innovation, particularly women who regarded it as an additional opportunity to help effectively in the ministry of the Quakers. Initially the responsibilities of Women's Meetings included taking care of and distributing funds to the poor, fatherless, widows and others who were suffering because of their family members being gone on ministry journeys. They also began to take on added responsibilities to admonish and exhort women in their local smaller meetings, as well as help in the approbation of marriages. Women's Meetings, according to Fox, were to be a place where 'the loose and disorderly reproved and admonished in the fear of the Lord; the clearness of persons proposing marriage more closely and strictly inquired into in the wisdom of God'.[273]

The beginning, expansion and establishment of separate Women's Meetings varied largely from place to place. It is suggested by some scholars that the earliest separate meetings of women appeared in London in the late 1650s, when Quaker Sarah Blackborow instigated what was called the 'box meeting', primarily set up to collect funds for the poor (the box being a literal box into which money was dropped), and a meeting called the 'Two Weeks' Meeting' for women was established.[274] A London Friend, Mary Elson, wrote in 1680 the first separate Women's Meetings took place 'betwixt three or four and twenty years ago' setting the date at 1656 or 1657, citing the overwhelming and desperate need to care for the poor.[275] Margaret Fell established and administered a fund collected at Kendal in 1654 for the distribution of funds to Quakers in need.[276] Led by women, these groups demonstrated women leading and organising separate from the men. Distribution of funds would become the eventual responsibility of future separate Women's Meetings.

---

[273] Fox, *Journal* (1952), 131.
[274] Braithwaite suggests the 'box meeting' was established as early as 1656 (Braithwaite, *The Second Period of Quakerism*, 273), while Mack places the advent of the 'box meeting' at 1659 (Mack, *Visionary Women*, 327).
[275] Kunze, *Margaret Fell and the Rise of Quakerism*, 145.
[276] Mack, *Visionary Women*, 220.

In October 1671, Women's Meetings were officially established at Swarthmoor Hall, directed by Fell and her daughters.[277] Braithwaite maintains Fox's concern with firmly establishing separate Women's Meetings occurred sometime this same year, when he wrote an epistle in June, strongly recommending their establishment.[278] Fox mentioned Women's Meetings in 1668 in an epistle exhorting followers to 'do true judgement, justice and truth, righteousness and equity, in all your men and Women's Meetings, without favour or affection to relations, kindreds, and acquaintance, or any respect of persons'.[279] He further warned 'take heed of hurting any concerning marriages, through any earthly reasoning, if the thing be right, lest they do worse', indicating that at least one if not both meetings were dealing with marriage approbation at this time.[280] In 1669, Fox pressed for more regular Women's Meetings:

> And now, Friends, as many Men's monthly meetings as you have in your county, so many Women's monthly meetings you may have; and if once a year, at least, a general Women's meeting, it would be well; for in some counties they have as many Quarterly Women's meetings as Men's, and in others they have only two in the summer time, because the ways are foul and days short in winter.[281]

While women felt the need to care for the poor and thus began to move in the direction of setting up meetings, Fox and Fell supported them and advocated Women's Meetings as an instrumental role in Quaker church government.

In 1672, Fox wrote an epistle entitled 'To All Women's Meetings' in which he clearly sets out his scriptural and spiritual reasons for the advancement of Women's Meetings:

> Keep your women's meetings in the power of God, and take your possession of that which you are heirs of, and keep the Gospel order. For man and woman were helps meet in the image of God, and in righteousness and holiness, in the dominion before they fell; but after the fall, in transgression, the man was to rule over his wife; but in the restoration by Christ, into the image of God, and his righteousness and holiness again, in that they are helps meet, man and woman, as they were before the fall. Sarah obeyed Abraham, and called him lord. Abraham did also obey the voice of his wife Sarah, in casting out the bondswoman and her son ... So women are to keep in the government of Christ, and to be obeyers of Christ; and women are to keep the comely order of the Gospel as well as men; and

---

[277] Glines (Ed.), *Undaunted Zeal*, 406.
[278] Braithwaite, *The Second Period of Quakerism*, 273.
[279] Tuke, *Selections from The Epistles, &c. of George Fox*, 180.
[280] Ibid, 182.
[281] Ibid, 196.

to see that all that have received Christ Jesus, do walk in Christ Jesus; and to see that all that have received the Gospel, do walk in the Gospel.[282]

Fox utilised his notion of the 'restoration by Christ' in the argument of removing the implications of male headship as a result of the Fall, in the government of the church. He encouraged women to be 'obeyers of Christ' in fulfilling their responsibility to take their rightful place in church government, and to admonish those in the church body, including their unbelieving husbands if the case may be.

By the end of the 1670s, records indicate the Quarterly Women's Meetings (i.e. Women's Meetings which met four times a year) took hold as a more permanent fixture in Quaker organisation not only throughout England and Scotland, but around the world. In 1676, Fox wrote an epistle from Swarthmoor to Quakers in Barbados which included a strong encouragement to establish as many Women's Meetings as Men's Meetings:

> And my desire is, that you may, in the power of God, encourage all the faithful women in your island, in the work and service of God; and now you have six men's meetings, if you had as many women's meetings, it would include all the faithful women in all corners of your island; and some of your ancient faithful women to go from meeting to meeting, till they are settled in the power of God, and that will keep all alive in the Lord's working power and life.[283]

With concern that women in Barbados were not actively participating in the Meetings, Fox encouraged all women to be involved, and requested that the more 'ancient' women go 'from meeting to meeting' probably to settle the meetings in 'good order'. In 1680, he spoke to a General Meeting of Quakers in London, calling for the direct participation of women in the marriage approbation process, 'And when things are clear before all parties, lay it twice before the women's Meeting and twice before the men's, that all may be clear in the sight of God and man.'[284] Evidently, Fox directed Women's Meetings everywhere to help manage marital approbation.

For Fox, perhaps more important to him than practical motives, believed he had received a direct revelation and command from God to advocate separate Women's Meetings, claiming he 'was moved of the Lord to recommend to Friends for the benefit and advantage of the church.'[285] Bonnelyn Kunze

---

[282] Ibid, 217–18.

[283] Fox, *To Friends in Barbados: Swarthmore, Lancashire, 25th of 8th Month, 1676.* (Tuke, *Selections from The Epistles, &c. of George Fox*, 180.)

[284] *George Fox's Sermon at Wheeler Street, 1680.* (Barbour and Roberts [Eds], *Early Quaker Writings*, 510.)

[285] Fox, *Journal* (1952), 131.

however attributes the advocating of Women's Meetings to Fell, stating she had likely seen how well they worked in London, and subsequently suggested to Fox that they be a main part of Quaker organisation. Kunze further suggests that Fell consciously attributed the creation of Women's Meetings to Fox in an effort to promote him as 'the divinely called founder of the Quakers', the leader and innovator who should not be questioned.[286] Many epistles written by Fox regarding Women's Meetings and women's role in leadership were composed during his time at Swarthmoor, further supporting Fell's probable great influence in the development and promotion of women's involvement in church government. Fell's direct influence on, and ardent belief in, the advent of separate Women's Meetings was clearly delineated in a document entitled *From our Country Women's meeting in Lancashire to be Dispersed abroad, among the Women's meetings every where.*[287]

Likely put in writing by Sarah Fell, the clerk of the Lancaster Women's Meeting, it delineated the biblical, spiritual and ministerial bases for separate Women's Meetings, including a list of their specific responsibilities. The document begins with a thorough combing through of scriptures relating to women in ministerial roles throughout the Old and New Testaments. Fell and the women of Lancaster believed God held women accountable to ministry in the church, that Jesus held women in high regard, and that in God's final restoration of humanity out of the Fall, women were to be helpmeets to not only men, but God.

> We may be all helps meet for God in the restoration, and co-heires with Christ Jesus ... who is no respecter of persons, but hath a care, and a regard unto all, the weak as well as the strong, that he may have the glory of his own work ... And that every particular of us, may be ready, and willing to answer what the lord requires of us; in our several places and conditions.[288]

Weakness, a term often used against women in derision, they contended was not condemned by God but used for furthering the kingdom. Women, regardless of social status and place, were encouraged to minister.

Fell worked with Fox in administering responsibilities bestowed upon the Women's Meeting which included a significant role in the marital approbation process.

---

[286] Kunze, *Margaret Fell and the Rise of Quakerism*, 165.

[287] The exact dating of the composition of the document is difficult to ascertain. Milton D. Speizman and Jane C. Kronick, whose edited version is quoted here, and Margaret Fell biographer Isabel Ross date it between 1675–80.

[288] *From our Country Women's meeting in Lancashire to be Dispersed abroad, among the Women's meetings every where* ('A Seventeenth Century Quaker Women's Declaration'), 235.

> In faithfull obedience to the truth, that according to the order of the Gospell that is established, that they bring their Marriages twice to the womens meetings, and twice to the mens: the first time they are to come to the womens meetings that the women of the meeting, do examin both the man and the woman, that they be cleare and free from all other persons, and that they have their parents, and friends and Relations, consent; And that enquiry be made of their clearness in each particular meeting to which they do belong, before their next appearance in the womens meeting.[289]

As with the Men's Meetings, women were to first look into the 'cleareness' of the couple to be married, alleviating some of the burden of the Men's Meetings. After an intention of marriage was brought to the Women's Meeting twice, if the couple seemed clear for approbation a woman from the meeting would then introduce the couple to the Men's Meeting, at which time the likelihood of being granted approbation increased. The process of going to the Women's Meeting twice allowed for adequate time for any concerns to arise from those in the community. After the couple's first appearance, if confirmed clear for marriage, Fell instructed:

> If nothing be found, but that they come in clearness to the next monthly meeting, then they may proceed according to the order of the Gospell, and perfect their marriage in the meeting of friends, as friends which they belong to sees it Convenient.[290]

However, if anything was indicated in the two meetings that the couple was not clear to marry, Fell offered a firm warning:

> But if anything be found that they are not clear, but that others lay Challenge, or Charge to them, either by promise or otherwise that then they do not proceed, till they have given satisfaction both to the parties, and friends, concerning that matter, according to the order of the Gospell; and that if any thing be amiss concerning the woman, examin it, and look into it, which may not be proper for the men.[291]

Propriety regarding any matters which might embarrass a woman in front of men was considered necessary in the meeting process. Propriety was also perhaps needed to be sure decorum or modesty did not inhibit anyone from speaking up regarding any potential obstructions to clearness and approbation.

---

[289] Ibid, 242.
[290] Ibid.
[291] Ibid.

Though these instructions were given in the 1670s, the rate at which Women's Meetings took on the formal role of taking part in marriage approbation varied amongst the various Quaker meetings in the latter half of the seventeenth century. Russell Mortimer, the editor of the *Minute Book of the Men's Meeting of the Society of Friends in Bristol*, notes there is evidence that on 12 March 1688, women Friends were present at the Men's Meeting when a marriage was proposed, suggesting perhaps this was done 'in order to set on foot enquiries in the Women's Meeting'.[292] But it was not until 1698 that a direct reference to the active participation by the Women's Meeting in the process of marriage approbation appears in the Bristol record.[293] A statement issued by the Women's Yearly Meeting at York in 1688 suggests women there had direct influence on the marital approbation process. It was an exhortation for orderly approbation, and an encouragement to unmarried Quakers not to rush into marriage, but rather to wait on God and to know Him first as the 'husband and bridegroom of your souls':

> Friends, be not concerned in reference to marriage, out of God's fear, but first wait to know your Maker to become your husband and bridegroom of your souls ... O Friends! This state is happy, and blessed are they that attain it and live in it; the Lord is not unmindful of them, but in his own time, if he see it good for them, can provide meet-helps for them. Then will your marriage be honourable, being orderly accomplished with the assent of parents and the unity of Friends and an honour to God and comfort to your own souls.[294]

Some of the earliest extant records of Women's Meetings come from the Swarthmoor Monthly Women's Meetings set up by Fell. Manuscripts of the minutes begin from the beginning of the meetings in 1671. Much of their occupation dealt with the distribution of goods or money to the poor (particularly widows and the sick), maintaining 'good order' as 'one family', as was recorded in the following minutes from a meeting in 1677:

---

[292] Mortimer (Ed.), *Minute Book of the Men's Meeting of the Society of Friends in Bristol 1686–1704*, xviii.

[293] Ibid.

[294] *Women's Yearly Meeting at York: A Testimony for the Lord and his Truth* (1688). (See the website qfp.quakerweb.org.uk/qfp19–56.html.) (From *The Book of Christian discipline of the Yearly Meeting of the Religious Society of Friends [Quakers] in Britain*, chapter 19, section 56.)

Approbation and 'Clearness': The Early Quaker Marriage Discipline 105

> This day, the need and necessity of several poor friends belonging to the meeting have been enquired into ... That soe the poore that are in necessity may bee assisted, and all kept in good order as one ffamily.[295]

They also dealt with various 'disorderly walking' amongst the members of local meetings, including people paying tithes to their local church, as was apparently the case with two local Quaker widows in 1675.

> This day wee have Admonished & reproved Eliz Barrow & Mary Stones widdowes, both of Cartmell Meetinge understandinge they have not been altogether faithfull in their Testimony against payment of Tythes, and have warned them to bee more faithful therein, for the time to come, as they tender their owne good, & the honour of truth.[296]

The minutes show the women of Lancashire evidently encountered the same issues the men of Bristol and other areas of England had encountered in regards to marriage approbation. They both regularly handled marriage approbation proposals, as well as reprimanded any 'disorderly walking' in relationship to marriage, particularly in the cases of couples marrying by a priest. An example of the latter can be found on the opening pages of the minutes dated to the year 1674. When news had reached the Women's Meeting that a Quaker couple, James Hathornthwaite and Bridgett Cowell, had gone to a priest to marry, it was ordered that a testimony against the couple be written (which was incidentally signed by Fell and others) and delivered to both the couple and to the priest who married them:

> Whereas it was ordered at our last weomens Meetinge ... that a paper should bee given forth as A Testimony against James Hathornthwaite and Bridgett Cowell, for goeinge to the Priest to bee Married – which was done, & was this day Reade.[297]

The testimony against the couple was copied in the meeting minutes, but unfortunately the right half of the page was torn. What remains reads as follows:

> Whereas James Hathornthwaite and Bridgett ... transgressed against the holy Law of God ... and the Testimony of Jesus which did shine in their Consciences ... have several times been admonished by us.[298]

---

[295] *Swarthmoor Women's Monthly Meeting Minutes 1671–1700*, 4. Copy of minutes held at The Society of Friends Library, London, Reference number 16 b 4. (Original copy at Cumbria Record Office, Barrow.)
[296] Ibid, 35.
[297] Ibid, 29.
[298] Ibid.

Evidently, the couple had been warned and reprimanded for their behaviour, as well as instructed to show evidence of contrition, else they be disowned by the Quaker fold. In response, James wrote a letter of contrition, not unlike the letters seen in the abovementioned Bristol minutes, which according to the following minutes the Bristol Meeting had received from the couple:

> Alsoe a paper was sent to us, from the aforesaid James Hathornthwaite & Bridgett his wife, both which papers were coppied in this booke next followeing under written and its that fitt that our paper they reade to the Preist, & publish at Markett if they have a desire to come amongst Ffreinds.[299]

Public demonstration of contrition, in writing, amongst Friends as well as in front of the priest and general public, was required of James and Bridgett.

James' letter of contrition explains the difficult quandary in which the young couple found themselves when faced with the 'temptation' to marry by a priest:

> Deare Ffriends, This is in love to you all, and I would have you take it soe, being that wee in this condition, that wee is in at this time; But I hope that the Lord will have mercy upon us; ffor truly wee were drawn by wicked people, & by the Preist; hee said to us, that wee cold not heive any of my Hashell(?) Estate; if wee was not married by him or some such like; And soe they Tempted us, beinge that wee were younge & easy to be drawne, which is & hath beene a sadd trouble to us both: soe wee desire you to take it into consideration, ffor wee know that if wee should goe to any other place wee should keep noe benefit, nor profit for our poore souls as wee doe desire that wee may come to true Repentance, ffor as we have done truly, it is a sadd Burden to us, and wee doe feel that it has been very hard for our ffriends, & a great offence to the truth, wee are very sorry, that the truth should suffer for our evildoings.[300]

The issue of marrying by a priest for the couple was not just a religious one, but one which ensured their financial sustenance. However, James and Bridgett appear very contrite concerning their behaviour, and desire to be accepted back into the Quaker community. The Women's Meeting response was carefully recorded in the following minutes excerpt:

> The paper above, wee have Reade & Considered; And wee doe hereby send you our Testimony in writinge, touchinge your hasty Running Together in Marriage; Soe if you cann joine with what wee write, come to Repent, & Returned, & see the Evill you have done, and Retell him yourselves; that you owne it to bee true,

---

[299] Ibid.
[300] Ibid.

> (you having given a Publicke occasions) In your Returne & Repentance wee can receive you.[301]

Following their orderly procedure, they sent what they called their 'Testimony in writinge' in response to the couple's written letter of contrition. If the couple truly repented, they had to not only provide written documentation of this repentance, but also 'Retell' the priest the 'Evill' they had done. If the couple returned and repented, the Women's Meeting could forgive the 'Evill' committed, and allow them back into the Quaker community. Thus repentance and forgiveness, acceptance or rejection were considered a public and communal affair. The need for clear, written documentation of every action is once again evident in their Women's Meetings, as was the case in other Quaker Meetings.

The problem of going to a priest to marry, as well as exogamy, was apparently also a continuing difficulty for the Women's Meeting of Lancashire. Two years later, the Meeting Minutes tell of a Quaker called Sarah Fell, who was married by a priest to 'one of the world', John Fell.[302] Sarah provided written evidence of repentance to the Women's Meeting. In the minutes, they indicate having received and read aloud Sarah's 'paper of contrition':

> This day is read in our Meetinge A paper of Condemnation from Sarah Fell the wife of John Fell of Ulverstone ... of her sence and sorrow of the transgression that shee fell into; in being married by a Priest to one of the world, which wee are glad of and gives thankes to the Lord in her behalfe, that hee hath broken her heart, & brought her to a sence of her Condition; which paper is hereafter Recorded.[303]

As they did with James' paper of condemnation, a member of the Women's Meeting copied the letter into the Minutes. In her letter, quoted here in full, Sarah detailed both her process of repentance as well as her hope that she might be brought 'backe againe, into unity' with God and her fellow Quakers:

> Ffriends: The Lord through his great love, & mercy, hath opened that eye, that was blinde, through Transgression, and hath lett mee see the error of my wayes, and that I have done contrary to the truth, in marrying amongst the Professors, by which I have caused the Lords truth to bee dishonoured, and evill spoken of; ffor which I am sorry, and doe Judge & condemne that Spirritt, that caused mee soe to doest; ffor by the Light of the Lord, I am come to see them all out of the truth, where I have been alsoe, but I hope the Lord will bringe mee backe againe, into unity with himselfe, and alsoe with you his people, soe that I may leave A

---

[301] Ibid, 30.
[302] John and Sarah Fell were not relations of Margaret Fell.
[303] *Swarthmoor Women's Monthly Meeting Minutes 1671–1700*, 48–9.

> testimony against them in my measure. – As for my Husband, hee did never strive to stay mee, but is willing, that I should come amongst you againe, ffor my trouble was never great, until I went away, and then I was sore troubled both for my Husband and my selfe; Soe I desire that I may come into unity with the Lord, and you his people, and that I may bee an Example to all Backsliders, and that this may goe as farr as the report of my Transgression. Ffrom your Ffriende, Sarah Fell.[304]

In her letter, Sarah acknowledged first that God, 'by the Light of the Lord', had helped her see the error of her actions, which she believed 'dishonoured' the 'Lords truth'. Her actions, she explained, were brought about by a 'Spirritt' that 'caused' her to do the evil deed of marrying with the world by a priest. By such actions she essentially saw herself 'out of the truth' and longed to be brought back into the 'truth' and an example to all 'Backsliders'. Interestingly, her non-Quaker husband was willing for her to return to Quakerism. Additionally, the Quaker women did not advocate a divorce or request proof of his repentance; John Fell was not one of them. But for Sarah, though now married to a non-Quaker, because she evinced true contrition in writing, she was forgiven and brought back into 'unity' with 'the Lord, and you his people'.[305]

Sarah's letter provides insight into the individual Quaker's deeply felt sense of inner temptation and backsliding, followed by an inner sense of being reprimanded by God. When the Women's Meeting documented the Lord had 'broken her heart, & brought her to a sence of her Condition' they too were acknowledging an inner battle between good and evil. If one 'fell into transgression' this was cause for 'dishonour' to the Lord's truth, and a threat to the unity of the person with the divine. The inward condition of following either a spirit of good or a spirit of evil subsequently affected one's unity with not only the divine, but also with the group. Though Sarah had an inward 'sense' of her 'evil' action, this inner, private repentance was not enough to completely restore her to unity with the divine or with the group. Her inward 'sence of her Condition' and subsequent repentance were not a private affair, but rather a public and communal event experienced by all Quakers involved. Written and public contrition, followed by communal and documented forgiveness, was the only means to the restoration of 'unity' Sarah desired.

The continued communal involvement in the marriage approbation process was also evident in the Women's Meeting. Their minutes indicate a relatively regular practice of couples bringing the approbation proposal to them first, then to the Men's Meeting, followed by a second time to the Women's Meeting. This procedure can be seen in the following minutes from a meeting in 1677:

---

[304] Ibid, 49.
[305] Ibid.

Approbation and 'Clearness': The Early Quaker Marriage Discipline 109

> This day, Christopher Simpson, & Issabell Birkett both of Swarthmore Meetinge, have declared their Intentions of Joininge together in Marriage as ffriends sees Convenient, & leaves it to their Consideration, for their Consent or otherwayes as in the truth & wisdome of God is seene meett; And thy have declared before us their clearance of being ingaged to any other upon that Account; soe wee desire them, to observe the order of truth, in layinge it before the Mens Meetinge, & to come to our next Weomens Meetinge at Swarthmore, where they may receive our Answer and Advise in it.[306]

Seemingly observing the 'order of truth', Christopher and Issabell appeared to be on the road to a fairly smooth marriage approbation procedure as they attempted to do everything as the Quakers instructed. However, when they brought their 'Intention of Marriage' to the Women's Meeting a second time one month later, a problem apparently arose which brought the approbation process to a halt:

> This day Christopher Simpson & Issabell Birkett came ... to lay their Intentions of Marriage before us; and there appearinge somethinge not to bee cleare to us, touchinge Issabell Birkett, who formerly kept company with Edmond Cooper as upon that Account Wee doe therefore order Mary Taylor & Elizabeth Sharpe to speake to Edmond Cooper that hee bee at the nearest Mens Meetinge at Swarthmore and there to satisfy ffriends what hee hath to say Against her marriage with Christo: Simpson. And if it then Appeare that all bee clear, they may proceed Accordingly to truths order, they having already their consent and Approbation of their Parents & Relations.[307]

Like the Men's Meeting of Bristol, when something appeared which could obstruct the marriage approbation process, two people from the meeting were sent to speak with the person or persons who might provide further clarification on why or why not a couple should be married. In this case, two women were sent to request that Edmond Cooper appear at a Men's Meeting at Swarthmoor, where he could elaborate his position against the proposed marriage. Interestingly Edmond was not requested to appear at the Women's Meeting, suggesting more delicate matters were deferred to the Men's Meeting, perhaps to save the man from embarrassment. In this case, it appears all went well, as an Isabell Simpson was active in the Women's Meeting the following year.[308]

Another instance of the Women's Meeting deferring a case of marriage approbation to the Swarthmoor Men's Meeting appears in 1680, in the minutes concerning the proposed intentions of marriage between a widow and a widower.

---

[306] Ibid, 33.
[307] Ibid.
[308] Ibid, 68.

The pressing issue was provision for the children of the widower whom he had with his late wife:

> This day Edward Saterthwaite Widdower, and Agnes Nickolson Widdow, both belonging to Hawkshead meetinge; have acquainted us with their Intentions of Mariage, with each other, desiring ffriends consent and approbation; – And upon our Enquiry of them; they doe declare themselves cleare from all other men and women; and its desired by this Meetinge of him; that hee taken care to provide for his Children which hee had by his former wife; which hee assures us off; and wee leave it to the Mens Meetinge to see it performed. – And we find, that they have the consent of ffriends & relations on both sides; and a good account is given of them both by ffriends of their owne Meetinge and of their orderly and discreet Management thus farr.[309]

In addition to 'leaving it to the Mens Meeting' to ensure adequate provisions were provided for the children, the Women's Meeting commended the couple for having friends and relations consent on both sides, as well as for 'their orderly and discreet Management' of their marriage proceedings which was reported by their local, regular Meeting in Hawkshead. Though all seemed to be in good order, as the people responsible for approbating the marriage the Women's Meeting wanted to be sure Agnes Nickolson was indeed 'cleare' for marriage, ordering that 'Dorothy Beck and Mary Walker be sent to inquire into her clearnesse from all other men'.[310] Happily for Agnes and Edward, she was indeed found clear in the Men's Meeting, as a month later, the Women's Meeting minutes read, 'All is found clear ... and they have approbation to marry'.[311]

In the minutes, there are further instances of pairs of women being sent from the Meeting to either investigate or verify 'clearness' of individuals seeking approbation for marriage, a practice which continued and appeared in the Women's Meeting minutes almost twenty years later. In 1691, when Quakers John Benson and Issabell Fforest sought approbation for marriage, Isabel was subsequently visited by Friends appointed to investigate their 'clearness' for marriage:

> This day John Benson and Issabell Fforest have againe layed before this meeting there Intenshons of maridge and those ffriends apoyented by our last meeting to Enspect the sade Issabell's clearness frome all other mene: gives an account to this meeting that they finde noething but that shee is clare from all others on the account of marriage ... so wee are satisfied of the Bretherins care concerning the

---

[309] Ibid, 97.
[310] Ibid.
[311] Ibid, 98.

sade Johns Clearness from all other woman. So this meeting doeth Consent and agree that they sade John Benson and Issabell Fforestt may proceed to Consumatt there intended marriage in convenient time: according to the order of truth.[312]

Hearing from the Men's Meeting that John was clear as well, the Women's Meeting provided approbation to John and Isabel, to marry 'in convenient time: according to the order of truth'.

Finally, beyond the scope of simply approbating marriages, the Women's Meeting had concern for, and investigated, any *possible* 'disorderly' marriages with the 'world'. Often coming to the Meeting word of mouth, they diligently followed up rumours with personal, face-to-face inquiry. In a Women's Meeting in 1695, attended by Margaret Fell and two of her daughters, after hearing of rumours of 'disorderly walking' of a young woman, some women of the Meeting were 'apointeth to enspect the walking of ffriends'. In the following minutes, the women documented clearly the rumours they had heard, and what action they would take. In addition to other women of the Meeting, the minutes were also signed by Margaret Fell and her daughter Mary:

> Some ffriends of Swarthmore meeting gives an account of a younger woman called Mary Dungley whoe have bee frequented there meeting for sum yeares; have of latte kept company with a younger man of the world in order to marriage as its feared; severall ffriends of that meeting having labored much with her in the love of truth and admonished her to beewayer of that temptation and snare that shee is in danger to fall in to; if not timely withstood at order account heare of may bee given to our next meeting.[313]

At the Meeting the following month, the women discuss the results of the investigation:

> Ffriends appointed to enspectt ffriends walking... as becomes truth; have answered there particular queries consarning things committed to them to enspectt – and wee understand: that friends at Swarthmore meeting have continued there care according to truths order in admonishing the young woman mentioned at our last meeting, and allso some friends of that meeting have spoke to the mades mother; to restraine her Daughter from accompanying with the sade young man; and deallth plainly and truly with her as to the Danger and so every way shee is like to come to; if shee further entangle herself therewith.[314]

---

[312] Ibid, 173.
[313] Ibid, 191.
[314] Ibid, 192.

The phrase 'enspectt friends walking as becomes the truth' appeared frequently throughout Meeting minutes, especially near the end of the century. Certainly, this was the primary occupation of the Monthly Women's Meetings, in which early Quaker women ensured 'truth's order' was upheld through careful and thorough documentation and investigation, with reproach or warnings if necessary. Proposed marriages were scrutinised methodically and meticulously. Every possibility of 'disorderly walking' was not left untouched, even regarding marriages that had not yet been proposed. Preventing their members, and the young impressionable women, from 'falling' into temptation and other evil dangers, the Monthly Women's Meeting worked hard to ensure 'orderly walking' and a 'love of truth' within the marriages and daily lives of their fellow Quakers. 'Order' and 'truth', two practical and theological conceptions engrained in the marriage approbation process, will be discussed at length in the following chapter.

Conclusion

In their efforts to avoid external criticisms of immorality and maintain spiritual purity and unity through being betrothed with solely their fellow Quakers, the early Friends developed and refined a system of maintaining order through which they attempted to exercise a degree of social control. It was a system requiring diligent documentation. Certificates providing proof of such things as contrition, clearance, consent or marriage were recorded and produced when needed. Investigating the 'truth of the matter' when fellow Friends were suspected of 'walking disorderly' was not questioned, and discipline was expected and accepted. If the wayward were not repentant, however, disownment would follow. If anything was done in secret, including clandestine marriages that would not gain approbation, this was seen as a serious breach to the order and unity of the Quaker fold. Quaker historian Rufus Jones suggests (nearly laments) that the early Friends' preoccupation with order led them to spend 'their precious lives, not in propagating the living principles of spiritual religion in the great life of the world, but in perfecting and transmitting a "system" within the circle of the Society'.[315] Yet this bureaucratic process was the very foundation of early Quaker spirituality which served as a means of ensuring their spiritual and moral ideals were kept and met within the movement. For Fox, Fell and other early Friends, spiritual unity necessitated producing orderly Quakers and maintaining an orderly Quaker community. The 'good order of the Gospel' was manifested in the Meeting process, finding fruition in the marital approbation process. With

---

[315] Jones, *The Quakers in the American Colonies*, xxiii–xxiv.

the paperwork aside, the theological and spiritual rationale that drove their marriage discipline will now be considered.

Chapter 2

The True Church Coming out of the Wilderness: The Theological and Conceptual Foundation of the Early Quaker Marriage Discipline

I was moved to open to the people the state of our marriages ... how God did join man and woman together before the Fall. And man had joined in the Fall but it was God's joining again in the restoration ... And then I showed them the duty of man and wife how they should serve God, being heirs of life and grace together.[1]

George Fox, *Journal* (1666)

Concerning Marriage: How God made them Male and Female in the beginning, and how he joyned them together, before they were drove from God into the Earth, and then the manner of Marriage before the Law, and then the Marriage in the Law, and the Marriage amongst the Christians in the Primitive times; And the Marriage of the Apostate Christians, and Jews and Gentiles, where hardness of heart was, there men put a sunder: But where God joynes together, let none put a sunder, that is as it was in the beginning before man was driven from God into the Earth, out of the defiled Bed into the Dominion, in the unity with all Saints, so not to be hid from them.[2]

George Fox, *Concerning Marriage* (1661)

Early Quaker marriage doctrine and practice provide a helpful rubric through which their theology and apocalyptic vision of the world can be better understood and more fully examined. Fox explained to fellow Quakers his own pending marriage to Margaret Fell would be a 'figure or testimony ... of the church coming out of the wilderness'.[3] He later reflected on the universal ramifications of marriage, stating in his *Journal* he married as 'a testimony, that all might come up into the marriage as was in the beginning' and as a testimony that all 'might come up out of the wilderness to the marriage of the Lamb'.[4]

---

[1] Fox, *Journal* (1952), 506.
[2] Fox, *Concerning Marriage* (1661), 1. Even though it was only published in 1661, George Fox wrote the pamphlet in 1659.
[3] George Fox, *Letter of George Fox Concerning his Marriage* (2 October 1669). (Cadbury [Ed.], *Narrative Papers of George Fox*, 79.)
[4] Fox, *Journal* (1952), 557.

For Fox, Quaker marriages tangibly reflected the 'true church' coming up out of the wilderness. But what was the wilderness? When Fox used the image of 'wilderness' throughout his *Journal*, epistles and letters, he most often referred to it as the place of exile of the 'true church'. Fox believed every Quaker, after responding to the inward light within one's conscience, enjoyed everlasting unity with the divine and with every member of the 'true church', which was in their day coming up out of the 'wilderness'. The state of matrimony for Quakers provided one *modus operandi* for the restored 'unity' or 'matrimony' between the divine and the 'true' church coming up from the wilderness of exile. Quaker marriages were a microcosm of the macrocosmic event of the 'marriage of the Lamb' – their collective exodus from the 'wilderness' to a place of restored spiritual unity with each other, and with their Creator. In this chapter, the early Quaker belief that their marriages helped demonstrate and define their exodus from the 'wilderness' will be more fully explored.[5]

As discussed in chapter one, the restoration of unity between the divine and the created was demonstrated in part by the early Quaker marriage approbation process, including the Quaker requirements that the couple 'have a sense' of being commanded by God to marry through an inner connection with the inward light, and that the marriage be approbated in 'unity'. This 'unity', as will be further discussed in this chapter, was a spiritual unity between every Quaker and with the divine, often described as unity in the 'light' or unity in the 'seed', both metaphors for Christ's presence 'within the conscience'.[6] What was of paramount importance within early Quaker doctrine and practice was the collective maintenance of their perceived spiritual unity with the divine through the inward light. Rosemary Moore reminds us the union the early Quakers experienced was ' ... not just a vague sense of undefined spiritual unity; body and spirit were one with Christ'.[7] Taking part in the necessary communal approbation of marriages within Quaker meetings ensured marriages were conducted in a manner that reflected this very real unity with the inward presence of Christ.

---

[5] See p. 122.

[6] For a full explication of the early Quaker understanding of 'light in the conscience' see Moore, *The Light in Their Consciences*. Moore explains Fox's meaning of unity with Christ through the light in the conscience: 'Belief in a real union with Christ, however expressed, remained the keystone of Fox's theology. Fox's theology was, however, obscure. The light was not Christ, but brought people to Christ ... What was this light, or "that of God", in everyone's conscience? Fox clearly did not equate it with the Holy Spirit, and while plenty of examples can be found of Fox equating the light with the spiritual presence of Christ, he by no means always did so ... Most often he described the light as something that comes from Christ or God ... without actually being Christ or God' (Moore, *The Light in Their Consciences*, 109). The meaning of the inward light within the conscience, and its bearing on the marriage approbation process, will be further explicated in this chapter. See pp. 149ff.

[7] Moore, *The Light in Their Consciences*, 78.

Marriages conducted with 'nothing hidden', from either each other or from the divine, further reinforced their perceived unity with the divine and amongst themselves in the True Church. But, as we have seen, if a marriage was done in secret, without communal approbation, this was a means of discord and disunity, making all 'clandestine marriages' or 'hidden' marriages strictly forbidden by Fox and the early Quakers.[8] Exogamous marriages and marriages by a priest or magistrate were also partly rejected on the same premise – they were signs of engagement with the 'false church' and the fallen world. Contributing further to disunity with the divine, these practices were prohibited.

As Quakers believed they were members of the 'true church', they strove to lead lives that were indicative of a people no longer living in the fallen state, uncovering the notions of defilement and dishonour. All marriages outside the Quaker fold, considered 'in the fall' and in the apostate state, were seen as 'dishonourable', and their beds 'defiled' by sin. On the contrary, marriages in the True Church, 'weighed and tried in the Light' and 'joined by God', were considered 'honourable' by the early Quakers. Fell wrote in 1654 of the honourable state of marriages amongst Quakers:

> And all the Children of Light which see god, & are of god, doth the marriages see, that be honourable, [while] ... the marriage that is not honourable; is with the Light seene, & Judged ... in which Light, all the Children of the Light dwell; & have unity.[9]

Those outside the 'true church', not open to direct revelation from God within their conscience and within the community, could not know whether or not their marriages were being brought together by God alone.[10] These marriages were thus vulnerable to judgment from God, and defiled by sin. But those who quickened to the 'light' could have the security of knowing their marriage was indeed brought together by God alone, and was thus undefiled by sin. When Fox proclaimed God would join him to Fell 'in the honourable marriage and in an undefiled bed' in God's 'seed and everlasting covenant of life and light', he believed his marriage would be 'undefiled' because he and Fell were now 'undefiled' by sin as Quakers.[11] The meaning of 'honourable' marriages, including 'undefiled' sexuality within marriage, will be further explored in this chapter.

---

[8] Fox, *Journal Vol. 1* (1836), xviii. In the preface, William Penn wrote of the Quaker approbation process, ' ... their care and checks bring so many, and such, that no clandestine marriages can be performed among them'.

[9] Margaret Fell, *Letter to Judge Hugh Wyndham* (1654). (Glines [Ed.], *Undaunted Zeal*, 109.)

[10] Fell, *To Friends, an Epistle on marriage*. (Glines [Ed.], *Undaunted Zeal*, 195.)

[11] Fox, *Letter of George Fox Concerning his Marriage*. (Cadbury [Ed.], *Narrative Papers of George Fox*, 78.)

The theological underpinnings of 'good order', the cornerstone of the Quaker marriage approbation process, also contributed to early Quaker spirituality and marriage doctrine. Interestingly, more is written about maintaining the 'good order' of marital approbation than guidance regarding the marital relationship itself. Perhaps this is partly because marriage approbation and endogamous marriages were so critical in maintaining unity and membership within Quakerism, issues which were of central concern in the latter half of the seventeenth century for the early Quakers. Later in this chapter we will discover that Fox wrote at length (particularly near the end of his life) about raising children within Quakerism, and keeping 'good order' within families. With the first generation of converts having children, a new generation of children being 'born into' Quakerism was emerging. Lacking the spiritual fervour of their parents, some children strayed from the Quaker fold of their family. Thus raising children in Quaker families in addition to marrying within Quakerism were two significant ways Quakers could maintain their membership.

Finally, 'good order', also described as 'Gospel Order', within marriage approbation was one means of insurance for the early Quakers that their meetings maintained 'unity in the light' through unanimous, communal consent for proposed marriages. In chapter one, the early Quakers' rigorous attention to investigation, approbation and documentation of marriages have become evident. Because the Quaker community, as the unified True Church, believed themselves the only True Church, their marital unions were considered 'honourable marriages', as Fell indicated in an epistle written in 1656:

> Friends in the truth, who in the light seeth joining together in marriage, let it be done in order as followeth ... declare it to the other party to bee tryed, & weighed in the light, that each may have a sure testimony in the light, & life which cannot bee blotted out. And so having unity in the light & life, & a clear sight of being joined in the lord, then declare it to the church, to be tryed in the light, which is one in all, that so the church may have unity with it in the same light & life ... And if friends in the meeting who dwells in the eternall light & life ... finde the thing mencioned by the partyes to be out of the light, & out of the unity, let it be condemned with the light.[12]

The Quakers' religious adherence to 'good order' was not only a necessary basis for a spiritually sound marriage 'in the light & life'. Fox and Fell, amongst their early Quaker contemporaries, had a strong sense of 'Gospel Order', a notion that God is not a God of chaos but that throughout the scriptures, holy men and women met in orderly meetings. An exploration of the meaning and significance of 'Gospel Order' will provide further insights into the Quaker

---

[12] Fell, *To Friends, An Epistle on Marriage*. (Glines [Ed.], *Undaunted Zeal*, 195.)

mindset regarding matrimony, as well as their understanding of 'Gospel Order' as a critical component of their own spirituality.

The 'true church' rising up from the 'wilderness', 'unity in the light', 'Gospel Order' and 'honourable marriages' with beds no longer 'defiled' by sin: such were the interconnected themes throughout the writings of Fox and Fell regarding Quaker marriage doctrine. As these themes arise, further questions come to the fore. What were the spiritual and marital implications of the 'true church coming out of the wilderness' according to Fox and Fell? What were the identifying marks of the 'true church'? Why were unity and 'good order' crucial components of holy matrimony and living? How did coming back to 'paradise' result in an 'honourable' marriage with an 'undefiled' bed? To explore these questions, this chapter will begin with an analysis of Fox's use of the word 'wilderness' within his *Journal* and various other writings. After a brief summary of seventeenth-century thought regarding 'Paradise', apocalyptic imagery of the 'true church' leaving the 'wilderness' and its influence on early Quaker marriage doctrine will be discussed. This will be followed by an analysis of the various themes arising in early Quaker marriage rhetoric and thought. Finally, how these themes and beliefs practically influenced early Quaker marriages, as well as Quaker marriages in the contemporary context, will be considered.

Up from the Wilderness: The Return of the True Church

As seventeenth-century popular culture was steeped in biblical literature, people interpreted their surrounding political and social circumstances through the scriptural accounts of humanity's creation, fall and eternal salvation.[13] The Quakers too looked to scripture to inform their own identity, as scriptural references ran throughout the writings of many early Quakers including Fox and Fell.[14] The scriptural imagery, including the notion of 'wilderness', carried various symbolic meanings. At the time Fox described his own marriage as a testimony to the church rising up out of the 'wilderness', the symbol of 'wilderness' already having had a long tradition in Christianity. In the Old Testament book of Exodus, the 'wilderness' or 'desert' was a place of exile and barrenness, where Israel wandered for forty years, finally encountering God which was symbolised

---

[13] Hill, *The English Bible and the Seventeenth-Century Revolution*, 18, 185.

[14] Though the early Quakers did not value the academic study of scripture, nor did they see scripture as the sole vehicle of God's revelation but often fought against scriptural literalism, many did generally embrace scripture as God's revelation. Catie Gill notes, ' ... though the Quakers might be seen to have been reacting against other Protestant faiths, specifically those that overestimated the importance of reading, their writers do venerate the Bible' (Catie *Gill,* 'Identities in Quaker Women's Writing', *Women's Writing*, 9 no 2 [2002]: 267–84; p. 278).

by miraculous appearances of water or gardens in the desert.[15] 'Wilderness' was also seen as a place of refuge for the Israelites who were in the desert after being delivered from slavery in Egypt. The 'wilderness' was thus a place of 'purgation and restoration', 'punishment' and 'a return to Godliness'.[16] In the New Testament narratives, it could represent a place of temptation, as Jesus was 'led of the spirit into the wilderness to be tempted of the devil' (Matthew 4:1). It was a place of reckoning between good and evil: in the wilderness Jesus resisted evil, thus foreshadowing his victory over Satan's powers. John the Baptist, a 'voice calling in the wilderness' (Matthew 3:3), called people to repentance and baptised them in the wilderness, setting a pattern of retreating to the desert for repentance and cleansing.[17]

In the early church, Christians living in the Graeco-Roman pagan society could no longer identify with their surrounding pagan world. The theologian Andrew Louth explains the early Christians thus identified themselves with Old Testament characters who 'acknowledged that they were strangers and exiles on the earth' (Hebrews 11:13), therefore making the world for Christians 'if not a desert ... a foreign country'.[18] Contrarily, when Christianity became increasingly conventional, particularly after Emperor Constantine brought Christianity to the Roman Empire, the 'call of the desert' drew the highly spiritual away for contemplation, prayer, ascetic practices and solitary encounters with the divine.[19] Thus emerged the desert fathers during the 3rd and 4th centuries, most famous amongst them Antony the Great (d. 356). After Antony lived in solitude in the desert for twenty years, seldom seeing others, he soon became well known for his asceticism and attracted many followers. Louth explains Antony's simple and solitary lifestyle indicated 'the natural state of man, as God intended it, in paradise, in the Garden of Eden', as the desert had become for Antony a 'way to paradise, to the lost state of harmony and perfection'.[20] For the early desert fathers, and subsequent monastic movements, the theme of 'wilderness' was often seen as a place to which one withdrew from the world and encountered the divine. The desert or wilderness was, in effect, the way to Paradise. While we do not have proof Fox read the writings of the early desert fathers, his exposure

---

[15] Andrew Louth, *The Wilderness of God* (London: Darton, Longman & Todd, 2003), 29–35.

[16] David Ross Williams, *Wilderness Lost: The Religious Origins of the American Mind* (London: Associated University Presses, Inc., 1989), 25.

[17] Ibid, 25–6.

[18] Louth, *The Wilderness of God*, 43–5.

[19] Ibid, 45.

[20] Ibid, 47.

to mystical thought in general may well have informed in part his understanding of the True Church emerging from the wilderness and returning to Paradise.[21]

In the mystical tradition of medieval western Christianity, the desert or 'wilderness' could represent an inward 'wilderness of the soul' in which one could experience divine insight in solitude. Within medieval monastic tradition, the 'wilderness' was a symbol of an internal, mystical state of consciousness, where one could be prepared to encounter and have union with Christ through a total detachment from all created things and carnal desires.[22] Wilderness in this sense was thus considered a positive state through detachment from the essentially evil world. This interpretation would also be used in the sixteenth century by St Teresa of Avila and the Carmelite St John of the Cross.[23] Contrarily, in the sixteenth century some Protestant reformers used the term 'wilderness' as a negative symbol of the chaotic and evil world, representing the temptations and trials one goes through before coming to repentance and conversion.[24] This particularly negative view of 'wilderness' carried into the seventeenth century in England, where the term 'wilderness' frequently similarly symbolised either the contemporary chaotic situation of humanity or the evil 'world'. Particularly during the Civil War and Interregnum, popular hopes rose of Christ's second coming – the time when God would once and for all save humanity from the evil worldly 'wilderness' and return them to 'paradise', the restored Garden of Eden where humanity could finally experience God's redemption in full.

Within popular seventeenth-century literature, Milton and Bunyan, amongst other writers of this time, reflected the eschatological hopes of many of the seventeenth-century sectarians.[25] Christopher Hill refers to Milton's *Paradise Regained* as a work that elaborated upon dissenter beliefs that 'man can attain to his pre-lapsarian state here on earth'.[26] Digger turned Leveller Gerrard Winstanley, along with many Ranters, believed Christ's second coming was through his 'spirit in men', making the historical Christ comparatively less important, and paradise on earth a viable event.[27] However, after the restoration

---

[21] Rufus Matthew Jones, *Spiritual Reformers in the 16th and 17th Centuries* (London: Macmillan, 1914), xxxi–xxxii, 208–34.

[22] Louth, *The Wilderness of God*, 86–97.

[23] Evelyn Underhill, *Mysticism: A Study in the Nature and Development of Spiritual Consciousness* (Mineola, NY: Dover Publications, 2002), 110, 173.

[24] Williams, *Wilderness Lost*, 27–32.

[25] Hill, *The World Turned Upside Down*, 398.

[26] Ibid, 398. 'If we were not so over-awed by Milton the great poet we should long ago have recognized his role as a precursor of the Ranters ... In his *Treatise of Education* Milton hoped that learning would undo the consequences of the Fall ... His hatred of priests, an established church, forms, ceremonies and tithes was as fierce as that of any of the radicals' (Hill, *The World Turned Upside Down*, 395–6).

[27] Hill, *The World Turned Upside Down*, 206–7.

of the monarchy many dissenters questioned the timing of paradise being 'founded now' in their own generation, as they had eagerly anticipated. Yet while many dissenting groups faded after the restoration of the monarchy, Fox remained on the spiritual landscape, retaining his rhetoric of the Quakers being a people rising from the 'wilderness'.[28] After Cromwell's death in 1658 and the restoration of Charles II to the throne in May 1660, Fox encouraged his fellow Quakers:

> All Friends, let the dread and majesty of God fill you. And as concerning the changing of times and Governments, let not that trouble any of you, for God hath a mighty work and hand therein ... in vain shall powers and armies withstand the Lord, for his determined work shall come to pass.[29]

Fox believed God's 'determined work' of restoring the 'true church' was still being accomplished on earth through the Quaker movement.[30]

In regards to marriage being a testimony to the 'church rising up from the wilderness', Fox's specific interpretation of 'wilderness' signified a place of exile for the communal 'true church', while the apostate, established church was in power. Fox maintained after the time of the primitive, apostolic Christian church, the 'true church' went into the 'wilderness', remaining hidden and not active while the 'false' or 'apostate' church rose to and remained in power. The early Quakers largely held that the 'false church' had remained in power until ultimately the rise of the Quaker movement. The 'false church' was not only the Catholic Church but also the established Church of England and by the end of the 1650s anyone outside of the Quaker circle.[31] 'Wilderness' was also attributed to one's personal spiritual exile from God's presence. Personal conversion, rising up and out of spiritual exile, was inextricably linked to the communal Quaker exodus from the 'wilderness', and was considered a necessary first step in coming into unity with the True Church. One's individual emergence from the 'wilderness' and a

---

[28] Ibid, 14.

[29] Fox, *Journal* (1952), 386.

[30] Rosemary Moore notes the persecution Quakers encountered after the restoration of the monarchy: 'During the following years the royalists and Anglicans, powerless during the Interregnum, viciously repressed all kinds of religious dissent, with Quakers taking the brunt of the persecution' (Dandelion [Ed.], *The Creation of Quaker Theory*, 56).

[31] Moore, *The Light in Their Consciences*, 131. 'Many people at this time thought that the true church had been lost since the days of the Apostles, but Quakers declared that not only had the true church reappeared but that it was exclusive to their movement'. See also Thomas Hancock, *The Peculium: An Endeavor to Throw Light on Some of the Causes of the Decline of the Society of Friends* (London: Smith, Elder and Co., 1859), 8. 'In 1658 there was not a Quaker living who did not believe Quakerism to be the one only true Church of the living God'.

return to God's presence within was the spiritual substance which the Quakers believed set them apart from the apostate church, a separation that was in part encouraged through marriages.

The Communal Rise of the True Church

Let us next consider Fox's interpretation of the communal True Church rising up from the wilderness. In 1655, Fox had already developed the notion of the emergence of the True Church in a letter (which he preserved and reprinted in his *Journal*) he wrote to 'all Professors' (or people who claimed to be religious through education) of the new age coming forth.[32] Fox argued while the 'priests' and 'professors' had 'talked' of such things as truth, Christ, the glory of God, the Son of God, and unity, all of these realities had not truly been 'possessed' in the 'false church'.[33] For Fox 'the fullness of knowledge' and the 'secrets' of God were now 'made manifest' to the 'children' of God.[34] The same year, fellow Quaker William Dewsbury wrote similar words of the hidden 'Sion' being redeemed forth by the Lord, after 'her long enthralled captivity in Babylon's kingdom' where she had 'fettered in the cloudy and dark day, into forms and observations'.[35] Four years later in 1659, Fox challenged a variety of contemporary religious groups including 'Anabaptists, Independents, Presbyters, Ranters, and many others', claiming all had 'manifested themselves not to be of a true descent from

---

[32] Fox, *Journal* (1952), 204.
[33] Ibid.
[34] Ibid. Fox wrote, ' ... the power that is now manifest, and doth overturn the world, and did overturn the world, to the exalting of the Lord, and to the pulling down of the kingdom of Satan and of this world, and setting up of his own kingdom, to his everlasting praise ... The priests incense all the ignorant people for fear their trade should go down; and the professors they show forth what is in them, full of rage ... Truth hath been talked of, but now it is possessed. Christ hath been talked of, but now he is come and is possessed. The glory hath been talked of, but now it is possessed, and the glory of man is destroyed. The Son of God hath been talked of, but now he is come, and hath given us an understanding. Unity hath been talked of, but now it is come ... to them that fear thy name the secrets of thee are made manifest, the treasures of wisdom are opened and the fullness of knowledge; for thou dost make thyself manifest to thy children'.
[35] William Dewsbury, *A true prophecy of the mighty day of the Lord* (1655). (Barbour and Roberts [Eds], *Early Quaker Writings*, 93.) 'The Lord is redeeming Sion forth of her long enthralled captivity in Babylon's kingdom, where she hath been fettered in the cloudy and dark day, into forms and observations, and their kept by priests, and teachers of the world, who ran when God never sent them. Now is the Lord appearing in this day of his mighty power, to gather His elect together'.

the true Christian Churches'.[36] Fox did not perceive the Quakers as *part* of the True Church, but as the *sole* True Church of their age.

Fox elaborated the idea of the 'age' of the True Church coming out of the wilderness in his *Journal*, in which he described the end of a 'long night of apostasy'.[37] In the following passage, Fox suggested the True Church had been sent into exile 'since the apostles' days'. Delivering a harsh criticism to the established Church of England who persecuted those of the True Church, Fox wrote the following strong admonition against 'false prophets' in 1656:

> The false prophets ... these are they that the world wonders after! These who have drunk the blood of the martyrs, prophets, and saints, and persecuted the true church into the wilderness! ... all nations have drunk of her cup of fornication; the blood of the martyrs and saints they have drunk, and the true church hath fled into the wilderness: and all this since the apostles' days.[38]

Fox regarded the established church as the harbour of 'false prophets' and 'antichrists' which arose, as Christ had predicted. Margaret Fell likewise believed God was bringing the True Church up from the wilderness in her lifetime, ending the 'night of apostasy'. In 1667, Fell wrote a lengthy treatise criticising *'the ministers of the Gospel whose time and day hath been in the last ages past, or rather in the night of apostasy'*.[39] In it Fell elaborated in a similar fashion to Fox

---

[36] George Fox, *The Great Mystery of the Great Whore Unfolded: and Antichrists Kingdom Revealed unto Destruction* (London: Thomas Simmons, 1659), 1.

[37] The idea of an 'age of apostasy' was not only promoted by Fox. Philipp Jakob Spener and Gottfried Arnold, both seventeenth-century German Pietists, also pointed to the moral decline of the clerical authorities into apostasy, calling for inner spiritual renewal which would reform the church. Spener in his work *Pia Desideria* encouraged people to meet together and discuss scripture, collectively praying and meditating, with the hope of reforming the corruption and passivity within the established church through encouraging a true priesthood and piety within the individuals. In Book One of his *Die Erste Liebe*, Arnold likewise called for reforms in the morally decaying established church. He argued the church had slipped into an age of apostasy after experiencing a spiritual decline since the Constantinian era, leading to a Christianity dependent on external forms rather than a life of true inner piety as a result of an inner union with Christ. In *Unpartheyische Kirchen und Ketzer-Histoire* (1699–1700), Arnold further attacked the established church as being religiously hypocritical, Pharisaical in practice, and overly dependent on academia and polemical theology. Encouraging a mystical union with the divine, Arnold believed the Christian community would be renewed and restored to pre-Constantinian Christianity (Peter Erb, *Pietists, Protestants, and Mysticism: The Use of Late Medieval Scriptural Texts in the work of Gottfried Arnold* [1666–1714] [London: The Scarecrow Press, Inc., 1989], 14–15, 60–64, 77–8).

[38] Fox, *Journal Vol. 1* (1836), 385–6.

[39] Fell, *A touch-stone, or A perfect tryal by the Scriptures*, 1.

on the 'night of apostacy' in her attack on the compulsory payment of tithes. Fell explained it as a time:

> When the Power and Spirit of the Lord Jesus was lost, and the Revelation of Jesus, by which the Apostles preached; then when the Apostacy come in, those that got up into the Popes Chair, took upon them to find out a way, whereby they might compel people to maintain them ... And thus they have laid a weight of Oppression upon poor people, ever since the dark Night of the Apostacy came on.[40]

Fell argued, like Fox, that in her day amongst the Quakers, the True Church was rising from the wilderness, out of 'bondage' and 'captivity', to end the 'Night of Apostacy' of the 'false church'.[41]

Fox's vociferous notion of ending the dark night of apostasy through the Quaker movement was echoed by a number of Fox's fellow contemporary Quakers. Quaker apologist Robert Barclay agreed the 'true church' and her 'truth' was being established in his day. Defending the Quakers in 1676, he declared them:

> Faithful witnesses and messengers, whom God has raised up in this day to witness for his truth, which hath long been in a great measure hid, but now again is revealed, and many brought to be witnesses of it, who thereby are come to walk in the light of the Lord.[42]

In 1679, Quaker Ambros Rigge criticised 'pretended Christians' for following the practices of their 'Fore-fathers, who lived in the Dark Night of the Apostacy'. In defence against people calling the Quakers a 'Noval start-up Religion', Rigge argued the Quakers were in fact a people in whom Christ was 'manifested' and 'followed the steps of the Antient & true Christians', and therefore knew the hope that 'hath been a Mystery hid from Ages and Generations'.[43] He accused the established church of following and upholding a religion that had been largely established upon the 'Heathen-like' traditions of their forefathers, without considering if these traditions were right or good. 'Apostate' Christians

---

[40] Ibid, 71.
[41] Ibid, 33. 'Yet for the Seed of God sake, which is kept in Bondage, and in Captivity, in and by this Power of Darkness, that hath lodged in this body of Teachers and Preachers, who have called themselves Christian, both Papists and Protestants, in this Night of Apostacy, that the True Church of God hath been in the Wilderness, and the Witnesses prophesied in Sackcloth; this hath been a Night of Darkness, but the Day is Springing'.
[42] Robert Barclay, *The Anarchy of the Ranters and Other Libertines* (1676). (Barbour and Roberts [Eds], *Early Quaker Writings*, 516.)
[43] Ambros Rigge, *True Christianity Vindicated* (1679), 27.

followed these traditions simply because they were 'Antient' and practised by their forefathers. But these forefathers, Rigge believed, lived not only in the 'Dark Night of the Apostacy', but also in 'Degeneration from the Life, Marrow, and Quitesence of true Christianity'.[44] Whether it was during the Civil War, the Interregnum or after the restoration of the monarchy, the Quakers consistently believed they were God's True Church, proclaiming God's truth, coming forth out of hiding, regardless of external political or social circumstances.

A helpful summary of the rise and fall of the True Church comes from William Penn. In his preface to Fox's published *Journal*, Penn summarised what he saw as historical sequence of the rise, fall and return of the 'true church'. The rise of the True Church began when God gave to humanity the knowledge of Himself in the appearance of Jesus Christ, a time identified by the Quakers as the days of the apostolic church.[45] At this time God wrote 'his law in the heart, and put his fear and Spirit in the inward parts', a fulfilment of the prophecy of Jeremiah, which the Quakers wholeheartedly believed was coming to fulfilment again amongst themselves.[46] The interruption of this direct knowledge of God came when 'human inventions and novelties, both in doctrine and in worship, crowded fast into the church', which thus gave rise to the 'false church'.[47] It was at this time, according to Penn, that the 'true church fled into the wilderness ... to a retired, solitary, and lonely state; hidden and as it were out of sight of men, though not out of the world'.[48] The direct experience and knowledge of the divine, not accepted in the 'false church', went into hiding, effectively in the hearts of the few who longed for something more spiritually. While in the wilderness, the True Church attempted several returns, which were 'blocked up', with the waters 'too high' for the church to succeed, due to persecution of the established 'false church'. Though not elaborating on who they were exactly, Penn noted many of the True Church's 'excellent children in several nations and centuries fell by the cruelty of superstition, because they would not fall from their faithfulness to truth'.[49] In his full summary of the history of the church from the time of Christ and the apostolic era to his current day, Penn supported the notion that the Quakers represented and embodied the victorious children and the True Church's triumphant return from the 'wilderness'.

Finally, in establishing the 'true church', any physical signs of the 'false church' were shunned, including all external forms of worship. William Dewsbury exhorted 'every particular inhabitant of England' to 'come out of Babylon,

---

[44] Ibid.
[45] Fox, *Journal Vol. 1* (1836), xviii.
[46] Jones, *Spiritual Reformers in the 16th and 17th Centuries*, 348.
[47] Fox, *Journal Vol. 1* (1836), xviii.
[48] Ibid.
[49] Ibid.

all forms, and observations, and traditions'.[50] Minding 'the Light in your conscience' and examining one's heart was considered the true form of worship, turning worship from the outward to the inward. This shift from outward forms of worship to true inward revelation from God was considered a sign of the beginning of the Lord's restoration of creation, as Dewsbury proclaimed, 'for the Lord will make the Earth as the Garden of Eden, and hath begun His great and strange works in this nation'.[51] In 1677, Fox warned of the Lord's coming through the 'true light' by which He was calling his church to do away with old symbols and images used in worship. According to Fox, any external images and symbols, including crosses, pictures and formal liturgical practices, deterred a person from following Christ in their hearts.[52] Through bringing down the images, symbols and signs of the apostate church, Fox believed the True Church would have 'victory' over the reigning 'false church' which had been 'inwardly ravened from the spirit of God'.[53] In their rejection of all external forms of worship, including the forms traditionally present within the marriage ceremony – the church building, the priest, the rings, the decadent celebrations – the early Quakers attempted to solely embrace the communal and personal witness of

---

[50] William Dewsbury, *A true prophecy of the mighty day of the Lord* (1655). (Barbour and Roberts [Eds], *Early Quaker Writings*, 100.)

[51] Ibid. 'Come out of Babylon, all forms, and observations, and traditions, which are set up by the will of man … examine your hearts, and mind the Light in your conscience … for it is the heart the Lord requires; He will no longer be worshipped in words, forms, and observations, but in spirit and in truth and in sincerity in the inward parts … for the Lord will make the Earth as the Garden of Eden, and hath begun His great and strange works in this nation'.

[52] George Fox, *A Warning to the Magistrates, Priests, and People, of the City of Hamburgh, to humble themselves before the Lord, and not to be high-minded. Amsterdam, the 19th of the 7th month, 1677.* (Reprinted in Fox, *Journal Vol. 2* [1836], 483.) 'And the Lord is come to bring his people off all the world's crosses, pictures, images, and likenesses, to know that the power of God is the cross of Christ, which crucifies them to the world, and brings them up into the likeness and image of God, that man and woman were in before they fell; and so to Christ that never fell'.

[53] George Fox and Francis Howgill, *Papists strength, principles, and doctrines* (London: Thomas Simmons, 1658), 9. '… for the true Church of the Apostles did never command that men should abstayn from meats, or set up a crosse of wood or stone, or worship Images, or Saints, or names, or bow down to them, but worship God, and worship not the Angels. Now these things hath been sett up since the dayes of the Apostles, in the Apostacy from the true Church, which has made war against the Saints and over-come them, but now is the Saints and the Lamb come to have victory, and now the Lamb and Saints will have victory, who is come to reign and the holy Prophets and the Saints shall rejoyce over you: sing and rejoyce ye heavens, and rejoyce ye Saints and holy Prophets over her Thats your Church which is inwardly ravened from the spirit of God, and has reigned'.

the inward presence of Christ, and thereby further establish and define their identity as the separate True Church.

Individual Exodus from the Wilderness

As the 'wilderness' was considered a place of exile of the True Church, so too was it described by Fox as a place of exile experienced by individuals who had turned away from 'the seed' of Christ within the conscience. When Quakers individually first turned inward, towards the 'light' or 'seed' of Christ within, and experienced inward judgment and redemption through an encounter with the 'light' or 'seed' of Christ within, the 'true church' began its return. Previously noted, the terms 'light' and 'seed' as used by the early Quakers signified the presence of Christ within the conscience – the inception of an inward spiritual encounter with the divine.[54] But this inward experience of the divine was not solely a solitary event. As each Quaker was converted personally, he or she was embarking on the collective exodus out of the 'wilderness', which brought about outward judgment, redemption and the purification of the True Church.[55] The early Quakers placed each individual conversion in a larger context, holding firm to the conviction their collective conversions were part of a broader apocalyptic event. As Quakers quickened to the 'light in their conscience' they were a part of the collective exodus of the 'true church' coming out of the wilderness. The 'night of apostasy' was coming to an end through personal, inward conversions, leading to communal unity with the divine. In 1656, Fox encouraged his fellow Quakers to 'witness Christ in them ... the mystery, that had been hid from ages and generations':

> Which was revealed to the apostles, and is revealed now, after this long night of apostasy ... now again, the everlasting Gospel must be preached to all nations ... that they may come into the pure religion ... the Gospel from heaven, and not from men.[56]

Fox's account of his own personal conversion experience echoes the same discovery and conviction:

---

[54] See p. 116.

[55] Dandelion, *The Creation of Quaker Theory*, 160. Dandelion explains Quaker conversion as it related to the whole of the Quaker community: 'In Quakerism, salvation might be found outside the church, but the measure of perfection could only be realized within the purified church. Unlike other individualistic radical groups, who taught perfectionist doctrines, Quakers were concerned about both individual rebirth and the rebirth of the true church'.

[56] Fox, *Journal* (1952), 339.

> The Lord God let me see, when I was brought up into his image in righteousness and holiness, and in the paradise of God, the state how Adam was made a living soul, and also the stature of Christ, the mystery, that had been hid from ages and generations.[57]

The 'mystery' of Christ, no longer hidden, was now being fully experienced by the Quakers, as their 'long night of apostacy' was finally coming to an end through personal conversions.

Like Fox, Margaret Fell also regarded unity with the divine and the coming of the True Church as inseparable. In 1653 Fell boldly wrote a letter to Oliver Cromwell in which she explained the Quakers' beliefs and exhorted him to 'harken' to the light of Christ within the conscience.[58] In Fell's warning to Cromwell, she was convinced God's True Church was manifested as 'that of God' became realised within the conscience. Fell also often described the return of the True Church as the 'seed' of Christ within set free. In an epistle to Friends written in 1655, Fell wrote of Christ calling his 'seed … out of bondage' in her description of the True Church coming forth in her era:

> Friends, whom the Lord God hath called unto the Light which is Eternal, which the Lord God hath sent, to bring his Seed out of Bondage, and out of the House of Darkness … .the Lord God of Life and Power hath visited you, and sent his Servants to awaken you, and to raise you from the Dead, that Christ might give you Life, who is now come, and coming to redeem Israel.[59]

Fell maintained the True Church, or seed of Christ, was coming out of the bondage of the 'false church' as Israel had come out of slavery. Similarly, two years earlier in 1653 Fell wrote a letter to Justice Anthony Pearson, a Commissioner in the North of England who was a Quaker, but apparently had been 'getting into the world's spirit', in which she compared the 'fleshly man' to

---

[57] Ibid, 32.

[58] Fell wrote to Cromwell: 'I warne thee … that thou beware how thou stands against the mighty dreadfull god that is now made manifest in his people, for that shalt thou & all that stands up against the Lord Anoynted … which he sends forth into the rude world to make manifest his great name and power will he overturn the oppressors … For to the first nature that all the world lives in[,] God is unknowne, & they are ignorant of that in the Conscience … for the seeds sake in thee with which I have unitie, have I written these things to thee, to the Informing of thy mind, the Lord God of power enlighten thy understandings that thou may be guided by that of god in thee which cannot erre'. Margaret Fell, *Letter to Oliver Cromwell* (1653). (Glines [Ed.], *Undaunted Zeal*, 38–9.)

[59] Margaret Fell, *An Epistle to Friends* (1655). (Glines [Ed.], *Undaunted Zeal*, 170.)

the taskmasters of Egypt keeping the seed of God in bondage.[60] In her letter, in which she encouraged the Judge to repent, Fell again likened the Quakers to the 'seed coming out of bondage', drawing from the Old Testament narrative of the exodus of the Jews out of slavery in Egypt led by Moses:

> And see if that which is of him in thee been not in bondage in Egipt, in darknesse under pharoh which is A taskmaster [Exod. 1:11], the fleshly man, which keepes the seed of god in bondage, but my dear hart, waite upon the Lord in the light of god in thee, which is Moses, and it will bring the seed of god out of prison if thou harken to it and be obeydient to it, and the Lord will … bring forth his owne seed that it may serve him in the Land of the liveing.[61]

Exhorting the Justice to 'wait on the light within', Fell believed this inward act would make the Justice aware of the evil of the outward world:

> Raise up the witnesse in thee, which shall testifie against the world and all the profession in the world, and all the worshipps in the world and the god of the world, and it will lead thee to another kingdome which is not of this world.[62]

In the other 'kingdome' God would be their 'King' while all the 'worships and professions' of the 'world' would pass away.[63] In this dichotomy, the 'light within' was considered the key to establishing God's Kingdom on Earth, while the world's kingdoms and false churches would eventually be defeated. Hearkening to the 'light within' was the necessary first step in both inward personal repentance and the outward establishment of the True Church.

---

[60] Braithwaite, *The Beginnings of Quakerism to 1660*, 463. Braithwaite makes the following summary regarding Judge Pearson's questionable actions in the eyes of his fellow Quakers, as well as remarks regarding Fell's abovementioned letter: 'There is a letter from Margaret Fell (Spence MSS, vol. iii. fol. 52, 53) which warns him to beware of the betrayer which lies near him, and shows her consciousness that he was slipping back into the world. Pearson, during his years of Quakerism, had retained his keen political interests, and his activity in 1659 against the Royalists had compromised him. In an hour of weakness and fear he made terms with the Royalist power that sent his political leader, Sir Arthur Hesilrige, to the Tower, and his friend, the great Sir Henry Vane, to the block. There is, however, no record … which suggests bitter personal feelings towards him on the part of Friends, or towards Friends on his part. His name died away in silence' (Braithwaite, *The Beginnings of Quakerism to 1660*, 463).

[61] Margaret Fell, *Letter to Justice Anthony Pearson* (1653). (Glines [Ed.], *Undaunted Zeal*, 21.)

[62] Ibid.

[63] Ibid.

Fell wrote a similar warning and exhortation to one Jeffrey Elletson in 1656. A Quaker called John Clayton had served with Elletson 'in the Army in Scotland', and after later becoming a Quaker, Clayton subsequently received harsh criticisms and difficult questions from Elletson regarding his new-found beliefs. Clayton requested that Fell write a letter to Elletson as a response to his challenges, including his assertion that Quakers were 'deluded' in following the light of God within.[64] In response to Elletson's accusations, Fell argued the 'light of God' in Elletson's own conscience would enable him to see that all the 'Gospel teachers' he followed were not following the real Christ within but a 'Christ without them', causing him to continue to live in sin.[65] Asserting that the mystery of Christ was 'hid ... from generation ages past', Fell maintained, like Fox, that the mystery was now in her day being 'revealed' through the 'Light within'.[66] According to Fox and Fell, while everyone had the 'light' or the 'seed' of Christ within, each person also had the power to either ignore it or submit to it, the latter bringing judgment followed by the restoration of the individual in Christ's image. Fell encouraged Elletson, 'Harken to the Light of God in thy conscience, which shewes thee thy sin & condemnation ... and that will lead thee out of thy sin ... into puritie up to god'.[67] The same year, Fox, like Fell before him, warned Cromwell to take heed of Christ within:

> Did not Christ say he would come again to his disciples & make his abode with them & did not say I in you, & the spirit of the father which speaks in you ... Therefore take heed, I am moved to warn you ... doth not the Apostles in their several epistles which have been read among you speak that Christ is in you and of their being the sons of god and the son of god revealed in them and the spirit of the father in them ... is he not the Lamb of god, and are not they against him where he is made manifest within that would not have him to speak, and such as would not have him to reign, here you may see what hath been lost since the Apostles.[68]

---

[64] Margaret Fell, *Letter to Jeffrey Elletson* (1656). (Glines [Ed.], *Undaunted Zeal*, 177.)

[65] Ibid, 181. Fell wrote to Elletson, 'The light of God in thy conscience ... will let thee see all thy Gospell teachers not to be built upon the rock which is christ the Light, which hath enlightened everyone that comes into the world, but are talking of A Christ without them, and soe thou and they are yet in your sines, And thou shalt never know the living god ... but Jesus xt [Christ] is risen and revealed and made manifest in these, whom thou and thy Gospell ministers calls deluded people, glory and praises be to the glorious god for ever, who hath hid these things from generation ages past but hath revealed them to us'.

[66] Ibid.

[67] Ibid.

[68] Fox, *Journal Vol. 1* (In two volumes. Norman Penney and T.E. Harvey [Eds] [Cambridge: Cambridge University Press, 1911]), 264-6.

Fox and Fell had the same message. If one did not succumb to the judgment and transformation of 'Christ within', one was against Christ. However, when one chose to succumb to 'Christ within', the individual took part in the larger movement which ushered forth God's collective 'kingdome' or 'the true church'.

Fox's Predecessors and Influences: Eschatological Hopes and Personal Conversion

With individual, personal conversion and the establishment of the collective 'true church' so closely linked, it is useful to take pause and consider Fox's specific beliefs and possible influences regarding personal inward conversion, as well as the communal experience of the 'light' within. While early Quaker ideas about the establishment of the 'true church' and a return to an inward experience of God were not wholly new, Fox promoted and utilised these notions by establishing the True Church through rigorous meetings, careful documentation and mutual accountability. Linking a personal inward experience of the divine with the communal exodus and establishment of the True Church, Fox created a movement that was distinctive and enduring, outlasting many other seventeenth-century sects.[69]

In a climate of dissatisfaction with the established church, Fox along with other seventeenth-century spiritual seekers and dissenters grappled with the notions of a return to a prelapsarian state and purifying the church.[70] As addressed in the introduction, while it is difficult to conclude that Fox gleaned directly from his contemporary dissenters (or those in preceding centuries) his doctrine of the 'light' and the return of the True Church, when one compares Fox's writings with the writings of many of his contemporaries, the similarities are striking. A common thread of thought which emerged amongst seventeenth-century sectaries, though taking varying forms and implying slightly different results, was the belief that the second coming of Christ could occur (or indeed was occurring) within the individual in their lifetime. Rather than anticipating the historical, physical return of Christ in an external, future 'second coming', one could inwardly experience the return of Christ, a presence which brought inner individual judgment and restoration as well as judgment against the established church.

Notions of 'resurrection within' were circulating long before the Quaker movement. Followers of Jakob Böhme in the sixteenth century contended

---

[69] Hill, 'Quakers and the English Revolution'. (Mullett [Ed.], *New Light on George Fox*, 23.)

[70] Allen, *Quaker Communities in Early-Modern Wales*, 24.

heaven and hell existed within the conscience.[71] By the seventeenth century, modified versions of this idea emerged. In 1650, a Seeker called Richard Coppin declared Jesus' resurrection was currently happening within the individual saints of his day, which thus gave them access to greater revelation than the prophets and apostles, and brought them to a pre-lapsarian state which was greater than Adam's in Paradise.[72] Another well-known Seeker, William Erbery,[73] wrote in his *Testimony* in 1658 of the saints being 'be-wildernessed' out of the 'Apostacy' of the current world.[74] A Seeker turned Leveller, Gerrard Winstanley, asserted in his 1648 work *The Saints Paradise*:

> If you expect, or look for the resurrection of Jesus Christ, you must know, that the spirit within the flesh is the Jesus Christ, and you must see, feel, and know from himself his own resurrection within you ... for everyone hath the light of the Father within himself, which is the mighty man Christ Jesus. And how he is rising and spreading himself in these his sons and daughters, and so rising from one to many persons.[75]

While it is difficult to know if Fox had direct encounters with the abovementioned spiritual seekers, the likelihood of some cross meetings is

---

[71] Christopher Hill, 'The Religion of Gerrard Winstanley', *Past and Present: Supplement 5* (Oxford: The Past and Present Society, 1978), 14–15.

[72] Ibid.

[73] William Erbury's daughter, Dorcas Erbury, was a fellow prisoner of James Nayler who allegedly 'believed herself to be raised to life by Nayler laying his hand on her head', though Nayler later denied this act while on trial. She was also one of several women who praised Nayler during his Jesus-like entry into Bristol (Braithwaite, *The Beginnings of Quakerism to 1660*, 247, 252–3).

[74] William Erbery, *The testimony of William Erbery, left upon records for the saints of succeeding ages. Whereunto is added, The honest heretick being his tryal at Westminster* (London: Printed for Giles Calvert, 1658), 100–01. '*I will allure her and bring her to the wilderness, and speak comfortable to her.* (Hosea 2.14) Communion of Saints and the company of men is sweet to flesh, sweet to man to walk with men, but that's no wilderness where company or path is before us; but when we can see none with us but God, and God leading us in a way we know not of, this is sweet to a Saint in Spirit; therefore God is said to allure before, to allure us from the sweetness of man, to the sweetness of himself, and of his divine presence dwelling with us and in us. For truly in that Apostacy we now are ... *fear the Lord and his goodness in the latter daies*, that it, when we are be-wildernessed, and at a losse in all things, that we cannot look on any man, nor find God in any means, then we will seek the Lord our God, *God dwelling in us* ... God in our flesh'.

[75] Gerrard Winstanley, *The Saints Paradise or, the Fathers teaching the only satisfaction to waiting souls. Wherein many experiences are recorded, for the comfort of such as are under spirituall burning. The inward testimony is the souls strength* (London: Giles Calvert, 1648), 83–4.

plausibly high. The historian Winthrop S. Hudson noted the Quakers shared a publisher, Giles Calvert, who 'kept shop at the sign of the Black Spread-Eagle ... and was the publisher of the worlds of Saltmarsh, Dell, Winstanley, and the Quakers'.[76] Hudson argued the shared publishing house likely constituted a 'very tangible point of contact' where it is likely there was 'a considerable interchange of ideas and mutual influence'.[77] Certainly, Fox himself described years of soul searching and speaking with other spiritual seekers, making mutual influence highly likely.[78] Homes, ale houses and publishers all flourished with dissenting conversation amongst and between various people who sought alternatives to the established Church of England, and exchanged various views regarding theology and spirituality.[79] Likewise, as dissenting conversation thrived so too did the publishing and circulation of 'unorthodox' books, pamphlets and other printed literature.[80] To what extent Fox borrowed from his fellow, contemporary dissenters is uncertain, as he did not quote them directly. But it is likely and plausible that he was at least influenced by the various dissenting views and thoughts at his time.

What is possibly most intriguing is a look at Fox's extant library at the time of his death, which notably included fifteenth-century works by Henry Nicholas and Sebastian Franck.[81] Franck, a German radical reformer, did not define the

---

[76] Winthrop S. Hudson, 'Gerrard Winstanley and the Early Quakers', *Church History*, 12 no 3 (September 1943): 177–94; p. 181.

[77] Ibid.

[78] The historian William Braithwaite notes the early Quaker William Penn recommended to a young Quaker a reading list of authors whom he believed were predecessors to Quakerism. The authors recommended by Penn included 'J. Saltmarsh, W. Dell, W. Erberry, C. Goad, R. Coppin, and J. Webster' (Braithwaite, *The Beginnings of Quakerism to 1660*, 544).

[79] Hill, 'Quakers and the English Revolution'. (Mullett [Ed.], *New Light on George Fox*, 24.) Christopher Hill reminds us of the 'liberation of religious discussion' during the revolutionary decades of the 1640s and 1650s when 'illegal groups were now free to meet where they could – in private houses, in ale-houses, in the open air – to discuss what they wanted to discuss'.

[80] Ibid, 23.

[81] John Nickalls, 'George Fox's Library', *Journal of the Friends Historical Society*, 28 (1931): 2–21; pp. 9, 18. 'George Fox's possession of this book by Henry Nicholas [Den Spegel der Gerechticheit, dorch den Geist der Lieffden, unde den vorgodeden Mensch H[enrick] N[iclaes] uth de Hemmelische Warheit betuget], the founder of the Family of Love or Familists, is of great interest. So far as is known he cannot have read the volume himself, but if he used it he must have made use of a translator. Nicholas (fl 1502–1580) made many converts in the Netherlands and in France and, by the later part of the sixteenth century, in England also. In their insistence on righteousness of life and their views on outward sacraments and silent waiting, Fox and Nicholas had much in common' (Nickalls, 'George Fox's Library', 9).

ultimate emergence of the 'true church' embodied by a specific group as Fox did; but like Fox, Franck made a link between an inward mystical experience of God as a sign of being a member of the 'true church':

> The true Church is not a separate mass of people, not a particular sect to be pointed out with the finger, not confined to one time or one place; it is rather a spiritual and invisible body of all the members of Christ, born of God, of one mind, spirit, and faith ... It is a Fellowship seen with a spiritual eye and by the inner man.[82]

As the inward experience of the divine took precedence, like Fox and others before him, Franck held that since the apostolic church, the True Church 'vanished from the earth' with no external church to take its place:[83]

> I am fully convinced [by a study of the early Church Fathers] that, after the death of the apostles, the external Church of Christ, with its gifts and sacraments, vanished from the earth and withdrew into heaven, and is now hidden in spirit and in truth, and for these past fourteen hundred years there has existed no true external Church and no efficacious sacraments.[84]

While Franck believed the True Church became a purely spiritual and inward presence of the divine alone, Fox believed the inward presence of the divine translated to the outward establishment of a purified and distinct external True Church.[85]

---

[82] Jones, *Spiritual Reformers in the 16th and 17th Centuries*, 58.

[83] This view was prevalent within Protestantism and developed amongst various reformers, including the Lutheran reformer Matthias Racius Illyricus (1520–75) in *Catalogus Testium Veritatis* (Basel, 1556). 'The *Catalogus Testium Veritatis* formed the blueprint for all subsequent Protestant histories of the True Church' (Raymond A. Mentzer and Andrew Spicer [Eds], *Society and Culture in the Huguenot World 1559–1685* [Cambridge: Cambridge University Press, 2002], 37).

[84] Ibid, 59–60.

[85] Henry Cadbury also points to Fox's extant library, which held works by Nicholas and Franck, to suggest Fox was likely influenced by these predecessors: 'Fox certainly claims that truths came to him by revelation. There was an immediacy and self-evidence about them which made them seem original, though he admits he subsequently found them in the Scriptures. I think he also subsequently found them in pre-Quaker writers like Boehme ... How otherwise shall we account for the presence in Fox's limited library of the *Looking Glass of Righteousness* by Henry Nicholas (in German) or of John Everard's English translation of Sebastian Francks' *Forbidden Fruit*, and of the treatises against the supremacy of the established church, against tithes, etc., by earlier English non-conformists like Tyndal, John Canne, Giles Randall, and Thomas Collier?' (Cadbury, 'An Obscure Chapter of Quaker

Henry Nicholas, the founder of the Family of Love, also advocated an inward experience of the divine over and above the external dead practices of the established church, believing the second coming of Christ was already occurring in the inward consciousness of each human. Familists were accused of allegorising the Fall, resurrection, second coming and judgment as all occurring within the individual, taking place in their lifetimes.[86] While Fox never quoted or referred to Nicholas directly in his writings, similarities emerge between the writings of both men.[87] Like Fox, Nicholas felt he was in unity with the divine, coining the phrase 'begodded'.[88] Penetrated with the divine, he saw himself as a prophet, with a divinely inspired call to tell others about this new revelation of the true fulfilment of Christ's redemption on earth, by being conformed to God's image inwardly.[89] Like the early Quakers, Nicholas regarded all outward ceremonies and sacraments of the established church as undesirable and moot forms, while his 'church' was the only True Church of his age. In his work *First Exhortation*, Nicholas wrote words strikingly similar to Fox's own phrases:

> 'Now in the last time ... through the appearing of Christ, God hath raised up His community of holy ones', which is 'the only true seed and witness of Jesus Christ in the world'.[90]

For Fox and other early Quakers, their understanding of 'last times' and the 'second coming of Christ' was through the individual's experience of the 'seed of Christ' within, which were signs of the end of the old age, or night of apostasy, and the beginning of the new age of the True Church. The Quaker sociologist Pink Dandelion best sums up early Quaker eschatology by describing it as a '*realising* eschatology, an unfolding of the endtime experienced inwardly'.[91] The future expectation of an external return of Christ was beginning to be realised through an inward experience of Christ in the seed or light.[92] The historian

---

History', 202–3; *Journal of the Friends Historical Society*, 28 [1931], 3–21; 29 [1931], 64, 66; and 30 [1931], 12).

[86] Hill, *The Religion of Gerrard Winstanley*, 15.

[87] Braithwaite, *The Beginnings of Quakerism to 1660*, 23.

[88] Rufus Matthew Jones, *Studies in Mystical Religion* (London: Macmillan, 1936), 431.

[89] Ibid, 431, 434.

[90] Henry Nicholas, *First Exhortation*, 23, 24. Cited in Jones, *Studies in Mystical Religion*, 439.

[91] Dandelion, *An Introduction to Quakerism*, 31. For a full discussion of the notion of second coming and early Quaker theology, see Dandelion, *An Introduction to Quakerism*, 30–36.

[92] Ibid, 33. Dandelion explains the Church of England understood its role as being a help to humanity in remaining faithful as they lived in 'an anticipatory adolescence of the adulthood to follow', while for many early Quakers 'the future collided with the present

Rosemary Moore explains that by the 1650s 'most typical was the belief that while the Kingdom of God was already beginning to be present in the Quaker movement, a final consummation in the (probably near) future was also to be expected'.[93] In light of this, it comes as no surprise that an opponent of Fox's, Roger Williams, made the following attack against the Quakers because they refused to partake in such ceremonies as baptism and the Lord's Supper:

> The Baptisme was within, and only the Baptisme of the Spirit and of Fire: The Lords Supper appointed by the Lord Jesus to be a Spiritual Feast remembering him until his coming was with them nothing else but Spiritual joy, which they have ... by the second coming of the Lord Jesus to them, who they said was come again to the Apostles the second time, and unto themselves also.[94]

As we have seen, Fox, Fell and others all attested to inward renewal through the coming of Christ in their inward consciences, making the way for the return of the Kingdom of God through the rise and establishment of the True Church.

Fox's self-perceived prophetic call to raise up the True Church, particularly through an individual quickening to the inward light of Christ within, may not have been wholly original. Yet the early Quakers' rigorous meeting system, which propagated mutual and communal accountability, was their distinctive way in maintaining the rising up and the purity of the True Church. The links between inward unity with the divine, and the rising up of the True Church were, for them, inseparable. As Fox explained in 1669, Quaker marriages, like Quakers themselves, were restored in Christ, 'the one who never fell', and were above 'all the marriages in the fall':[95]

---

and all the temporary and pragmatic outward forms of helping humanity remain faithful in the meantime were over now that the meantime had become the endtime' (Dandelion, *An Introduction to Quakerism*, 32–3).

[93] Moore, *The Light in Their Consciences*, 68. This partly accounts also for the early Quaker preoccupation with the conversion of the Jews. See Sylvia Brown (Ed.), *Women, Gender, and Radical Religion in Early Modern Europe* (Leiden: E.J. Brill, 2007), 51. 'A distinctive feature of Quaker apocalypticism of the 1650s was the readiness of Friends to live as if 'the ends of the world' had already come ... For the Quakers of this period, the Second Coming was an historical event that was happening within each convinced believer'. See also Christopher Hill, "Till the Conversion of the Jews', in Richard H. Popkin (Ed.), *Millenarianism and Messianism in English Literature and Thought, 1650–1800* (Leiden: E.J. Brill, 1988).

[94] Roger Williams, *George Fox Digged Out of His Burrowes* (Boston: John Foster, 1676), 65.

[95] Fox, *Letter of George Fox Concerning his Marriage*. (Cadbury [Ed.], *Narrative Papers of George Fox*, 78.)

> And so it is in the seed that restoreth all things out of the Fall ... so it is in the restoration ... And so I say that the marriage in him, or his marriages, is above all the marriages of Adam and his sons and daughters in the Fall ... the marriage in him that never fell nor never will fall nor never will change, who destroyeth the Devil and his works, who was before the Devil was, or Adam was.[96]

Quaker Isaac Penington echoed the same sentiment two years later in 1671:

> Whom God hath joyned together let no man put asunder; and those which he joynes he joynes with his Power, even by his Immortal Power, with a Band over and above the State which is in the Fall.[97]

As God had restored individuals and subsequently the True Church so too had God restored the marital bond. The evidence that the early Quaker was living out of the Fall and in the restored True Church was evinced through the Quaker marriage approbation process.

Maintaining the True Church: A Return to Paradise and Purity

While Fox, not unlike others before him, longed to see the end of the age of apostasy, Fox further believed the True Church needed to evince a state of communal purity, as evidence that they indeed were living in a restored state. Purity within the individual alone was not enough. Purity evidenced in the community was essential. This concern for purity led to a call of repentance to his fellow 'apostate' Christians who were members of the 'false church'. Fox warned in 1677:

> So God in Christ is bringing people to the pure and undefiled religion, that will keep them from the spots of the world, into the new and living way, Christ Jesus; and to the church in God, which Christ is the head of, as he was in the apostles' days.[98]

Holding firm to the belief that they had returned to the purity of the apostolic church by experiencing an inner direct connection with God, Fox proclaimed the Quakers were leading the way 'with the light, who now speaks to his people

---

[96] Ibid, 78–9.

[97] Isaac Penington, *Some Principles of the Elect People of God in scorn called Quakers* (London: 1671), 44.

[98] George Fox, *A Warning to the Magistrates, Priests, and People, of the City of Hamburgh*, 471.

by his Son, as he did in the apostles' days; it was the same God that was the speaker to Adam and Eve in paradise'.[99]

As the True Church emerged from the wilderness, individual and communal purity by conforming to the image of Christ or the 'Second Adam' was essential, a process which was often described by Fox as 'coming up into the state of the second Adam'.[100] During a sermon delivered to Quakers in London in 1681, he preached that it was necessary for the Quakers to come into the image of the Second Adam before entering Paradise:

> Now in Adam all died, and so were plunged into his death and imperfection. Now comes Christ, the second Adam, of whom it is said: he shall baptize you with fire and the Holy Ghost ... Now everyone must know this baptism with the Spirit before they can come up into the garden in Paradise again.[101]

Over twenty years earlier in 1659, Margaret Fell in the same way addressed all 'Saints, Brethren, and Sisters' as coming up into the image of the Second Adam:

> The Second Addam, the lord from Heaven, whose power is now Resen, and whose Light is now Shininge in the Consciences of men, but Especelly in his Saints, in whom he is to be Glorified, and Admired, as his name and Nature Ariseth and growes in them, and as his Image is Renewed.[102]

The inward presence of Christ was, according to Fell, at work in the conscience, restoring the 'Saints' to the state and image of Christ.

In his *Journal*, Fox wrote in 1673 of the 'three states and three teachers' of humanity in relation to God and Paradise. In the first state of humanity, God was the first teacher in Paradise, under whom the state of 'man was happy'. After the Fall, Fox explained, 'man followed the teaching' of the second teacher, the serpent, by which man fell into a state of 'misery'. Finally, the third teacher, Jesus Christ, brought man and woman into the state before the Fall, renewing them into the image of Christ:

> So as man and woman come to God, and are renewed up into his image, righteousness, and holiness by Christ, thereby they come into the Paradise of

---

[99] Ibid.

[100] 'Second Adam' was a term frequently used by Protestants in reference to Christ.

[101] *George Fox's Sermon at Wheeler Street, 1680*. (Barbour and Roberts [Eds], *Early Quaker Writings*, 506.)

[102] Margaret Fell, *To the Saints, Brethren, and Sisters* (1659). (Glines [Ed.], *Undaunted Zeal*, 266.)

God, the state which man was in before he fell; and into a higher state than that, to sit down in Christ that never fell.[103]

Three years later in 1676, Fox elaborated further on the states of humanity. He not only addressed Adam and Eve's fall in the Garden of Eden; Fox further asserted the Jews fell from God's grace after failing to follow the Mosaic laws, as well as the 'many Christians' who also 'fell from their prophecies, and erred from the faith'. Yet despite these failures by Jews and Christians alike throughout the ages, Fox affirmed 'the Spirit, grace, faith, and power of God remains'.[104] He concluded, 'Many such states have I seen within these twenty-eight years; though there is a state, what shall never fall, nor be deceived, in the Elect before the world began'.[105] Fox exhibited his understanding of the three states of humanity and their relation with God: the state at the point of creation, the fallen state, and the return to a pre-Fall state in which humanity is brought back into the image of Christ, the Second Adam. For Fox, every Quaker was expected to exhibit the qualities of this renewed, pre-Fall state. Being in the image of Christ, the Second Adam, the Quaker experienced the light of Christ within, and by this presence of Christ was thus enabled to conform to the holy qualities of Christ and have direct revelation from God. Quakers came back to the original intention, and thereby were made Friends of God once again.[106]

The notion of leaving the wilderness and returning to the state of the 'pre-fall Adam' was not a mystery to early Friends. As discussed earlier in this chapter, many early Quakers believed the inward light was a fundamental and essential sign of the Quakers' exodus from the wilderness, and a return to the state of

---

[103] Fox, *Journal Vol. 2* (1836), 183. 'So here were "three states and three teachers" ... God was the first teacher in Paradise; and whilst man kept under his teaching, he was happy. The serpent was the second teacher; and when man followed his teaching, he fell into misery, into the fall from the image of God, from righteousness and holiness, and from the power that he had over all that God had made; and came under the serpent, whom he had power over before. Christ Jesus was the third teacher'.

[104] Fox, *Journal Vol. 2* (1836), 220. 'Though Adam and Eve fell from Paradise, the Jews fell from the law of God, and many Christians fell from their prophecies, and erred from the faith, the Spirit, and the grace; and the stars have fallen, as was spoken in Revelations: yet the Spirit, grace, faith, and power of God remains ... Many such states have I seen within these twenty-eight years; though there is a state, what shall never fall, nor be deceived, in the Elect before the world began'.

[105] Ibid.

[106] *George Fox's Sermon at Wheeler Street, 1680*. (Barbour and Roberts [Eds], *Early Quaker Writings*, 503.) Referring to the book of Genesis, Fox explained, 'Now after Adam and Eve had eaten, they were naked, and hid themselves in the trees of the garden. Then they heard the voice of the Lord God, in the Cool of the day: "Adam, where art thou? While thou keptst in my image thou wert my Friend"'.

unity with God.[107] Leaving the wilderness was an image of a very real condition the Quakers believed themselves to be living in as a result of the 'light' within them. Before the Quaker re-entered Paradise, the 'light of Christ within' first brought judgment on the individual, as Fox explained:

> Man and woman came then to be driven out of the garden, and a flaming sword placed every way with two edges to keep the way of the tree of life. So every one must come through this two-edged flaming sword before they can come into the Paradise of God. They must know this sword to cut down the transgressing life and earthly wisdom and to burn it up, before man can inherit life.[108]

After going through 'the flaming swords', or the judgment of God experienced by the Quaker during his or her conversion, all Quakers could come back to Paradise, or the state of reconciliation with God, in which they enjoyed direct revelation from God in silence. William Dewsbury, an early convert and leader amongst Quakers, wrote in 1655 a warning to all of England of the coming of 'Lord in the light':

> It is the heart the Lord requires: He will no longer be worshiped in words, forms, and observations, but in spirit and in truth, and in sincerity in the inward parts ... Now you have time, prize it, in waiting on the Lord in the light, to make your calling and selection sure ... in so doing you shall escape the wrath of God ... for the Lord will make the Earth as the Garden of Eden, and hath begun His great and strange words in this nation.[109]

Elizabeth Hendricks wrote from Amsterdam a letter entitled *An Epistle to Friends in England, To be Read in the Assemblies in the Fear of the Lord* (1672) in

---

[107] See pp. 128–32.

[108] *George Fox's Sermon at Wheeler Street, 1680.* (Barbour and Roberts [Eds], *Early Quaker Writings*, 503, 506.)

[109] *From the Spirit of the Lord, written by one whose name is in the flesh William Dewsbury, called Quaker with the people of the World, who live in the perishing nature: A true prophecy of the mighty day of the Lord* (London: Printed by Giles Calvert at the Blackspread Eagle at the west end of Paul's, 1655). (Barbour and Roberts [Eds], *Early Quaker Writings*, 100–01.) 'It is the heart the Lord requires: He will no longer be worshiped in words, forms, and observations, but in spirit and in truth, and in sincerity in the inward parts ... Now you have time, prize it, in waiting on the Lord in the light, to make your calling and selection sure, in putting off the old man and his deeds, and putting on the Lord Jesus Christ in righteousness and holiness ... in so doing you shall escape the wrath of God, which is coming upon the children of disobedience in this nation and elsewhere; for the Lord will make the Earth as the Garden of Eden, and hath begun His great and strange words in this nation'.

which she asserted the light within was condemning the world, and ushering in a new age of a renewed Paradise:

> The Spirit of the world ... is out of Truth, and by the Truth, the Light of God it is condemned. This is he that appeared in Adam and Eve in the beginning after the Fall: and so Friends, You who are called to come out of the Fall, let nothing that is of that spirit and nature be cherished nor regarded; but that all may be judged in the Light.[110]

Hendricks was familiar with the direct correlation between coming out of 'the Fall' with the experience of the work of the 'Spirit of Truth' or 'Light of God' within, believing the new state to be happening amongst her fellow Quakers, like Dewsbury almost twenty years earlier.

While the Quakers perceived themselves as the True Church which had come out of the wilderness into the state of the Second Adam, Fox believed those of the apostate church were still living in the 'Old Adam'. He wrote in 1676 that all Christians, like the Quakers, should 'serve God in the new Life, out of the Life of the Old Adam', but lamented there are some who 'profess Christ Jesus, and yet live in the Old Adam, and serve Sin and Evil' by denying God 'in their Works, Lives, and Conversations'.[111] Fox came to this conclusion in part because of the frustrations he had encountered during his early spiritual seeking as already mentioned. He wrote disparagingly in his *Journal* of the people he encountered who saw themselves, as well as the church on the whole, as remaining subject to sin in this world, in the state of the 'Old Adam'. Seeing others still living in the fallen state of disobedient Adam, he described this state as 'a dullness and drowsy heaviness upon people' amongst whom none 'could bear to be told that any should come to Adam's perfection, into that image of God'.[112] When Fox argued the 'true church' was coming out of the wilderness and into the state of

---

[110] Elizabeth Hendricks, *An Epistle to Friends in England, To be Read in their Assemblies in the Fear of the Lord* (1672). 'The Spirit of the world and is out of Truth, and by the Truth, the Light of God it is condemned. This is he that appeared in Adam and Eve in the beginning after the Fall: and so Friends, You who are called to come out of the Fall, let nothing that is of that spirit and nature be cherished nor regarded; but that all may be judged in the Light, which is springing forth of that Ground, the cursed Ground in which the Thorns and Briars, and the Weeds growes, and let the Fire Consume it'.

[111] George Fox, *Gospel Family-Order, Being a Short Discourse Concerning the Ordering of Families, both of Whites, Blacks and Indians* (London: 1676), 12–13.

[112] Fox, *Journal Vol. 1* (1836), 110. 'For all the sects in Christendom (so called) that I discoursed withal, I found none that could bear to be told that any should come to Adam's perfection, into that image of God, that righteousness and holiness that Adam was in before he fell; to be clear and pure without sin, as he was. Therefore, how should they be able to bear being told that any should grow up to the measure of the stature of the fullness of Christ,

the 'Second Adam' or the image of Christ, he believed the Quakers were coming into a state of being 'clear and pure, without sin'. Fox exhorted his fellow Quakers in Danzig in 1684:

> It is good to stand fast in the liberty of Christ Jesus, the second Adam, the Lord from heaven, who hath made you free out of snares, bondage, and limitations of the wills of the sons of old Adam.[113]

Members of the True Church, in the image of the 'Second Adam', could come up 'to the measure of the stature of the fullness of Christ', making 'Adam's perfection' possible on earth. Living holy lives in the image of the Second Adam, and holding others accountable to this holy living, was of utmost priority individually and communally.

As the dichotomies set up by Fox and his fellow Quakers between the 'false church' and the True Church, and the 'Old Adam' and the 'Second Adam' were central to his mission and message, so too were these dichotomies the focal points of Fox and Fell's marriage doctrine and theology. All means possible were taken to ensure that their marriages testified to 'the marriage of the Lamb' and were indicative of the True Church 'coming out of the wilderness'. Their strident efforts set them apart from their contemporaries, and perhaps helped them to survive. The historian Rufus Jones has suggested the Family of Love had 'weaknesses of system and method' which eventually 'hampered them and kept them from becoming a powerful people'.[114] In light of Jones' observation, the importance the early Quakers placed on the systematic checking of 'orderly walking' and endogamous marriages, within disciplined meetings, becomes more understandable.

Fox, Fell and other early Quaker leaders, unlike other dissenters and radical reformers with similar spiritual and theological beliefs, developed a thoroughgoing meeting and documentation system which held followers accountable to holy behaviour and participation in the group, maintaining what Fox and others perceived as the holy community of the True Church. Every aspect of a Quaker's life, most importantly marriage, was likely to be in either of the two categories: in the 'false church' or the 'true church'. The early Quaker marriage discipline reflected the True Church coming up out of the wilderness, into the image of the Second Adam through abolishing all outward signs and

---

when they cannot bear to hear that any should come, whilst upon earth, into the same power and Spirit that the prophets and apostles were in?'

[113] George Fox, *To the Suffering Friends at Danzig* (1684). (Barbour and Roberts [Eds], *Early Quaker Writings*, 500.)

[114] Jones, *Studies in Mystical Religion*, 448. The sect had died out by the end of the eighteenth century, but many of its followers, Jones argues, likely followed the movement of Fox as an alternative.

forms of the 'false church'. Many dissenters believed one could experience inner redemption on earth. But for Fox and the early Quakers, this inward conforming to the image of Christ, first through convincement then by the cultivation of good works and perfection in behaviour, led to both the rising up and the necessary *preservation* of the True Church as a whole. A precise, public and orderly marriage approbation process ensured endogamy and divinely directed matrimony, keeping the unity of the True Church and the divine intact.

Primitive Christianity: The True Church and Gospel Order

As I have demonstrated earlier, the Quakers sought to identify themselves with the qualities of the apostolic church, which they perceived as the original True Church.[115] The coming forth of the True Church was understood as the reawakening of primitive Christianity, where pure Christianity within the True Church was alive and well. The Quakers regarded the original apostolic Christians as followers of God who never relied on external forms in worship, but were only guided directly by God within.[116] A component of primitive Christianity, which the early Quakers believed was evinced in the apostolic age and which they heartily adopted into their own worship and marriage approbation process, was the concept of 'good order' or what would become known as Gospel Order. Pink Dandelion provides a useful summary of the term Gospel Order:

> This is the name given to the ecclesiastical system laid down by Farnworth, Fox, and Fell in the 1660s. It has been seen by historians and sociologists as pragmatic and shrewd, contributing to the survival of the group. Theologically, it was claimed that this was the gospel order, i.e. the divinely ordained structure for the chosen people to work within.[117]

Dandelion further elaborates that Gospel Order was 'the most significant element in the shift towards a consolidated sectarian spirituality' which was clearly interpreted by the Scottish Quaker apologist Robert Barclay.[118] In 1676,

---

[115] See pp. 122–44.

[116] The historian Howard Brinton explains, 'Both the religion of the prophets of the Old Testament and the religion of the early Christian Church were based, not on form and tradition, but … on the immediate experience of God in the soul' (Brinton, *Friends for 300 Years*, 17).

[117] Dandelion, *An Introduction to Quakerism*, 48. Richard Farnworth was a prominent early Quaker from Yorkshire who died in 1666 (Barbour and Roberts [Eds], *Early Quaker Writings*, 591).

[118] Dandelion, *An Introduction to Quakerism*, 53.

Barclay introduced a defence of Quakers with the intention of vindicating them from 'those that accuse them of disorder and confusion on the one hand, and from such as calumniate them with tyranny and imposition on the other'.[119] Barclay stated he also wanted to demonstrate how the Quakers were a people engaged in the restoration of the order of the apostolic church:

> As the true and pure principles of the Gospel are restored by their testimony, so is also the ancient apostolic ORDER of the Church of Christ re-established amongst them, and settled upon its right basis and foundation.[120]

Barclay, amongst other Quakers, based the Friends' adherence to good order on the examples set by their 'ancient' Christian spiritual ancestors, who for them set the example for Quaker harmonious meetings, in which all were originally 'led and guided by the Spirit of Christ'.[121]

Barclay also looked to scriptural accounts of the apostolic church for support of the benefits of 'good order', contending 'the apostles and primitive Christians did practice order and government' as in the 'history of Acts' where one can read about the first meeting 'the apostles and brethren held together after the ascension of Christ' in which they had to choose who would replace Judas.[122] This meeting was followed by a series of other meetings addressing various doctrinal and practical issues such as financial distribution to the poor and the appointment of men to lead this work. When religious issues such as whether or not to circumcise were discussed in meetings, Barclay praised the 'primitive Saints' for not following 'their own minds and wills' but rather 'told their judgments and came to a positive conclusion' in unity, which 'pleased not only them, but the Holy Ghost'.[123] Like his fellow Quakers, Barclay believed God was a 'God of order, and not of confusion'.[124] Based on this view he maintained 'the Spirit of God doth now as well as in the days of old lead his people into those things which are orderly, and of a good report'.[125] As God was restoring the church through the Quakers to the pure state of Christianity so too was God restoring order. Barclay contended as the Lord 'has again restored the Truth unto its primitive integrity and simplicity', the Lord has 'also gathered and is

---

[119] Barclay, *The Anarchy of the Ranters and Other Libertines* (1676). (Barbour and Roberts [Eds], *Early Quaker Writings*, 515.)
[120] Ibid.
[121] Ibid.
[122] Ibid, 524.
[123] Ibid.
[124] Ibid, 530.
[125] Ibid.

gathering us into the good order, discipline and government of his own Son the Lord Jesus Christ'.[126]

Barclay further believed some in the Quaker fold had been granted by God specific responsibilities of 'watching for the souls of their brethren'.[127] In their meetings and marriage approbation process, we have seen Friends 'watching for the souls of their brethren' and giving thorough account of their actions and preparedness for marriage through investigation and papers of condemnation and contrition, as well as their careful certificate procedure. Barclay warned of the repercussions of being out of the watchful eyes of one's community, and the happy outcome for those who do submit to such order:

> Those who through unwatchfulness, the secret corruption of their own hearts, and the mysterious or hidden temptations of the Enemy, have fallen into his snares ... who being seasonable warned by those that keep their habitation, and faithful overseers in the Church, have been again restored by unfeigned repentance ... [and] have rejoiced that others watched over them for their good.[128]

Shortly after Barclay wrote his abovementioned work defending the benefits and primitive purity of good order, in 1682 Quaker William Gibson wrote a general epistle to all Quakers in which he likewise encouraged the model of 'order' for marriage which he believed was found in scripture.[129] Gibson commended the Quakers as 'Servants of God' who were joined in marriage by God in 'a comely Order'.[130] Gibson believed following an orderly, public process in marriage approbation, as followed by the 'true Christians', prevented both clandestine marriages and any possible hurt or wrong that befell one getting

---

[126] Ibid, 521. 'Now He, that was careful for his Church and people in old times hath not been wanting to us in our day; but as he has again restored the Truth unto its primitive integrity and simplicity ... the Lord hath also gathered and is gathering us into the good order, discipline and government of his own Son the Lord Jesus Christ. Therefore he hath laid care upon some beyond others, who watch for the soul of their brethren, as they that must give account'.

[127] Ibid.

[128] Ibid.

[129] Gibson, *A General epistle given forth in obedience to the God of peace for the preservation and increase of charity and unity*. This is the same epistle referred to in chapter one (pp. 89–90) in which Gibson, like Fox and Fell, expressed his rejection of the use of the wedding ring.

[130] Ibid, 82. 'Observe something briefly concerning the Marriage of the Servants of God, as recorded in the holy Scripture ... Their Marriages are not clandestine, dark or hidden, but they are joyned together by the Lord God, to whom only belongs the right of joyning his People in Marriage, and the great God of Order carries on this work in a comely Order'.

married.[131] Gibson defended the Quakers as 'true Christians' who restored 'order' to marriage.

An orderly marriage approbation process followed by an orderly wedding provided the Quakers with a viable vehicle through which they could demonstrate they were involved in the re-establishment of the True Church of the ancient apostles. Marriages approbated by God and the community, conducted in front of witnesses within ceremonies void of any external forms, followed by the production of certificates – all of this was a reflection of the Gospel Order of the primitive church. Within Fox's framework of the several stages of the church – the age of primitive Christianity, the night of apostasy, followed by the subsequent rise of the True Church through the Quaker community – he believed marriages amongst Christians followed similar stages. After the Fall, when humanity was driven from Paradise, Fox explained marital unions went through several phases or 'manners' including:

> The manner of the Marriage amongst the Christians in the Primitive times; And the Marriage of the Apostate Christians, and Jews and Gentiles, where hardness of heart was, there men put a sunder.[132]

As the True Church ended the night of apostasy, the Quakers brought back the 'true' marriage form practised by the primitive church: the manner of 'Marriage amongst the Christians in the Primitive times' in which a couple was joined by God where 'there were people present as witnesses'.[133]

In 1679, during one of his stays at Swarthmoor, Fox wrote a twenty page epistle entitled *The true marriage declared* in which he summarised scriptural examples of 'holy men and women' who were never married by priests (even the 'High Priest' Jesus Christ) but rather were married before witnesses, followed by a recording of the marriage in a book:[134]

> Did Christ or any of his Twelve Disciples marry them in Cana of Gallile, where they were called to the marriage, He that was a Priest higher then the Heavens did He, or His Disciples use that Ceremony to marry them ... you cannot prove neither in the Old nor New Testament, that either Priest or Bishop, or Jews Priests

---

[131] Ibid, 83. 'Notice is given in a publick manner among the People of God several times, to prevent wrong or hurt to any thereby (as much as in us lies) this in short concerning Marriage, as it is owned and practiced amongst the true Christians, who have been and yet are by many (reproachfully) called Quakers'. See also chapter one, p. 42.
[132] Fox, *Concerning Marriage* (1661), 1.
[133] Ibid, 3.
[134] George Fox, *The true marriage declared* (London, 1679), 7.

or Christ or his Apostles married any, But Gods people tooke one another before wittnesses, and Recorded it in a Booke.[135]

Fox further praised all marriages done 'according to the practice of the holy men ... in the Scriptures of Truth', which included good documentation:

> God Joyneth and marrieth and his people are witnesses, and then in the same Meeting a Certificate of their so takeing one another is drawne up and Recorded in a Booke, with the place, day and yeare to satisfie all that it may Concerne.[136]

In 1681 Fox instructed Friends in Birmingham to not 'goe disorderly together in marriage ... contrary to the practice of the holy men of god', but rather when they 'goe together' in marriage, 'let there be noe less than a dozen of friends & relations present (according to former order)'.[137] Looking to the pattern of the apostles, Fox and the early Quakers believed they evinced 'primitive Christianity' through a marriage process of approbation which reflected 'good order' through clear documentation of the entire process from approbation to marriage.

Adherence to a scriptural orderly process of marriage 'according to former order' was a means by which early Quakers could combat the fear that their 'adversaries might the more boldly accuse' the Quakers as 'overturners of all human and Christian order'.[138] Gospel Order, evident in the apostolic church, was not only a practice that ensured no one could accuse the Quakers of disorder, but was also an identifying marker of the True Church.[139] In his 1681 sermon in Birmingham mentioned above, Fox, like Barclay and Gibson, believed the orderly meetings, once held by the primitive Christians, fell away when the 'Church fled into the wilderness':

> [Amongst] the Christians in the first age there was a man's meeting set up at Jerusalem to see that nothing was lacking, which was the gospel order according to Jesus. And this continued as long as they lived in the spirit of life and power of god, but when the apostasy came in then the true Church fled into the wilderness.[140]

---

[135] Ibid.

[136] Ibid, 8. As noted in chapter one, Fox's assertion of a biblical precedent of recording marriage in a book is historically erroneous. See p. 49 n. 87.

[137] George Fox, *The Epistles and Advices of George Fox to Birmingham Friends* (1681). (Cited in Lloyd, *Quaker Social History*, 177.)

[138] Barclay, *The Anarchy of the Ranters and Other Libertines*. (Barbour and Roberts [Eds], *Early Quaker Writings*, 533.)

[139] Ibid.

[140] Fox, *The Epistles and Advices of George Fox to Birmingham Friends*. Cited in Lloyd, *Quaker Social History*, 177.

Thus, with the return of Christ and His 'true church' came the return of Gospel Order.

For Fox, the Quaker orderly process of marriage collectively testified to the inward witness of God, 'salvation' and the preservation of 'unity' between God and his 'true church':

> And the true Church come up out of the wilderness and the man child which was caught up into heaven come down againe to rule all nations with a rod iron. Then the mariage of the Lamb is come and the lamb and the saints shall have the victory and the everlasting gospel shall be preached againe [as] was amongst the apostles; and the gospel order shall be set up amongst them; and a mans meting as was at the first conversion & soe that nothing be lacking in the Church.[141]

Christ the Lamb reunited with his bride, the True Church, resulted in harmonious, unified meetings that reflected Gospel Order.

Marriage of the Lamb: Unity and Witness in Quaker Marriages

Fox and Fell also built a marriage discipline which required all Quakers to be married in good order in front of witnesses. Fox dissuaded his followers from clandestine marriages by pointing to what he perceived was a clear scriptural precedent of marriage by witnesses. He wrote in 1659 of the marriages of Isaac, Jacob, Boaz and David found in the Old Testament, showing biblical precedence for marriage by God in front of witnesses.[142] He further noted the marriage at Canaan in the New Testament, which was witnessed by many including Jesus and his disciples:

> There was a marriage in Canaan, and Jesus his Mother and his Disciples were called to it; So you may see there were people present as witnesses; things were not done in a corner or in a hole.[143]

---

[141] Ibid, 179–80.

[142] Fox, *Concerning Marriage* (1661), 2. Fox wrote of the Old Testament precedence for marriage: 'The manner of Isaacks taking a wife ... People were present when he took a wife, and Rebekahs friends blessed her and said, be thou Mother of Thousands; and Isaac took her into his Mothers Tent, and there took her to Wife. At the marriage of Jacob, Laban gathered together all men of the place (and so there was people) Gen. 29.22 ... At Boaz and Ruth all the People and Elders that were in the Gates were witnesses, and said, *we are witnesses* ... And David sent his servants to Abigail, and communed with her to take her to wife, and she came with five Damsels, and became his wife, 1 Sam. 25.39.42'.

[143] Fox, *Concerning Marriage* (1661), 3.

Marriages in 'a corner or in a hole' or 'clandestine marriages' were not only undesirable due to the risk of marriages between those not legally available to marry, they were also unscriptural according to Fox, and were not the type of marriages primitive Christians conducted. In effect, Fox suggested those who did not follow the scriptural examples of marriage by witnesses were essentially contradicting the behaviour of the prophets, including Christ himself.[144]

Fell used similar reasoning early in the Quaker movement. In 1654, when Quaker Cuthbert Hunter was charged with adultery and sent to prison by Judge Hugh Wyndham for being married in a Quaker meeting rather than by a priest or magistrate, Margaret Fell defended Hunter's manner of marriage in front of witnesses as being in accordance with the examples found in scripture amongst the 'holy men of god':

> And for the false accusation, of the said Judge windham; which did accuse Cuthbert Hunter, for Adultry & fornication, because he took a wife; before witnesses; & was not marryed with the priests of the world, which marry people for money; & for giving of them a forme of words ... but took a wife according to the mannour found in scripture; (witnesses;) the holy men of god, & did not goe to the priests to give them money: for marrying, for there is noe such example in scripture.[145]

When Judge Wyndham argued their manner of marriage was contrary to the 'Law of god' and 'Contrary to the Law of man' she stated his accusations were unfounded, declaring his accusation false 'for the law of God witnesses the same' and 'the holy men of god witnesses the same'.[146] The law of God, according

---

[144] Contrary to many Protestants, who believed the biblical days of God's direct revelation to humanity were over, the Quakers identified with the prophets of Israel believing they were also receiving direct revelation from God (Brinton, *Friends for 300 Years*, 16). Prophetic activity and writings abated after the restoration of the monarchy (Gill, *Women in the Seventeenth-Century Quaker Community*, 2). Thomas Hamm explains, 'Public demonstrations like interrupting church services and going naked as a sign faded away. The Lamb's War no longer looked toward political and social apocalypse. The basic framework of Quaker belief – the ministry of all believers, spiritual equality, direct revelation, waiting worship – remained the same. But it would be less exuberant, more structured' (Thomas Hamm, *The Quakers in America* [New York, NY: Columbia University Press, 2003], 25–6). I argue the Quakers' self-identity as the True Church remained in fact after the restoration of the monarchy, and was largely perpetuated through their Meeting system and marriage discipline.

[145] *Margaret Fell to Judge Hugh Wyndham* (1654). (Glines [Ed.], *Undaunted Zeal*, 108–9.)

[146] Ibid, 109.

to Fell, overrode the law of the apostate Church of England and the civil law, making the Quaker marriage system legitimate.

Fox further argued while the 'heathen went together like beasts, and the Apostate Christians since the daies of the Apostles, have done the same', the Quakers, being joined by God in front of witnesses, were 'redeemed from the Gentiles marriages and the Apostate Christians marriages' through their meeting practice which ensured God's joining.[147] Fox believed the Quaker discipline of marriage by witnesses, as in the days of the apostles, ensured God joined the couple 'as it was in the beginning', in a way not available to 'apostate' Christians.[148] As each Quaker believed they had the 'witness of God' within them they felt they were sensitive to knowing the desires of the divine.[149]

Evidence of having 'unity with' the intended marriage was thus of utmost importance. In her epistle on marriage written in 1656, Fell stressed repeatedly the need for the meeting having 'unity with' an intended marriage. 'Having unity' could be evidenced only after a marriage was brought to a meeting to be 'tryed and weighed in the light, that each may have a sure testimony in the light, & life, which cannot be blotted out'.[150] As demonstrated in chapter one, the early Quaker approbation process allowed for an ample amount of time to ensure that no one 'sensed' a leading contrary to the couple's leadings, or had any negative feelings or legitimate concerns about the union, whether legally or spiritually. When the time came to marry, those in the meeting who felt moved could then testify to the positive sense they had that God was indeed joining the couple. As Fell instructed, once the couple felt 'unity' with the Spirit to join in marriage, they were to bring it to the meeting, to 'try and weigh' it in the light, to see if the meeting as well had 'unity with it'.[151] As the Bristol Meeting minutes testified, if the couple did not gain 'unity in the light' with the meeting, their marriage

---

[147] Fox, *Concerning Marriage* (1661), 6.

[148] Ibid, 5–6. Fox instructed, 'After a convenient time, and the thing be seen, felt, and had unity with, and an Assembly of about twelve Friends met together, they may speak their Testimony (that all may take notice who are the persons) as they are moved, how the Lord hath joyned them together in Marriage ... And that those things that cannot be owned by all Friends, & have unitie with all in the Power and Spirit of God, may not be recorded, and Unrighteousness, and Filthiness, Fornication, Whoredom, and Adultery may be shut out, that the witness of God in all Friends may in that which is done be answered'.

[149] Ibid.

[150] Fell, *To Friends, An Epistle on Marriage*. (Glines [Ed.], *Undaunted Zeal*, 195.)

[151] Ibid. 'And so having unity in the light & life, & a clear sight of being joined in the lord, then declare it to the church, to be tried in the light, which is one in all, that so the church may have unity with it in the same light & life. Let there bee a space after the first declaration to the meetings, that if any have any thing to object against the things, they may have time to speak in the fear of the lord ... [in the meeting] that so friends ... may try and weigh the objection in the light, & if it be found contrary to the truth, let it be condemned

would be condemned and not approbated, but if it was 'feelt in the unity' they were free to marry. Fox, like Fell, believed collective listening and testifying to the witness of God in meetings ensured all things were 'done in the Power, Life, Truth, and Wisdom of the Lord God, and in Unity' in order to 'serve God in a New life, and one heart'.[152] According to Fox, collective testimonies also served to 'shut out' all 'Unrighteousness, … Filthiness, Fornication, Whoredom, and Adultery' – both within the marriage itself and within the collective Quakers' experience of the 'marriage of the Lamb'.[153]

Being attentive and obedient to the light within was a way the early Quaker could be faithful to Christ their husband, the 'Lamb', and thereby maintain their collective and individual unity with the divine.

> And all that live in the Spirit of God have a Testimony, & unity with the marriages whom God Joyns together, with his spirit and truth in the restoration.[154]

With 'the witness of God in all Friends', or the light of Christ, they could thus witness and affirm that indeed the marriage was 'of God', marking them as a people reinstating the primitive True Church of the apostles, set apart from the false, apostate church.[155] As we have seen, the 'marriage of the Lamb' was not a future event waiting to unfold for the early Quaker, but was rather perceived to be their present condition, as the prominent early Quaker Edward Burrough explained in 1660:

> The marriage of the Lamb *is* come unto many … and here is his wife that made herself ready, and is prepared for the Bridegroom … for this is the Virgin unto whom he is joyned, that hath put away all other lovers, and loveth the Lord with all the heart … who is clothed with perfect beauty and innocency, and covered with Divine Righteousness, in which there is no spot, being delivered out of the wilderness, and freed from her mourning state, is no more separated from her husband … and is married to the Lamb.[156]

---

with the light … But those who in the fear of the lord … felt in the unity … they may take each other in the meeting, & speak what the unlimited power & spirit gives utterance'.

[152] Fox, *Concerning Marriage* (1661), 6.
[153] Ibid.
[154] Fox, *The true marriage declared*, 10–11.
[155] Fox, *Concerning Marriage* (1661), 6.
[156] Edward Burrough, *A general epistle to all the saints being a visitation of the Fathers love unto the whole flock of God: To be read in all the assemblies, of them, that meet together to worship the Father in spirit and truth* (Henry E. Huntington Library and Art Gallery, Wing B 6005), 7–8. Italics mine. Burrough did not quote biblical passages directly, but was likely borrowing from John 3:29 in which there are images of Christ the Lamb as the bridegroom

Fox in 1679 echoed the belief that the True Church was presently married to Christ, and further suggested this relationship enabled the Quakers to hear God's voice:

> For the Saints, that are Marryed to Christ, and receive him, they are his Sheep, that hear his Voice, and according to his promise, he will dwell in them ... for they that are Marryed to Christ do enjoy him in his Light and Spirit.[157]

The metaphorical language of Christ and his bride employed by many early Quakers to demonstrate the union between Christ and his church is reminiscent of the language of the Song of Songs. Sharon Achinstein notes how the Quaker Thomas Ellwood used the image of the marriage bed in a devotional poem, where in 'his imagination he became the loyal bride to his God' as he described 'his devotion with the marital imagery common to Song of Songs'.[158] The Quaker poet Mary Southworth Mollineux likewise utilised the imagery of the love between Christ and his bride, the True Church, from Song of Songs. Achinstein describes how Mollineux, in her poetry, used romance and erotic desire as an agency to communicate her devotion to Christ.[159] The imagery of the early Quakers as the True Church married to Christ the Lamb was also illuminated both in Fox and Fell's description of their own marriage and in the various testimonies shared during their marriage approbation process, all of which will be further explored in the following chapter.[160] But for now, it is important to highlight the early Quakers' connection between their identity as the True Church married to Christ the Lamb, and how this identity was believed to have effected both direct revelation from God through the inward light and spiritual unity amongst one another in the Quaker community. Marriage with

---

to his church, and also from Revelation 19:7–9 which describes 'the marriage of the Lamb' for which 'his wife hath made herself ready'.

[157] George Fox and John Burnyeat, *A New-England-fire-brand quenched something in answer unto a lying, slanderous book, entituled George Fox digged out of his burrows, &c. printed at Boston in the year 1676, of one Roger Williams of Providence in New-England* (London, 1678), 18. Henry E. Huntington Library and Art Gallery, Wing F 1864.

[158] Sharon Achinstein, 'Romance of the Spirit: Female Sexuality and Religious Desire in Early Modern England', *English Literary History*, 69 no 2 (Summer 2002): 413–38; pp. 419–20. Achinstein explains, 'Although the biblical poem Song of Songs represents erotic desires through powerful, concrete imagery of two lovers, in Christian interpretation that erotic relation was allegorized as a tale of Christ's love for his Church as well as the mystery of the apocalypse' (Achinstein, 'Romance of the Spirit: Female Sexuality and Religious Desire in Early Modern England, 428).

[159] Ibid., 435. 'Romance became deployed by a feminine devotional tradition precisely because it worked to accommodate erotic desires as agency'.

[160] See pp. 199ff.

the Lamb carried with it immediate and tangible results. 'Married to the Lamb' through the inward light of Christ within the conscience of the individual, early Quakers believed each Friend was in effect a physical representative of God's truth.[161] Without witnesses stating they had 'unity' in agreement that a couple was led by God to be married, there was no communal confirmation that God had indeed joined the couple. The presence of the inward light, through the members of the True Church, thus had to confirm in unity God's leading them to marry. The marriage certificate and its signatures by witnesses provided evidence on paper of God's presence and leading in the marriage. Through the communal approbation process of endogamous marriages joined by God in front of witnesses, the Quakers demonstrated their belief in the unifying presence of the divine and practically set themselves apart as the bride of Christ, the True Church, which has fled from the wilderness.

Threat to the Marriage of the Lamb: Marriage with the World

As discussed in chapter one, marriage with someone outside of the Quaker community posed several serious threats to the early Quakers. First, if a Quaker married an 'apostate Christian', it was evidence that the offending Quaker was being unfaithful to the True Church, had turned from the light of Christ within, and thereby was adulterating the True Church's 'marriage to the Lamb'. Second, exogamous marriage posed a threat to the spiritual unity of the Quaker community, which they believed they shared amongst one another as the True Church married to the Lamb. Making an intimate bond with someone from the world, or the 'false church', allowed the spirit of the world to enter and thus disrupt the spiritual unity of the Quakers with each other and with the Light. Returning to the spiritual dichotomies of Fox, one was either a member of the 'false church' or the True Church. All exogamous marriages were considered marriages with the 'false church', as the Quaker community sought to be set apart from the world and its fallen customs, including the prohibition of marriage with non-Quakers. Quoting the apostle Paul from the New Testament epistle of First Corinthians, Fox reminded his followers, 'The Apostle saith, "be not unequally yoaked with unbelievers, for what fellowship hath Believers with Infidels", 1 Cor. 6'.[162]

Fox cited Numbers 25, which tells of the Israelites who married women from other tribes. According to Fox, this offence was so grave it led to God's destruction of the world:

---

[161] Dandelion, *An Introduction to Quakerism*, 46.
[162] Fox, *Concerning Marriage* (1661), 3.

The Old world was destroyed and the beginning of their destruction was thorow their bad Marriages. The Jewes who broak the Law of Marriage that took them Wives of other Nations and Religions, God destroyed three and twenty thousand of them in one day 1 Cor. 10.[163]

For the Quakers in the seventeenth century, as for the ancient Israelites, Fox believed exogamy was such a severe offence it could result in one's spiritual destruction:

> But such as mingled with the heathen and unbelievers, and followed strange flesh, they went from the spirit, they lost the sonship ... and such as marry with unbelievers and heathen, go contrary to the law of God, and grieve him and their righteous parents.[164]

Fox concluded those who disobediently marry unbelievers 'grieve the Lord and corrupt the earth and themselves when they goe against his good Spirit ... and goe from God's joyning into bad marriages'.[165] Going 'contrary to the law of God' which forbade 'following strange flesh' and marrying unbelievers, which caused grief to both God and possibly to one's 'righteous parents', was thus to be avoided at all costs, as Quakers strove to be obedient to God. Faithfulness and fidelity to the Lamb, as evinced in unity and witness, was their identifying mark as the True Church.

Resisting Exogamy on Spiritual Grounds: The Proposal of Colonel West to Margaret Fell the Younger

A very early and telling slice of history, which exhibits the above theological and spiritual concerns of Quakers regarding exogamy, comes from Margaret Fell's daughter, Margaret Fell the Younger. In 1656, the same year Fell wrote her first epistle on marriage, Margaret Fell the Younger received a proposal of marriage from Colonel William West. Colonel West, a non-Quaker and a member of parliament, was a friend of the Fell family. His proposal of marriage was approved by Judge Fell but rejected by his daughter on religious and theological grounds. The written responses from both Fell and Margaret Fell the Younger provide an apropos illustration of some of the earliest signs of theological grappling with marriage, relying largely on the 'living metaphor' of being essentially married

---

[163] George Fox, *Right Marriage* (1679), Swarthmore Manuscripts, vol. V, folio 44 (The Society of Friends Library, London).

[164] Fox, *Epistle CCLXII*. (Hopper, *The Works of George Fox Vol. 1*, 334.)

[165] Ibid.

to the Lamb.[166] As Colonel West was not a Quaker, the younger Margaret was in a position of trying to explain to both her father and Colonel West why she, as a Quaker, could not marry a non-Quaker. Fell, having been approached by Colonel West to explain their 'peculiar' practice of marriage within meetings, wrote a letter justifying the Quaker marriage process on theological grounds.

Explaining the Quakers as a people redeemed from 'under the worlds wayes', Fell argued they were in a position of obeying God while disobeying the law of the land which required marriage by priest or magistrate. Both Fell and her daughter grounded their respective arguments on the theological notion that as Quakers, they were to obey God over parent or law. Fell began her letter to Colonel West stating she could 'see A trouble upon thee as Concerning our friends, in that wee cannot Consent to submit to your Law to Come under it'.[167] West had apparently written to Fell asking why Quakers married in a peculiar way – within meetings, and without clergy or magistrate. Fell set up her entire response with the dichotomy between his laws, which he followed as a member of both parliament and of the world, and the laws of God, which the Quakers followed. She wrote the Quakers were not subject to the laws of parliament in regards to marriage, but rather subject to the laws of God, their 'Lawgiver':

> Who is the Judge of the world, who Judges in righteousness & equity, And to this we are subject & by this are wee guided … And soe under the Lawes of man, which is made in the will of man, wee cannot Come, nor stoop to that Law which is made by the Carnall mind, which the Apostle saith is not subject to the law of god[,] neither can wee, who are guided by the Law of god, & subject to it, wee cannot be subject to that which is contrary to this Law.[168]

For Fell, the 'Law of god' could potentially override the laws of the world, or parliament, when they contradicted each other.

In the case of marriage, the laws of the world and parliament were indicative of the 'graven' images of the apostate church and fallen world. Fell appealed to the 'witness' of the light within West's 'conscience' not to follow the laws of the fallen, cursed world, which went contrary to both the law of God and to the scriptures:

> For wee doe not come under the curse, for our Law saith[,] cursed be the man that maketh any graven or molten Image, which is an abomination to the Lord,

---

[166] 'Living metaphor' is a term I am borrowing from Ng, *Literature and the Politics of Family in Seventeenth-Century England*, 200–202. See introduction, pp. 26–7.

[167] Margaret Fell, *To Colonel William West* (1656). (Glines [Ed.], *Undaunted Zeal*, 189.)

[168] Ibid, 189–90.

> And whether this Law bee, not an Image, which hath bene set up and acted out of the Light, & out of the Truth of god[,] I appeale to that in thy Conscience which cannot beare false witness, but is A swift wittnesse against the Idollator & false swearer[;] & this witness wittnesseth against this Law, which is acted Contrary to scripture, & Contrary to all that ever was or is taught of god.[169]

According to Fell, if one was listening to the 'light' within one's conscience, one would be against all aforementioned forms and images of the fallen world and 'false church', including the laws which forced people to marry by priest or magistrate.

Fell further explained to West if Quakers were prosecuted for not following the law of the world, they would be protected by God for 'keeping from under the curse':

> And if wee suffer by this Law, it is nothing to us, soe Long as wee keep in that where the blessing is, from under the Curse, through our enemyes Come in one way[,] ... they shall be smitten before our face, and this wee know for our god is A faithfull god.[170]

Like Fox, Fell believed those who did not marry according to God's instructions – joined by God, with a fellow Quaker, in the presence of witnesses – would be subject to punishment by God, just as the disobedient Israelites before the flood. Following the laws of God, as opposed to the laws of the 'false church', set marriages amongst God's True Church apart from the marriages of the world. For Fell, the Quaker way of marriage was indicative of the 'free' True Church:

> And soe now here I have clearly laid before thee, why wee cannot Come under the Law which is made in the house of darkness & bondage ... the children of this world marry & are given in marriage, & ever did before the flood, there they were found, & before the comeing of the son of man their they are found; but the children of Light is not of this world[,] for the Light is the Condemnation of the world; and beares witness against the world that the deeds thereof are evill, And this redeemes from under the worlds wayes and Customes.[171]

Fell concluded her letter, 'Our marriages which is in the Light, whom the Lord Joynes together no man can putt asunder', as the 'wayes and Customes of the world' allowed.[172] If the Lord's will brought the couple together, rather than

---

[169] Ibid, 190.
[170] Ibid.
[171] Ibid, 190–91.
[172] Ibid.

one's personal will, the anticipated outcome was a marriage that would last, as no human will or action could undo what God had done.[173]

The same year Fell wrote the above letter, her daughter Margaret wrote two letters in which she explained her reasons for refusing to marry Colonel West. The first was addressed to her father, Judge Fell, and the second was addressed to Colonel West. Her refusal of such an offer was unusual for the time, particularly because the Colonel was an esteemed member of society, a friend of Judge Fell and his family, and the Judge's first choice for his daughter. It is plausible to suggest Judge Fell had difficulty understanding his daughter's decision, as he was not a Quaker, and the younger Margaret's letter appears to be an attempt to defend Quaker perceptions of marriage. Additionally, it is worth noting that the Judge did not force his daughter to marry against her wishes, likely because he appeared to be tolerant of Quaker sentiments and allowed some freedom to his wife in these matters. Apparently he afforded his daughters the same flexibility, but perhaps not without a little resistance as the following letter suggests. The younger Margaret's letter at the very least showed her great concern that her father completely understood her reasons for not marrying Colonel West.

Strikingly, the younger Margaret began her letter with a rather forthright and challenging question, which appears to verge almost on reproach:

> Why will not thou trust god who hath been good and gracious unto thee, and tenderly, and faithfully preserved thee from many dangers, whose long suffering & patience, is exercised every day, towards thee, though thou goe on in transgression and rebelion against him, it is his mercy that preserves or else the transgressor would bee consumed.[174]

Challenging her father for his disobedience to God, she echoed her mother's warning to Colonel West for not following God's laws but rather the laws of the world. The younger Margaret appeared to be upset that her father had

---

[173] Thomas Clarkson, *A Portraiture of Quakerism, Taken from a view of the moral education, discipline, peculiar customs, religious principles, political and civil economy, and character of the Society of Friends in Three Volumes* (London: R. Taylor and Co., 1807). According to the Quaker Thomas Clarkson, at least up until 1807 divorce amongst Quakers was virtually unknown in the British Courts. Clarkson wrote of the Quaker marriages, 'As married, they may said to be a happy people. Hence the detailers of scandal have rarely had it in their power to promulgate a Quaker-adultery. Nor have the lawyers had an opportunity, in our public courts, to proclaim a Quaker-divorce' (Clarkson, *A Portraiture of Quakerism Vol. 2*, 4). The Quaker demographer Richard Vann concurs with Clarkson's conclusion about divorce and its virtual non-existence in the early Quaker record (Vann and Eversley, *Friends in Life and Death*, 84 n 8).

[174] Margaret Fell the Younger, *To Judge Thomas Fell and Colonel William West from Margaret Fell, Jr.* (1656). (Glines [Ed.], *Undaunted Zeal*, 192–3.)

encouraged her to take Colonel West's hand in marriage even though he was not a Quaker. When the younger Margaret disagreed with her father, she demonstrated a measure of freedom and independence. She opposed her father's will and chose to obey God instead.[175]

Thus began the younger Margaret's explanation to her father about the dangers of disobediently marrying a person who was not a Quaker. She defended her refusal with the following argument:

> Would thou have, thy children to forsake xt ... Jesus, the husband of his church, and chosen ones, for a husband of the world, in this his day, wn [when] many that hath husbands is made to deny theire will for xt who hath said[,] he that will not forsake wife and husband or father and mother for me is not worthy of mee.[176]

If she married a 'husband of the world', she would be forced to 'forsake' her 'husband' of the True Church, Christ. Just as Fox and Fell instructed Quakers to be faithful to 'the marriage of the Lamb', the younger Margaret argued she could not marry a person of the world, and be faithful to Christ. All Quakers, male and female, were required to be faithful and obedient to their husband, Christ the Lamb, head of the True Church.[177]

Apparently Judge Fell was not happy when he had first heard of the younger Margaret's choice not to marry West. The younger Margaret responded with the following to her father:

---

[175] The historian David Cressy suggests fathers in the gentry class may have experienced a loosening of power over their daughters during the social upheaval of the mid 1600s: 'Sir John Oglander's reluctant acquiescence to the marriage of his daughter Briget to a husband of whom he disapproved reveals the power of the convention of matrimonial arrangement among the gentry, even in its violation. In 1649, with the traditional order shattered, the royalist gentry debased, and his own fortune and authority undermined, Oglander could not even rule his daughter' (Cressy, *Birth, Marriage, and Death*, 242). There is no evidence of a great disruption of Judge Fell's authority in the household, save the above correspondence, as well as Margaret Fell the Elder's active leadership in a movement that was largely outside of Judge Fell's domain. However, familial harmony and Judge Fell's legal and social protection of his Quaker family are apparent.

[176] Fell the Younger, *To Judge Thomas Fell and Colonel William West from Margaret Fell, Jr.* (Glines [Ed.], *Undaunted Zeal*, 193.)

[177] Though Fell the Younger remained within a gendered role of obedience, she used a metaphor that included all Quakers, male and female. Achinstein points out that Thomas Ellwood in a poem utilising the imagery of Song of Songs had a 'flash of gender transformation' as he took on the 'female role in marriage' and pledged 'sexual chastity to a husband' as marriage provided 'the best metaphor for the desire of a human for the divine' (Achinstein, 'Romance of the Spirit: Female Sexuality and Religious Desire in Early Modern England', 420). See pp. 152–4 of this work for a discussion of Christ as husband of the bride, the True Church.

> And what is it that thou children doe, that thou saith they kill thy heart any more[,] but forsake the world for xt sake, which all must doe that will have him and they that have Christ for there husband[,] have they not enough, but with this thou art not content.[178]

She further reproached her father for not being 'willing to waite upon him, until hee give them husbands in Christ'.[179] She was certain if she remained 'chaste to the lord', Christ would bring a husband in his time and therefore posed the question to her father 'what reason had thou to murmer at this condition' when 'the apostle [Paul] gives his testimony of it to bee the best, not to chuse but what the lord chuseth?'[180] Thus, in line with the Quaker practice of waiting on God to bring a mate, as God had brought Eve to Adam, the younger Margaret effectively told her father she longed to marry not whom he chose, but whom God alone chose.

In her letter to Colonel West, the younger Margaret was not as reproachful as she was to her father. Instead, she focused on explicating why she, as a Quaker, could not marry a man who was not a Quaker. She began with the following assertion:

> They that will owne us, must first owne god, to bee theire guide and teacher, and come into the unyty of the spirit[,] where the marriage of the lamb is.[181]

Like her fellow Quakers, she believed if she married a person who was not a Quaker, she would be marrying someone who was not in 'the unyty of the spirit[,] where the marriage of the lamb is'. Exogamous marriage was out of the question for the younger Margaret. If she married a man of the world, she believed she would be directly disobeying God's command and thus be unfaithful to the marriage of the Lamb. She explained:

> We cannot transgress against the command of the lord, who did command us not to make marreges with the heathen[.] deutrimeny 7[:]3 and 4[,] Josua 23 the 12 and 13[.] this was that, that brought the flood and caused the lord to complean, who said my spirit shall not always strive with man which is but flesh. It was this that caused the wrath of the lord to fal upon the children of Israell when they joyned themselves to the heathen. And the apostle[,] when he spake as unto his children[,] saith be not unequally yoked together with unbelievers.[182]

---

[178] Fell the Younger, *To Judge Thomas Fell and Colonel William West from Margaret Fell, Jr.* (Glines [Ed.], *Undaunted Zeal*, 193.)
[179] Ibid.
[180] Ibid.
[181] Ibid.
[182] Ibid.

Using an almost identical scriptural defence against exogamous marriages that, as we saw in the previous section, Fox would use almost three years later in his epistle on marriage, the younger Margaret believed scriptural evidence indicated those who married with the 'heathen' were in danger of destruction, while those who married believers were thus 'equally yoked' and obedient to God. Though the Quaker marriage discipline was in its infancy, the younger Margaret's refusal, and her reasoning behind it, fit the ideal picture of the Quaker marriage doctrine promoted, particularly by Fell the Elder at the time and for the remainder of her lifetime.

In the Quaker historical record, it was Margaret Fell and her daughter who were the forerunners in articulating this necessity for Quakers to forsake the laws of the world, and instead be faithful to the laws of God through their 'peculiar' marriage doctrine and practice. It appears from the very outset of the movement they believed it was necessary to marry a person who was likeminded spiritually, thereby obediently keeping within the 'true church'. They had a clear notion of waiting on God to bring one's spouse, and being faithful to God. Finally, in the younger Margaret's closing comment she referred to Christ as the one who 'created the male and female in his owne Image, which is undefiled'. Possibly in collaboration with her mother and Fox, the younger Margaret made clear theological links between human marriage, the marriage of the Lamb, the story of creation and the undefiled image of Christ.

'As it was in the beginning': Honourable Marriages and Undefiled Beds

As the Quakers rose from the 'wilderness', they believed their state of marriages mirrored the original marriage of Adam and Eve in the Garden of Eden – created, restored and brought together by God – and were thus often described as 'honourable marriages' with 'undefiled beds'.[183] While the terms 'honourable' and 'undefiled' differed slightly in meaning, they were often used together, and seen as inextricably linked. Marriage was considered honourable because it was God's ordinance, given by God at the time of humanity's innocent state. As the Quakers considered themselves restored to the image of the Second Adam, they believed their outward behaviour and actions, including marriage, exemplified this 'honourable' inward state. Their marriages, done by God and in the presence of God, were thus honourable as was the honourable marriage of Adam and Eve in the beginning. Likewise, their marriage-beds, indicating both marriage and the sexual act, were subsequently considered undefiled by sin. To understand better how early Quakers viewed their marriages as honourable, and their marriage-beds undefiled, it is useful to explore first both the meaning and

---

[183] Fox, *Concerning Marriage* (1661), 1.

theological implications of the terms 'honourable' and 'undefiled' which were so frequently used to describe Quaker marriages, and to consider second the theological implications of 'honour' and 'undefiled' in relation to sin.[184]

Various aspects regarding the notion of 'honour' appeared throughout early Quaker writings and applied to different aspects of their spirituality. Fox often juxtaposed God's honour with 'man's' or 'worldly' honour, encouraging his followers to seek only the honour of God.[185] Conferring honour to a social superior was strictly forbidden, as this action went directly against the Quakers' adherence to spiritual equality before God. An example of this can be found in the early Quaker practice of refusing 'hat-honour', the social ritual of taking off one's hat in the presence of those with a higher title or rank, believing this 'honour' was due only to God. In his *Journal*, Fox wrote of Quakers being imprisoned for resisting hat-honour, a practice he believed was 'of men':[186]

> As to the hat-honour, because I could not put off my hat to them [priests and professors], it set them all into a rage. But the Lord showed me that it was an honour below, which he would lay in the dust, and stain; – an honour which proud flesh looked for, but sought not the honour which came from God only; – an honour invented by men in the fall, and in the alienation from God ... but Christ saith, 'How can ye believe, who receive honour one of another, and seek not the honour that cometh from God only?'[187]

Fox argued Quakers 'saw how God would stain the world's honour and glory', while they were instructed 'not to seek that honour, nor give it' for they know 'the honour that cometh from God only'.[188]

In light of the above, the Quakers identified one's honour with the inward presence of God in the conscience. A person who had not succumbed to the

---

[184] Though it cannot be substantiated as a conscious semantic decision, it is possible to speculate the Quakers chose the term 'undefiled' rather than 'chaste' because 'undefiled' stresses the absence of sin *in toto*, while 'chaste' may be more directly associated with sexual purity.

[185] Faramerz Dabhoiwala, in a paper presented at Cambridge University in 1995, explained the function and importance of honour in early modern England, ' ... honour and reputation ... were part and parcel of how individuals in this society conceived of the relationship between the personal and the public. More particularly, they lay at the heart of two crucial issues: how people thought about social status, and about the differences between man and woman' (Dabhoiwala, 'The Construction of Honour, Reputation and Status in Late Seventeenth- and Early Eighteenth-Century England', *Transactions of the Royal Historical Society*, 6 no 6 [1996]: 201–13).

[186] Fox, *Journal Vol. 1* (1836), 329.

[187] Ibid, 114–15.

[188] Ibid, 321.

light or seed of God within was not honourable, while the person who had succumbed to the inward light was in effect in God's presence, and was thereby considered 'honourable'. In other words, honour came from God within, not from society or humans without. This notion is demonstrated in a letter by Fox to a magistrate in 1655, in which he contended that 'which is of God in every man's conscience' was the source of honour for all men:

> To the measure of God's Spirit in thee I may speak, that thou mayest consider, and come to rule for God; that thou mayest answer that which is of God in every man's conscience: for this is that, which bringeth to honour all men in the Lord.[189]

Similarly, William Penn juxtaposed the 'honour' of 'The Mind of the Holy Ghost' with the 'Age of Fools' relying on human wisdom in his day and age, making reference to the Gospel of Mark (7:21) which reads 'For it is from within, from the human heart, that evil intentions come':

> I was the more willing to add these Passages, to shew the Difference that there is between the *Mind of the Holy Ghost*, and the Notion that those Ages had of Fools, that deserve not *Honour*, and that which is generally meant by *Fools* and *Folly* in our Time; that we may the better understand the *Disproportion* there is between *Honour*, as then understood by the *Holy Ghost*, and those that were led thereby; and the Apprehension of it, and Practice of these latter Ages of Professed Christians.[190]

Penn, like Fox, associated 'honour' with the presence of God in the mind versus the dishonourable state of relying on the human mind, as the 'Fools' in his 'time' did during the ages of the 'false church'. The honourable state of the Quakers, the True Church, contradicted the dishonour of the apostate Church of England.

In the early Quaker mindset, an honourable state was not an unchangeable condition, but rather had to be maintained through virtuous behaviour and living. Therefore, an individual could, in effect, shun the light of God within. Once this happened, not only would that individual slip into what they considered dishonour and disrepute but they could potentially threaten the honour and reputation of the Quaker community. Losing honour through disorderly behaviour went hand in hand with losing one's restored unity with the divine and with one another, often described as being outside of the truth. In 1658, Fox wrote to his fellow Friends of staying 'in the truth', and thereby staying

---

[189] Ibid, 303.
[190] William Penn, *No Cross, No Crown. A Discourse Shewing The Nature And Discipline Of The Holy Cross Of Christ* (1668). (Printed in William Penn, *A Collection of the Works of William Penn, Vol. 1* [London: J. Sowle, 1726], 317.)

'in the honour', warning them against losing that honour by going outside of the truth:

> So that all Friends being kept in the truth, they are kept in the honour, they are honourable, for that will honour them: but if any lose the power, they lose the life, they lose their crown, they lose their honour ... and by losing the power, the Lamb comes to be slain.[191]

Staying in the honour and 'truth' was essential for the Quaker, while the danger of losing that crown of honour was ever present. As seen in their lengthy approbation process and orderly meetings, the early Quakers diligently tried to avoid disunity and dishonourable behaviour. In 1669, Fox wrote an epistle in which he reminded all Quaker meetings:

> For all the talkers of Christ and his gospel, that do not walk in him, dishonour him. And all uncleanness and looseness in all your meetings, judge and condemn with the light, power, and spirit of Christ; so that nothing may reign among you, but that which doth glorify Christ.[192]

Margaret Fell likewise exhorted her fellow Quakers in 1667, 'God will render to every man according to his deeds; to them who by patience continue in well doing, seek for glory, and honour, and immortality, and eternal life'.[193] The Quakers' occupation of investigating 'disorderly walking' and 'miscarriages' within their community exemplified their concern for the maintenance of individual and subsequently communal honour. As seen in chapter one, the Quaker preoccupation of protecting that God conferred honour in their marriage discipline, and conducting only honourable marriages, was critical to maintaining the honourable state of the True Church.

When Quakers spoke of honourable marriages, the theological implications of honour Quakers attributed to marriage differed slightly from their Protestant contemporaries. To bring in sharper relief the Quakers' particular interpretation of 'honourable marriage', it is useful to compare it to how the term was being used amongst other English Protestants. Like the Quakers, Protestant Puritans did not regard marriage as a sacrament but did believe the marital union merited honour because it was an ordinance of God.[194] After the Reformation, celibacy was no longer considered a more honourable and holy estate than procreation, as

---

[191] Fox, *Journal Vol. 1* (1836), 469.

[192] Fox, *Epistle CCLXII*. (Hopper [Ed.], *The Works of George Fox Vol. 1*, 331.)

[193] Margaret Fell, *A touch-stone, or, A perfect tryal by the Scriptures* (1667), 20.

[194] Though marriage was not considered a sacrament by the Church of England, sacramental elements remained in the Protestant marriage ceremony (Cressy, *Birth, Marriage, and Death*, 294). As seen in chapter one, these elements were eschewed by the

clerical marriages were increasingly embraced and encouraged.[195] In the *Second Prayer Book of Edward VI Issued 1552*, marriage was affirmed as:

> An honourable estate, instituted of God in Paradise, in the time of man's innocency, signifying unto us the mystical union that is betwixt Christ and his Church: which holy estate Christ adorned and beautified with his presence, and first miracle that he wrought, in Cana of Galilee, and is commended of Saint Paul to be honourable of all men.[196]

In 1622, a generation before the beginning of Quakerism, the English Puritan clergyman William Gouge asserted in his popular manual on domestic life, *Of Domesticall Duties*, marriage was an honourable estate because it was instituted by God in Paradise:

> It is a most honourable thing ... No ordinance was more honourable in the first institution thereof ... The *Author* and first Institutor of marriage was the Lord God ... The *Place* was Paradise ... glorious [and] honourable ... The *Time* was the most pure and perfect time that ever was in the world, when no sin or pollution of man had stained it ... Purity addeth much to the honour of a thing.[197]

Though the Quakers acknowledged, like their fellow Protestants before them, that marriage was an 'honourable estate' due to it being ordained and instituted by God in Paradise, the Quakers took the notion of 'honourable marriage' a step further in their unique belief in the restoration of a direct relationship with God as Adam and Eve originally enjoyed in the Garden of Eden. Quakers perceived

---

early Quakers. For a full discussion of matrimony within the Church of England, see Cressy, *Birth, Death, and Marriage*, 285–97.

[195] Theologian Rosemary R. Ruether reminds us that while the reformers' sweeping 'away of the system of celibacy and monastic life overcame the hierarchy of the celibate over the married, elevating the status of marriage', women were spiritually 'defined as having only one calling, to be wife and mother' (Rosemary Radford Ruether, *Introducing Redemption in Christian Feminism* [Sheffield: Sheffield Academic Press, 1998], 41). As already noted, though the early Quakers did not intend to overturn all gendered roles in family and society, early Quaker women were seen as spiritual equals, actively involved in ministries outside of the domestic realm and the sole role of mother and wife.

[196] Alan Macfarlane, *Marriage and Love in England: Modes of Reproduction 1300–1840* (Oxford: Basil Blackwell Ltd, 1986), 153. As the historian David Cressy reminds us, ' ... the opening remarks from the "form of solemnization of matrimony" in the Book of Common Prayer reflect the determination of the church to impose religious solemnity on an undertaking that was often coloured by secular concerns' (Cressy, *Birth, Marriage, and Death*, 294).

[197] Gouge, *Of Domesticall Duties*, 148–9.

their marriages as honourable because they believed they had returned to the state of Adam and Eve before the Fall – restored to God's presence and able to hear God's voice. Contrarily, marriages 'in the fall', i.e. all marriages outside the Quaker fold, were not considered honourable as they were not innocent in God's eyes and were still living outside of paradise in the fallen world and in the 'false church'.

Let us consider the subtle differences between William Gouge's comments and the position of the Quakers. Gouge was a well-known clergyman and author whose works on marriage and domestic life, including *Of Domestical Duties* (1622), were widely read during the thirty or so years leading up to the beginning of Quakerism.[198] His views, which likely largely represented the views of the Church of England, provide a useful comparison between the views of the established church and the early Quakers regarding the wedding ceremony and marriage. The contrasts are subtle, but important. In regards to the marriage ceremony, Gouge claimed since marriage was an honourable ordinance, it should be solemnised in an honourable space, within the walls of the church.[199] As we have seen, for the Quakers, honourable marriages were solemnised amongst witnesses, the people who constituted the 'true church', who were in the honour of God. While Gouge claimed marriage was instituted in Paradise, and therefore honourable, Quakers further affirmed they had returned to the paradisiacal estate in their lifetime on earth, which in spirit made their marriages honourable. While Gouge believed God joined male and female together in paradise through the creation of Eve, the early Quakers (based on their belief in direct revelation from God) took the notion of God's joining of male and female literally in their present day. The Quaker couple, like Adam and Eve in Paradise, quite literally knew through their 'inner leadings' that God was indeed the matchmaker. As already discussed, these inner leadings from God through direct revelation had to be verified practically and communally, through meetings of silence and discussion.

Believing their Protestant contemporaries did not fully accept the notion of 'Christ within', Quakers understood the implication of the 'mystical union that is betwixt Christ and his Church' carried more sweeping implications. Having an understanding of Christ within the individual and subsequently within the community, Quakers saw marriage as signifying the virtual union between Christ and the church, as well as the union amongst one another in Christ. The approbation process which verified that God brought the couple together and joined them in marriage and embodied the Quaker spirituality of unity was

---

[198] Ng, *Literature and the Politics of Family in Seventeenth-Century England*, 2.

[199] Ibid. 'Solemn ordinances are made in honourable places. Thus with us marriages are solemnized in Churches, not in private houses'.

essential in verifying an intended marriage was honourable, as Fox affirmed in 1663:

> When Lovers are moved and guided by the Light in coolness and moderation, waiting in Gods counsel, then the honourable marriage may be known in the Light, and all children of Light will have unity with it.[200]

The honourable nature of the Quaker marriage did not rest only on it being conducted in a church by a priest, nor did it rest solely on the precedent of God's original intention as demonstrated in Paradise. Their marriages were honourable because they were brought together by God in their present day and confirmed in community and in unity by the inward 'light' which they enjoyed as a result of the full restoration of the Quakers out of the Fall. The union between the True Church and the divine, coupled with the union between each other through the divine light within, couched their marriages in honour.

The issue of honour subsequently dealt directly with the issue of human will versus the divine will. For the Quakers, those in the world, outside of the True Church, who sought out humanly appointed, paid ministers, were engaging in dishonourable marriages, since they did not rely on the light within to lead and bring together these marriages. Bound to manmade practices of the 'false church', the marriages of the world were considered still in the Fall, and therefore dishonourable. Quakers perceived worldly marriages fallen not only because they were conducted by priests in churches, using forms of the 'false church', but also because their marriages were clearly motivated by human will rather than God's will. Because the 'false church' rejected hearing from God directly, in the inward conscience through unity with the divine, their marriages were outside of God's voice, presence and will. The union of wills, between each other and the divine, was perceived by the early Quakers as a necessary consequence of being restored out of the Fall.[201] Fox wrote in 1678:

---

[200] Thomas Lawrence and George Fox, *Concerning Marriage. A Letter Sent to G.F. And with it, a Copy of an Answer to a Friends Letter Concerning Marriage. And some Queries, and his Reply to the Answer and Queries, and an Additional to G.F.'s. Reply, containing 13 Queries concerning Marriage; Also the manner how the parties intending Marriage are to go together* (London: Benjamin Lawrence, 1663), 1.

[201] William Penn wrote in 1673 regarding the human will: ' … by the Will of man we do not understand Will subjected, but the Will absolute, and that we exclude. The Will of Man in that case is swallowed up in the Will of the Spirit, as the Apostle Paul's Life was swallowed up in Christ; It is not I Paul that live, but Christ in me' (William Penn, *The invalidity of John Faldo's vindication of his book, called Quakerism no Christianity being a rejoinder in defence of the answer, intitled, Quakerism a new nick-name for old Christianity* [s.l., 1673], 243).

If God walketh in the mid'st of his Creation, where is it, if it be not in the hearts of people in his Light? And if he writes his will in the Tables of the fleshly hearts, then therein they do know his will.[202]

Marriage and the marriage approbation process demonstrated this union and harmony of wills between humanity and the divine.

Verifying if a proposed marriage was rooted in God's will was not a simple task. As seen in chapter one, the extensive meeting system, investigations and documentation of communal approval were tantamount in upholding this key spiritual component of their unified community. It was through this waiting period on the part of both the couple and the Meeting that hopefully allowed for confirmation that it was indeed God's will, rather than the will of just the couple hoping to get married. If a couple wanted to marry each other, but the community did not sense an inner spiritual confirmation about the union, then the union would not gain approbation.[203] This conflict of wills, particularly when one was convinced that God was indeed commanding the marriage while others did not, was to be avoided.[204] But how did one know if they were hearing from God correctly and were indeed pursuing, or in, an 'honourable' marriage restored out of the Fall?

The issue of certainly and accurately knowing God's will in regards to marriage was addressed in 1663, in a correspondence between Fox and an inquiring couple regarding marriage and knowing whether or not one was hearing from God correctly. Fox responded to their queries, which were then transcribed, and interpreted with the help of a Quaker leader from Marlborough, Thomas Lawrence. The couple[205] inquired whether any 'may know Gods will absolute and infallible concerning their marriage, as whether such a person be appointed of God to be a fit help.'[206] The couple further noted, 'Forasmuch as some have

---

[202] Fox, *A New-England-fire-brand quenched*, 19.

[203] This was the case with Martha Plats. See chapter one, pp. 60–1.

[204] Phyllis Mack explains, 'Quakers shared a profound sense that the community of Friends formed one single living organism' (Mack, *Visionary Women*, 209). Mack further states however in regards to the Meeting system, 'Clearly, the system of meetings established by Friends was both supportive and repressive, and clearly the two functions were linked; the support of the community was conditional on the individual's willingness to conduct his or her private and public life within the parameters set by the meetings' (Mack, *Visionary Women*, 285). In light of Mack's assertions, while ideally Quakers desired unity in marriage approbation, if the Meeting did not grant approbation, the couple would be forced to sacrifice their personal wishes, or marry outside the Quaker Meeting.

[205] The names of the couple were not disclosed.

[206] Lawrence and Fox, *Concerning Marriage*, 7.

been so perswaded, yet failed'.[207] Fox and Lawrence asserted affirmatively that throughout the Bible, many knew for certain God's command:

> *Adam* knew Gods appointment, *Abraham* knew Gods appointment, and said, God will send his Angel, and thou shalt take a wife for my son from thence. Laban and Bethuel knew Gods appointment, and said, This thing is proceeded of the Lord, for this cause (Gods wil manifest, Gods appointment, Gods ordinance) shall a man leave father and mother and cleave to his wife.[208]

As Adam, Abraham, Laban and others knew infallibly that God had appointed a particular person for them to marry, so too could the Quakers, in the like direct relationship with God, have infallible access to God's voice and direction. Lawrence and Fox admonished people who 'marry in their own wills, and said it is Gods will', confirming that Quakers claim to have the ability to know the difference between their own will and God's will in their new restorative state.

Fox and Lawrence confirmed being in the light, restored 'out of the fall', a Quaker joined his or her will with that of God's, and in this unity, there could be no doubt of God's command.[209] They further acknowledged however that being out of the Fall, and hearing from God clearly, was a 'growing condition' after 'long trial' but would come after waiting on God, and submitting their desires to the community of Quakers. The assurance of God's will they concluded could be applied to marriage but also to all other areas of Quaker life:

> This one thing is to be noted especially, although this doctrine of absolute and infallible assurance, is here occasionally applyed to marriage; it is also true in all other things, prophecies, promises and revelations, things spiritual and temporal, and all conditions.[210]

When the couple inquired further, 'How may one come to know this infallible assurance in himself, and not be deceived?' the response of Fox and Lawrence was again equally grounded in the doctrine of the 'light'.[211] They stated one knew 'the time of discerning God's stirrings to marriage clearly ... after the coming out

---

[207] Ibid.
[208] Ibid.
[209] Ibid. 'Who abides in the light, are in the unity; joyed to the Lord, are one spirit, one in desire, delight and sweetness, one will; what man wills, God wills; if ye abide in me, and my words abide in you, saith Christ ... Jews, Gentiles, Christians; Gods stirring have been in all generations, and all Gods stirrings are absolute and infallible; and when any one is restored out of the fall, his assurance may be infallible also'.
[210] Ibid.
[211] Ibid.

of Egypt, out of darkness into light, and they have put away sin'.[212] One could only know God's joining clearly if one was out of transgression. As discussed earlier, some Quakers (e.g. William Caton) spent months waiting even before mentioning the notion to another, for fear they were not hearing correctly from God.[213] The marriage approbation process thus had the potential of creating some anxiety and anguish for the early Quakers who were striving to live honourable lives and in the light.

The notion of honourable marriages brought together by God's will through the inward light was also illuminated in the aforementioned case of Cuthbert Hunter's Quaker marriage in 1654.[214] When Judge Wyndham had judged it as adulterous and invalid due to its not being conducted by a priest, Fell wrote a letter to the Judge in which she ardently argued all Quaker marriages were 'honourable' because they were 'joyned by God ... in the light'.[215] She began her letter by chastising Judge Wyndham who had declared the 'light within', which the Quakers follow, was a principle that 'doth Lead into all manner of sin'.[216] Her opening remarks challenged his criticism. Delineating the theological meaning of the 'light' for the Quakers, she stated it was this light that would in fact judge him for his wrongdoings:

> The Light which Comes from xt ... which he doth enlighten everyone ... is the Condemnation of all sin, wickedness[,] uncleanes & ungodliness, & the Light which is our principle, as hee Calls it; in every man, will witness against the said windham who is Called a Judge, & doth witness aginst sin ... And the Light in every mans Conscience which Comes from xt; will & doth witnesse against thee; that thy Judgment is false.[217]

Looking to the Gospel of John, Fell accused Judge Wyndham 'thou art darkness & doth not comprehend the Light ... the scripture is filled upon thee, the saying of John, Light shines in darknes & darknes doth not Comprehend it [John 1:5]'.[218] Fell argued the 'Light in every mans Conscience' witnessed against and condemned all manner of sin, including the ruling against Quaker marriages:

---

[212] Ibid.
[213] See chapter one, p. 56.
[214] See chapter one, p. 150.
[215] *Margaret Fell to Judge Hugh Wyndham.* (Glines [Ed.], *Undaunted Zeal*, 109.)
[216] Ibid, 107.
[217] Ibid.
[218] Ibid, 108.

> That which Judge Windham Calls Adultry, soe whome the Lord Joyneth together, Lett noe man put asunder [Mark 10:9]; the marriage that is honourable; Contrary to the Light, god doth not Joyne together; that marriage is not honourable.[219]

The crux of 'honourable' marriage for Fell rested not only on God's ordinance in Paradise, but also on the belief that God led a man and woman together to pursue marriage through the light in the inward conscience. Because God brought together the marriage, in a very literal sense, this deemed the marriage honourable.

Fell further explained to the Judge, a marriage which was done contrary to the Light was 'to be Condemned; & not honourable; for there the bed is defiled'.[220] When God does not join man and woman in marriage, that marriage is 'not honourable' and subsequently the marriage 'bed is defiled'. Contrarily, if the marriage is brought together by God, it is honourable, and therefore the bed is 'undefiled'. Fox used similar language in respect to marriage and the marriage-bed:

> That bed is defiled; all that is Joyned there; in that Nature; Contrary to the Light, together with that which is Contrary to the Light; all this is with the Light, to be Condemned; & not honourable; for there the bed is defiled; All Covetousnes, & whoremongers, & Adulterers; such marriages Contrary to the light; god doth not Joyne together; but is with the Light seene & Condemned; the bed that is defiled, is not honourable; & there is hardness of heart; & putting asunder.[221]

Though neither Fox nor Fell in the above passages quoted the biblical verse directly, the language they used is strikingly similar to, and most likely borrowed from, Hebrews 13:4, 'Let marriage be held in honour by all, and let the marriage-bed be kept undefiled; for God will judge fornicators and adulterers'.[222]

In this discussion, it is useful to compare again Quaker views with those of William Gouge. In his commentary on Hebrews there are slight variations between his interpretation of the biblical notions of honourable marriage and the undefiled bed when compared to the beliefs of Fox and Fell.[223] Gouge argued the married couple and the marriage-bed were not undefiled by sin *in toto*:

---

[219] Ibid.

[220] Ibid, 109.

[221] Fox, *Letter of George Fox Concerning his Marriage*. (Cadbury [Ed.], *Narrative Papers of George Fox*, 78–9.)

[222] Bible, *New Revised Standard Version*.

[223] Citing William Gouge, Matthew Griffith and William Whately, historian David Cressy summarises the general seventeenth-century Protestant outlook on marriage and sexuality: 'Marriage ... was a sexual safety valve, an alternative to sin [adultery, fornication, incest, rape or sodomy], as well as an honourable and delightful estate to be entered for its own more positive merits' (Cressy, *Birth, Marriage, and Death*, 297). See also Gouge, *Of*

> The marriage-bed is called *undefiled*, not simply, as if in the act of married persons there were no manner of pollution, no sin at all; but in regard of God's ordinance, and of the act considered in itself, and exempt from the frailties and faults of them that use it. Adam and Eve might have used it in their innocent estate. It is no more a defiled act, than to eat and to drink are. Well, therefore, is it here opposed to acts of uncleanness: namely to whoredom and adultery. In this respect married persons may live as chastely as single persons, whether male or female, if not more chastely ... That which in itself is undefiled ought to be used, so far as in us lieth, without any pollution or defilement. Though the marriage-bed be itself the bed undefiled, yet by licentiousness it may be, and useth to be, too much defiled. We must, therefore pray that it may be sanctified to us; and we must use it with moderation and sobriety, having an eye to the right ends thereof, and carefully observing the directions of God's word thereabout.[224]

According to Gouge, only Adam and Eve were at one time innocent and undefiled, and therefore were the only humans who could have had a marriage-bed completely undefiled by sin before the Fall. Additionally, the undefiled nature of the marriage-bed as described in Hebrews, Gouge maintained, was solely the result of it being an ordinance of God. In other words, sexuality within marriage was undefiled in and of itself, but the defiled couple could defile sexual relations through 'licentiousness', 'whoredom and adultery'. In his *Of Domesticall Duties*, Gouge reminded his readers that marriage, and one can infer sexuality within marriage, was instituted by God to avoid fornication 'whereby we keep our bodies undefiled' in 'matrimonial chastity'.[225]

Fox and other early Quakers held a variant view regarding the undefiled bed. Like Gouge, as seen above, Fox and Fell warned of licentiousness, whoredom and adultery – figuratively, as in relationship to the church forsaking Christ, and literally, within the marital bond. In his sermon to London Quakers in 1680, he encouraged chaste living till 'the day of their marriage and time of death':

> Now let all Friends be careful to keep in the holy chaste life over all lust and uncleanness of filthy fornications ... those that profess the truth should know more virtue and dominion over the filthy lusts, and keep their bodies clean till

---

Domesticall Duties, 182–4, 209; Matthew Griffith, *Bethel: Or a Forme for Famlies in which all sorts, of both sexes, are so squared, and framed by the Word of God, as they may best serve in their severall places, for usefull pieces in God's building* (London: Richard Allot, 1633), 223, 237, 240; and William Whately, *A Bride-Bush. Or a Direction for Married Persons Plainely describing the duties common to both, and peculiar to each of them* (London: Benjamin Fisher, 1623), 3, 18–20 Cited by Cressy in *Birth, Marriage and Death*, 546 n 39.

[224] William Gouge, *A Commentary on the whole Epistle to the Hebrews Vol. 3* (1655) (Edinburgh: James Nichol, 1867), 283–4.

[225] Gouge, *Of Domesticall Duties*, 154–5.

the day of their marriage and time of death, that all may be kept in chasteness and purity to God's glory.[226]

Chaste living, in and out of marriage, was advocated by Fox, but the nature of the individuals in the chaste state as understood by Fox differed from Gouge's view: for Gouge, the couple remained in transgression; for Fox and the early Quakers, they were no longer in bondage to the curses of the Fall. The couple was considered undefiled. As Fell's daughter Margaret noted in her letter to Colonel West concerning marriage:

> Soe with xt jesus, wee are satisfied, who is our beloved, whom wee have found, who will Give husbands in his time[,] who created the male and female in his owne Image, which is undefiled.[227]

Unlike Gouge who suggested the bed was undefiled (i.e. a refuge from sin) while the couple nevertheless remained defiled by sin, the early Quakers made no special allocation of the 'undefiled' state solely to the marriage-bed, as Fox and Fell advocated the *couple* had already 'witnessed transgression finished' in their restored state.[228] Returning to the original innocence of Adam and Eve, the early Quakers could now know innocence in all areas of their lives, including the marriage-bed.[229] Seeking refuge from sin was considered a moot action. While Gouge and many of his Protestant contemporaries viewed marriage and the marriage-bed as means to avoid sin, Fox rather saw it as a product of God's eradication of sin. In Christ's image – the Second Adam – the Quakers could enjoy the undefiled nature of marriage and its bed, just as the original, innocent couple did in the Garden of Eden; no longer ashamed, early Quakers believed each marriage embodied an honourable union between two undefiled individuals, who were brought together by God.

The idea that marriage should be between two persons who have 'witnessed transgression finished' was explicated in greater detail in the aforementioned correspondence in 1663 between Fox, Friend Thomas Lawrence and an

---

[226] *George Fox's Sermon at Wheeler Street, 1680.* (Barbour and Roberts [Eds], *Early Quaker Writings*, 509.)

[227] Fell the Younger, *To Judge Thomas Fell and Colonel William West from Margaret Fell, Jr.* (Glines [Ed.], *Undaunted Zeal*, 194.)

[228] Lawrence and Fox, *Concerning Marriage*, 1, 3.

[229] Rosemary Moore explains the Quaker use of the term 'innocence': 'The process of salvation was often described as a return to the state of innocence of the Garden of Eden. The Fall of Adam and Eve was treated as taking place in the hearts and minds of people, who had to come through and out of the Fall ... Quakers could describe salvation as being in the Covenant of Light, or as a matter of attending to the light in the conscience, or as having returned to the state of innocence before the Fall' (Moore, *The Light in Their Consciences*, 86, 88).

inquiring Quaker couple who had questions regarding marriage.[230] In this correspondence, the early Quaker understanding of the relationships between 'honourable marriage', an 'undefiled bed' and 'transgression finished' can be better understood. Lawrence opened the published correspondence with a copy of the following words from Fox regarding honourable marriage and the undefiled bed:

> Marriage is Gods Ordinance, which is joined in, and by the Lord. The honourable marriage is when the bed is undefiled, transgression finished, freedom from sin witnessed, victory over the world known, and the enmity kept under, an absolute divorce from all that the first nature hath been wedded to, and committed uncleanness with, in the time of ignorance.[231]

But what of those who did not follow the light within and witness transgression finished? Fox explained anyone who did not 'witness transgression finished' could not be joined by God, and subsequently was defiled, for marriage was instituted 'before sin was' and was a joining of 'nothing but that which is pure'.[232] Additionally, 'hasty' marriages or ones brought together by 'fleshly motions', or 'carnal desires, and self-ends, the usual provocations to the Worlds marriages' according to Fox, could not possibly be of 'God's moving'.[233] Lawrence lamented that some of his fellow Quakers did not grow 'in truth' but, rather, were in the process of 'losing the condition' (i.e. the condition of staying within the Quaker fold and being in the image of the Second Adam), went after exogamous marriages and subsequently grew in 'deadness'.[234]

The above passage from Fox prompted further queries from the couple and Lawrence, as it was apparently met with quizzical brows from the couple who

---

[230] See pp. 168–70. Fox, *Concerning Marriage*.

[231] Lawrence and Fox, *Concerning Marriage*, 1.

[232] Ibid. Fox explained, 'But for any that cannot witness transgression finished, nor scarcely know what it is, who live in sin, and say God hath joyned them in marriage, is it not a lie against God and his Ordinance? God instituted marriage before sin was, and doth it when sin is done away, and is the same for ever, who joyneth nothing but that which is pure; all that is hasty and hankering after fleshly motions, is not Gods moving: some have been observed not to have grown in truth, but deadness, and losing the condition, have followed after marriage; nothing defiled is to be owned, much less to be endeavoured after'.

[233] Ibid, 13.

[234] As already discussed, without the careful watchful eye of the Quaker community, one could potentially witness transgression returned. The 'true church', as the early Quakers understood it, made a consistent effort to maintain their holiness and unity. Within marriage and marriage approbation, there was no exception. But as Fox and Fell ardently believed, if a couple brought their intention to the group, and all was done in the 'light', purity and unity could be maintained.

felt Fox's answer was 'a parable; and to the thing in question, but little answer'.[235] When told this, Fox replied he often 'did usually answer to the ground of a thing rather than the words'.[236] To help the couple further understand Fox's meaning, Lawrence wrote a letter in which he addressed each question they had posed to Fox, answering it in his own words with references to Fox's initial response.[237] What follows is Lawrence's interpretation and reiteration of Fox's words. Endorsed by Fox, this correspondence also indicates others like Thomas Lawrence understood clearly Fox's restorationist theology as it applied to marriage.

The first question addressed to Fox by the couple was, 'Whether the joyning together in marriage by such as cannot witness freedom from all sin, be God's ordinance, or of the World?'[238] The couple's concern struck at the heart of Fox's restorationist theology in relation to marriage. Lawrence reiterated the terms set out by Fox – a couple could only be joined by God who had been redeemed by God 'out of the fall':

> Gods joyning is a state out of the fall again, by the power of God and his image ... Such as are redeemed out of the fall into the image of God, and marry, is God's ordinance; and such as are in the War, who cannot as yet witness freedom from all sin, yet if they do believe there is such a freedom, and do endeavor to attain it, who can witness growth, and do abide faithful, and marry, this may be God's ordinance also.[239]

Lawrence followed the above with a comparison between the days of the apostate church, or the age of 'ignorance' before God's truth was made known through the church, and the age of the True Church:

> In the time of ignorance God winked; but now such as do not only deny freedom from sin after they have been admonished to the truth, but contend against it, affirming that none can be free from sin on this side of the grave, and not only live in sin, but profess they must do so: if such marry, their marriage is of the World, in the fall, out of the power of God and his image, not as God joyns.[240]

---

[235] Lawrence and Fox, *Concerning Marriage*, 3.
[236] Ibid.
[237] The historian Arnold Lloyd explains, 'Fox was often asked for advice ... When his advice had to be communicated at a distance it sometimes proved to be so obscure that it had to be interpreted. Thomas Lawrence, a well-concerned Quaker of Marlborough, published Fox's answer to some queries which he had submitted for resolution' (Lloyd, *Quaker Social History*, 53).
[238] Lawrence and Fox, *Concerning Marriage*, 2.
[239] Ibid, 3.
[240] Ibid, 3–4.

For Lawrence and Fox alike, there were no excuses in the age of the True Church, during which the light and truth were being made known, for anyone to marry in the manner 'of the World, in the fall' as a result of denying 'freedom from sin ... this side of the grave'.

Concerning those outside of Quakerism (or perhaps their own reticence to accept the notion of 'transgression finished'), the couple proposed an additional question, 'Whether the marriage-bed be undefiled whilst any kind of sin remaineth?'[241] This particular question puts into question Gouge's assertion that the undefiled nature of the marriage-bed was separate from the married couple who remained defiled by sin.[242] Lawrence's response, again based on the thoughts of Fox, clearly reiterated and clarified that the undefiled nature of the marriage-bed was the result of the undefiled nature of the married couple, who had returned to the state of Adam and Eve before they fell.

> He that believes, hath passed from death to life, and so from the sin, and overcome the sin ... To know marriage as it was in the beginning before man fell, is a state before defilement was ... and such as live in sin, and say they never look to be otherwise in this life, are not they in the defilement? Is not all sin defilement? Is not their bed defiled, and all that they do? *To the unclean all things are unclean*, though they may be faithful each to other concerning bodily act. Here the honourable marriage of Gods joyning, out of transgression, goes over the head of the Worlds marriages of mans joyning in the sin, though they boast and mock at the simplicity of truth, and them that live in it.[243]

Passing 'from death to life', Quakers were no longer seeking refuge from fornication within the marriage-bed.[244] Their marriages, which were considered 'out of transgression' and above all marriages in the Fall, were completely out of the defiled state. For Lawrence and Fox, those still living in the Fall remained 'unclean' and thus their marriage-bed was defiled, despite marital and physical fidelity.

Following the above question regarding the undefiled state of the marriage-bed, the couple further inquired about the offspring of such unions, 'Whether the children of Parents that are both or either of them free from transgression, are conceived and born in sin, or are they clean and holy?'[245] The answers given by Fox and Lawrence addressed not only the notion of original sin, but also the

---

[241] Ibid, 2.

[242] See pp. 171–3. The couple could still potentially defile the marriage-bed.

[243] Lawrence and Fox, *Concerning Marriage*, 4.

[244] The historian Arnold Lloyd explains, 'For those who, like himself [Fox], came into subjection to the Spirit of God there was no longer any need to think of marriage as a refuge from sin' (Lloyd, *Quaker Social History*, 49).

[245] Lawrence and Fox, *Concerning Marriage*, 4.

quandary of the defiled or undefiled state of the marriage when one partner has not witnessed transgression finished. Lawrence responded:

> There is a state where the believing wife sanctifies the unbelieving husband, and the believing husband sanctifies the unbelieving wife; else were your children unholy, but now they are clean, which is through the sanctification, which is through the belief; he that believes, hast passed from death to life, and so from the sin, and overcomes the sin.[246]

When one came to the Quaker fold through turning to the light within, submitting to and believing in God's restorative work, and coming into the sanctified state, this individual restoration could have salvific implications for the rest of the family, particularly those who were not Quakers. As in the above case, a believing spouse could positively affect the sanctification process of the other spouse.

It is worth noting briefly the distinct implications and significance honour and defilement carried for English women in the seventeenth century, particularly related to sexuality. As the historian Joanne Bailey reminds us, in English law and institutions, there was a deeply rooted double-standard, as 'women's pre-marital and extra-marital sex would appear to be punished far more harshly than men's and carried far greater social consequences'.[247] If a woman committed sexual misconduct, she would be socially deemed dishonourable, but if she was 'passive, chaste, and obedient' she would then be the epitome of honourable femininity.[248] Chastity was a virtue which could be embraced by single women and married women alike. A single woman remained sexually chaste through celibacy, while a married woman would remain chaste through fidelity to her husband.[249]

Though men and women were expected to live chaste lives, there is some evidence that feminine honour, in the explicit form of reputation, was expected in the form of chastity.[250] In 1668, William Penn associated feminine 'honour'

---

[246] Ibid, 4–5. Reference to 1 Corinthians 7:14.

[247] Joanne Bailey, *Unquiet Lives: Marriage and Marriage Breakdown in England, 1660–1800* (Cambridge: Cambridge University Press, 2003), 140. See also Keith Thomas, 'The Double Standard', *Journal of History of Ideas*, 20 (1959): 195–217; p. 195.

[248] Laura Gowing, 'Women, Status and the Popular Culture of Dishonour', *Transactions of the Royal Historical Society*, 6 no 6 (1996): 225–34; p. 225.

[249] Ibid.

[250] The historian Phyllis Mack notes, 'Friends were also restrained in their sexual behaviour. Historians have understandably dwelt on the salacious pamphlet literature that labelled both Quakers and Ranters as antinomian and described women and men cavorting through the countryside during the upheavals of the Civil War and Interregnum, claiming to be Adam and Eve or the Messiah and his adoring disciples. The fact is however that of the

with maintaining a 'reputation' of virtuous living, referencing Proverbs 11:6, 'A gracious woman (according to Solomon) retaineth honour; that is keeps her Credit; and by her Virtue, maintains her Reputation of Sobriety and Chastity'.[251] However, if a man had sexual relations with a woman prior to, or outside of, marriage, he could also in effect 'defile her'. This was an issue directly addressed by Fox in 1669. Fox provided the following course of action for Meetings if such an event occurred:

> If any man should defile a woman, he must marry her ... for he must fulfil the law of God, for the law of God commands it, that he must marry her, and condemn his action, and clear God's truth. But no such marriages, where the bed is defiled, we bring into our meetings; but some Friends (if such a thing happen) draw up a certificate, and they to set their hands to it, that they will live faithfully together as man and wife, and fulfil the law of God. And this I write, if ever such a thing should happen; but I hope that Friends will be careful, and keep in the fear of the Lord, that they may have an esteem of the Lord's truth, and their own bodies, and of the honourable marriage, where the bed is undefiled.[252]

Interestingly, in this case Fox believed this particular marriage-bed was not completely undefiled. The marriage, having been brought together by physical attraction over God's direction, resulted in a bed defiled still by the fallen state. But if a woman was defiled by a man physically, according to Fox, the man was obliged to marry her, albeit outside of the meeting. It is an intriguing example of Fox grappling with the sinful state of the world, granting options for those who have succumbed to worldly temptations to still have a means of marriage and be members of the Quaker community.[253]

---

hundreds of Quaker prophets and visionary writers active during the 1650s, only one man was formally accused of sexual misconduct' (Mack, *Visionary Women*, 133).

[251] Penn, *No Cross, No Crown*. (Penn, *A Collection of the Works of William Penn, Vol. 1*, 317.)

[252] Fox, *Epistle CCLXII*. (Hopper [Ed.], *The Works of George Fox Vol. 1*, 337–8.)

[253] Russell Mortimer, editor of the *Minute Book of the Men's Meeting of the Society of Friends in Bristol*, explains how the Bristol Meeting dealt with disownment and readmittance: 'For persistence in an offence, or for denial of the authority of the meeting in a matter affecting the reputation of Friends, the ultimate penalty was a minute of disunion ... excluding the offender from participation in the business of the Society, and disowning him until he should come to a true sense of repentance and wish to be reunited with Friends' (Mortimer [Ed.], *Minute Book of the Men's Meeting of the Society of Friends in Bristol 1667–1686*, xii). No offence was unforgivable or without the possibility of readmission by the Quakers, particularly if repentance was adequately demonstrated. See also J.D. Marietta, *The Reformation of American Quakerism, 1748–83* (Philadelphia, PA: University of Pennsylvania Press, 1984), 10. Pink Dandelion explains 'Disownment did not mean not

In British society at the time, sexual relations with a betrothed may not have been so severely judged; but as seen above, with the Quakers it was discouraged and generally frowned upon.[254] This in part was due to the early Quaker belief that marriage was first and foremost based on one's inward spirituality rather than on the motivation for procreation.[255] But this did not necessarily translate into celibacy. On the contrary it opened the possibility of sexual relations being chaste, and the bed being undefiled, without the necessity of procreation. With or without the hope of bearing children, the Quaker bed was undefiled. Likewise, the Quaker couple was expected to refrain from sexual relations until after the marriage was verified by the communal body of witnesses. The bed undefiled could only be within a marriage which was brought together by God, through communal approval, within the True Church in which each member was expected to have witnessed transgression finished. The people of the True Church, who emerged from the wilderness, came into the image of the Second Adam, Christ, and in this image, males and females alike 'witnessed transgression finished'.[256]

In the above correspondence between Lawrence, Fox and the inquiring couple, Lawrence asserted if all parents seriously weighed 'what their children do inherit from them in the seed', it might be a motive for parents to pursue sanctification 'for their childrens sake'.[257] However, the woman who had witnessed transgression finished was also in a unique position as a mother. Submitted to the sanctifying light within, the Quaker mother could transmit this sanctification in the light to her child in the womb. Referencing the story of John the Baptist's birth in the New Testament, Lawrence supported his argument by pointing to Zachariah and Elizabeth who were both 'just before God, and John was filled with the Holy Ghost from his Mother's womb'.[258] Lawrence and Fox did not refute original sin.[259] But their collective response indicates a strong

---

being able to attend a Meeting, which was, after all, public. It meant the ex-Friend could not call themselves a Quaker, attend a Meeting for Worship for Church Affairs (i.e. Business Meeting), and could not have recourse to Meeting funds' (Dandelion, *An Introduction to Quakerism*, 73). Thus, if Friends were readmitted by a Meeting they had access to the full privileges of membership.

[254] Dandelion, *An Introduction to Quakerism*, 70. See also Marietta, *The Reformation of American Quakerism*, 6–7, 11, 13; Bailey, *Unquiet Lives*, 140; Adair, *Courtship, Illegitimacy and Marriage in Early Modern England*, 92–3.

[255] Vann and Eversley, *Friends in Life and Death*, 162.

[256] Lawrence and Fox, *Concerning Marriage*, 1, 3.

[257] Ibid, 5.

[258] Ibid.

[259] The Quaker conversion experience was rooted in coming out of the fallen state and moving into a restored state through the work of the inward light and the larger Quaker community. See also Dandelion, *An Introduction to Quakerism*, 60, 196.

belief in the presence of the light within having a positive effect on the child within the womb. While they were not technical in how this transmission could take place, they essentially put forth the notion that a Quaker woman could give birth to a child who was exposed to the light in the womb, and thus be born more inclined to being submissive to that light. It was still left to both the child's parents and the Quaker meetings however to check and maintain the orderly behaviour of the children of Quakers. As we will see in the following section, this task became increasingly important as the first generation of children born to Quaker parents began to make religious decisions of their own, some of whom began leaving the fold altogether, and marrying with the world.

Gospel Family-Order in Households of Faith

Early Quaker marriages formed the cornerstone of Quaker families, which would increasingly become important in the spread of Quakerism. Though the Quaker family and child rearing within Quakerism were concerns for Fox since the earliest years of the Quaker movement, Fox's preaching and teaching on 'family order' became more prevalent after the 1660s. The historian Richard T. Vann notes that publications dealing with the rearing of children were not common during the original generation of spiritually fervent Quakers:

> The early Quakers for the first 25 years had almost nothing to say about the religious upbringing of children. Only a handful of titles out of the flood of books published in this period referred to the proper care of children.[260]

Over twenty years after the beginning of the movement, during which time Quakers had personal conversions, the first generation of Quakers who were essentially born into their Quaker faith were coming into adulthood.[261] The immediate familial unit increasingly became for the Quakers a mirror of their spiritual family of the True Church embodied by the local and regional Meetings, and a critical venue for the propagation of Quakerism by the beginning of the eighteenth century.[262]

---

[260] Richard T. Vann, 'Nurture and Conversion in the Early Quaker Family', *Journal of Marriage and Family*, 31 (November 1969): 639–43; p. 641.

[261] Ibid. There was a decline in conversions by the mid-eighteenth century, and according to Vann, 'As a consequence … the Society of Friends is revealed by family-reconstitution analysis to have been in the mid-eighteenth century from 80- to 90-percent composed of children of Quakers'.

[262] Dandelion, *An Introduction to Quakerism*, 56. 'The children of Quakers were necessarily to be brought up in the true church even whilst they had not yet made a voluntary

The Quakers came to be in a time when the Protestant family ethic, as a result of the Reformation, was in effect. After the Reformation, matrimony and the familial unit were elevated in their practical efficacy to help foster the spread and maintenance of the Gospel, as the family was regarded as an agent for moral training and a model of Christ and his church.[263] Multiple homilies and marriage manuals were circulated to instruct on the meaning of the marital estate. In Archbishop Thomas Cranmer's 1549 prayer book he stated the chief reasons for marriage were 'mutual society, help and comfort'. In *The Book of Common Prayer* (1559) of George Fox's youth, the three purposes of marriage were listed as: 'the procreation of children, the remedying of sin, and the mutual help of the partners'.[264] Procreation, mutual aid and comfort (physically and financially) as well as spiritual edification (in the form of 'remedying of sin' as aforementioned) were considered essential ingredients to a happy and respectable marriage.

Procreation and the proper education of one's offspring in the established church amongst seventeenth-century Protestants were perceived as praiseworthy occupations, particularly for women.[265] Being a nurturing mother, who procreated and instructed children in spiritual matters, was considered by some a woman's highest calling and vocation.[266] Marriage was largely considered the most honourable spiritual estate for women, particularly for women who no longer had the convent as a means for independent spiritual pursuit outside of marriage.[267] The husband was considered the head of the wife and family, as

---

confession of faith. In a world beset by continuing apostasy and spiritual corruption, the home and the Meeting House became the twin cloisters of spiritual renewal and purity'.

[263] The historian Susan Wabuda explains various effects of the Reformation on marriage and family: 'Marriage, as the mirror of the relationship that bound Christ to his church, was deeply affected ... Once Protestants embraced Christ as the sole mediator between a sinful humanity and a reconciling God, and argued that faith meant placing active confidence in Christ's promises (trusting God's goodness alone), the prestige of a host of mediators was reassigned ... The celibate priesthood, whose propitiations were offered on behalf of the rest of society, were now supposed to become preaching ministers who taught their flocks and raised their families' (Susan Wabuda, 'Sanctified by the Believing Spouse: Women, Men and the Marital Yoke in the early Reformation'). Cited in Peter Marshall and Alec Ryrie (Eds), *The Beginnings of English Protestantism* (Cambridge: Cambridge University Press, 2002), 111–28.

[264] *The Book of Common Prayer* (1559) http://justus.anglican.org/resources/bcp/1559/Marriage_1559.htm (accessed 7 April 2011). Cited by Lloyd in *Quaker Social History*, 48.

[265] Mendelson and Crawford, *Women in Early Modern England*, 67.

[266] Ibid. 'Preachers explained that the biblical texts defined the ideal state for a woman as marriage and motherhood – never idle, reared her children in piety and obedience, home is life', while a mother was considered 'tender and loving, transmitting her own good qualities to her offspring by her breeding of the child in her womb, and by her nursing it at her own breasts'.

[267] Ibid, 225. 'The Reformation eliminated most of the formal linkages between religious ritual, female collectivities, and the yearly cycle of village life which had been a feature of

Christ was head of the church.[268] *The Book of Common Prayer* (1559) exhorted wives: 'submit yourselves unto your husbands, as unto the Lord, for the husband is the wives head, even as Christ is head of the Church'.[269] Gouge wrote in *Of Domesticall Duties* (1622), the wife was to be 'a joint governor with her husband' over the children and servants, as long as she remained obedient to her husband.[270] The raising of children within the church, while teaching them morals in the familial microcosm of the macrocosmic church, helped ensure the salvation of their offspring.

The household of the early Quakers was likewise a harbour of teaching spirituality to one's offspring. Similar to their contemporaries, the patriarchal structure of family was generally left intact amongst the Quaker families.[271] Quaker women, though on the most part considered spiritually equal and capable of prophesying and preaching, remained largely associated with their familial responsibilities. Phyllis Mack explains:

> As mothers in Israel, Quaker women were defined as gendered, social beings, embedded not only in their own spiritual community but in biological families and physical neighbourhoods ... As public prophets, however, Quaker women were utterly distanced from traditional forms of female self-definition.[272]

During the decrease of prophetic activity amongst both male and female Quakers after the restoration of the monarchy, women's activities became more clearly

---

medieval life'. Mendelson further makes the following note regarding the significance of the early Quaker Women's Meetings: 'Apart from informal settings – private gatherings for childbirth, prayers at each other's houses, and separate rooms at christenings – there were no female religious associations until the separate Quaker Women's Meetings of the 1670s' (ibid, 225).

[268] Wabuda, 'Sanctified by the Believing Spouse', 117–18.

[269] *The Book of Common Prayer* (1559) http://justus.anglican.org/resources/bcp/1559/Marriage_1559.htm (accessed 7 April 2011). Cited by Jacqueline Eales in *Women in Early Modern England 1500–1700* (London: UCL Press Limited, 1998), 24.

[270] Gouge, *Of Domesticall Duties*, 7. Cited by Eales in *Women in Early Modern England 1500–1700*, 25. Women were not always submissive to their husbands. A Russian visiting London in 1645–6 remarked that women ruled their husbands and their households. See Hill, *World Turned Upside Down*, 309.

[271] Rosemary Moore explains, 'Family life at this time was based on a patriarchal model with some flexibility in practice, and the Quakers generally followed this pattern ... On the other hand, the Quaker marriage declaration, in which the man and woman used the same words to take each other, indicated greater equality between men and women' (Moore, *The Light in Their Consciences*, 120).

[272] Mack, *Visionary Women*, 238.

established in their separate Meetings.[273] In addition to the Meetings, women's nurturing roles within the family became increasingly important, as the family became the locus of spiritual upbringing. Fox and Fell encouraged women to wisely look after their households, and likewise agreed women were in touch with domestic affairs that equipped them with handling marriage approbation.[274]

An early example of Fox's concern with the proper rearing and teaching of children within Quakerism can be found in a pamphlet written in 1657. Fox exhorted both teachers and parents to teach and raise their children in the fear of the Lord by encouraging their children 'to depart from sin, and to depart from evil', and by teaching them 'to know the witness of God in them, which lets them see sin and transgression'.[275] He warned parents about their wayward and worldly habits in childrearing:

> Your young men and maidens are light, and vain, & wild, and heady, and this hath dishonoured me, though they profess my name: So that both old men and young men, and old women and young women have both dishonoured their profession: young men and young women have both been trained up without my fear, that thy be as wild as ever ... yee old men and old women have spoiled your children; you have served the desires of your mindes, & served the desires of your childrens mindes, whereby they are given to vanity, following the fashions and lusts of ignorance.[276]

Concluding with a prophetic backing to his words, 'This is my word to you all saith the LORD', Fox from a very early stage took seriously the necessity of training children by demonstrating behaviour that was unlike the mind and the ways of the world.[277]

The early Quaker insistence on endogamous marriages ensured a parental unit that could effectively raise children in the Quaker tradition; a microcosmic familial unit within the greater family of the Quaker Meetings. As Quaker marriages and the offspring they produced were considered illegitimate, and thus under great criticism particularly at the beginning of the movement, so too

---

[273] Catie Gill notes, 'The post-Restoration period saw a decline in the prophetic activity that had characterized early Quakerism ... Post-restoration Quakerism also established duties and responsibilities for women to carry out in the separate women's meetings' (Gill, *Women in the Seventeenth-Century Quaker Community*, 3).

[274] See chapter one, pp. 94ff.

[275] George Fox, *A Warning to all Teachers of Children, Which are called School-Masters and School Mistresses, and To Parents, which doth send their Children to be taught by them: That all School-Masters and School Mistresses may train up Children in the fear of God* (London: Thomas Simmons, 1657), 2–3.

[276] Ibid, 6.

[277] Ibid, 8.

were their families susceptible to scrutiny by some of their suspicious Protestant contemporaries. In 1673, John Faldo (1633/4–91), a non-conformist minister educated at Cambridge, wrote an anti-Quaker tract in which he accused Quakers, amongst other things, of not having 'Gospel-Prayers' within their families. Faldo described 'Gospel-Prayers' as 'the soul uttering its wants and desires to God, by way of humble supplication; with an audible voice, when it is exercised solemnly in a Congregation, or Family', but also as 'without an audible voice, when a person is private: but always in the name, and for the sake and merits of Jesus Christ'.[278] Faldo contended 'Gospel-Prayer' was a duty that the Quakers had disowned.[279] Critical of the Quaker silent prayers in worship, Faldo argued the Quakers also did not use 'prayer [audibly at least] with their Families daily', something easily discovered 'by all that have opportunities of so conversing with them'.[280] Faldo attacked the Quaker neglect at saying the Lord's prayer amongst their families and in worship, calling it a 'sin against our Saviours Directory'.[281] Finally, he accused the Quakers of not saying daily 'Family-Prayers' when gathered around a table for meals, 'That they crave not God's blessing, nor express their thankfulness at set-meals for their Table-mercies, is as notorious as the other'.[282] Faldo argued that the omission of these spiritual practices, which were apparently practised amongst other Protestant families, was suspect. According to Faldo, if the Quakers were not following these disciplines, set out by Christ, either in worship or amongst their families, they had to be going against the Gospel.

William Penn quickly rebutted Faldo's charge of the Quaker 'denial of Gospel-Prayer … as well in Families as Meetings, and at Meals' by arguing all forms of prayer 'wherein God's Spirit is not the first and chief Mover and Assister' were false.[283] While the early Quakers were not following forms of prayers in their families, they did believe in 'Gospel-Prayer' as Penn explained:

> No Prayer that ascends to God without the Leading of God's Spirit, and which is not by, and in the Light, can be acceptable with him; consequently, Gospel-Prayer is only from the Motions of the Spirit of God, and by and in the Light of Christ.[284]

---

[278] John Faldo, *Quakerism no christianity, clearly and abundantly proven out of the writings of their chief leaders* (London: Ben Griffin, 1673), part II, chap. XIII, 23–4.
[279] Ibid, 24.
[280] Ibid.
[281] Ibid.
[282] Ibid.
[283] William Penn, *Quakerism, a new nick-name for old Christianity being an answer to a book entituled Quakerism no Christianity, subscribed by J. Faldo* (s.l., 1672), 121.
[284] Ibid, 123.

What constituted 'Gospel-Prayer' was not the form or place, whether it be in church or at the family meal, but the motivation and foundation of the prayer. Penn believed prayer was a 'Gospel-Ordinance ... that is not only Good, but Necessary to be used', wherever a Friend might find himself or herself, within a Meeting or in the home.[285] What mattered to the early Quaker was whether or not the prayer came from human invention or tradition, or from God within, as Penn affirmed:

> Those who have not Words, especially in Publick Places, have Sighs and Groans, and a deep and silent Exercise of the Spirit God-wards ... That is the duty of all to wait upon God, and that not only at Publick Meetings, but at their own Houses also, and therein as well at their Meals as at all other times for Worship. If any have the Motion of God's Eternal Spirit upon their Hearts, let it be answer'd, to God's Praise, and the Edification of others.[286]

The spiritual disciplines of silent prayer and listening to God, as well as spontaneous, unscripted audible prayers in private or in public, were encouraged by the early Quakers, not just within the walls of the home or worship, but throughout all spheres of the life of the Quaker.[287]

Fox and others set out the responsibilities of parents regarding the spiritual welfare of their families within the framework of 'Gospel Family-Order' in a 'household of faith'.[288] As previously discussed in this chapter, the 'Gospel-Order' of primitive Christianity was promoted in support of the Meeting system and the marriage approbation process. Likewise Fox promoted Gospel Family-Order in a transcribed discourse at a Men's Meeting during his trip to Barbados in 1671 entitled *Gospel Family-Order, Being a Short Discourse Concerning the Ordering of Families*. In this discourse, Fox extolled the 'holy men of God' who followed the 'command of the Lord ... to order their Families' as Abraham was commanded by God 'to keep his Covenant between him and his Seed'.[289] Here Fox made a reference to Genesis 17, the biblical narrative which tells of God making a covenant with Abraham that he will be an ancestor of many nations and his succeeding generations will follow God, in addition to instructions of circumcision as a sign of the covenant and a symbol of separation from the gentile world. As God commanded Abraham to order families, so too was God commanding the Quakers to order their families through Quaker disciplines and spirituality, as Fox explained:

---

[285] Ibid.
[286] Ibid, 126.
[287] Ibid.
[288] Fox, *Gospel Family-Order*.
[289] Ibid, 3.

> And so are not all you Christians now, and Masters and Mistresses of Families now to look to your Families, to see that you and your Families do serve the Lord in the Circumcision of the Spirit of God?[290]

Upon the biblical precedence of Abraham propagating his 'seed', the Quakers tendered the spiritual seed of Christ within each member of the family, setting the True Church apart from the 'false church'. Fox exhorted his followers to 'therefore mind and consider this in your Families, and gather them altogether, and teach them the Way of the Lord, and the New Covenant'.[291] Teaching Quaker spirituality and disciplines to one's children was critical in sustaining the True Church in unity.

Ten years later, Fox continued advocating the necessary Gospel Family-Order of raising children in the New Covenant, as Abraham had raised his family in the old covenant. In his sermon at Wheeler Street in London in 1680, Fox wrote of the necessity of both mothers and fathers, as well as male and female elders in the church, to train up their children, in their homes and in their Meetings. Fox reminded his London listeners of the importance of elder women in the church and home, spiritual mothers and physical mothers, taking on the mantle of spiritually nurturing the youth:

> Paul the Apostle said, 'I permit not a woman to speak in the Church' ... yet he appointed Titus to ordain elders, and the elder women must be teachers of good things. So he ordains the elder women; then he did not stop them. So the elder women must teach good things: that is their duty incumbent upon them. So it must be in every family.[292]

Not only the women but the men as well were responsible for the right upbringing of their children as Fox instructed:

> Men and women are to train up their children to walk in the New Covenant, as the Jews did in the Old Covenant ... so here is the particular service of every man in his family and every woman in her family.[293]

Fox stressed both the father and the mother as having a share in the responsibility of the moral and spiritual training of their children. As in the government of the church, women and men were expected to have a share in the government of the

---

[290] Ibid, 5.
[291] Ibid.
[292] *George Fox's Sermon at Wheeler Street, 1680.* (Barbour and Roberts [Eds], *Early Quaker Writings*, 504.)
[293] Ibid.

home. Just as in the Meetings, the watchful care of the elders or parents of both sexes in the context of family would ensure sound spiritual care and guidance. In the home, again utilising the story of Abraham as a model, the nurturing and propagating of the 'seed' through family was necessary, as Fox instructed, 'Have your children in submission' and train them well:

> So that they may be plants of God round about their tables, all growing up to the praise of the pure God ... So first, here is your duty in families; then come to take care of the church of God; then fathers and mothers in Israel which comes farther than fathers and mothers in a family.[294]

While the familial unit was seen as indeed important by Fox, even crucial to the maintenance of Gospel Family-Order of the Quaker movement, he saw it as complementary to the greater whole. The Mothers and Fathers in Israel, who tended and watched the spiritual state and orderly behaviour of the spiritually and physically younger, were considered elders and parents of the household of God.[295]

Evidence that many of the first younger generation may have been going astray from the Quaker doctrines and practices in the 1670s can be found in the following written testimony given forth by the Quarterly Meeting in London. The title is in itself quite telling: *A short testimony from some of those that are come to the Obedience of the Gospel, Against all false Liberty in Youth (or whom it may concern) amongst us that make the cross of Christ of none Effect, and the pretious way of Truth seem a light thing, and evil spoken of by them which are without, etc.* The London Quarterly Meeting expressed they were in a 'deep sense concerned' and made the following exhortation to the youth in their midst who had not yet taken seriously the Quaker way of life. They encouraged the 'young ones':

---

[294] Ibid.

[295] The term Mother in Israel was used more frequently than Father in Israel, and denoted a gendered role of nurturing in the Quaker community. Catie Gill explains, 'The "mother in Israel" was a role assigned to venerable women in the Quaker community, and it invokes domestic notions of the caring, nurturing role of women. This role prioritized domestic activities and, furthermore, ensured that male power was protected' (Gill, *Women in the Seventeenth-Century Quaker Community*, 168). As we have seen, the gendered role of domesticity was used in the promotion of the Women's Meeting role in managing marriage approbation. See chapter one, p. 94ff. Margaret Fell also used the metaphor of 'household' for the early Quaker community as Catie Gill explains, 'For Margaret Fell, the Quakers enact the Galatians notion 6:10 of the church as a "household of faith"' (see Margaret Fell, *False Prophets, Antichrists, Deceivers* [London: Giles Calvert, 1655], 21. Cited by Gill in *Women in the Seventeenth-Century Quaker Community*, 118).

That never yet took up the cross of Christ to stay your minds out of the lusting Eye and cain Desires, but are at Liberty in your affections, which is the product of the spirit of the World.[296]

The 'Liberty' in affections likely referred largely to the continued problem of exogamous marriages. The family, along with the Meetings, was now considered a viable and critical avenue for suppressing this disorderly behaviour. Ordered families equalled ordered Quaker life, the Gospel Order as God intended. Disordered families on the other hand, particularly amongst the youth, indicated disorder in the Quaker family, as the London Quarterly Meeting of 1677 solemnly declared, "'Tis our Godly care for young Ones Preservation in the Truth in their particular, and our woeful Experience of Youths miscarriage in this present day'.[297] These words of concern and caution were echoed by the Quaker prophet Mary Waite, leading Quaker and friend of Margaret Fell's daughter Isabel Yeamans, in her pamphlet *A Warning to All Friends* (1679), 'I warn and exhort all parents not to winke or connive at any sin in your Children as you tender that everlasting well being'.[298] Like Fox had written in his Gospel Family-Order decree a few years prior, she encouraged 'all Masters and Mistresses of Families' to 'keep in the Dominion of Truth, that in it you may Rule over every unclean thing ... keeping your own houses in the good Order'.[299]

Another female Quaker, Katherine Whitton, wrote to her fellow Friends in 1681 of the benefits of 'comely order' in the 'house' of the heart, as well as one's literal household:[300]

> To be truly arrayed in the White-Linen which is the righteousness of the Saints, is very decent, and to have this house (to wit, our hearts and inward parts) clean swept, and all its furniture of righteousness set in good and comely order, in carefulness, is very commendable and consistent with good housewifery too.[301]

She concluded her epistle with the exhortation, 'So Friends let us be Faithful to the Lord, and careful over his household and family ... giveing them Meat

---

[296] *A short testimony from some of those that are come to the Obedience of the Gospel, Against all false Liberty in Youth (or whom it may concern) amongst us that make the cross of Christ of none Effect, and the pretious way of Truth seem a light thing, and evil spoken of by them which are without*, etc. (From *The Quarterly Meeting in London, the 8th of the 8th month* [1677], 2.)

[297] *A short testimony from some of those that are come to the Obedience of the Gospel*, 5

[298] Mary Waite, *A Warning to All Friends* (1679), 6.

[299] Ibid, 7.

[300] For further reading concerning seventeenth-century women's spirituality and housewifery see Mack, *Visionary Women*, 305–50.

[301] Katherine Whitton, *An Epistle to Friends Everywhere* (London: Printed for Benjamin Clark, 1681), 6.

in due Season, Feeding the Hungry, Cloathing the Naked', while relying on the 'Heavenly Wisdom' bestowed upon God's sons, daughters, 'Servants and Handmaids'.[302] Whitton, like her fellow Friends Fox and Waite, connected good order in the home to good spiritual order and righteousness within the heart and community, or as Fox put it, 'Christ's government in the hearts of his people'.[303]

Finally, Fox added another very important component to the notion of Gospel Family-Order, as can be seen in his previously mentioned discourse from Barbados in 1671. Fox explicitly stated to the Men's Meeting, which included heads of families and plantations, that they should teach the 'Way of the Lord, and the New Covenant' to their families and children, *as well as* to 'those you bought with Moneys, and the Strangers, and such as are born of them in your House'.[304] Gospel Family-Order, according to Fox, necessitated the inclusion of slaves as members of the True Church. All members of the entire family of God – Meetings, plantations or homes – all were included in the household of God regardless of race or social status. Fox's paternalistic vision of an Abrahamic family unit which regarded slaves as fellow human beings, particularly as a vehicle for the perpetuation of the True Church, stood in stark contrast to the practices of most planters and masters in Barbados at the time. The historian Hilary McD. Beckles asserts Barbadian planters had abandoned the 'traditional values and ideologies of paternalistic master-servant relations', and thus did not 'conceive of their servants socially and emotionally as integral parts of the family or household, but instead viewed them as an alienated commodity which could be recruited and exploited'.[305] At a time when slaves were considered less than human or mere property, Fox's assertion that slaves were essentially Second Adams, equal members of the True Church, worthy of education and inclusion in worship is noteworthy. As we will see shortly, though Fox did not advocate slaves rebelling against their master or running away, he did advocate humane treatment of slaves as fellow members of the spiritual household of God.[306]

---

[302] Ibid.

[303] Fox, *Gospel Family-Order*, 3.

[304] Ibid, 5.

[305] Hilary McD. Beckles, *White Servitude and Black Slavery in Barbados, 1627–1715* (Knoxville, TN: The University of Tennessee Press, 1989), 5.

[306] There is some argument about the extent of Fox's anti-slavery sentiment amongst Quaker scholars. In 1947, Herbert Aptheker acknowledged that while Fox had advocated the education of slaves as early as 1657 in his letter 'To Friends beyond the sea that have Blacks and Indian Slaves', the first reference to slavery from a Quaker, he laments the letter 'is not antislavery but merely maintains that since God made all the nations of the earth one blood, all are entitled to hear his message. Fox therefore asks that the slaves' religious instruction should not be neglected' (Herbert Aptheker, 'The Quakers and Negro Slavery', *The Journal of Negro History*, 26 no 3 [July 1940]: 331–62; p. 333). Aptheker argues in his article that while Quakers as a body have historically been seen as a force for the abolition of slavery, the process

After arriving in Barbados in 1671, Fox realised Barbadian Quaker masters were not treating slaves as members of the True Church and household of God. The education of slaves was overall largely neglected, they were not encouraged to worship, nor were they encouraged, as we will discuss shortly, to pursue monogamous relationships in honourable marriages. Grieved by this, Fox explained to them he was very troubled 'to see that Families were not brought into Order, for the Blacks are of your Families'.[307] The number of slaves who belonged to Quakers on Barbados was not small. The historian Larry Dale Gragg notes by 1680 out of the 2,593 property holders in Barbados, 120 were Quakers who, incidentally, were also quite prosperous on the island.[308] Gragg explains 14, or 6 per cent, of the 'big planters' on the island were Quakers, averaging 223 acres, 113 slaves and 3 servants, while the 'middling' Quaker planters (who made up 11 per cent of the middling planter class on the island) averaged 79 acres, 35 slaves and 2 servants, and the Quaker 'small planters' (5 per cent of the 1,041 small planters) averaged 24 acres, 9 slaves and 1 servant.[309] When Fox arrived in Barbados, he stayed his first week with one of the most powerful planters on the island, a Quaker called Lewis Morris, whose holdings reached 400 acres and 200 slaves.[310] Fox's assertions regarding each slave's humanity and membership within each Quaker family were thus directed to hundreds upon hundreds of people in bondage.

In a paper addressed to the Governor of Barbados he acknowledged the great number of slaves on the island and the heavenly repercussions that would follow the mistreatment of them:

---

of developing anti-slavery sentiment amongst Quakers was slow. In more recent scholarship, the sentiment is generally the same, if not a little more gracious to Fox in acknowledging he was at least ambiguous about anti-slavery. The Quaker historian J. William Frost wrote in 1991 that while Fox's contributions to anti-slavery are embarrassingly scant, and never 'addressed the morality of slavery, *per se*', Fox did 'advocate the humane treatment of slaves, proclaimed that Christ died for all people – whites, blacks, and Indians', making his attitudes 'appear very progressive as compared to virtually all other Quaker and non-Quaker visitors to the West Indies' (J. William Frost, 'George Fox's Ambiguous Anti-slavery Legacy'. From Mullett [Ed.], *New Light on George Fox*, 69–70).

[307] Fox, *Gospel Family-Order*, 19.

[308] Gragg, *The Quaker Community on Barbados*, 64.

[309] Ibid. Gragg explains, ' ... while they had substantial acreage and many slaves, the Quakers may not have been as affluent as the other "big planters". Still, they were men of great substance'.

[310] Ibid, 65–6.

> Now Negroes, Tawnies, Indians, make up a very great part of the families in this island; for whom an account will be required by him who comes to judge both the quick and the dead, at the great day of judgment.[311]

As Fox contended that slaves were equally viable members of the True Church and of the Quaker family, every slave was thus under Christ's order, law and government – all signs, according to Fox, of the righteousness of the Quaker community:

> I had much trouble, how that Righteousness might be brought through in the thing, and Justice and Mercy set up in every Family and in *every* Heart, that so God might be honoured in every Family, who is the Creator of *all*, and hath given his Law to *all* ... and so I leave these things to your serious consideration.[312]

Upholding Christ's government in *all* persons was necessary to uphold and perpetuate God's True Church and Gospel Family-Order. The full inclusion of slaves into the household or family of God was the critical foundation of that task.

Again turning to the example of Abraham, Fox supported his view through exhorting Quaker families to embrace God's covenant of maintaining and governing families through the inclusion of slaves in the household, as well as through regular worship and meetings amongst the slaves. In a letter from Maryland in 1672, Fox wrote a letter to Barbados, 'Touching the Government of Families', in which he again exhorted masters and mistresses:

> And in all your Family Meetings be not negligent among your whites and Negroes, but do your Diligence and Duty to God and them, which you will not neglect, if you keep the faith of Abraham.[313]

The following year, Fox wrote from London two years after his trip to Barbados:

> Dear Friends, keep your meetings, and your Men's and Women's, and your Fortnights Meetings among your Blacks, and train them up in the fear of the Lord, and spread the Truth abroad, and instruct your Families, as Abraham did.[314]

---

[311] George Fox, *For the Governor of Barbados, with his Council and Assembly, and all others in power, both civil and military in this Island; from the People called Quakers* (1686). (Printed in Fox, *Journal Vol. 2* [1836], 152.)

[312] Fox, *Gospel Family-Order*, 19. (Italics mine.)

[313] George Fox, *Letter from Maryland, the 4th Day of the 12th Month, 1671*. (Fox, *Gospel Family-Order*, 20.)

[314] Fox, *Letter from London, the 14th day of the 7th Month, 1673*. (Fox, *Gospel Family-Order*, 21.)

As in the household of Abraham, Fox encouraged Barbadian Friends to set up a largely paternalistic family order, consisting of humane treatment of slaves in the households as well as their inclusion in Quaker Meetings.

While it is unclear how the slaves received this order, there is evidence some slaves at least attended Quaker meetings and engaged in dialogue with Fox and other Quakers. During his trip to Barbados in 1671, Fox spent a great deal of time amongst the slaves in the plantations. A Friend called John Stubbs wrote to Fell from Barbados, explaining Fox's preaching and teaching with the local slaves, and the legacy of which was picked up by Stubbs and a man called Solomon:[315]

> The Truth is freely preached, both to white people and black people. Solomon and I have had several meetings among negroes in several plantations, and it's like must have more yet. But thy husband, it's like, hath had more than any of us; we feel the Lord's presence and power in that service, as well as when we speak among the white people, and that's enough. Thy husband had the first meeting with them, and then after a while, it fell upon me and Solomon.[316]

The legacy of including slaves in Meetings, education and worship left by Fox encouraged Friends to appreciate that 'the power of God' could equally be felt amongst both the slaves and the white Friends of Barbados, as all were equally spiritually restored and under Christ's order and government in the True Church. This legacy apparently remained after Fox's departure from the island. In 1677, a wealthy Quaker planter called Richard Sutton was arrested in Barbados for allowing thirty black slaves to be present at a Meeting.[317]

The perpetuation of the household of God, under Christ's government, also extended to implementing the marriage discipline amongst the slaves like that of their Quaker masters – with both the practical process and the spiritual significance being the same.[318] As we have already seen, the marriage discipline was considered evidence of Gospel-Order, and was a primary vehicle for the

---

[315] Ibid. It is not clear from the text, but it is possible Solomon was a slave.

[316] *John Stubbs to Margaret Fox, Barbados: 2nd 10th mo. [Dec.], 1671*. Reprinted in Fox, *Journal* (1952), 601–2.

[317] Herbert Aptheker, 'The Quakers and Negro Slavery', 334; Gragg, *The Quaker Community on Barbados*, 138; Norman Penney (Ed.), *The Short Journals and Itinerary Journals of George Fox* (Cambridge: Cambridge University Press, 1925), 346 n 187.

[318] Frost briefly acknowledges Fox 'insisted upon the necessity of treating the marriages of blacks like those of whites' but does not address the spiritual implications of this necessity, nor does he further explicate on Fox's views of marriage in association with slavery save his intriguing passing comment Fox 'condemned the lack of marriage and frequency of adultery in slavery, holding the masters and blacks responsible, but never mentioned the pervasive physical cruelty and near-starvation of the slaves' (Frost, 'George Fox's Ambiguous Anti-slavery Legacy'. From Mullett [Ed.], *New Light on George Fox*, 73). Frost's comment begs the

maintenance of the True Church and Gospel Family-Order reflecting the pragmatic orderly process and certification of marriage approbation, as well as the high spiritual discipline of honourable marriages with undefiled beds. In Barbados Fox instructed that all slaves who desired to marry were required to 'take one another before Witnesses in the presence of God and the Masters of the Families, in the Name of Jesus, the Restorer of all Things'.[319] Fox regarded slave marriages on the same grounds as the marriages amongst the free. The slaves were thus not only considered spiritually equal to their white masters, based on the foundation of the Quaker perception of the restoration out of the Fall, but this spiritual equality had physical and practical ramifications: honourable marriages done in the presence of God and witnesses.[320] Monogamy was likewise encouraged amongst the slaves:

> Let not I say … such as you have bought with Money, suffer them not … to take Husbands and Wives at their Pleasure, and then leave them again when they please … this is not well; this may bring judgment of God upon you … yea, this manifests your Families to be unclean and adulterous … this is the Law of God, and of Jesus Christ, the great Reformer and Restorer.[321]

The 'Law of God' permitted no adultery amongst the entire household of God, whether slave or free.

Fox and the early Quaker encouragement of slaves forming monogamous relations and marrying is stunning in light of the fact, as Beckles reminds us, that 'Seventeenth–century Barbados planters did not encourage either slaves or servants to form stable monogamous relationships within family structures.'[322] Beckles explains the planters' reasons for discouraging monogamy and their fears of religious groups supporting such relationships:

> The planters believed that the stabilization of family and sexual relations, with the support of religious dogma, interfered with their objective of reproducing an efficient, obedient labour force. Furthermore, it was felt that the emotional ties resulting from family relations diminished servants' ability to accept subordinate position.[323]

---

question why, and on what grounds, marriage amongst slaves was so important to Fox, but Frost does not attempt to provide an answer in his essay.

[319] Fox, *Gospel Family-Order*, 17–18.
[320] Ibid.
[321] Ibid, 17.
[322] Beckles, *White Servitude and Black Slavery in Barbados*, 83.
[323] Ibid.

Fox on the contrary explicitly called on masters to encourage monogamous relations amongst slaves by providing means for slaves to marry in the Quaker way, just as it was in the 'Beginning':

> God made them Male and Female, not one Man and many Women, but a Man and a Woman, and they were to continue and consort together as long as they lived, and not to break the Covenant and Law of Marriage (nor defile the Marriage Bed) as long as they lived.[324]

At a time when slaves were discouraged to form personal bonds, Fox was not only recommending they form monogamous attachments, but upheld their unions to the same spiritual plane as that of their masters' marriages: honourable marriages with undefiled beds.

The early Quakers of Barbados, owing much to their outspoken encouragement of slaves to participate in religion as well as marry, were susceptible to scrutiny and criticisms from the other planters and masters of the island. Fears abounded amongst planters and masters of Barbados that their slaves would rebel, escape and run away from the island, making it virtually impossible for them to find and recapture their slaves.[325] These fears were a component of accusations against Quakers in Barbados that they were encouraging slaves to run away. The same year Fox had voiced his concerns to the Men's Meetings regarding marriage and Gospel Family-Order, Fox and fellow Friends in Barbados addressed a paper to the Governor and Assembly at Barbados in which they defended themselves from the 'slander and lie' that they were teaching 'the negro to rebel, a thing we do utterly abhor and detest in and from our hearts':[326]

> For that which we have spoken and declared to them is to exhort and admonish them to be sober and to fear God, and to love their masters and mistresses, and to be faithful and diligent in their masters' service ... and that their masters and overseers will love them and deal kindly and gently with them ... it's no transgression for a master of a family to instruct his family ... it is a very great duty incumbent upon them, as Abraham and Joshua did.[327]

According to their justification, just as Abraham instructed his extended family, including slaves, so too were the Quakers, encouraging harmonious relations

---

[324] Fox, *Gospel Family-Order*, 18.

[325] Beckles, *White Servitude and Black Slavery in Barbados*, 83.

[326] George Fox, *To the Governor and Assembly at Barbados* (1671). Reprinted in Fox, *Journal* (1952), 604.

[327] Ibid.

within the familial unit. But this was not where Fox's advocacy amongst slaves ended.

It is clear at this time that Fox never directed or encouraged slaves to rebel and leave their masters. However, he did harbour hope that the masters of the slaves, after instructing their slaves about God and encouraging times of worship amongst them, would effect a very physical outcome from the spiritual restoration of the slaves – their eventual physical freedom. To be sure the Friends in Barbados were indeed following the Abrahamic example of instructing their slaves, Fox made the following remarkable request: 'send me over a Black boy of your instructing that I may see some of your Fruits, and as I shall see, I shall make him a free Man, or send him to you again'.[328] In light of this request, it is not wholly implausible to consider Fox's call for the teaching of slaves could potentially lead to slaves being called out of bondage, both spiritually and physically, with the help of the masters.[329]

Fox also explicitly exhorted masters of slaves to set the slaves free after a period of years of service, a striking precursor to later Quaker involvement in the abolition of slavery:

> Let me tell you, it will be doubtless very acceptable to the Lord, if so be that Masters of Families here would deal so with their Servants, the Negroes and Blacks, whom they have bought with their Money, to let them go free after a considerable Term of Years, if they have served them faithfully: and when they go, and are made free, let them not go away empty handed, this I say will be very acceptable to the Lord.[330]

In support of his argument, Fox likened the situation to the plight of the slaves of Israel, asking the masters to try to put themselves in the position of the slaves and consider their plight:

> If you were in the same Condition as the Blacks are (and indeed you do not know what Condition you or your Children, or your Children's Children may be reduced and brought into, before you or they shall dye) who came as Strangers to you, and were sold to you as Slaves; now I say, if this should be the Condition of you and yours, you would think it hard Measure; yeah, and a very great Bondage and Cruelty.[331]

---

[328] Fox, *Letter from London 18th of 12th Month, 1673*. Reprinted in Fox, *Gospel Family-Order*, 22.

[329] A slave rebellion occurred in Barbados in 1675, resulting in the enactment of anti-Quaker laws and increased suspicion of practicing Quakers and their activities amongst slave labour (Aptheker, 'The Quakers and Negro Slavery', 334).

[330] Fox, *Gospel Family-Order*, 16. This is a possible reference to Leviticus 25.

[331] Ibid, 18.

Teaching the 'way of the Covenant', and God's promises for freedom, did not only entail bringing slaves under the order of Christ's government within the family, but also entailed the following through of physical freedom for all of God's children in that family. However, as Gragg reminds us, on seventeenth-century Barbados 'any question raised about slavery posed a profound and troubling challenge to a labour system indispensable to the success of sugar planters', which led to a very slow evolution from slave owner to abolitionist for most Quakers throughout the Atlantic world.[332]

Fox therefore understood 'family' within multiple contexts – families of parents and children, families of entire households, including servants, 'strangers' and people 'bought with money', or persons marrying into a family, and finally the family of the Quaker Meetings in the broader communal context. In all of these cases, each person, slave or free, was considered a member of the household of God, spiritually equal, and restored into the honourable image of God, enjoying God's presence within their conscience with the equal responsibility to respond to and to obey that of God within. Fox concluded his remarks to the Men's Meeting in Barbados:

> And so I leave these Things to your serious consideration ... for indeed when any shall marry into your Family ... then you may admonish them all of God and of Christ, and know the true Marriage which is honourable in all things to beat down the Evil and Vile; for Marriage is of God, and so honoured by him.[333]

The 'true Marriage' for Fox, the marriage between Christ and his True Church, embodied both spiritual and physical freedom for all, while marriages between Friends encouraged and strengthened righteousness within families and unity between all members of the family of God. The spiritual household, both in the home and in the Meetings, was the foundation of the True Church. Quoting again the book of Revelation, Fox further explicated over a decade after his trip to Barbados:

> They are living members, living stones, built up a spiritual household, children of the promise, and of the Seed and flesh of Christ; and as the apostle saith, 'Flesh of his flesh and bone of his bone.' ... They sit together in heavenly places in Christ, are clothed with the Sun of Righteousness, Christ Jesus, and have the moon under their feet, as Rev xii ... And they that are quickened by Christ, are the living stones, living members, and spiritual household and church, or congregation of Christ, who is the living head and husband.[334]

---

[332] Gragg, *The Quaker Community on Barbados*, 121.
[333] Fox, *Gospel Family-Order*, 19.
[334] Fox, *Journal Vol. 2* (1836), 387, 393.

In the next chapter, we will explore how the 'true Marriage' was, for many Quakers, exemplified through the honourable marital union between George Fox and Margaret Fell.

Chapter 3
The Marriage of Margaret Fell and George Fox

We took each other in marriage, the Lord joining us together in the honourable marriage, in the everlasting covenant and immortal Seed of life.[1]

Though the marriage approbation of Fox and Fell was largely subject to the same order and process as all other Quaker marriages, the spiritual implications of their marriage were largely elevated in much of the Quaker mindset, as the leading Quaker prophet married one of his most important converts, who was also a great leader. When the 'father' of Quakerism married the 'Mother in Israel', many early Quakers regarded the Fell/Fox union as spiritually significant in that it testified to a fulfilment of the Quaker aspiration of returning to Paradise, a fulfilment of God's covenant of life. Evidence suggests that the motivation for the marriage of Fox and Fell was not simply to unify the leadership of the movement. Fox and Fell shared a vision of marriage that reflected and fulfilled their doctrine of marriage. According to Fox and Fell, their marriage was motivated by spiritual 'leadings from the Lord', a requirement for all early Quaker unions, but was additionally to be accomplished as a 'testimony that all might come up out of the wilderness'. Not purely practical or without emotion, as can be seen in the testimonies at their wedding, their marriage was motivated by both theological and personal reasons. There was an apparent genuine affection shared by each other, as evidenced particularly in their exchange of letters. In addition to these letters, a variety of resources regarding the matrimony of Fox and Fell have been at best only briefly touched upon by scholars. Yet these documents not only shed light on the significant theological underpinnings of Fox and Fell's marriage theology, but also help to explain how their marriage uniquely reflected early Quaker perceptions of a restored creation. In this chapter, an analysis of the development of their relationship and the approbation of their marriage, including their particular wedding vows, will be considered. This will be followed by an examination of the biblical and apocalyptic imagery used by Fox and Fell in regards to their marital union, including their understanding of the images of the new Adam, the Lamb and the New Jerusalem, and the subsequent spiritual and theological implications of their marriage. Finally, we will discuss the Fox/Fell marital relationship, their day-to-day life and correspondence as a married couple, noting whether their relationship changed after their marriage,

---

[1] Fox, *Journal Vol. 2* (1836), 118.

and how their marriage was received and perceived by their contemporary Quaker communities.

The Royal Seed and the Book of Revelation

Before examining the writings and testimonies regarding the marriage approbation of Fox and Fell, it will be helpful to take pause and review their perceptions of the world specifically through scripture, particularly the book of Revelation. While Quakers were often attacked by their opposing counterparts, as well as being seen historically as a group largely giving precedence to direct revelation over scriptural revelation, the language of the early Quakers was saturated with scriptural imagery and references to scripture. As previously noted, many early Quakers, like many of their seventeenth-century contemporaries, spoke and wrote with biblical imagery believing it to be a very real rubric in understanding the world around them. In their day-to-day life as well as in their perceptions of the beginning and end of the world, and their role in cosmic events, scriptural narratives and imagery thus informed practically every part of their lives in the Quaker mindset. The biblical images used throughout the following testimonies are indicative of the Quakers' fluid use of scriptural language, utilised to give meaning to their current surroundings and spiritual events, including the momentous occasion of the marriage between Fox and Fell.

Throughout Fox and Fell's written works they frequently inserted scriptural references in the margins of their writings as biblical support for their arguments and ideas. As previously mentioned in chapter two, the biblical books frequently referred to by Fox and Fell included the first and last books of the Bible: the Old Testament book of Genesis and the New Testament book of Revelation. The book of Genesis relays the creation of the world and humanity, as well as its 'fall', and was also important for Fox and Fell in its recounting of God's original intentions of having a direct relationship with humanity in a 'pure and innocent' state. The book of Revelation provides in apocalyptic imagery the course of the end of the old world, and God's restoration of the new world, what Fox referred to as a return to 'Paradise' or the fulfilment of the 'New Covenant'.[2] Fox provided a thorough summary of the history of the world and cosmos in a sermon he delivered in London in 1680. Fox began with the story of creation as told in Genesis, how God 'placed man in a blessed habitation in the beginning

---

[2] Rosemary Moore provides a useful summary of the way Quakers read the scriptures: ' ... a reader of early Quaker tracts is left with certain impressions. Quakers interpreted the whole sweep of the Old and New Testament story, from Genesis by way of the prophets through to Christ and the Book of Revelation, in such a way as to show that the story rightly ended with the mid-seventeenth-century gift of the Spirit to the Quakers, the same spirit that had inspired the prophets and apostles' (Moore, *The Light in Their Consciences*, 53).

... and made him perfect'. But this 'blessed concord' between humanity and God was lost by the work of the 'Serpent'. After God had set humanity in 'Paradise his garden of pleasure', the serpent went to the woman, convinced her to eat from the forbidden tree of knowledge, and then 'man entering temptation also, they both lost the blessed estate, the concord'. The result of humanity's disobedience was 'Adam died, Eve died' and they 'knew not God', a broken state which could only be resolved with the coming of Christ, as Fox concluded, 'And here came the Lamb to be slain from the foundation of the world'. After humanity had disobeyed God and eaten from the 'Tree of Knowledge', Fox affirmed 'man and woman came then to be driven out of the garden, and a flaming sword placed every way with two edges to keep the way of the tree of life'.[3]

Fox's firm conviction that humanity in this world and in his time had the opportunity to pass through the 'flaming swords' and re-enter paradise was an event he claimed to have experienced first hand. Fox saw himself as perhaps the first one to experience this in his age. His conversion subsequently set the precedence for others, as he considered himself as a sign of the new age of the True Church coming forth and 'innocency' being renewed in humanity. In Fox's early description of his conversion, originally written in 1648, he elaborated on his personal spiritual experience of leaving the wilderness and entering Paradise:

> Now was I come up in Spirit through the flaming sword, into the paradise of God. All things were new, and all the creation gave another smell unto me than before, beyond what words can utter. I knew nothing but pureness and innocency and righteousness, being renewed up into the image of God by Christ Jesus, so that I say I was come up to the state of Adam, which he was in before he fell ... I was immediately taken up in spirit to see into another or more steadfast state than Adam's in innocency, even into a state in Christ Jesus that should never fall. And the Lord shewed me that such as were faithful to Him ... should come up into that state in which Adam was before he fell ... as people come into the subjection to the Spirit of God, and grow up in the image and power of the Almighty, they may receive the word of wisdom that opens up all things, and come to know the hidden unity in the Eternal Being.[4]

As discussed in the previous chapter, all Quakers were ideally returning to Paradise. So too was Fox. In the above vision, Fox believed he had returned physically to the state in 'which [Adam] was ... before he fell', and witnessed paradise first hand. As we have seen, while many of his Protestant contemporaries were preaching humanity's state of total depravity outside Paradise, Fox was

---

[3] *George Fox's Sermon at Wheeler Street, 1680.* (Barbour and Roberts [Eds], *Early Quaker Writings*, 502–3.)
[4] Fox, *Journal Vol. 1* (1836), 105–6.

preaching that humanity had the option of being fully restored and return to the interior of Paradise, where they once again would be 'innocent'. This belief that humanity could be in the state of Christ 'that should never fall' infiltrated Fox and Fell's perceptions of their own marital union and its proceedings. In 1659, Fox exhorted Quakers who married in the 'power of God' that they may 'know it to be as it was in the beginning, the true Marriage; God made them Male and Female, the honourable Mariage ... which was before the fall'.[5] Written ten years before his marriage to Fell, this idea of the restored relationship before the Fall will be considered later in this chapter, in an analysis of the testimonies shared by Fox, Fell and other Quakers at their wedding and during the approbation process. Their marriage was 'the honourable marriage' and the archetype for all Quaker marriages.

Another biblical image, largely based on Genesis and Revelation, that appears frequently throughout the writings and testimonies surrounding the Fox/Fell marriage is the concept of marriage in 'the seed'. Metaphors of the 'seed' and 'sin' were already abundant, particularly amongst a variety of sectarians, by the seventeenth century.[6] The Quakers likewise utilised the metaphor of the 'seed' in varying ways, largely in relationship to their understanding of the fall of humanity, the later restoration of humanity, and the True Church coming up out of the wilderness. As noted in the introduction, the early Quakers often used the terms 'light' and 'seed' interchangeably. Both terms represented the presence of Christ within the conscience. Fox and Fell often referred to the 'seed' of God in every human being, frequently using phrases regarding Quakers as being the 'seed of God' or the 'Royal Seed'.[7] Additionally, based on the Genesis narratives

---

[5]   Fox, *Concerning Marriage* (1661), 7.

[6]   Philip C. Almond, *Adam and Eve in Seventeenth-Century Thought* (Cambridge: Cambridge University Press, 1999), 174–5. 'Influenced by Boehme a number of the sectarians saw the serpent's attack on Eve as resulting in conception, in the birth of Cain and in his reprobate progeny – the seed of Cain ... the first-born Cain was the very seed or spirit of that reprobate Serpent Angel in the body of Eve, and the first born [sic] child or son of the Devil ... Doctrine of the two seeds was traditional among the radicals. It occurred in the writings of Jon Saltmarsh, Gerrard Winstanley, Abiezer Coppe, George Fox, and elsewhere'. Though Fox and Fell used the term 'seed' frequently, they did not follow the Behmenist thought, never referring to the impregnation of Eve and rarely mentioning Cain.

[7]   Moore, *The Light in Their Consciences*, 82. 'Fox made more use of "seed" to mean the people of God and Christ within them, from the 1660s onwards'. Margaret Fell wrote to her fellow Quakers in 1656, 'Therefore, dearly beloved children, consider what ye are called to, and what ye are made to partake of, a living, and pure and holy priesthood, a peculiar people ye are, and of the holy nation and of the Royal Seed' (Margaret Fell, *An Epistle to Convinced Friends* [1656], 88). The following year, Fell wrote 'Dear Friends, this I write unto you in tender and in dear love to the Seed of God in you all, for which my soul travails' (Margaret Fell, *An Epistle to Friends* [1657], 96). In Margaret Askew Fell Fox, *The life of Margaret Fox. Wife of George Fox. Compiled from her own narratives, and other sources; with a selection from*

regarding ancestry and God's covenants and promises with his chosen people, the term 'seed' was connected to the greater cosmic battle between Satan and God. The historian Rosemary Moore notes 'Fox generally linked [seed] to Genesis 3.15, where the "seed of the woman", meaning Christ, is contrasted with the "seed of the serpent", or to Genesis 24, where the seed of Isaac is contrasted with the "seed of the bondswoman", or Ishmael'.[8] In Genesis chapter three, after Eve and Adam were deceived by the serpent and ate of the Tree of Knowledge, God pronounced a sentence on the serpent, as Fell summarised in 1666, 'See what the Lord saith in verse 15 … I will put Enmity between thee and the Woman, and between thy Seed and her Seed; it shall bruise thy Head, and thou shalt bruise his Heel'.[9] This 'enmity' continued to exist, throughout the history of the world, between the 'seed of the serpent' or Satan, i.e. all those who commit evil actions and turn away from God, and the 'seed of the Woman'. This was first Eve, then subsequently Sarah (the wife of Isaac referenced in Genesis 24), and eventually the Virgin Mary who would give birth to Jesus. Fox and Fell perceived a world where these two seeds, 'the seed of the serpent' and the 'seed of the Woman', were in opposition.[10]

These images provided a concrete context to their understanding of the great cosmic battle, between God and Satan, and the subsequent 'Lamb's War' between the 'seed' of God, the Quakers and the 'seed' of Satan (i.e. those who were not Quakers). In 1680, Fox referred to the Genesis account of God's covenant with Abraham that all nations would eventually be 'blessed' through the 'seed' of Abraham: 'This was the gospel to Abraham: "in thy seed all nations shall be blessed". So all nations shall come to the blessing of the Seed'.[11] The Friends believed they came from the line of Isaac, and subsequently the line of Jesus, not by blood, but by spirit. This was both an outward and an inward battle. In Fox's 1647 recollections from his *Journal*, he explained:

> So Christ, the Word of God, that bruised the head of the Serpent the destroyer, preserved me, my inward mind being joined to his good Seed, that bruised the

---

her epistles, etc. (Philadelphia, PA: Association of Friends for the Diffusion of Religious and Useful Knowledge, 1859).

[8] Moore, *The Light in Their Consciences*, 83.

[9] Fell, *Womens Speaking Justified*, 1.

[10] Rosemary R. Ruether, *Introducing Redemption in Christian Feminism*, 54. Ruether explains, 'Following the tradition of that the "seed of the woman" is Christ, Quakers divided humanity between the "two seeds", those who are in the light, who belong to the "seed of the woman". And those who remain alienated from God, who belong to the seed of Satan'.

[11] *George Fox's Sermon at Wheeler Street, 1680*. (Barbour and Roberts [Eds], *Early Quaker Writings*, 505.)

head of the Serpent the destroyer. And this inward life did spring up in me, to answer all the opposing professors and priests.[12]

Joining his 'inward mind' to God's 'good Seed', Fox essentially experienced that seed of Christ within 'springing forth' and battling the seed of the serpent in the professors and priests.

The notion of *marriages* 'in the seed' provided a context to their understanding of the redeemed male/female relationship, as Fox elaborated upon in his aforementioned sermon in 1680:

> Now it's said 'the seed of the woman' ... shall bruise the Serpent's head ... This was the first Gospel promise, in which all the faithful did believe in and hope that this should come to pass. Therefore you see the Apostle, in the 11th to the Hebrews, reckons up to Enoch and Abraham and Abel and all these died in the faith, not receiving the promised that is, the Seed was not yet come. But to us and in our day, the Apostles' day, the Seed did come that inherits the promise, and the saints in the Apostles' days enjoyed that Seed that was come to bruise the Serpent's head ... So here, in the resurrection and restoration of man up again into the image of God, Christ, (who bruiseth the Serpent's head that defiled man, and sanctifies and renews up into the heavenly image, as Adam and Eve were in before they fell); here they come to be meet helps.[13]

Returning to his 1659 work *Concerning Marriage*, Fox encouraged his fellow Quakers to be 'a Royal seed, a peculiar people zealous of good works, and to know God's joyning together, which is over and above mens putting asunder'.[14] A marriage 'in the seed' was joined together by God, a picture of the restored relationship between the divine and humanity, and an act of victory of sorts of the 'Royal seed', which again was the basis of Fox's perception of his marriage to Fell.

Another crucial element when examining the language used during their marriage approbation process and testimonies is to bear in mind the Quakers' prolific use of imagery from the book of Revelation. The image of the Lamb and the New Jerusalem comes largely out of this last book of the Bible, which recounts in apocalyptic imagery the second coming of Christ and the restoration of creation. Interestingly, a passage in Revelation addressed 'to the angel of the church of Philadelphia' gives an encouragement to that church which has

---

[12] Fox, *Journal* (1952), 13.
[13] George Fox, *The True Church Restored* (1680). (Barbour and Roberts [Eds], *Early Quaker Writings*, 504–5.)
[14] Fox, *Concerning Marriage* (1661), 7.

remained faithful to God, including the phrase the 'New Jerusalem', a self-descriptive name consistently used amongst Quakers:

> I am coming soon ... If you conquer, I will make you a pillar in the temple of my God; and you will never go out of it. I will write on you the name of my God, and the name of the city of my God, the new Jerusalem that comes down from my God out of heaven.[15]

As evidenced in the following wedding testimonies, we will see Margaret Fell referenced Revelation in her testimony, shared at her marriage to Fox, in which she refers to herself as 'the Lamb's wife, whose Light is as a jasper stone, clear as crystal', echoing references to Christ in Revelation 4, 'And there in heaven stood a throne ... And the one seated there looks like jasper ... and in front of the throne there is something like a sea of glass, like crystal'.[16]

Some imagery borrowed from Revelation by the Quakers has been too quickly attributed to solely 'hermetic and occultist thought', an argument Jacques Tual puts forth. Tual argues early Friends viewed their marriages as a microcosm of the 'macrocosmic alchemical pairing of the Sun and the Moon, of Heaven and Earth, of Nature and God', indicating that 'hermetic and occultist thought' found its way into 'the movement's reflection', the symbolical significance of which 'underlies George Fox's marriage to Margaret Fell'.[17] It would be interesting to see where Tual found Quakers using occultist or hermetic language in their weddings, as he does not provide information on or examples of how these images were used, nor any historical references to their use amongst any specific early Quaker marriages. The testimonies shared at Fox and Fell's wedding, as well Fox's epistle on his marriage to Fell, are infused with biblical imagery that had been used by the Quakers from the beginning of the movement, as the juxtapositions mentioned by Tual were often set in a biblical context. The image of 'Heaven and Earth' for example was based largely on Fox's reading of Revelation, in which Fox interpreted the final cosmic battle between God in heaven and evil on earth, at the end of which the 'New Jerusalem' replaces the 'Old Jerusalem'. The juxtaposition of heaven and earth, of Godly wisdom and earthly wisdom, are found throughout Fox's writings and sermons, including in his sermon in London, in which he encouraged his listeners:

> Look up and have the wine of the kingdom and receive the spring of life from heaven ... these have their bread from heaven, all looking upwards and not downwards ... for those who look downwards look for the bread in the house

---

[15] Bible, *New Revised Standard Version*, Revelation 3:12–13.
[16] Ibid, Revelation 4:2–6.
[17] Tual, 'Sexual Equality and Conjugal Harmony', 165.

of the old Adam ... But in the son's house, the second Adam, there is living unleavened bread.[18]

While the image of the 'sun and moon' in correlation with the marriage partnership was not used during the marriage of Fox and Fell, the image of the church being 'clothed with the sun' appears in early Quaker writing. An example of the church being 'clothed with the sun' is found in an introduction to the 1672 edition of Fox's work *The Great Mystery of the Great Whore Unfolded* (originally published in 1659). Written by Edward Burrough just two years after Fox married Fell, it reads 'as our minds became turned, and our hearts inclined to the Light' the Friends came to know:

> The perfect estate of the Church; her estate before the apostles' days, and in the apostles' days ... And her present estate we found to be as a woman who had once been clothed with the sun, and the moon under her feet, who brought forth Him that was to rule the nations; but she [the Church] was fled into the wilderness, and there sitting desolate ... when the time of her sojourning was towards a full end, then *we* [Friends] were brought forth.[19]

Like Burrough, Fox also frequently described the 'true church', i.e. the Quakers, as being 'clothed with the sun' with the 'moon under her feet'. This image comes from Revelation chapter twelve, a selection of which reads as follows:

> A great portent appeared in heaven: a woman clothed with the sun, with the moon under her feet, and on her head a crown of twelve stars. She was pregnant and crying out in birth pangs ... And she gave birth to a son ... who is to rule all the nations ... But her child was snatched away ... and the woman fled into the wilderness.[20]

Fox referenced this passage in his comparison between Christ's True Church and the changeable 'things that are in the World', explaining the 'good Seed' have 'put on the Lord Jesus Christ':

> and so are clothed with the Sun of Righteousness, Christ Jesus, and have the Moon under their feet, as Reveleation 12 ... So all changeable things that are

---

[18] *George Fox's Sermon at Wheeler Street, 1680.* (Barbour and Roberts [Eds], *Early Quaker Writings*, 511.)

[19] Jones, *Spiritual Reformers in the 16th and 17th Centuries*, 338. Cited from Edward Burrough's introduction to the 1672 publication of George Fox's work *The Great Mystery of the Great Whore* (1659).

[20] Bible, *New Revised Standard Version*, Revelation 12:1–2, 5–6.

in the World ... are as the Moon: For the Moon changes, but the Sun doth not change. And so the Sun of Righteousness never changeth, not sets, or goes down.[21]

Interestingly, Edward Burrough compared Fell to the church, the 'woman' in Revelation 12, in a letter he had written to her in 1659:

> O thou daughter of God and a mother in Israel, a nourisher of the fathers babes and children, who are begotten by the everlasting world thou art comely in thy beauty clothed with the sun, and the moon under her feet.[22]

With this image firmly fixed in the Quaker psyche, some saw Fell as a symbol of the church coming forth. Though there was not a direct reference to this image during the extant records of Fox and Fell's marriage proceedings, it would not be far-fetched to assume that Fell represented mother in Israel of 'the restored church', while further, it would not be surprising to see Quakers use this analogy in their marriages, which they considered to be a reflection of the union between Christ and his redeemed church.

While many Quakers were spiritual seekers and therefore likely exposed to hermetic and occultist thought, most Quakers including Fox and Fell predominantly emphasised scripture, including footnoting scriptural references throughout their writings, perhaps in part to avoid criticisms from their contemporaries of being 'unscriptural'. Additionally, the language utilised during the proceedings of the Fell/Fox marriage rings more of Revelation than occultism, as the predominant themes include the coming of the 'New Jerusalem', the marriage of the 'Lamb and his church', innocence, purity, a marriage that was 'in the seed' and was 'above all marriages in the fall'.[23]

---

[21] George Fox, *A Journal or Historical Account of the Life, Travels, and Sufferings, Christian Experiences and Labour of Love in the Work of the Ministry of that Ancient, Eminent and Faithful Servant of Jesus Christ, George Fox. The Second Part.* London: J. Sowle (1709), 464.

[22] *Letter to Margaret Fell, from Dublin* (September 1655). (Barbour and Roberts [Eds], *Early Quaker Writings*, 477.)

[23] There is evidence of some early Quakers being influenced by Behminism, as other sectarians were at the time. There was a copy of Hendrik Nicklas in the Swarthmoor Library, but beyond this it is difficult to assess if Fox or Fell read and incorporated hermetic and Behmist material into their theology and spirituality. However, Rufus Jones in his work *Spiritual Reformers in the 16th and 17th Centuries* notes: 'There is at present no way of proving that George Fox ... had actually read the writings of the Teutonic philosopher [Jacob Böhme] or had consciously absorbed the views of the latter, but there are so many marks of influence apparent in the *Journal* that no careful student of both writers can doubt that there was some sort of influence, direct or indirect, conscious or unconscious. The works of Boehme were, as we have seen, all available in English during the great

The frequent references to the 'Lamb of God' in their marriage proceedings is an image that can be found throughout the New Testament, including Revelation, serving for them a fitting picture of the conquering 'Christ within' who comes to be with his bride, 'the Church'. On the title page of Fox's aforementioned *The Great Mystery of the Great Whore Unfolded*, he introduced his volume:

> In Answer to many False Doctrines and Principles ... being held forth by the professed Ministers, and Teachers ... in England, Ireland, and Scotland ... sent forth by Them ... against the despised People of the Lord called Quakers, who are the Seed of that Woman, who hath long fled into the Wildernes.[24]

For Fox, and many early Quakers, the 'whore' was the defiled, disobedient church who 'knew not God' while the innocent, undefiled, 'spotless bride', the 'woman who fled into the wilderness' was the true, redeemed church, fulfilling the covenant promised to Abraham and Isaac, that a 'seed' will come to 'crush the serpent's head'.

In the following testimonies and Fox's epistles regarding his marriage, we will see Fell and Fox refer to these themes repeatedly. Fell claimed she stood 'pure and spotless, chaste and undefiled to the Lord', while Fox claimed his marriage to Fell was grounded on 'the Church's coming up out of the fall in the seed which was before all: and Is over all; in which seed he was clear and pure and free from all'.[25] As we will see in the following sections, the underlying spiritual foundation of their marriage was the 'pure heavenly marriage' of Christ 'the Lamb' and his church, as William Penn testified in Bristol in an approbation meeting for the Fell/Fox union, ' ... so is this marriage ... the true character, resemblance, and express image of that innocent marriage of the Lamb ... that pure marriage which with the Church and the seed has been in the wilderness and is now come out from thence'.[26]

The Courtship and Marriage Approbation Process of Margaret Fell and George Fox

By the time Margaret Fell and George Fox were married in 1669, they had known each other for nearly twenty years, forming an allegiance, friendship and partnership in leadership for almost two decades. During these years they

---

formative period of Fox's life, from 1647 to 1661' Jones, *Spiritual Reformers in the 16th and 17th Centuries*, 220).

[24] Fox, *The Great Mystery of the Great Whore Unfolded*, 1.
[25] Cadbury (Ed.), *Narrative Papers of George Fox*, 84.
[26] Ibid, 87.

had begun building the theological and spiritual framework of the Quaker movement, dealing with the movement's internal struggles and external persecutions, and at times sharing prison sentences. Though respected as leaders amongst many of Fox's party, their close partnership sometimes prompted criticism, even within the Quaker fold. In 1663, a disgruntled, and eventually disowned, Quaker from Yorkshire called John Harwood publicly accused Fox and Fell within the Quaker circle of questionable behaviour, making innuendos regarding their close working relationship:

> His [Fox] being shut up in a room in Newgate-Market with Margaret Fell, several hours, and none suffered to come into them, thou several endeavoured it, hath not the favour of honesty in it; but I shall leave that to the Lord to judge of, who will reward them according to their works. And it is also reported amongst friends, that the said George Fox & Margaret Fell did so carry themselves each to other, and walk so unseemly and undiscreetly at the House of Elizabeth Trott when they lay there, that she questioned their honesty, and was weary of their company; and what this doth signifie, let truth and innocency judge.[27]

Fox swiftly responded to Harwood's potentially damaging accusations:

> And as for M.F. thou art not worthy to take her name in thy mouth, a virtuous woman, when thou sayest, *being shut up in a room neer Newgate several houres*; this is thy malitiousness, wickedness, for there was her Son in law, and her Daughter was passing to beyond the Seas, where they had something to speak together, where several Friends desired to come in and could not, because I had some businesse to speak with them before they went beyond the Seas, which was the occasion for stopping some Friends; and this is like thy reports at Elizabeth Trotts house, thy false reports: And as for her being weary of my company, or questioning any such thing, or questioning me or she, this is like thy rest, and I believe she will tell it to thee to thy face, for what is to be looked for from thee, & what thou hast acted, with that same line.[28]

Though Harwood was quietened, and in the end was not a threat to the reputation of Fox and Fell or their leadership, this exchange indicates they

---

[27] John Harwood, *To All People That profess the Eternal Truth of the Living God This is A true and real demonstration of the cause why I have denied, and do deny the Authority of George Fox, which is the original ground of the difference betwixt us* (London, 1663), 7.

[28] George Fox, *The spirit of envy, lying, and persecution made manifest for the sake of the simple hearted, that they may not be deceived by it: being an answer to a scandalous paper of John Harwoods, who in words professeth God, but in his works doeth deny Him, as may appear by what is herein written* (London, 1663), 11.

encountered some sceptical questioning before their marriage.[29] In his *Journal*, Fox recollected at the time he was preparing to approach Fell regarding marriage, there was 'jumble in some minds' regarding their personal relationship, 'but the Lord's power came over all and laid all their spirits; and some after confessed it'.[30]

In the years leading up to their marriage in 1669, the Quakers were in the middle of what was arguably the harshest period of Quaker persecution.[31] Five years prior to their marriage, Fox had been arrested at Swarthmoor and sent to Lancaster prison charged primarily for refusing to take the Oath of Obedience.[32] Fell gathered a larger meeting at her house after the arrest, which, according to local magistrate Daniel Fleming, she had done 'on purpose, as 'tis generally thought, to affront our authority'.[33] She was then also arrested on two charges: violation of the Conventicle Act which forbade any meeting of more than five persons outside of the household, designed by the government to quell any possible conspiracies, and like Fox, her refusal to take the Oath of Obedience, which was perceived as a sign of disloyalty by the government. In the trial, Fell still refused to stop the Quaker meetings at Swarthmoor Hall and to make an Oath of Obedience.[34] Being found guilty, Fell was imprisoned at Lancaster Castle in February 1664, and, despite a brief respite at Swarthmoor, was not released until June 1668.[35] After Fell joined Fox in prison they continued their partnership

---

[29] Fox mentioned John Harwood in his *Journal*: 'John Harwood ... turned Apostate from the truth' (Fox, *Journal Vol. 2* [1911], 336). Harwood apparently became a separatist who 'had run out' in 1660 (Braithwaite, *The Beginnings of Quakerism to 1660*, 578).

[30] Fox, *Journal* (1952), 557. See also Kunze, *Margaret Fell and the Rise of Quakerism*, 55.

[31] Horle, *The Quakers and the English Legal System 1660–1688*, xi. Horle argues the harshest period for the early Quakers, particularly in terms of legal prosecutions and imprisonment, occurred between the years of 1660 and 1689.

[32] Fox, *Journal Vol. 2* (1836), lxvii. See also William Cobbett and David Jardine, *Cobbett's complete collection of state trials and proceedings for high treason and other crimes and misdemeanors from the earliest period to the present time, Volume 6: Comprising the period from the reign of King Charles the Second, A.D. 1661, to the thirtieth year of the said reign, A.D. 1678* (London: R. Bagshaw, 1810), No. 218 'The Trial of Margaret Fell and George Fox, for not taking the Oath of Obedience: 16 Charles II A.D. 1664', 629–45. In the Quaker view, taking an oath was against the biblical mandate of never swearing, and also was considered useless by Friends who believed one should always tell the truth.

[33] Braithwaite, *The Second Period of Quakerism*, 33.

[34] Cobbett and Jardine, *Cobbett's complete collection of state trials and proceedings Vol. 6*, 629–45.

[35] Glines [Ed.], *Undaunted Zeal*, 254. Bonnelyn Kunze notes, 'Fortunately for Margaret the king did not seize Swarthmoor, and the Fell daughters continued to live there while their mother was in prison. Her oath trial became a well-remembered show trial for nonconformity. Margaret Fell was a widely known sectarian gentlewoman when she entered Lancaster Castle for an incarceration that began in August 1664 and lasted until June 1668' (Kunze, *Margaret Fell and the Rise of Quakerism*, 18).

in preaching and defending their beliefs. One encounter in particular was with a fellow prisoner, a Baptist called John Wigan, who vehemently opposed the Quaker practice of mixed gender assemblies. Wigan complained one 'may hear not onely men, but women-teachers ... Teaching lyes in the name of the Lord, and causing their weak captivated disciples to erre by their lyes, as that woman Jezebel did, Rev. 2.20'.[36] As a mixed gender leadership team, Fox and Fell countered his arguments, while their shared time in prison likely punctuated and deepened their partnership.[37]

This was the last time they would spend together at length before their marriage. Fox had a 'shorter but harsher confinement' during which he was quite ill and physically weakened. He was finally freed in September 1666, while Fell remained almost two years longer.[38] While Fell's family continued in their attempts to secure her release, Fox visited Fell who, as he explained, 'being a prisoner at Lancaster, got leave to come up to the meeting and went with me to Jane Milner's in Cheshire'.[39] At the end of March 1668, shortly before Fell's release, Fox travelled through Bristol where he participated in 'several powerful meetings' after which they 'settled the Men's Monthly meeting there and the Women's meeting'. Fox then went to London where he 'was moved to exhort them to bring all their marriages into the Men's and Women's Meetings'.[40] Not long after Fell was finally freed, she witnessed the marriage of her daughter Mary to Thomas Lower, and then travelled throughout the North and western parts of England, Bristol, Devon and Somerset with her daughter Rachel. In the winter of 1668, she travelled with Rachel to London, where Fox was preaching, and returned again the following summer of 1669.[41]

It was during this time in London Fox recollected he would 'first mention' marriage to her, and though he felt the time was drawing near for them to

---

[36] T.L. Underwood, *Primitivism, Radicalism, and the Lamb's War: The Baptist-Quaker Conflict in Seventeenth-Century England* (Oxford: Oxford University Press, 1997), 92.

[37] Braithwaite, *The Second Period of Quakerism*, 262. Braithwaite makes the following speculation regarding their shared time in prison: 'Fox was now a man of 45 and his strenuous service and heavy sufferings had already left their mark. There can have been little to choose between him and Margaret Fell, who was ten years his senior but would survive him eleven years. It seems probable that the idea of marriage had been formed while both were prisoners at Lancaster in 1664 and 1665'.

[38] Ibid, 37. It was during this imprisonment that Fell penned her well-known pamphlet *Womens speaking justified* published in 1666 (Kunze, *Margaret Fell and the Rise of Quakerism*, 19). In January of 1665, the Swarthmoor estate was granted to her estranged non-Quaker son George Fell by Charles II (Kunze, *Margaret Fell and the Rise of Quakerism*, xii).

[39] Fox, *Journal* (1952), 514.

[40] Ibid, 519.

[41] Ibid.

marry, he believed he had to go to Ireland first.[42] Fell recalled when Fox initially mentioned marriage to her after her release from Lancaster prison:

> I went down into Cornwall with my son and daughter Lower, and came back by London to the yearly meeting; and there I met with him again; and then he told me the time was drawing on towards our marriage, but he might first go into Ireland ... So into Ireland he went, and I went into Kent and Sussex, and came back to London again; and afterward I went to the west, towards Bristol, in 1669, and there I stayed till he came over from Ireland.[43]

Eleven years after Judge Fell's death, according to Fox it became increasingly clear to him, particularly through a vision and a 'leading' from God, that he should ask Fell to be his wife. Fox explained in his *Journal* that he had sensed he should marry Margaret Fell long before, but did not feel 'clear' to follow through on this leading for quite some time:

> I had seen from the Lord a considerable time before that I should take Margaret Fell as my wife ... But though the Lord had opened this thing unto me, yet I had not received a command from the Lord for the accomplishment of it then. Wherefore I let the thing rest, and went on in the work and service of the Lord as before.[44]

When Fox returned from Ireland and met Fell in Bristol, just a year after Fell had been released from prison at Lancaster, it was at this meeting he believed 'it opened in me from the Lord that the thing should be now accomplished'.[45] This language indicates that he felt commanded by God to take Margaret Fell to be his wife, similarly to the courtship practices he had promoted others should follow. Without hurry, but patiently waiting on God for a 'command' was the ideal taught by Fox and Fell. In their retrospective writings about their marriage process, they emphasised this dimension of their courtship and marital proceedings. According to Fox, their 'sense' of God's desire for this marriage to take place took many years to develop, reflecting the ideal of waiting on God before pursuing marriage.

Fox and Fell then 'discoursed the thing together', as Fox inquired whether 'she also was satisfied with the accomplishing of it', exemplifying the necessity for the woman to be in agreement with the inner sense of God's desire for the

---

[42] Ibid, 554. See also Braithwaite, *The Second Period of Quakerism*, 262.
[43] Margaret Fell (Fox), *The Testimony of Margaret Fox, Concerning Her Late Husband, George Fox: Together with a brief account of some of his travels, sufferings, and hardships endured for the truth's sake*. Reprinted in Fox, *Journal Vol. 1* (1836), lxviii.
[44] Fox, *Journal* (1952), 554.
[45] Ibid.

marriage to take place.[46] Fell had responded that she too had felt they would marry.[47] After Fox and Fell were in agreement, she sent for her children, as Fox explained:

> When the rest of her daughters were come I was moved to ask the children and her sons-in-law whether they were all satisfied and whether Margaret had answered them according to her husband's will to her children, in which if she married they might suffer loss, whether she had answered them in lieu of that and all other things. And the children made answer and said she had doubled it, and would not have me to speak of those things. I told them I was plain, for I sought not any outward advantage to myself.[48]

Here Fox followed his own advice to fellow Quakers, namely the necessity of verifying that the children of a marriage between a widow and a single man would be well provided for, a Quaker ideal he attempted to establish in the marriage approbation process.

After Fox, Fell and her children felt 'confirmation', they then went through a series of meetings in Bristol for their own marriage approbation.[49] Attempting to follow the guidelines they had given to their fellow Quakers, they took their marital approbation requests before at least two meetings. They first brought their intention of marriage to the regular Two Weeks' Men's Meeting in Bristol, bringing with them Fell's daughters, sons-in-law and friends to offer affirming testimonies regarding their intended marriage.[50] In the minutes of the first meeting on 18 October, the intention of their marriage was recorded with relatively more pomp and circumstance as compared to other marriage intention publications in the Bristol Men's Meeting minutes. A more lengthy and poetic description, this publication was considered an important spiritual event:

> George Fox and Margaret Fell hath this day proposed to this assembly of the people of the Lord their intentions of beinge joined in the honourable marriage which in the power and presence of the Lord they have both declared to have arisen and to stand in the everlasting seed, in the covenant of life which is from everlastinge to everlastinge. John Rowse & Margaret his wife, Thomas Lower and Mary his wife, Issabell Yeamans and Rachell Fell, daughters of the said Margarett

---

[46] Ibid.
[47] Ibid.
[48] Ibid.
[49] As discussed in chapter one, these meetings allowed time for members to wait on God for clarity and guidance regarding the intended union, while a slow approbation process also provided an opportunity for the bringing forth of any reasons why the couple should not marry. This provision, as demonstrated earlier, was not taken lightly, and frequently utilised.
[50] Cadbury (Ed.), *Narrative Papers of George Fox*, 76.

Fell, have all of them one by one not onely declared their free assent to said intended mariage butt also have for the most of them signifyed that they have had a sence that the thinge intended to bee accomplisht doth stand in the covenant of light and life, & therefore doe rejoice for that the accomplishment thereof draweth nigh.[51]

A possible reason for this more effusive entry is that the members of the Bristol Meeting attached greater spiritual (and practical) import to the marriage between their prominent leaders, as compared to other fellow Quaker followers who sought approbation. Other entries do not include such a long explanation, nor the spiritual language of a couple standing 'in the seed' or 'in the covenant'. The Meeting's claim that the couple were standing in the 'everlastinge seed' and 'the covenant of life' reflects Fox's efforts to set his marriage and Quaker marriages in general in the context of a pre-Fall, paradisiacal state. This language, though its specific meaning was not elaborated upon in the Meeting minutes, conceivably points to the high doctrine of marriage that was being developed by Fox and Fell before their marriage took place. It is clear from this first publication of intent that the Bristol Meeting regarded and recognised the marriage of Fox and Fell as a spiritually significant event.[52]

Though the historical record tells us at least five meetings took place, the Bristol Men's Meeting minutes mention only four. The first meeting, mentioned above, was followed by a second meeting, likewise of mixed gender, on 21 October.[53] The marriage was then announced at a general public meeting for worship on 22 October by a leading Quaker called Dennis Hollister. This was then supposedly followed by a final large public meeting before the marriage ceremony itself on 27 October.[54] Throughout these various meetings, a number of testimonies were shared by Fox and Fell's accompanying friends and family who had journeyed to Bristol in order to take part in the approbation and marriage publication. While these testimonies were not recorded in the Bristol Men's Meeting minutes, there are extant manuscripts of portions of what was shared. Exploring these extant manuscripts will help us better understand the theological perception Fox and Fell's fellow Quakers had of their matrimonial union.

---

[51] Mortimer (Ed.), *Minute Book of the Men's Meeting of the Society of Friends in Bristol 1667–1686*, 24.

[52] The description 'honourable marriage' was applied to all Quaker marriages, as discussed in the previous chapter.

[53] Cadbury (Ed.), *Narrative Papers of George Fox*, 76.

[54] Ibid. See also Mortimer (Ed.), *Minute Book of the Men's Meeting of the Society of Friends in Bristol 1667–1686*, 24–5: 'On the 22th day, their intentions of mariage was publisht in our publick meeting, by Dennis Hollister & on the 27th day of said month in the power and spirit of the Lord they were joined together in the honourable marriage'.

The Marriage Approbation and Wedding Testimonies

Though apparently not all the words shared at these meetings could be recorded, what remains clear from these few manuscripts of the Fox/Fell marriage is that their approbation process, publication meetings and the wedding itself were not typical of other Quaker marriages. The atypical nature was in part due to the large number of witnesses and testimonies given. The marriage was witnessed by over one hundred Quakers, ninety-four of whom signed the marriage certificate. The testimonials given during the approbation proceedings and their marriage meeting evince a marriage approbation and wedding which carried great spiritual significance and was composed of spiritual events such as shaking, visions and previsions. Although all Quakers were expected to attend meetings and to wait on God for confirmation, the actual proceedings were not usually, if ever, this dramatic. At the marriage itself, Fox was described as unable to stand under the weight of the Spirit during the marriage meeting.[55] As will be demonstrated, the spiritual exaltation of Fox and Fell's marriage is evinced in the Quaker testimonies shared at the various approbation meetings as well as at the wedding meeting itself.

Fox noted in his *Journal* the number of attendees at the wedding, perhaps to provide proof that it was accepted and approved in unity within the Quaker community, and also enthusiastically affirmed that 'several large testimonies' were shared at his wedding:

> There was a large meeting appointed of purpose in the meeting house at Broad Mead in Bristol, the Lord joining us together in the honourable marriage in the everlasting covenant and immortal Seed of life, where there were several large testimonies by some Friends. Then was a certificate, relating both the proceedings and the marriage, openly read and signed by the relations and by most of the ancient Friends of that city, besides many other Friends from divers parts of the nation.[56]

Curiously, no record is extant of these testimonies Fox mentioned, save a small fragment of manuscripts in the Society of Friends Library in London.[57] Within

---

[55] Ibid, 80.
[56] Fox, *Journal* (1952), 554.
[57] Fox, *Journal Vol. 2* (1911), 416. Norman Penney writes regarding the testimonies, 'No record of these Testimonies is now to be found in the Spence Manuscripts, but in D [Society of Friends Library Manuscripts], where it has probably rested for two centuries, there is a fragment of manuscripts once forming a thick quarto book, giving an account of the Fox-Fell marriage and extracts from the Testimonies of numerous Friends regarding it. This interesting survival is composed of fourteen pages, numbered 403–416, and has neither beginning or ending'. Also later edited from the *Journal* by Ellwood were several accounts

these manuscripts there is an explanation (almost an apology) for the relative lack of a written account:

> But the life and power of the Lord was so over all that the words was not written, Friends being so filled and overcome with the power of the Lord, and testimonies that arose in themselves to the honourable marriage then made mention of, that they could not write G.F.'s words, where he largely opened the several states of marriages; – And the ground of his – The Church's coming up out of the fall in the seed which was before all: and is over all; in which seed he was clear and pure and free from all.[58]

Though not all were written many testimonies which were supposedly taken down and recorded are virtually absent from the historical record.

In his edited and transcribed collection of Fox's narrative papers, the Quaker historian Henry Cadbury attempts to shed some light on the confusing circumstances surrounding their absence:

> The small oblong volume of Fox's letters ... originally contained, as the index shows, both Fox's letter ... and 'Testimonies thereunto and the manner of their proceedings therein &c ... ' It can be no accident that both these sections have been torn out ... and the whole account was torn out of the Maria Headley MSS (V), though pages of the 403–416 of the original 401–420 pages have been separately preserved in Portfolio 10.[59]

Cadbury transcribed these surviving pages within Portfolio 10 at the Friends Library in London.[60] These important surviving testimonies show Quakers filled with awe, sharing a sense that something new and spiritually groundbreaking was taking place at the marriage of George Fox and Margaret Fell. These testimonies include Margaret Fell's vows to Fox, as well as words from Quaker family and friends including George Whitehead, William Penn and Thomas Salthouse. We find both men and women sharing their thoughts and feelings about the marriage, testifying primarily that it is a marriage commanded by God and approved of and consented to, in unity, by the Quaker community. Furthermore, most testimonies indicate that within the Quaker community they had some prior revelation or knowledge that the marriage would eventually take place.

---

of meetings between Fox and Fell or Fox and Fell's daughters, to perhaps further curb the accusations that their relationship was somehow not appropriate (Fox, *Journal Vol. 2* [1911], 417).

[58] Ibid, 84.
[59] Cadbury (Ed.), *Narrative Papers of George Fox*, 74.
[60] A close examination of the original manuscripts prove Cadbury's transcriptions reliable.

These spiritual previsions, and presentiments, helped embellish the spiritual gravity of Fox and Fell's marriage, and firmly placed it within the context of a restored creation.

The beginning of the manuscripts detail a summary of the approbation proceedings, giving us a glimpse of the spiritual happenings surrounding the process of publishing the marriage. Also included is a noteworthy stress on the fact that women were present at each meeting:

> When the command came to George Fox concerning Margaret Fell and him ... on the 2nd day afterwards it was published at the Men's Meeting where about a dozen women Friends went with Margaret and her daughters: where there was a great power of the Lord amongst Friends in the Meeting of both men and women. And several Friends and her daughters and sons were moved of the Lord to stand up and testify to the thing, many of whose words were not taken in writing at that time ... And the second time it was published in the Men's Meeting, where ... many women came with Margaret, and a great power of the Lord there was, and several testimonies and prophecies, which were not take in writing ... the 4th time it was published ... William Penn was moved of the Lord to speak; but many of the testimonies were not taken in writing that were spoken that might have been serviceable. The 5th time there was a meeting ... where there was a multitude of Friends ... where there was a mighty power of the Lord God among Friends that did so overcome them that there was many testimonies could not be taken, and there was such a mighty power that George Fox had like to have fallen down, but that he laid his hand upon another; for he could not tell whether he had a body or not a body.[61]

The intentional inclusion in this record that Fell brought to the first Men's Meeting 'about a dozen women Friends ... and her daughters', and 'many women' came again with Fell to the second meeting is significant. It is possible Fell and Fox made a point of bringing a group of women in order to avoid criticism for not taking their proposal of marriage to a Women's Meeting first, a practice they expected of their fellow Quakers. Significantly, the second meeting, held on 21 October, was also specifically set up to expedite the approval of the marriage, an unusual occurrence.[62] Though many women were brought to this second meeting as well, the expedition and omission of first going to a Women's Meeting drew later criticism from within the Quaker fold. Over a decade after their marriage, Quaker William Rogers, who had attended the approbation meetings and had provided an affirming testimony, argued against marriages being brought to Women's Meetings, and defended his argument by pointing out

---

[61] Cadbury (Ed.), *Narrative Papers of George Fox*, 79–80.
[62] Ibid, 76.

Fox did not submit his own marriage to a Women's Meeting, though, according to Rogers, they existed in Bristol at the time of their marriage.[63] The absence of this necessary first step helped make their marriage process go much more quickly than normal. Though the Women's Meeting had been set up by the time of their marriage, in 1669 the practice of approaching the Women's Meeting first for marriage had not yet been thoroughly integrated in the Bristol approbation process. As seen in chapter one, the direct involvement of Women's Meetings in marriage approbation in Bristol does not appear in the historical record until the year 1698.[64] Whether or not Rogers' argument was entirely valid, Fox and Fell made an effort to have women present throughout their approbation process, perhaps as well in an effort to incorporate women Friends in the process more directly.

The expedition of their marriage, and perhaps other concerns regarding their union, may have encountered more discussion than the Bristol Men's Meeting minutes allude to. In the extant manuscripts of their marriage approbation, there appears a rather important footnote. Dennis Hollister, in the meeting of 22 October, stated the marriage of Fell and Fox had been 'already propounded according to the order of Friends at several men's meetings'.[65] This is a curious statement, considering the minutes of the Bristol Men's Meeting indicated that prior to 22 October, their marriage had only been brought to two other meetings.[66] However, tucked away in the corner of the manuscript, the unknown author wrote, 'There was one or more men's meetings more particular, and private than the men's public meeting'.[67] A transcription of these private meetings not mentioned in the Bristol Men's Meeting minutes is unfortunately no longer extant.[68] But if these additional private meetings did indeed occur, it is reasonable to infer that if they were required, the marriage of Fox and Fell may not have been so wholeheartedly accepted, without any questions or reservations from the Quaker community, as some remaining resources suggest. Nevertheless,

---

[63] William Rogers, *The Christian-Quaker Distinguished from the Apostate* (London, 1680). Part I, Sig H 4V, 64. See also Ng, *Literature and the Politics of Family in Seventeenth-Century England*, 213. Almost ten years after Fox's marriage, William Rogers helped instigate a movement challenging Fox's leadership (Mack, *Visionary Women*, 294).

[64] See chapter one, p. 104.

[65] Cadbury (Ed.), *Narrative Papers of George Fox*, 86.

[66] Mortimer (Ed.), *Minute Book of the Men's Meeting of the Society of Friends in Bristol 1667–1686*, 24–5.

[67] Cadbury (Ed.), *Narrative Papers of George Fox*, 86.

[68] This omission was perhaps a result of the editing activities of Fox or the Morning Meeting.

as Hollister confirmed, because the marriage was tried by these meetings in the presence of God, the marriage was still considered divinely approbated.[69]

During the first public meeting in which their marriage was proposed on 18 October, Fox 'signified his intention of marriage' followed by attendees who all had 'stood up in the power of the Lord and bore testimony to the thing, that it was of God: and the accomplishing of it would be to his glory'.[70] Various testimonies were given by members of Fell's family, including four of Fell's daughters and their husbands. Two of the daughters stated they were 'satisfied' with their mother's marriage to Fox, Margaret Rous testifying, 'I am satisfied that in the life and power of God this thing hath been proposed and I have unity with it', while Mary Lower stated simply, 'Truly I am very well satisfied with the thing and do believe the Lord requires it at your hands'.[71] Rachel Fell briefly concurred, 'I am of the same mind with my sisters and give my consent', while Isabel Yeamans gave the lengthiest consent of the four sisters:

> I must bear my testimony for the Lord and to his truth in this matter, and that the life and power of God in me hath perfect unity, and fellowship with it. And I have long desired to see it accomplished, and now rejoice in its accomplishing, and therefore do freely assent unto it.[72]

As many others testified, Isabel noted that she had hoped for some time that her mother would marry Fox. Her reasons though were not expressed as solely personal, but rather as in unity with God's command that it be accomplished, underlining the importance of marriage being directed by God alone.

Other testimonies included Margaret Jr's husband John Rous, who also stated that he had long hoped for their marriage to pass, and believed it to be ordered by God:

> It was that which was sealed long before in my heart in relation to that which is laid before you. That the presence and power of him who is the orderer thereof would evidence whose work it is, which I see more and more evidenced to all the faithful.[73]

Mary's husband Thomas Lower further testified to hoping for this marriage for several years, acknowledging he believed it was 'of the Lord', and that it would

---

[69] Mortimer (Ed.), *Minute Book of the Men's Meeting of the Society of Friends in Bristol 1667–1686*, 24–5.
[70] Cadbury (Ed.), *Narrative Papers of George Fox*, 80.
[71] Ibid, 81.
[72] Ibid.
[73] Ibid.

be accomplished after waiting on God's timing. He concluded having unity with it as well:

> Friends, that which hath been propounded unto you touching this intended marriage I have several years since seen and believed would be accomplished in the Lord's due time, which now I have this day heard published amongst you, at which my heart rejoices. And I do believe that this thing is of the Lord, and that in the farther accomplishment thereof the Lord's name and truth will be honoured and glorified, and I have in the measure of God's gift unto me perfect unity with it.[74]

There was also an important note of how, when the marriage was accomplished, God's 'name and truth' would be 'honoured and glorified' making it clear that this marriage was done without scandal or was not in any way out of the bounds of pure intentions, perhaps responding to some unease with the marriage that will be discussed shortly.

The Quaker George Whitehead was the first outside of the Fell family to share a testimony. He emphasised his belief that the Lord was bringing the marriage of Fox and Fell to pass, with additional musings on the nature of marriage itself within the Quaker fold:

> I believed that if it came to be accomplished it would be well and to the glory of God, if the Lord brought it to pass. And that such who knew that state in God's covenant should be made living examples and know an experimental testimony. All who are in the sense of the power of God will feel it and none but those whose spirits are seasoned with the power of God and have known a travail in the spirit are fit to judge of these things, or propound questions in such a thing. There hath been in many families so light communication and discourse of such matters that it hath let up an airy inconsiderate spirit that hath gone into marriage without the sense of God's power and so the truth comes to suffer through the want of that sense of the Lord's power which we have travailed to see Friends gathered into. I must yet again testify that it hath been and yet is my faith that the accomplishment of this thing will be to the honour and glory of God.[75]

Whitehead showed great concern with the 'airy inconsiderate spirit' which he apparently saw amongst other Quakers, while those who were 'seasoned with the power of God', such as Fox and Fell, provided testimony to the weightiness

---

[74] Ibid.
[75] Ibid, 82.

of marriage. Whitehead, as well as Fox, used their marriage approbation process as an opportunity to teach about the spiritual gravity of all Quaker marriages.[76]

Others shared at the first meeting that they had known for some time, in a vision or foreknowledge from God, that the marriage would come to pass. A Quaker called Miriam Mosse had apparently foreseen the coming of this marriage in 1657 during a visit with Fell at Swarthmoor Hall. Mosse described she 'was moved of the Lord to go into her [Fell's] garden', where while sitting in silence she had a vision of their marriage, but since it was while Judge Fell was alive, she would not dare mention it at the time.[77] Quaker Thomas Salthouse, a frequenter of the Bristol Men's Meeting, also believed he had known for some time the marriage would come to pass, stating the Lord hath done something wonderful which by some was not expected 'though by me it hath been believed that the thing in the Lord's time would be accomplished'.[78]

Some described having a sense that the Lord 'constrained' them to give testimony supporting this marriage. William Penn stated, 'I know that the power of the Lord that is everlasting constrains me to bear my testimony to it [the marriage]'.[79] John Moon, a regular member of the Bristol Men's Meeting, similarly testified:

> The power that I feel amongst us constrains me to give this my testimony that 'tis of the Lord, and had I never heard the parties before, yet feeling the power raised up amongst us makes me to give it as my testimony that 'tis of the Lord.[80]

Several other testimonies followed Moon's, including four given by other women Friends, all testifying that the Lord had brought the marriage to pass. Notably, Ann Whitehead claimed she 'was truly satisfied and refreshed in it'.[81] All testimonies indicated a sense that they were grateful to be witnesses of such

---

[76] George Whitehead (1636–1723) was himself a prominent Quaker. In the biographical index of *Early Quaker Writings*, he is described as a 'London grocer from about 1660 … [he] emerged after Fox and Penn as a leading Quaker organizer and spokesman to monarchs' (Roberts and Barbour [Eds], *Early Quaker Writings*, 614).

[77] Ibid, 83–4. Previsions were not uncommon amongst the early Quakers. Fox wrote in his *Journal* of visions of his coming to Lancaster: 'Margaret Fell had a vision of a man in a white hat that should come and confound the priests, before my coming into those parts', and 'a man had a vision of me that a man in leather breeches should come and confound the priests' (Fox, *Journal* [1952], 119).

[78] Cadbury (Ed.), *Narrative Papers of George Fox*, 79.
[79] Ibid, 82.
[80] Ibid, 82–3.
[81] Ibid, 83.

a momentous spiritual event, such as Moon who declared, 'And that we are eye witnesses of this matter is a joy to my soul'.[82]

Interestingly, the aforementioned William Rogers also shared a lengthy documented testimony in which he thoroughly supported their marriage, believing it to be from the Lord. Rogers furthermore acknowledged Fell and Fox as ministers who had refreshed 'many hearts' and had led particularly holy lives:

> I am perfectly persuaded in my heart that what they have declared unto us hath been in a living sense and feeling of that immortal life and power which lives forever, and through which they have often ministered unto us the word of Life, to the refreshment and consolation of many hearts. And in as much as there is a marriage that is truly honourable, there is none in whom it can be more honourable than in those who are redeemed out of the perishing objects of this fading world and comes to know a life that never dies, and are given up both in body, soul and spirit, to glorify God our Creator, and that these our worthy friends are arrived unto this holy state I am this day for the Lord made a living witness.[83]

Even in the eyes of Rogers, at least at this time, their marriage exemplified one in which 'there is none in whom it can be more honourable' than between two individuals who were 'redeemed out of the perishing objects of this fading world ... to know a life that never dies'.[84]

The apocalyptic and prophetic implications of Fox's marriage are clearly apparent in the aforementioned testimony of William Penn, which he shared at the approbation meeting on 21 October:

> The marriage that is according to God is in the Light and it is God's work of life to all people; that whosoever marry out of it marry in the Fall; upon whom is the woe, and where is the curse, and as for our dear Friend George Fox, I am constrained to testify that as by him God in these last days first brought forth the knowledge of his pure light, and seed of life; which had been in the wilderness for many generations, so is this marriage by him proposed to be accomplished, the true Character, Resemblance and Expressed Image of that innocent Marriage of the Lamb, the seed that was before the Fall; or the Curse; for all marriages hath been in the false and apostate state from the pure heavenly marriage of the Lamb; but as the Church, and seed, is come out of the wilderness state; and that instrumentally by our dear Friend G.F., so is this marriage likely to be betwixt our

---

[82] Ibid.
[83] Ibid.
[84] Ibid.

dear Friends G.F. and M.F. that pure marriage which with the Church and the seed has been in the wilderness is now come out from thence.[85]

Penn utilised apocalyptic language in expressing the particular sanctity of Fox's marriage, with an additional emphasis on the exaltation of Fox's marital union with Fell in terms of Fox's role as a prophet. Penn believed Fox the prophet 'first brought forth the knowledge of [God's] pure light, and seed of life; which had been in the wilderness for many generations'; likewise, Fox's marriage exemplified 'the true Character, Resemblance and Expressed Image of that innocent Marriage of the Lamb, the seed that was before the Fall'.[86] For Penn it was obvious that, as the Quakers had witnessed the church coming out of the wilderness, so too could they witness this particular marriage as a symbol of that perceived exodus out of the fallen state.

The great spiritual import of the marriage was stressed further by Penn, who concluded his testimonies with a warning against anyone who rose up against the marriage:

> And whatever envious or prejudiced reasonings may get up in any, this I testify from the sense of the weighty truth, that they are all wrong, and will bring darkness over those who let them in, for God Almighty knows him, and his crowning presence with him, and hurts shall attend all that rise against him.[87]

These were strong words, but indicative of the restorationist perception Penn held of this union of the Quaker movement's leaders. For Penn, being against the marriage of Fox and Fell was equated to being against God's prophet who enjoyed God's 'crowning presence', and in effect being against God himself.[88]

The exalted language of other testimonies shared during the approbation meetings echoed passages from the New Testament narratives of the birth of Jesus. Isabel Yeamans, Fell's daughter, claimed that 'many shall come from the east and from the west and from the north and from the south and shall call them blessed'.[89] Following her testimony, John Rous made a similar declaration 'that blessed is the womb that bare them, and the paps that gave them suck, and

---

[85] Cadbury (Ed.), *Narrative Papers of George Fox*, 84. See also Mortimer (Ed.), *Minute Book of the Men's Meeting of the Society of Friends in Bristol 1667-1686*, 24, and MS in Portfolio X in the Friends Reference Library, p. 53.

[86] Ibid, 87.

[87] Ibid.

[88] Opposition to their marriage will be more thoroughly discussed shortly. Penn's strong words could indicate that opposition may have occurred and necessitated the probable additional private meetings which were held during their approbation. See p. 231.

[89] Cadbury (Ed.), *Narrative Papers of George Fox*, 84.

the children that are yet to be born shall call them happy and blessed'.[90] These testimonies resemble the New Testament narrative of Elisabeth's declaration to Mary, the mother of Jesus, 'Blessed are you among women, and blessed is the fruit of your womb ... and blessed is she who believed that there would be fulfilment of what was spoken to her of the Lord'.[91] Thus in their mindsets, this marriage was a sign of the birth of a living demonstration of redemption and restoration in their age. Dennis Hollister, similar to Rous and Yeamans above, also likened their marriage to the narrative of Mary and Jesus:

> The same Lord God Almighty by his eternal powerful word of wisdom ... hath brought and is bringing to pass amongst you a marriage which is truly honourable, between our beloved and truly honourable Friends in God's everlasting truth and covenant, who is become truly honourable in all the churches of all the saints, George Fox and Margaret Fell ... for I may truly say, as I heard the voice of its salutation, the babe immortal leaped in the womb from joy, etc.[92]

Perhaps the most telling of all testimonies were the ones shared by Margaret Fell, who set their marriage squarely in the metaphor of the marriage of the Lamb and the church. In the first meeting of 18 October, Fell stood up and testified:

> Friends in that everlasting immortal word of Life and Power, which was in the beginning, in which God created all things, the male, and the female in his own pure image which was from everlasting and will be to everlasting I have my testimony sealed in my heart unto this thing in God's everlasting covenant.[93]

In her first words of the approbation process, Fell referenced the Genesis story of paradise as the prototype of their own marriage, in which each party is effectively innocent, and brought together by God. In the following meetings, Fell would continue to locate their marriage clearly in the context of God's covenant with humanity of the restoration of creation and a return to Paradise, in line with Fox's adherence to their marriage as a testimony to coming out of the wilderness. At the following meeting on 21 October, Fell further elaborated on the glorification of the male and female 'in the seed':

> Whereas being many which were not at the last meeting, it may be some will expect that I should confirm my testimony in the everlasting light and in the word, which was in the beginning with God, by which the heavens were made and

---

[90] Ibid, 85.
[91] Bible, *New Revised Standard Version*, Luke 1:42, 45.
[92] Ibid, 86.
[93] Ibid, 80–81.

the earth and all things therin, by which word God created man in his own image: male and female in Christ Jesus; in this seed which was glorified with the Father before the world began. In this everlasting covenant and word of life I stand pure, spotless, chaste and undefiled to the Lord, and am clear and free from all that is below the marriage of the Lamb.[94]

In the above passage we find Fell likening herself to the church (pure, spotless, chaste, undefiled) and Fox to the Lamb (Christ). Using the familiar metaphor of the marriage between Christ and his church, she clearly likewise believed her marriage to Fox was a representation of the restored union between God and his people, the fulfilment of the covenant, the church and the Lamb reunited.[95]

In Fell's prayer at the meeting of their marriage, she again placed their marriage in the context of restoration and the fulfilment of God's covenant, using the metaphor of the marriage of the Lamb and his bride:

> Oh Lord God omnipotent, who reigns over all: and whose glory is over all, whose covenant shines to the ends of the earth, thou hast set thy King upon the holy hill of Sion and crowned him with glory and honour: and thy Jerusalem is come down from heaven, the city of the Great King; the bride, the Lamb's wife, whose Light is as a jasper stone clear as crystal, whose freeborn of that womb of eternity is coming out of the wilderness to be comforted and nourished, and to be nursed and clothed with the eternal free spirit of the living God … And though thou art made higher than the heavens yet thou hath left thy gifts amongst men for the gathering and for restoring and for the bringing back the captivity and for building up of that which hath fallen down.[96]

Fell does not explicitly state that she is the 'bride' and Fox is the 'Lamb', but her symbolic references, here in the context of her earlier testimonies, do at least suggest that she did see her marriage as a physical representation of the restoration God had begun to accomplish. Since Fell regarded herself as a 'Mother in Israel', her language in the above passage fits her self-perception as a spiritually attuned individual, leading with Fox the procession of 'Jerusalem is

---

[94] Ibid, 85.
[95] Ng, *Literature and the Politics of Family in Seventeenth-Century England*, 203, 207. Ng notes both Fox and Penn likened the Fox/Fell marriage to the 'marriage of the Lamb'. Braithwaite explains, 'Fox wrote that the marriage was commanded him as a figure or testimony of the Church coming out of the wilderness and of the marriage of the Lamb before the world was. He witnessed this marriage of the Lamb in the restoration which had come to him out of the Fall and in the Seed of Life' (Braithwaite, *The Second Period of Quakerism*, 263).
[96] Cadbury (Ed.), *Narrative Papers of George Fox*, 88.

come down from heaven' into the hearts of her fellow Quakers – the 'free born ... coming out of the wilderness'.

In addition to Fell's prayer, from their wedding two other fragments of shared testimonies have survived.[97] The testimony of long-time Quaker Jeremiah Hignell appears first, which may have been the opening of the meeting. A native of Bristol, Hignell appears in the Quaker historical record as early as 1655. He had participated in the Bristol Men's Meeting for a number of years, including being assigned to disciplinary appointments from 1671 until 1691.[98] In the extant manuscript, Hignell offered an exhortation for 'all to wait to feel the unity of the spirit' that they may 'testify before the Lord that this thing is of him' followed by the following assurance, 'and so doing you will receive the answer of God, which shall be a testimony for him to his glory for ever'.[99] Believing the marriage to be of God, he sensed 'no opposition' in his 'spirit at all' concluding with the encouragement that 'the sense of the thing may be upon everyone's heart grounded and settled on the truth of God'.[100] Though some may have had concerns, Hignell affirmed after the various meetings and testimonies, all Quakers were in unity with 'the truth of God' in approbating the marriage of Fox and Fell.

The transcription of Fox's words at his marriage is incomplete. It appears Fox was beginning a summary of the course of events leading to his marriage to Fell, concluding with, 'I opened it to none but Margaret and' at which point the transcription is cut off.[101] What remains is Fox's brief proclamation, 'all meetings to me is but one meeting in the whole world who are gathered in the name of Jesus', followed by an acknowledgement that his marriage was coming to pass 'in this Meeting of which I knew little. Only some thing concerning Margaret's children pointed to me as the middle place'.[102] Fox indicated they married in Bristol for practicality, but in essence they could have just as easily married at any other meeting, as all meetings are 'one'. Fox thus took the opportunity to emphasise the unity amongst Quaker meetings across the world he had been encouraging. This emphasis is not surprising, given he and Fell were consistently pushing for a unified movement, in spirit and in practice. Finally, Fox's words emphasise also the unity the Quakers felt in affirming the marriage of Fox and Fell was being done in the presence and power of God. As Fox was an itinerant,

---

[97] Ibid, 87.

[98] Mortimer (Ed.), *Minute Book of the Men's Meeting of the Society of Friends in Bristol 1667–1686*, 203. His sister Temperance Hignell died in 1655, after being in prison for disturbing the minister at Temple church.

[99] Cadbury (Ed.), *Narrative Papers of George Fox*, 87.

[100] Ibid.

[101] Ibid.

[102] Ibid. They married at the public meeting at Broadmead Meeting House in Bristol, the same location of all the preceding meetings leading up to their marriage.

he could not know everyone personally at Bristol, which for him further confirmed their approbation in the context of the 'everlasting power of God this thing hath been laid before' them.[103]

It is evident from the extant records their marriage was an intriguing blend of being esteemed as a special, living embodiment of the restoration of creation, while at the same time, like all other marriages, being also subjected to an orderly meeting process which ensured unity and clear documentation. Their particular marriage approbation process largely followed the model set up by Fox and Fell years prior: marriage through approbation after multiple meetings, witnessed by fellow Quakers, conducted by neither priest nor justice, and joined together by God alone. Yet, as previously discussed, their marriage approbation process differed in that it was expedited, and was not technically submitted to a Women's Meeting first.[104] Nevertheless, while Fox, Fell and others claimed their marriage was one of high spiritual importance, in the end it was still subjected to the Meetings of Bristol and a unified approbation. Fox and Fell remained persistent in their reliance on and encouragement of spiritual revelation, written testimony and order within marriage, all of which we have seen constitute Quaker spirituality.

Coming up out of the Wilderness: The Lamb and the New Jerusalem

Retrospectively, both Fox and Fell described their marriage in relatively (and perhaps surprisingly) subdued terms. Bonnelyn Kunze notes Fell recollected her marriage in a 'matter-of-fact way':

> At Bristol he declared his Intentions of Marriage with me; and there was also our Marriage solemnized, in a publick Meeting of many Friends, who were our Witnesses.[105]

A lengthier quote can be found from Fell in regards to her marriage, but not with a great deal more spiritual or theological enthusiasm:

---

[103] Ibid.

[104] There is evidence that other marriages were expedited at the Bristol Meeting in exceptional circumstances after the marriage of Fell and Fox. In 1678, the marriage of Friends Jonathon Packer and Sarah Baugh was expedited due to his 'being suddenly bound away to Virginia' and 'it also being the earnest request of her now dyeing mother' (Mortimer, 'Marriage Discipline in Early Friends', 191).

[105] *A relation of Margaret Fell, Her Birth, Life, Testimony and Sufferings for the Lord's Everlasting Truth in her Generation* (1690), 8. Cited in Kunze, *Margaret Fell and the Rise of Quakerism*, 21.

> And so our intention of marriage was laid before Friends, both privately and publicly, to their full satisfaction, many of whom gave testimony that it was of God. Afterwards a meeting being appointed on purpose of the accomplishing thereof, in the public meeting-house at Broad Mead, in Bristol, we took each other in marriage; and the Lord joined us together in honourable marriage, in the everlasting covenant and immortal Seed of life.[106]

Curiously, Fell appears to tone down the great spiritual import of her marriage to Fox which is evident in the marriage approbation testimonies. Fox's recollections in his *Journal* are similar in brevity, and show an absence of any full theological explication of the event. Yet as the wedding testimonies demonstrate, the marriage of Fox and Fell was considered at the time a spiritually significant occurrence. Fox was so enthused, he wrote out an explanation of his forthcoming marriage in which he elaborated on its cosmic significance in apocalyptic terms.

On 2 October 1669 Fox sent out from Bristol this controversial letter to all Quaker meetings explaining his reasons for marrying Fell. In it lie additional keys to understanding his theological perception of his pending marriage to Fell. Amongst his contemporaries, it was controversial due to its cryptic nature, and the seemingly elevated language Fox used in reference to himself. But for Fox, his goal was to describe and explain to all meetings the theological and spiritual foundation of their marriage. In his *Journal* he recollected:

> Before we were married I was moved to write forth a paper to all the meetings in England both of men and women and elsewhere, for all meetings of Friends which were begotten to the Lord were but as one meeting time.[107]

In the letter, what appeared most important to Fox was his desire to express the great spiritual significance he felt their intended union possessed. Fox promoted his relationship to Fell by placing their marriage in the context of a great spiritual event, the image of the coming together of the church or 'New Jerusalem' and the 'Lamb of God', in a 'marriage in him that never fell' about which, Fox explained, 'more might be spoken which would be too large to be uttered'.[108] Their marriage was not a convenient marriage between two prominent leaders, but was presented by Fox as a significant event, the coming of which was almost beyond human comprehension.

The thematic contents of the controversial letter written by Fox were consistent with both the wedding testimonies and Fox's other writings regarding

---

[106] Fell Fox, *The life of Margaret Fox*, 50–51.
[107] Fox, *Journal* (1952), 555.
[108] Fox, *Letter of George Fox Concerning his Marriage* (2 October 1669). (Cadbury [Ed.], *Narrative Papers of George Fox*, 79.)

marriage. He again relied heavily on the Genesis story of God joining Adam and Eve in what Fox considered a 'pure marriage' before the Fall. In 1659, ten years prior to Fox's marriage to Fell, he wrote an essay in which he argued Quaker marriages were the only ones who were in effect living in a pre-Fall state and brought together by God 'as it was in the beginning':

> So Friends that be redeemed out of the Earth comes to know it as it was in the beginning again; and how God created the Male & the Female, and joyned together which no man can put a sunder ... But who comes together as it was in the beginning, comes over the Jews, Gentiles, and Apostate Christians, and that is the Marriage that is honourable, and there the Bed is that is undefiled.[109]

Though Fox considered all Quaker marriages in general as a return to the pre-Fall condition, he moved beyond this definition in his letter of 1669. Fox wrote of his own marriage as specifically 'testifying' to the restoration of the Lamb, or Christ, and his church, the New Jerusalem, coming out of the wilderness, and being the image of the 'heavenly marriage' of the Lamb and the church:

> Friends and brethren, in the power of the Lord God, that is from everlasting and over all to everlasting and in his seed and everlasting covenant of life and light, that G. Fox and M. Fell the Lord God hath brought it to pass to join us together by his power and command in his everlasting power and seed and life, light and truth, and in the honourable marriage and in an undefiled bed, in his everlasting seed ... the promised seed I do witness, who am free from all other outward covenants, promises, contracts and engagements of all men and women in the whole world concerning such a thing. And the which marriage is a figure or testimony which I am commanded to do, of the church coming out of the wilderness, and the marriage of the Lamb before the foundation of the world was.[110]

While Fox had long talked of Quaker marriages being a living symbol of the reunion of the church and the divine, here he suggested his marriage was a particular figure of the 'marriage of the Lamb *before the foundation of the world*

---

[109] Fox, *Concerning Marriage* (1661), 4–5. Unlike Bailey's suggestion that Fox considered himself alone to be living in a pre-Fall state, and thus dictated to himself higher ascetic standards, in the above passage Fox made clear all Quakers were to be in this pre-Fall state, in which all Quaker marriages were considered honourable and the marriage-bed (i.e. sexuality) was 'undefiled', rather than non-existent. The place of asceticism and celibacy in Fox's own marriage as well as other Quaker marriages will be discussed in the following section and chapter.

[110] Fox, *Letter of George Fox Concerning his Marriage* (2 October 1669). (Cadbury [Ed.], *Narrative Papers of George Fox*, 78.) The notion of 'undefiled bed', as discussed in chapter two, reflected the Quaker belief in the undefiled nature of sexuality within the restored creation.

was', seemingly ascribing a personal Christ-like, and perhaps self-elevated, status to primarily himself but also to Fell. This allusion appears in Fox's further claim:

> And here the everlasting seed [the light of Christ within] cometh up to the marriage of the Lamb, and in these bodies [Fox and Fell] which they shall have, which they had, and which was before the foundation of the world was, in Christ Jesus. Which marriage of the Lamb I do witness in the restoration out of the Fall and also with him that was in the beginning with the Lord and Father, before the foundation of the world was.[111]

Fox once again walked the fine line between witnessing divinity within and actually being divine. As a person inhabited by the light of Christ, he explained he personally not only witnessed the restoration out of the Fall, but also was with Christ before the foundation of the world. This marriage union between Fox and Fell, according to Fox, not only was a sign of the heavenly, cosmic union between the Lamb and his church – it specifically embodied it.

Fox's language is ecstatic in his description of his forthcoming marriage to Fell. Fox presented himself and Fell as forerunners of this new-found cosmic state of the restored creation. Through the witness of the light of Christ within, a heavenly marriage was going to occur through the physical marriage of Fox and Fell; it testifies not only to the church coming up out of the wilderness but also to the True Church coming into Paradise. Fox explained he had a personal revelation regarding this marriage of cosmic proportions and concluded his letter:

> And this thing the heavenly marriage I saw in the everlasting covenant ... I saw it many years past and I waited in the same everlasting covenant, and I waited for a command from God ... to perform and fulfil the things which came to me but of late, and of this thing you may hear more large.[112]

But no more follows in the historical record, save the exalted declarations in the marriage testimonies we have already seen.[113] Likely due to the close allusions of divinity with Fox, and its cryptic nature, the letter in general created a puzzled

---

[111] Ibid, 79.

[112] Ibid.

[113] Henry Cadbury notes Fox wrote two other epistles to Friends on marriage (one during the proceedings of his marriage approbation on 22 October and another on the day of his marriage, 27 October 1669) which are no longer extant (see Cadbury [Ed.], *Narrative Papers of George Fox*, 76).

response from the Quaker communities. Not well received, Fox's letter was 'recalled' and most copies were destroyed.[114]

A surviving copy of the letter was used as fodder for criticism in the hands of Fox's adversaries. Quaker opponents used the letter against Fox, including Quakers William Mucklow and Francis Bugg. In 1673, Mucklow cited the letter accusing Fox of vainly placing his marriage above all marriages and claiming to be the Second Adam:

> Such is the swelling pride of this Luciferian, that he gave forth a Paper, That his Marriage with Margaret Fell, was a figure of the Marriage between Christ and the Church. I may more justly believe it to be a figure of the great Apostacy from the Truth, and barrenness in the Truth ... He likewise declared, That his Marriage was above the state of Adam in his Innocency, in the state of the second Adam, who never fell. This Paper was so ill resented and so much dislik'd that it was call'd in again; and a rare thing it was to get a sight thereof, albeit through an accident, I had a view of it.[115]

Francis Bugg printed and used a copy of the letter, which he had received from an 'ancient Quaker', to attack the reputability of Fox and his followers forty years after Fox had written his perceived incriminating letter.[116]

Despite the controversial nature of the letter, it provides valuable insight into the Quaker understanding of 'the New Jerusalem' and why Fox attached such language to his own marriage. God was establishing a renewed church, which they sometimes referred to as the 'Jerusalem from above', a heavenly Jerusalem or the 'New Jerusalem'. Understanding the way this image was used and understood throughout the early years of the movement can help us better understand how it related to the context of Fox's marriage to Fell. We have a glimpse of the use of this image in a pamphlet written by George Whitehead in 1693 in which he attempted to explicate the reasoning behind the Quaker doctrine of the 'light':

> So that the light and life of the Son of God within, truly obeyed and followed ... does not leave men or women (who believe in the Light) under the first covenant, nor as sons of the bondwoman, as the literal Jews were, (when gone from the Spirit of God, and his Christ in them) but it naturally leads them into the new

---

[114] Cadbury (Ed.), *Narrative Papers of George Fox*, 74. Fox's self-perception will be dealt with in the following section.

[115] William Mucklow, *The Spirit of the Hat, or, The government of the Quakers among themselves as it hath been exercised of late years by George Fox and other leading-men in their Monday or second-dayes meeting at Devonshire-House* (London: F. Smith, 1673), 42.

[116] Braithwaite, *The Second Period of Quakerism*, 263. According to Braithwaite, the letter printed by Bugg seems genuine based on comparison with other sources.

covenant, into the new and living way, and to the adoption of sons, to be children and sons of the free-woman, of Jerusalem from above.[117]

The 'sons of the free-woman, of Jerusalem' were considered to be the Quakers, who were under the 'new covenant' and the 'new and living way'.

In his sermon to the London General Meeting in 1680, Fox gave an overview of the entire history and state of the cosmos in which he referred to the Quakers returning to the 'Jerusalem from above'. Beginning with a summary of the creation of Adam and Eve, whom God had placed 'in a blessed habitation in the beginning in a blessed and happy state' where there was 'a blessed concord and unity', Fox then moved to the temptation by 'the serpent', the subsequent fall of Adam and Eve, and their being driven from the 'Paradise of God'.[118] Fox claimed all people thereafter were 'baptised in death', a state of humanity 'in the wilderness' which remained until Christ came to reconcile humanity to God. Fox believed this 'reconciliation' was being truly experienced in the Quakers' day as it had been in the 'Apostles' day'.[119] Fox asserted that the Quakers have returned to 'Paradise', or the 'New Jerusalem', under the 'new covenant', as he preached to the Quakers in London:

> We are come to the New Jerusalem, Jerusalem that is above, the mother of us all, to Jesus the mediator; to God the judge of all the earth. Here is the Son's house, the heavenly Jerusalem. Have you a temple in your Jerusalem? Yes, the Lord God Almighty and the Lamb is the temple, and the Lamb is the Light of the temple ... So now have a distinction between the new covenant and the old; and have a distinction to know what family you are of; and so be substantial and grounded in the Spirit of Light and Life in Christ Jesus the rock of ages.[120]

The Quaker community was thus the embodiment of the heavenly New Jerusalem, the True Church set up and inhabited by the light of God. The New Jerusalem represented the True Church, the 'family' which one had to belong to in order to experience God's direct revelation and restored state of innocence. Similar words can be found amongst the writings of Margaret Fell, including a pamphlet written by Fell five years prior to her marriage to Fox:

---

[117] George Whitehead, *The Christian Doctrine and Society of the People called Quakers cleared &c.* (1693). (Barbour and Roberts [Eds], *Early Quaker Writings*, 562.)

[118] *George Fox's Sermon at Wheeler Street, 1680.* (Barbour and Roberts [Eds], *Early Quaker Writings*, 502.) Fox equated the 'Apostles' day' (i.e. the twelve disciples and Paul) with 'our day' (i.e. the time of the Quakers), reflecting a common belief amongst Friends that they were returning to the state and experiences of the primitive apostolic church, a state which had been 'dead' in the church for many generations after.

[119] Ibid, 504.

[120] Ibid, 508.

Adam, the first man which was made ... fell from and lost his Righteousness, lost his Holiness and Innocency and beauty, and his Dominion which he had ... and so he and his wife came under the curse, and the Earth became cursed for their sakes and the Serpent ... they were utterly deprived of, and drove out from the presence of the Lord, and shut out of the Garden, and the flaming Sword set ... so that there none enter back again ... but the Lords infinite bounty ... had a secret ... and knew how to recover them not only into the state they were in before, but into a state which shall never fall, even by Christ Jesus the second *Adam*.[121]

Fell explained further, similar to Fox, that Quakers through God's 'Light in their consciences ... may turn from their dark and fallen state to follow Christ Jesus' and 'come to the Law which goeth out of Zion, which is written in everyones heart, and to the word of the Lord which goeth from *Jerusalem*, which is from above, which is the mother of us all'.[122]

This perception of Jerusalem as 'mother of us all' we have seen appeared in the wedding testimonies, which suggests perhaps Fox made a possible conscious reference to Fell, as she symbolised the 'mother in Israel', the New Jerusalem, 'the bride, the Lamb's wife'.[123] In 1664, five years before she married Fox, Fell wrote about 'Jerusalem' arriving in the hearts of the Quakers, utilising the metaphorical language of the 'marriage of the Lamb' and 'the New Jerusalem' that she would use to describe herself in her wedding testimonies.[124]

Thus the language used by Fox and Fell in describing their marriage was language they had already been using years earlier. It was within this paradigm

---

[121] Margaret Fell, *A call to the universall seed of God throughout the whole world to come up to the place of publick worship, which Christ Jesus the great prophet hath set up, who took not upon Him the nature of Angels, but the Seed of Abraham, whereby he comes to raise up Adams House and fallen State, into an Estate that shall never fall* (London, 1665), 3–4.

[122] Ibid, 6, 12.

[123] Cadbury (Ed.), *Narrative Papers of George Fox*, 88.

[124] 'You are the Light of the World ... here is the great and high Mountain which is above all the Mountaines, the holy Jerusalem, the Bride, the Lambs wife descending out of Heaven from God, having the glory of God ... this is the new Jerusalem which comes down from Heaven ... which is the free Spirit, Son of the free Woman, which calls freely, and proclaimes freely, the everlasting Gospel of peace, which hath a witness in every heart' (Margaret Fell, *A Call to the universall seed of God throughout the whole world which Christ Jesus the great prophet hath set up, who took not upon Him the nature of Angels, but the Seed of Abraham, whereby he comes to raise up Adams House and fallen State, into an Estate that shall never fall* [London, 1665], 13). 'And this Lamb is now arising and raising up that which was fallen down, and quickening that which was slain, and is bruising and breaking the head and the power of him that slew him, and is removing that man of sin and son of perdition that hath so long sitten in the Temple of God, he is now coming to be taken away that hath long let, by the Lamb that hath been slain, by the spirit of his mouth and brightness of his coming will he slay that wicked one'.

of the New Jerusalem, already established, that they consciously placed their marriage. Fox's effusive language and the initial enthusiasm for their marriage in apocalyptic terms (that was shared by Fell, Fox and others who attended the wedding and marriage approbation proceedings) was, however, not to last.

Fox's enthusiasm demonstrated in the letter was indeed highly apocalyptic and unclear, making it understandable that it was widely rejected. While it was clear that their marriage was considered a very significant 'figure' of the True Church coming out of the wilderness, in his letter Fox's allusions of the embodiment of the Lamb and the New Jerusalem led to misunderstandings. While Fox did see his marriage at the time as spiritually significant, as did others, in retrospect, as we have seen, it was not as enthusiastically remembered by all those involved. Additionally, Fox did not seem to halt the destruction of the controversial letter, and mentioned it only once in his *Journal* without elaborating at length on its contents, suggesting perhaps even he had some reservations about his initial proclamation regarding his marriage. One can only speculate why Fox, Fell and much of the Quaker movement later quietly downplayed the early spiritual fervour associated with their marriage. Certainly the seemingly intentional omission of some of the marriage testimonies (as Cadbury attests) alludes that perhaps there were worries the sentiments shared would be misconstrued, or used against Fox in accusations of blasphemy, as we saw was the case with the Quaker critics Francis Bugg and William Mucklow when they had hold of Fox's controversial letter. Fox remained convinced, as his *Journal* shows, that his marriage was indeed a testimony to the church coming out of the wilderness, but the real, cosmic, heavenly implications of this marriage were not pursued or explained further. The task of Fox and Fell over the subsequent years was focused more on the work of partnering in the work of propagating, managing and unifying the Quaker movement, and regularising marriage within the meetings, so that marriage approbation could be a testimony, through good order, to the restoration of creation, and the union of the divine with the church.

'Marriage of the Lamb': Fox's Self-perception in Relation to the Divine

Considering Fox's persistent effort to promote the inward light of Christ within without necessarily being Christ incarnate, particularly in relation to his claims of his marriage being a figure of the marriage between the Lamb and his church, it is worth exploring Fox's self-perception as being the first to prophesy and experience the light of the Lamb within. The early movement of the Quakers was often self-described as the 'Lamb's war', an image of 'the Christ within' fighting against evil in general, a war ultimately against the 'serpent', or 'deceiver in the world'.[125] With such spiritual importance attached to their marriage as the marriage of 'the Lamb' and 'the New Jerusalem', by Fox, Fell and the witnesses present, it is necessary to understand the context and meaning of these images to appreciate fully the implication of their marriage. To begin to discover the imagery and meaning behind their wedding, it would also be helpful to take pause briefly to consider how Fell and other Quakers actually perceived Fox. Was he the actual embodiment of the second appearance of Christ, ergo the 'actual' appearance of the 'Lamb'? Such ambiguities concerned some of their contemporaries. Some fellow Quakers had justifiably cause for concern as Fox set his marriage in the context that he was indeed '*the* Lamb of God', the same self-proclamation that got James Nayler into so much trouble.[126]

Before the Nayler incident Fox himself was arrested in 1652 for allegedly similar claims. Francis Higginson, a Puritan pastor of Kirkby Stephen near Kendal and a vociferous opponent of Fox, helped aid this arrest by signing a Puritan petition calling for Cromwell to suppress the Quakers.[127] Amongst other accusations set before him at the Lancaster assizes, Fox was accused of proclaiming himself equal with God. After a defence against these accusations was presented in a document entitled *Saul's Errand to Damascus* (1653), Higginson responded later the same year with a condemning tract in which he claimed 'Fox, the father of the Quakers of these parts, hath avowed himself over and over to be equal with God', and he had multiple witnesses to Fox claiming 'I am equal with God'.[128] At the 1652 trial in Lancaster, Margaret Fell, Judge Fell and Colonel West were sympathetic to Fox, all refusing to draw up a warrant of blasphemy against him.[129] In *Saul's Errand to Damascus*, in response to the court's accusation that Fox 'did affirm that he had the Divinity essentially in him', was the answer:

---

[125] Barbour and Roberts (Eds), *Early Quaker Writings*, 19. Barbour explains the 'Lamb's War': 'The early Quaker movement, called then and since "The Lamb's War", combined in its impact a triple awareness: (1) Friends felt the spiritual and psychological power of a regional religious awakening in the north of England, which had rarely seen mass meetings; (2) they experienced the Spirit of Christ's Light of Truth, searching all hearts to expose and conquer inner evil in every self; and (3) early Friends saw the Spirit of Christ, the enthroned "Lamb" of Revelations 14, conquering worldwide social evil at a turning-point in history'.

[126] Hill, *The World Turned Upside Down*, 364.

[127] Barbour and Roberts (Eds), *Early Quaker Writings*, 64.

[128] Ibid., 66. From Francis Higginson, *A Brief Relation of The Irreligion of the Northern Quakers wherein their horrid principles and practices, doctrines and manners are plainly exposed to the view of every intelligent reader* (London: H.R., 1653).

[129] Ibid., 66, 251. Colonel William West was a friend and colleague of Judge Thomas Fell, as well as an influential and helpful aide to the Society of Friends, though he was not a Quaker himself. See also Glines, *Undaunted Zeal*, 397; Braithwaite, *The Beginnings of Quakerism to 1660*, 108; and Fox, *Journal Vol. 1* (1911), 63.

> For the word essentially, it is an expression of their own: but that the saints are 'the temples of God' (II Cor. 6:1), and God doth 'dwell in them' (Eph. 4:6), that [I witness and] the Scripture do [th] witness. And if God dwell in them, then the Divinity dwells in them. And the Scripture saith 'Ye shall be partakers of the Divine nature' (II Peter 1:4), and this I witness, but where this is not, they cannot witness it.[130]

Claiming to have the light of Christ within was difficult territory for the early Quakers to traverse, for Fox as well as his followers. While they affirmed they had the 'light' dwelling within them, this assertion often got them into trouble for blasphemy.

When Fell likened Fox to 'the Lamb' in her first and second testimonies during their marriage approbation meetings, this interpretation of Fox was a recognition of the 'Lamb's' presence in Fox, thus not making him equal to God, but a vessel of God's presence. This was not a new revelation for her, nor for others in the early Quaker movement. However, Richard Bailey argues in his recent study of Fox, that Fox believed himself to be the 'Son of God' while Fell, and other Quakers, believed him to actually be 'the Lamb' or the 'second appearance of Christ'.[131] Bailey cites an early letter from Fell to Fox in 1652, which included her use of superlatives reserved for Christ, as proof of Margaret Fell's exalted perception of Fox.[132] According to Bailey, Fell's various names for Fox in this letter included 'our dear father in the Lord', 'bread of life', 'our life', 'dear nursing father', 'fountain of eternal life' and 'father of eternal felicity', as well as claiming that he 'suffered for us', all have some measure of 'Christ-like' implications.

Arguing further that early Quakers ascribed to Fox a special status of 'divine sonship', Bailey offers other quotations from various Quakers: Howgill and Burrough referring to Fox as the one 'who art one with the Father'; Thomas Curtis calling him the one 'who was dead and is alive, and forever lives'; Ann Curtis referring to him as 'my dear father' and 'fountain of eternity'; Ann Burden addressing him as 'thou Son of God which the world knoweth not'; Richard Sale writing to him 'praises to thee for evermore, who was and is to come, who is god over all'; Thomas Holme referring to him as the one who 'owns the world'; and finally, Thomas Lower, the husband of Margaret Fell's daughter Mary, describing Fox in salutation as 'the second appearance of him who is blessed for ever'.[133]

---

[130] Barbour and Roberts (Eds), *Early Quaker Writings*, 253. Brackets inserted by the author.

[131] Ibid, 128.

[132] Bailey, *New Light on George Fox and Early Quakerism*, 127.

[133] 'Edward Burrogh to Francis Howgill to George Fox', Barclay MSS, No. 154; 'Edward Burrogh to Francis Howgill to George Fox' (21 January 1656); 'Thomas Curtis to George Fox' (1658) Swarthmore MSS, 3, No. 87; 'Ann Curtis to George Fox' (23 May 1660), in Elisha

Bailey refutes the Quaker historian Henry Cadbury's suggestion that these titles were an example of 'Fox's salutary influence on people', and Geoffrey Nuttall's conclusion that these were simply examples of a 'hyperbolic language used by those whose minds were filled with Biblical imagery', with his own argument that the various titles bestowed upon Fox exemplified his exalted self-promotion as, in Bailey's words, an 'avatar of the divine'.[134]

One oversight in Bailey's argument is his failure to acknowledge the exalted language to which he refers in reference to Fox was also used by early Quakers amongst themselves in reference to each other, particularly during the beginning of the movement. In 1677, Fell used similar exalted language in the introduction to a letter she wrote to William Penn:

> Dear & Faithfull: whom the Lord has chosen, & owned & honoured with his everlasting Truth ... Blessed art thou for ever ... who art a Noble, & faithfull Instrument, in the hand of the Almighty; for the spreading abroad of Truth, & for the exaltation of the Kingdome, O thy Name will be had in everlasting Remembrance, with all the Faithfull ... O: Beautiful is thy feet, that preaches Glad Tideings to the poor, & Libertie to the Captives [Isa. 61.1–2] Children yet unborn will bless the Lord for thee.[135]

In this letter, Fell used biblical imagery and parallels to Christ to exalt her friend William Penn.

Margaret Fell was frequently referred to as 'nursing Mother', and was addressed as 'Dear Mother in the eternal Truth of God' by John Camm and Francis Howgill in an early letter dated in 1654.[136] The following year, a grateful Thomas Holme wrote a thank you letter to Fell for her daughter Margaret's visit with him in Chester gaol. Holme's letter included much of the typically exalted language used in early Quaker correspondence:

Bates, *An Appeal to the Society of Friends* (London: Hamilton, Adams & Co., Whittaker & Co., and Edmund Fry & Son, 1836), 21; 'Anna Burden to George Fox' (1663), Swarthmore Manuscripts, 3, no. 102; 'Richard Sale to George Fox' (25 October 1655), Swarthmore Manuscripts, 4, no. 211; 'Thomas Holme to George Fox' (September 1654), Swarthmore Manuscripts, 4, no. 249; 'Thomas Lower to George Fox and Margaret Fell' (4 January 1675), Spence Manuscripts, 3, folio 174.

[134] Bailey, *New Light on George Fox and Early Quakerism*, 130–31. Bailey uses the Hindu term 'avatar', defined as 'descent of deity', as a description of Fox's self-perception. Though he acknowledges Fox would not appreciate the comparison, Bailey argues 'Fox was indisputably a manifestation of deity and he was exalted as such'. See Bailey, *New Light on George Fox and Early Quakerism*, xi.

[135] *Margaret Fell to William Penn* (October 1677). (Glines [Ed.], *Undaunted Zeal*, 421.)

[136] Barbour and Roberts (Eds), *Early Quaker Writings*, 382.

> Verily the glory of all nations is with you, and you do I honour with my life with my life and soul and not with feigned words ... for I know the presence of the glorious God is with you and before you no deceit can stand, yea glorious daughters of Sion whose faces shine like the sun at noon day ... A nursing Mother thou art who feeds the hungry with good things, but the fat with judgment, who kills and stays the living and raises the dead. Judgment is committed unto thy hands, and judgment thou gives to whom judgment belongs, and mercy to whom mercy belongs, power in heaven and in earth is given unto thee.[137]

As he had done in his address to Fox, as mentioned by Bailey, Holme likewise used biblical descriptive phrases, which would allude to the divine, in his addresses to Fell and her daughter. Edward Burrough, in a letter to Margaret Fell the same year, also utilised effusive language and biblical imagery in regards to Fell in his introduction:

> My dearly and eternally beloved Sister, in whom my soul and life is refreshed, by the remembrance of thee, Oh thou daughter of God, and a mother in Israel, a nourisher of the father's babes and children ... thou art comely in thy beauty clothed with the sun and the moon underneath thy feet. Thou art glorious and fair; thy raiment is of needle work and thy art full of glory within ... by whom I am ravished with love which burneth in my breast. Thou art in thy life and glory to be above all things to be desired after. I who am of thee and doth in the measure behold thee, and partake with thee of thy life and glory and fullness do dearly salute thee, in the everlasting fountain of life at whom I do drink with thee, and art daily nourished, and everlasting refreshed.[138]

In a footnote to this letter, the editor of this collection of Quaker writings, Hugh Barbour, makes the following note about ecstatic language in early Quaker letters:

> Such ecstatic affection is found in most early Friends' letters, but came to be an embarrassment after Nayler's 'Fall' in 1656, and was cut out by Ellwood and Whitehead [early Quakers who gathered and printed letters] from later printings of such letters, and by Fox even from some manuscripts.[139]

---

[137] Swarthmore MSS, 1, 197. Cited by Ross in *Margaret Fell*, 25.
[138] *Letters Leading to Co-ordinate a Quaker Mission: Edward Burrough, Letter to Margaret Fell, from Dublin, September, 1655.* (Barbour and Roberts [Eds], *Early Quaker Writings*, 477.)
[139] Ibid.

Though Barbour states this kind of language was largely edited out from the historical record, remnants, like those above, remain. Fox himself was likely involved in a good deal of editing out of exalted language from letters and epistles, both by himself and by other Friends, which could be incriminating or misunderstood. Using a broad nib pen, lines are crossed or scribbled through, while some edges and corners of pages are torn away. While we cannot know how many letters Fox did throw away, Quaker historian H. Larry Ingle asks the intriguing question, why did Fox keep the altered letters instead of throwing all of them out entirely? Ingle concludes, 'Fox and his successors consciously set out to colour the way people in the future would view the movement'.[140] With the possible implications of blasphemy in such close associations with divinity, some early Friends, including Fox himself, felt the necessity to edit out anything that could be construed by people outside the Quaker community as blasphemous behaviour or beliefs.

Because of this editing, an arrival at an accurate conclusion of Fox's self-perception is limited to what he wanted history to know. Perhaps we can glean from his personal portrayal what he, in the end, believed of himself. There can be no doubt he saw himself as a person with a unique prophetic call whose holy life and unity with the divine made him *a* son of God. But in the end, he exhorted all Quakers to this holy lifestyle as children of God, and desired to awaken in them a realisation of the light of Christ within. Thus it seems clear the early Quakers had ecstatic spiritual experiences of the divine within, believing their fellow Friends were communing closely with God as well, which they acknowledged and translated into exalted language. In light of this, using Bailey's language, *all* Quakers could be construed as believing themselves to be in effect 'avatars'.

Taking the above into account, there is some degree of truth in all of the arguments presented by Cadbury, Nuttall and Bailey. Indeed the Quakers of the seventeenth century were steeped in biblical imagery, using exalted biblical language not only throughout the testimonies at the Fox/Fell marriage but also amongst other early letters and writings, a way of thinking not only a part of the Quaker tradition but, as previously noted, a part of the seventeenth-century use of biblical passages in everyday life and worship. However, while one cannot escape the notion that many followers of Fox were particularly impressed with the presence of the divine within him, particularly after one had first met him and was 'convinced', their exalted titles towards Fox were not necessarily declarations of Fox being the second appearance of Christ, or as one exalted above everyone else, as Bailey concludes.[141] Fox's self-perception of having the

---

[140] H. Larry Ingle, 'Unravelling George Fox: The Real Person'. (Mullet [Ed.], *New Light on George Fox*, 38–9.)

[141] Carole Dale Spencer, 'Early Quakers and Divine Liberation from the Universal Power of Sin'. Jackie Leach Scully and Pink Dandelion (Eds), *Good and Evil: Quaker*

light of Christ within him was an expectation and hope he had for all Quakers.[142] Just short of being the second appearance of Christ, he was certainly perceived as the forerunner of experiencing 'the light', in his role as a prophet, as Penn described him. However, Fox did not claim that he was to be the only one who would come out of the wilderness, but rather saw his ministry, and his marriage, as a testimony, or indication, that *all* of his followers were to come out of the wilderness. In short, Fox thought of himself as a forerunning prophet who proclaimed the inward presence of the light of Christ.

Fox certainly continued to walk a thin line between his self-assertion of authority and the encouragement of authority in others, based on the light of Christ within. Within the Quaker fold, the aforementioned Friend John Harwood from Yorkshire argued Fox equated himself with Christ and claimed infallibility. Fox had disowned Harwood for causing disunity and asserting too much authority. In 1663, this tension between the two leaders came to a head when Harwood wrote a document which he directed was to 'only go amongst Friends' where 'Fox's papers of enmity against the innocent have passed'.[143] In Harwood's written defence he publicly questioned and criticised Fox's actions, claims and authority, explaining he wrote the document 'to signifie the several causes which I believe and know to be the chiefest substantial matter of the ground of George Fox's disowning of me'.[144] He accused Fox of asserting authority through claims of infallibility and equality with Christ:

> And whereas George Fox hath called himself the Son of God, and also said, I am the Seed, which he might as well have said, I am Christ; (for we know that the Seed is Christ) I do desire Friends to judge impartially of his fruits, whether or no the Son or Seed of God ever brought forth such things as these that follows: And whether or no such have not been, and are yet deceived, who have esteemed, and do esteem him infallible?[145]

Fox promptly responded to this accusation in the same year in a document entitled *The spirit of envy, lying, and persecution made manifest for the sake of the simple hearted, that they may not be deceived by it: being an answer to a scandalous paper of John Harwoods*. In his response, Fox did not deny claiming to be the son of God, but rather defended this assertion:

Perspectives (Farnham: Ashgate Publishing Limited, 2007), 43–58; p. 50. 'He [Fox] never claimed to be equal to Christ, though he and other Quakers were accused of blasphemy by the civil authorities'.

[142] Ibid. 'Fox never exalted his mystical raptures'.
[143] John Harwood, *To All People That profess the Eternal Truth of the Living God*, 1.
[144] Ibid.
[145] Ibid, 3.

And thou sayst, *G.F. calls himself the Son of God, &c.* And this thou calls a crime; thy actions and fruits hath manifested whose son thou art, and thy self to be ignorant of the Scriptures and the Spirit that gave them forth. And as for the esteem of thee, it was never much valued, though G.F. & many other friends, did exhort thee, that thou might have been preserved, as a civil man, & been kept out of these things, which were below many of the World.[146]

Affirming that he believed having that of Christ within made him the son of God, Fox argued that Harwood's actions showed 'whose son thou art'. Again, Fox does not claim to be the son of God as equal to the Christ incarnate or the second appearance of Christ. The issue for Fox was not equality with Christ, but rather a status of allegiance. One is either in union with Christ and a member of the True Church, or in disunion and a member of the 'false church'. By one's actions, one could either be the son of Satan or the Son of God, the seed of the Serpent or the seed of the woman.[147]

When Harwood further accused Fox that he 'should set himself in the high place, and throw down the others', Fox replied that God, rather than himself, had set him in a high place and gave him authority to lead and to judge as a prophet:

This is another of thy lyes, for it is the Lord that set him up, and not man, and such wicked unclean spirits as thine is, he doth not own, and such unclean spirits as thou art, are not Gods inheritance; for I do Judge and am above all such, and ever was, and ever shall be. And so thou art one fallen into diverse temptations,

---

[146] Fox, *The spirit of envy, lying, and persecution made manifest for the sake of the simple hearted*, 2.

[147] Fox in his early *Short Journal*, which would provide the basis for his later published *Great Journal*, wrote about an altercation with a drunk fellow with a club, after which Fox explained he said to him 'I was the Sonne of God, and was come to proclaim the everlasting truth of God' (Penney [Ed.], *The Short Journals and Itinerary Journals of George Fox*, 17). Editor Norman Penney footnotes this statement with a short note regarding Fox's term 'the' Son of God: 'For the expression "son of God" ... it is interesting to note that in the Ancient copy of *The Short Journal* of George Fox, written in the seventeenth century, the words were originally written "the Sonne of God", but at some later but early date a capital letter *A* has obscured the "ye" and at the apex of the letter appears a small *a*. It will be seen that the reference here to the expression "son of God" is omitted from the Cambridge and Ellwood Texts' (Penney [Ed.], *The Short Journals and Itinerary Journals of George Fox*, 279 n 17.2). Here we have another example of Fox not shying away from using the phrase 'the' Son of God, the use of which caused concern for later editors of early Friends' records, not necessarily as a cover-up, but arguably done to avoid it being misinterpreted or misconstrued. Nevertheless, this editing and omission, as I have argued, does not necessarily mean Fox originally claimed equality of essence with the divine, or with Christ, but rather he claimed to be restored into the image of Christ and therefore perceived himself to be a product and prophet of God as a result of this restoration.

and hurtful lusts, but thy heart is given up to the same which is come up to open view ... And the Seed of God doth condemn all that is contrary to it, & such actions & practices as thine, its set atop of the head of them.[148]

Fox again saw himself as a prophet of the new age and spiritually mature to hear God's voice. He juxtaposed an inward spiritual authority from God against the 'unclean' spirits at work within Harwood. The 'seed' within Fox was judging all that opposed the 'seed'. Fox did not assign the authority of the 'seed within' only to himself. As we have seen he claimed all Quakers to have Christ within. However, it was certainly true that at the same time, many revered Fox for his leadership and prophet-like status.[149]

A glimpse of early Quaker observations of Fox, including the notions Fox had Christ 'within' and was 'the Son of God', can be found in the oldest extant letter written by a Quaker in July 1652 by Richard Hubberthorne. Possibly having written this letter only two or three weeks after his first meeting with Fox and after his 'convincement', Hubberthorne made the following reflections regarding his struggles after conversion along with observations of Fox. Addressing Fox as 'Dear Brother', he wrote:

> Fleshly lusts wars against the soul ... strong enemies ... comes forth to devour that young and tender plant which is planted by the Lord ... I am led into the wilderness to be tempted, and strong temptations compass me about. But thou art above them all, and not ignorant of his wiles, but art in the liberty of the Son ... Pray that the tender plant may grow up to be the Son, to have power and strength over all his enemies ... that I may come out of all, to live in him who is invisible, pure and spiritual, which I have had a taste and sight of ... And the Son yet as a servant learning obedience, under sufferings; and he is calling me to forsake all ... Pray that I may be kept not to boast above my measure, but may stand in the easy and gentle leadings of the Lamb, and may drink of those rivers in which thou swims.[150]

Being in the 'liberty of the Son', free from the temptations of the world, was a longing of Hubberthorne, and something to which he aspired. He knew he would not become the Christ, but hoped he would experience the Son, or Christ, within himself more fully. Hubberthorne humbly regarded Fox as

---

[148] Ibid, 9–10.

[149] Rosemary Moore explains Fox's status as 'Son of God': 'Quakers made great use of the concept of one's own "measure" of the Light or the Spirit, and while Fox's "measure" may have been greater than anyone else's, it was not different in kind. Son of God he may have called himself, but he directed others toward the Christ in themselves' (Moore, *The Light in Their Consciences*, 78).

[150] Barbour and Roberts (Eds), *Early Quaker Writings*, 156–7.

someone who had led the way in this experience of having the light of Christ within; who swam in 'those rivers' from which Hubberthorne hoped to drink. While Hubberthorne revered Fox for his experience of 'the Son' or the light of Christ within, it was clear that both he and Fox were in the position of receiving from 'the Lamb', making no reference to Fox being the Lamb himself.

Further possible clarification can be found later in a 1681 work by the prominent Quaker leader George Whitehead, in which he defended the early Quaker meeting system as not an invention by man (i.e. George Fox) but as divinely ordained by God. In this defence, Whitehead delineated the difference between Fox and Christ:

> G. Fox's *Form of Church-government*, G.F.'s *Orders*, &c. These expressions we own not, they are not proper; for though we grant, that *He* hath been Instrumental in the hand of Christ for stirring up other to *Unity* and *good Order*, yet we are satisfied that the great Builder, Former and Orderer of the spiritual House, is Christ Jesus, and that HE is the Author and Foundation of that Christian Religion, Care, Over-sight and good Government among us.[151]

William Rogers, the author of the offending book to which Whitehead was responding, was uneasy with Fox's leadership in setting up the meeting system, and eventually sided with Wilkinson and Story in their separatist movement. This alone shows that there were some who were uncomfortable with the wielding of power they felt Fox was using in setting up a formalised meeting system. While this exchange arguably took place late in the early Quaker movement, perhaps after the exalted language started to subside in order to save the movement from appearing too radical, or as a group worshipping Fox, on the other hand, it shows quite clearly the struggle taking place within the movement of how to perceive Fox's authority. Whitehead answered this question with a resolute statement that Christ, not Fox, had set up the good order they followed, while Fox was simply an instrument used by God.

Similarly, Fell's admiration of Fox did not lie in the belief that he was the second appearance of Christ or 'the Son of God' equalling Christ in the flesh *per se*, but rather Fell saw Fox as an instrument used by God to usher in the Gospel

---

[151] George Whitehead, *The accuser of our brethren cast down in righteous judgment against that spirit of hellish jealousie vented in a great confused book, falsly entituled, The Christian-Quaker distinguished form the apostate and innovator, in five parts; the fallacy and force whereof being herein clearly detected & justly repelled* (London: John Bringhurst, 1681), 6. Whitehead wrote this work in response to *The Christian-Quaker distinguished form the apostate and innovator* (London, 1680) by William Rogers, a Bristol Quaker who was condemned by the Bristol Meeting, and who eventually sided with John Wilkinson and John Story in their resistance against formalised meetings, setting up their own separatist movement. See Kunze, *Margaret Fell and the Rise of Quakerism*, 149.

which she felt had been hidden for many generations. Fell perceived Fox as a prophet who was the first to experience the fullness of God's presence within. Her perception of Fox indicates a chasm between perceiving one as having revelation from God, and *being* God. Her vision would remain the same as she reflected after Fox's death in 1691:

> He was the instrument in the hand of the Lord in this present age, which he made use of to send forth into the world to preach the everlasting gospel, which had been hid from many ages and generations.[152]

Bonnelyn Kunze rightly notes Fell's intentional 'close parallel of Fox to Christ' in her writings and personal beliefs, quoting Fell's tribute to Fox after he passed away:

> It having pleased Almighty God to take away my dear husband out of this evil and troublesome world, who was not a man thereof, being chosen out of it, and had his life and being in another region, and his testimony was against the world.[153]

Like the biblical narrative recounts Jesus' earthly ministry and rejection, so too did Fell see Fox as one not of this world, but often rejected by it. But the demarcation between an elevated 'second appearance of Christ' or a unique 'son of God' and an instrument or a prophet of God remained intact for Fell. On her own deathbed Fell prayed:

> Oh! my sweet Lord, into thy holy Bosom do I commit my self freely; not desiring to live in this troublesome, painful world; it is all nothing to me: For my Maker is my Husband … [I am] very weak in Body, but alive to God.[154]

Fell loved and admired Fox. She loved him as a husband, whom she encouraged and upon whom, as we will discuss later, she relied on for support, counsel and guidance, while in turn Fox relied upon her in many ways. She revered him as a man filled with God's presence, who led her to what she felt was her real conversion. But in the final analysis, Fell worshipped God alone. She regarded God as her ultimate husband in spiritual terms, the Lamb married to the bride, his True Church.

The perception of Fox as a man who lived as a son of God but was not 'the' Son of God did not necessarily alter over time, or fade with the decreasing

---

[152] Kunze, *Margaret Fell and the Rise of Quakerism*, 24. From the Box Meeting MSS No. 43.
[153] Ibid.
[154] Ibid, 26. Quoted from Fell, *Works*, 'Some of Margaret Fell's Dying Sayings'.

apocalyptic and prophetic fervour within the movement. In the abovementioned 1652 Lancaster assizes where Fox was accused of blasphemy, Judge Fell came to his defence with an argument, that incidentally Fox did not discount, which illuminates Fox's early identity. In his *Journal*, Fox recalled on the way to court Judge Fell 'said to me he had never such a matter brought before him before: & he could not tell what to do in the business'.[155] At the examination of George Fox before Colonel West, Judge Fell and other Justices, Fox made the following defence against accusations that he had claimed to be 'as upright as Christ':

> That was not so spoken that I was equal with God, he that is sanctified are [all of] one, they are one in the father, and the Son, and of his flesh, and of his bone, this the scripture doth witness, and wee are the Sons of God, and the father and the Son are one, &c.[156]

Here Fox not only rejected that he ever claimed to be Christ, but he also clearly pointed out all who are sanctified are 'Sons of God'.

At this point, Judge Fell engaged in the following argument with Dr William Marshall from Lancaster, a Puritan who had been chosen to represent those prosecuting Fox. In the following exchange, Judge Fell challenges the accusations against Fox by questioning the implications of 'equality':

> *Judge Fell*: Equality shows Two distinct.
>
> *Doctor Marshall*: But he saith they are one they are equal.
>
> *Judge Fell*: I cannot tell what you should make of that, the same thing cannot be equal.[157]

In a rather cunning twist, Judge Fell helped save Fox from imprisonment. Fox concurred, he was not claiming to *be* Christ, but claimed to be unified with Christ. In Fox's personal response to the accusation he had claimed to be as upright as Christ he argued, 'As he is, so are we in this present World: That the Saints are made the righteousness of God'. To this Judge Fell replied, 'He that sanctifyeth and they that are sanctified are one, they are united', followed by Colonel West's conclusion, 'All this is not to say That is equal with God'.[158] It appears, at least from this trial, that Fox was suggesting one could be united with the divine, and in this unity one had a measure of authority. When Fox was

---

[155] Fox, *Journal Vol. 1* (1911), 62.
[156] Ibid, 64–5.
[157] Ibid, 65.
[158] Ibid.

also accused of claiming to be the 'Judge of the World', Fox replied, 'The saints shall Judge the World, the Scriptures witness it whereof I am one, and I witness Scriptures fulfilled'.[159] Having cleared Fox from the charges of blasphemy, Judge Fell, a thoroughgoing Puritan, seemed to grasp the fine line Fox was attempting to walk in upholding Christ's presence in the 'saints' in the present day, while avoiding blasphemous claims.

Working then from the framework that Fox did not claim to be 'the' Lamb, or the second appearance of Christ, but perceived himself, and was perceived by his followers, as God's *instrument* in testifying to the presence of 'the Lamb' within the conscience of each restored individual, we can better grasp Fox's assertion that his marriage to Fell was an instrument used by God 'as a testimony that all might come up out of the wilderness to the marriage of the Lamb'.[160] In summary, from the very beginning of Fox's ministry he considered the whole mission of Friends to be witnesses to a renewed reconciliation and unity with God through an inward encounter with the divine, of which he had personally lived through during his own spiritual conversion. Braithwaite explains Fox regarded himself as 'kept through the power and light of Christ in a state of perfection like that of Adam in Paradise'.[161] The foundation of his ministry was thus being a living testimony to this return to the state of the 'pre-fall Adam' and to the purity and innocence of Paradise. He did not see himself as the 'Second Adam' but as a man who represented the reality of living in a restored unity with God as it was with Adam before the Fall.

Likewise, he saw his marriage as a representation of that restored union. As Fox considered himself a prophet, leading the way for his followers to likewise become 'Second Adams', his particular state of marriage was not exclusive to himself or to Fell, but was rather a forerunner or prototype of marriage that was to be exhibited and experienced by all Friends. Many early Quakers regarded Fox as the forerunning prophet to the restored creation, and a person who had the qualities of someone living quite in that state. Fox, the first to bring the news of the Lamb, and Fell, being an early convert and subsequent leader, came together in a marriage which marked a significant moment when the reality of the church coming out of the wilderness could be a 'testimony that all might come up into the marriage as was in the beginning', a reality which would be testified to by all fellow Quakers before and to come.[162] A telling quotation from Quaker leader William Gibson indicates Fox's followers did indeed translate this state of matrimony to all Quaker marriages in general. He wrote in 1682,

---

[159] Ibid.

[160] Fox, *Journal* (1952), 557.

[161] Ibid, 39. Braithwaite notes that Fox's favorite seal was 'G.F. and the Flaming Sword'. (See Fox's Will, reprinted in Fox, *Journal Vol. 2* [1911], 355).

[162] Fox, *Journal Vol. 2* (1911), 154. Fox referenced Revelation 19:7.

'Marriage was the Ordinance of God in Paradice, before Transgression was; God Married *Adam* and *Eve*, or joyned them together in the Covenant of Marriage'.[163] Fox and Fell were fairly successful in getting the message across; their marriage and all Quaker marriages were a testimony to the New Covenant, a return to paradise and direct communion with God, as the Second Adam was joined together with a restored Eve by God.

The Undefiled Bed of George Fox and Margaret Fell

While it was believed their marriage was a testimony to marriage 'out of the wilderness', the marriage itself was not strictly spiritual or a cosmic event, or a purely spiritual and celibate union. Nowhere does Fox claim that his marriage (nor any other Quaker marriage) was or should be purely spiritual. Neither did he claim or suggest his marriage was celibate, or that other marriages should be celibate. An interpretation of the following passage from Fox's *Journal* has led some scholars to this conclusion. In Fox's subsequent travels shortly after his marriage, he encountered an elder Puritan called Walter Newton, who told Fox he had heard he was married and wanted to know the reason he had decided to marry. When Fox replied he married 'as a testimony that all might come up out of the wilderness to the marriage of the Lamb' Newton replied that he thought marriage was only for the procreation of children. Fox answered:

> I never thought of any such thing but only in obedience to the power of the Lord. And I judged such things below me, though I saw such things and established marriages; but I looked on it as below me. And though I saw such a thing in the Seed yet I had no command to such a thing till a half year before, though people had long talked of it, and there was some jumble in some minds about it, but the Lord's power came over all and laid all their spirits; and some after confessed it.[164]

Fox's response 'I judged such things below me' has posed questions for some scholars. It is referred to by Bailey and Tual as proof of George Fox's abstinence from sexual relations in his marriage to Fell. Both Bailey and Tual interpret Fox's comment to mean he viewed sexuality as 'below him'.

This conclusion however fails to take into account Fox's consistent high doctrine of the restored marriage which included an 'undefiled bed'. As discussed in the previous chapter, Fox taught the nature of all Quaker marriages was honourable in the sight of God, and would include sexuality that is undefiled. Fox argued the following:

---

[163] Gibson, *A General epistle given forth*, Section 2, 78.
[164] Fox, *Journal* (1952), 557.

So Friends that be redeemed out of the Earth comes to know it as it was in the beginning again ... that is the Marriage that is honourable, and there the Bed is that is undefiled.[165]

For Fox, this state of honour and purity of the Quaker marriage-bed (sexuality within marriage) was not a result of the act of celibacy between two married individuals.[166] Rather, in the restored creation, there was the transformation of the sexual act, as there was transformation of every area of creation. The marriage-bed was now undefiled as the Quakers themselves were believed to be undefiled, as all was restored to the prelapsarian state of humanity.[167] While he did not see procreation as the sole or primary purpose of marriage (for his or any other Quaker marriage), a belief common amongst the Quakers' Protestant contemporaries including the Puritan minister Newton, Fox held fast to the notion of the 'undefiled bed' as an integral component of a Quaker marriage, a bed which was undefiled not because of an absence of sexual relations, but because of an absence from sin.

In his 1669 letter explaining his reasons for marrying Fell, Fox asserted his marriage would include an 'undefiled bed' when he wrote, 'G. Fox and M. Fell the Lord God hath brought it to pass to join us together ... in the honourable marriage and in an undefiled bed.'[168] As he included the 'undefiled bed' in his own description of his marriage, Fox's rather perplexing statement that he believed 'such things' to be 'below' him could alternatively suggest he viewed the notion that marriage was *solely* for procreation (a belief frequently upheld by Newton and other Protestants) as a degradation of the full meaning of the marital union.

---

[165] Fox, *Concerning Marriage* (1661), 4–5. Unlike Bailey's suggestion that Fox considered himself alone to be living in a pre-Fall state, and thus dictated to himself higher ascetic standards, in the above passage Fox made clear all Quakers were to be in this pre-Fall state, in which all Quaker marriages were considered honourable and the marriage-bed (i.e. sexuality) was 'undefiled', rather than non-existent.

[166] The historian Thomas Hamm notes, 'For the first three hundred years of the Society of Friends, sexuality was not an issue. Whatever their doctrinal differences, Friends embraced the sexual ethics other Christians endorsed' (Hamm, *The Quakers in America*, 137).

[167] There is evidence that some early Quakers, particularly in the North American colonies, promoted celibacy within marriage. Joseph Nicholson wrote a letter to Fell in 1669 from Boston indicating a Quaker husband refused to lie with his wife, and two women refused to lie with their husbands. Itinerant preachers Dorothy Waugh and Mary Clark were also proponents of celibacy. Likely out of practical necessity, they chose single life as opposed to marriage (see Mack, *Visionary Women*, 227). The practice of celibacy was however rare. Celibacy never became an official, regular Quaker practice, nor was it promoted by either Fox or Fell.

[168] Fox, *Letter of George Fox Concerning his Marriage* (2 October 1669). (Cadbury [Ed.], *Narrative Papers of George Fox*, 78.)

To place marriage in the context of being solely for the procreation of children was perhaps an insult to his high doctrine of marriage, both to his own marriage with Fell and to all Quaker marriages in general.

Other clues as to what Fox meant by 'below me' may be found in Margaret Fell's testimony at her marriage to Fox. Using similar language as Fox did in his letter, she declared:

> God created man in his own image: male and female in Christ Jesus; in this seed which was glorified with the Father before the world began. In this everlasting covenant and word of life I stand pure, spotless, chaste and undefiled to the Lord, and am clear and free from all that is below the marriage of the Lamb.[169]

Fell's reference to being clear and free from 'all that is below the marriage of the Lamb' suggests she was engaging in a marriage that was not 'in the fall'. Her notions of being 'pure, spotless, chaste' are images relative to the purity of the church, or the bride being married with and wholly devoted to the groom, 'Christ', a figure of the marriage of 'Christ and his church' as previously stated by Fox. Using language like 'above' and 'below', there was a distinction for Fox and Fell between Quaker marriages representing the restored creation and the fulfilled covenant and the 'marriages in the fall' preceding the Quakers. Thus, this new highly spiritual perception of marriage did not shift the value placed on sexual activity within marriage, placing celibacy above procreation, but rather shifted the emphasis on the meaning and motivation behind marriage as a whole to a higher spiritual plane which included an undefiled bed.

Regarding the question of celibacy and asceticism in their own marriage, other historical references suggest a possibility that Fell may have been pregnant and miscarried, or had experienced a phantom pregnancy during her first year of marriage to Fox. Bonnelyn Kunze presents a letter discovered by Henry Cadbury which possibly alludes to a conjugal relationship between Fox and Fell:

> Quaker historian Henry J. Cadbury found a curious letter of 16 July 1670 in the Calendar of State Papers Ireland addressed to William Penn, who was in Ireland that year. The letter, written by a Quaker woman minister in London, was intercepted by government agents.[170]

The author wrote about Margaret Rous (Fell's daughter) meeting with Margaret Fell and about one of them being 'with child':

---

[169] Ibid, 84.
[170] Kunze, *Margaret Fell and the Rise of Quakerism*, 55.

> She hath bene here to mete Margaret Rouse About her Mouther's Besenes that is in order to Geat her relese and ... ouderstanden Margrett Foxes Condeshon and that she being weth child and so nere ass she is her time beingen out All Most they are veary endorstret [interested] to procure her liberty which I hope thay well done.[171]

Kunze notes that Fell biographers either have ignored this letter or did not know of its existence. If the woman 'weth child' was Margaret Fell, it would prove the existence of a conjugal relationship. Contrarily, the Quaker historian Henry Cadbury suggests it may be a misprint, noting Margaret Rous was pregnant with a son at the time the letter was written, making the reference 'being weth child' appropriately Rous. But on the other hand, Cadbury also points out the letter was written eight months after Fell married Fox, at which time she was incarcerated in Lancaster gaol, during which time Fell was fifty-five years old and apparently in ill health.[172]

Kunze's conclusions are equally speculative. She suggests that since there are virtually no letters in the Fell family records of a possible pregnancy, Cadbury's suggestion that the reference was a misprint could be accurate; but on the other hand, circulating rumours amongst their opponents regarding Fell and Fox could suggest she experienced a phantom or menopausal pregnancy.[173] Kunze further notes that if the above letter did refer to Margaret Fell the Elder, it would be supported by a hostile accusation by a vociferous Quaker opponent called Francis Bugg. In 1707 Bugg described Fox and Fell as having at one time been 'deluded' that they had mystically conceived a child:

> After many years' cohabitation, when George Fox and Margaret Fell were grown old, whether the spirit of delusion to whom they had given themselves up possessed them in a vain conceit that they were Abraham and Sarah I know not. But it is very certain that they both persuaded themselves that Margaret Fell, alias Fox, was with child, and the Lord would raise up Holy Seed of them. All preparations were made for old Maximilla's lying in, baby-clouts were prepared, the midwife was called and gave attendance for about a month together, but there came nothing forth, all proved wind.[174]

---

[171] Henry J. Cadbury, 'Intercepted Correspondence of William Penn', *Pennsylvania Magazine of History and Biography*, 70 (1946): 354–6, cited by Kunze in *Margaret Fell and the Rise of Quakerism*, 56.

[172] Kunze, *Margaret Fell and the Rise of Quakerism*, 56.

[173] Ibid.

[174] Ibid. Kunze notes, 'Much ridicule of Fell's and Fox's alleged belief in such a mystical conception circulated in the north country even after her death' (Kunze, *Margaret Fell and the Rise of Quakerism*, 56). The Maximilla which Bugg referenced here is probably the Maximilla who, with Montanus and Priscilla, co-founded Montanism. Bugg likely drew

It is difficult to assess to what time period Bugg referred, but it may be a reference to their essential co-habitation at Swarthmoor where Fox took breaks in his ministerial travels, further adding fuel to the opponents of Quakerism with regard to their relationship, which Fox called 'some jumble in some minds'.[175] The Quaker historian Larry Ingle runs with the evidence, stating forthright, 'After she returned north following ten days with her new husband, she began to notice signs that she was pregnant.'[176] When Fell was sent to prison the following April after their marriage (at which time she would have been allegedly six months pregnant), Ingle contends this unhappy situation presented further problems for Fell, as 'Giving birth to a child, however, was not something easily hidden, especially in the crowded jails of seventeenth-century England'.[177] According to Ingle, ' ... word had leaked out' as the 'pregnancy dragged on' and a 'handful of people came to know of her condition', including supposedly the woman who had written the aforementioned letter to Penn.[178] However, he concludes the 'baby never came' because there was 'no actual pregnancy', as Fell had 'convinced herself that she was carrying a child, a condition known as pseudocyesis, imaginary or false pregnancy'.[179]

While the speculations persist, the intercepted letter does seem to provide fairly clear evidence that she did in fact at least think she was pregnant. Further, the fact the letter was intercepted possibly points to an effort on the part of at least one well-meaning Quaker to keep intimate news regarding Fell and Fox at bay, and out of the hands of people who might misuse this information. The fact that there is no mention of the pregnancy amongst the extant Fell family letters is not necessarily proof she was not pregnant, as it is possible that those letters were destroyed in the sifting and endorsing of letters by Fox during his time at Swarthmoor. As Fox never claimed his marriage was celibate, nor did he cite celibacy as a crucial element of a marriage within restored creation, it seems the evidence supporting their relationship being celibate is lacking. If they were celibate and saw it as a valuable ascetic practice within their marriage, it is likely they would have preached and encouraged the same discipline amongst their fellow Quakers.

The fact Fox and Fell did not advocate celibacy as a mark of the restored state (nor was innocence within paradise thus associated with abstinence from sex),

---

a parallel between Fell and Maximilla in an effort to underscore what he perceived as the heretical beliefs and unorthodox behaviour of Fell. For further reading on Maximilla, see William Tabbernee, *Montanist Inscriptions and Testimonia: Epigraphic Sources Illustrating the History of Montanism* (Macon, GA: Mercer University Press, 1997), 19ff.

[175] Fox, *Journal* (1952), 557.
[176] Ingle, *First Among Friends*, 228.
[177] Ibid.
[178] Ibid.
[179] Ibid.

was also significant in light of popular accusations of antinomian tendencies within Quakerism as a whole. According to the historian Rosemary Moore, early Quakers did teach some antinomian tenets (literally 'opposed to the laws') or the 'belief that the elect were incapable of sin, being entirely protected by the righteousness of Christ', but emphasised 'the practical impossibility of sin for one united with Christ, and the real righteousness resulting, rather than a legalistic theory'.[180] Other historians, including William Braithwaite, and more recently Bonnelyn Kunze, argue Fox and Fell preached against antinomianism.[181] Fox and Fell were indeed in a position of distancing themselves, and other Quakers, from Antinomians, including the Ranters, who used their antinomian beliefs to justify behaviours such as sexual relations outside of marriage and with multiple partners.[182] The worry that Quakers were translating their prelapsarian status into immoral behaviours was certainly widespread.[183] Yet instead of acting as if moral behaviour in the material world was inconsequential, their perception of 'being united with Christ' and the resulting 'real righteousness' was infused into the physical realm, including the marriage-bed and the physical manifestation of the monogamous relations on earth. Thus they heightened the importance of moral behaviour. Interestingly, Quakers also faced criticism for their stress on good works, as the historian Rosemary Moore explains, 'The Quakers' call to turn to 'the light within', and their stress on the necessity of right conduct, was considered by their opponents to be advocacy of justification by works'.[184] But for Fox and Fell, these good works, including honourable marriages, brought together by God, with undefiled beds, were a direct result of the restored experience of Christ within. Purity was proven not in celibacy, but in the orderly process of marriage approbation and in the restored state of marriages as a whole.

Neither did Fox or Fell ever promote their marriage as an unattainable emblematic pinnacle. Theirs was a marriage that was spiritual, not wholly devoted solely to reproduction, but not necessarily celibate. Richard T. Vann, in his demographical study of Quaker marriages and births, argues when Fox married Fell, who was 'too old to have children', and when Fox justified their marriage 'as a spiritual union', Fox along with other Quakers crossed 'a crucial mental boundary ... that can eventually lead to the sanctioning of sex without

---

[180] Moore, *The Light in Their Consciences*, 100. Bugg's abovementioned parallel of Fell to Maximilla, the co-founder of Montanism, demonstrates popular hostility to the perceived antinomian tendencies amongst the Quakers.

[181] Braithwaite, *The Beginnings of Quakerism to 1660*, 164. Braithwaite explains Fox 'proved himself a skilled antagonist in disputes with Antinomians, Ranters, and parish priests'. Kunze argues Fell was against Antinomians in her *Works* (Kunze, *Margaret Fell and the Rise of Quakerism*, 20).

[182] Ibid, 100–101.

[183] Ibid, 100.

[184] Ibid, 100–101.

reproduction'.[185] Since marital love was linked directly with the union of the divine with his church in the Quaker mindset, Vann's conclusion is certainly a possibility. For the early Quakers, after experiencing the convincement and work of the light in their inward conscience, the physical realm was transformed into the spiritual realm. The marriage between Fox and Fell, like that of other Quakers, was a physical representation of the spiritual realm. As scholar Su Fang Ng explains, the Quakers were driven 'to spiritualize the mundane, turning everyday actions into symbols and living testimonies'.[186] The physical realm was not eradicated. The subsequent years of Fox and Fell's marriage illuminate a relationship that, though spiritualised as a living testimony of the redeemed marriage between Christ and his church, was in the end also incredibly interdependent and human – particularly in their shared tenderness and their desires to accommodate for the physical comforts and care of the other, as well as their dealing with the practical, daily, at times mundane problems any couple might face. In the following section, this very human marital relationship will be further explored through their correspondence.

The Marital Relationship of George and Margaret Fox

In this section, a biographic account of their marriage will be followed by a discussion of whether or not their marriage did indeed exemplify the marriage of the Lamb and the New Jerusalem. In the following description of their marriage and the issues they encountered in the movement, we will find they spent a great deal of time apart, worked independently for the spread and organisation of Quakerism, while depending on each other for guidance and support largely through their letter correspondence. A look at their marriage, and how it practically functioned, I argue illuminates a marriage not without tenderness. In addition, their marriage sustained a partnership that helped continue to bring about the rising of the True Church but in very pragmatic ways. In comparison to the wedding testimonies described above, the highly apocalyptic language regarding their union is not as apparent in their actual marriage, particularly as the years passed. Their marriage, as we will see, was not without some discord (both internally and externally), but was human in desires, disappointments and genuine affection for one another. As best as can be understood from the outside looking in, let us now consider the daily life of Fox and Fell as a married couple.

During their marriage, Fell and Fox not only faced external persecution but also had the task of consolidating the Quaker movement internally, in an effort to maintain a unified movement. After Fell and Fox were married in Bristol, Fell

---

[185] Vann, *Friends in Life and Death*, 162.
[186] Ng, *Literature and the Politics of Family in Seventeenth-Century England*, 204.

returned north to Swarthmoor while Fox travelled through Wiltshire and then on into Berkshire and finally to London, continuing his ministry and itinerant lifestyle.[187] With Margaret Fell in the North and Fox in the South in London, the two leaders were in better geographic positions to maintain unity in the movement.[188] However this geographic separation, that would subsequently be the rule rather than the exception throughout most of their twenty-two years of marriage, has been used by various scholars as proof that Fox and Fell's marriage was purely symbolic, and has also been used as fuel for criticism of the Fox/Fell union by their contemporary enemies.[189] Yet Fell did not necessarily prefer this arrangement, as she explained in her later recollections:

> And though the Lord had provided an outward habitation for him, yet he was not willing to stay at it because it was so remote and far from London, where his service most lay. And my concern for God and His holy, eternal Truth was then in the North, where God had placed and set me, and likewise for the ordering and governing of my children and family; so that we were very willing, both of us, to live apart some years upon God's account and His Truth's service, and to deny ourselves of that comfort which we might have had in being together.[190]

There is evidence that Fell was possibly annoyed with Fox for not trying harder to stay out of gaol and be able to return to Swarthmoor, particularly when Fox was sent to Worcester gaol from December 1673 to February 1675. Fell apparently believed Fox could have avoided the arrest. After he had been imprisoned, Fell left Fox in Worcester gaol, returning to Swarthmoor rather than staying on and caring for Fox while he was in prison, which was usually the custom amongst Quaker couples.[191] Fox wrote to Fell in January 1674:

> I received thy letter by Leonard Fell and another from Rebecca Travers from London. And she strangeth that thee hath not written to her, for she and the rest of London Friends generally think that thou are with me in prison and did stay,

---

[187] Kunze, *Margaret Fell and the Rise of Quakerism*, 54.

[188] Bruyneel-Padgett, *The Eschatology of Margaret Fell (1614–1702) and its Place in her Theology and Ministry*, 90.

[189] In his *Journal*, Fox explained he had tried to meet Fell in Leicestershire not long after they were married. This plan was thwarted when he discovered she had been sent to Lancaster prison, an imprisonment which will be discussed shortly. Fox explained, 'Intending to go as far as Leicestershire, I wrote a letter to my wife ... that if she found it convenient to her she might meet me there ... I turned into Leicestershire; where instead of meeting with my wife, I heard that she was haled out of her house to Lancaster prison' (Fox, *Journal Vol. 2* [1836], 120).

[190] Braithwaite, *The Second Period of Quakerism*, 264.

[191] Kunze, *Margaret Fell and the Rise of Quakerism*, 55.

and not gone into the North. And therefore thou should write to her and them, for they oft remember their love as though thou were here and do not think that thou art gone.[192]

Fox wrote again a month later:

Dear Heart, Thou seemed much grieved when I was speaking of prisons and when I was taken thou began to fall upon me with blaming of me, and I told thee that I was to bear it and why could not thee be content with the will of God. And thou said some words and then was pretty quiet ... The three pound thou sent up to me in love, for it I did speak to a Friend to send thee as much Spanish black cloth as will make thee a gown.[193]

In July, Margaret and her daughter Susan Fell would go to visit him in Worcester.[194] In this rather touching sequence of letters, the vulnerability of Fox and Fell to marital conflicts as well as desires to reconcile is evident. Fell seems to have been a wife wishing for her husband's safety and swift return home, while Fox felt his ministry lay in the South, and in prison if need be, making efforts to assuage her grief with a gift of 'Spanish black cloth'.

A few years later in April 1678, when Fox was still in the South of England and Fell was at Swarthmoor, Fox wrote to Fell that while he was in Bristol he bought 'as much scarlet as would make thee a mantle which thou may line it ... whether it be come I have not heard.'[195] Fell wrote to Fox the following July, perhaps in direct response to this present:

I received thy kind token by Leonard [Fell], which I did not expect, but I know it is thy true love to remember us [thus]. I thought to have sent something by Mary Fell to thee, but I considered thou would only buy something with it for me as

---

[192] *Letter by George Fox to Margaret Fell from Worcester Gaol (January 1674).* (Cadbury [Ed.], *Narrative Papers of George Fox*, 111.) See also Kunze, *Margaret Fell and the Rise of Quakerism*, 55.

[193] Ibid, 112–13. *Letter from George Fox to Margaret Fell from Worcester Gaol (February 1674).* In a letter dated in April 1674 Fox tells Fell of the whereabouts of the delivery of the said black cloth, in addition to 'black hair for cloth': 'The black cloth was gone by Henry Perfer, carrier ... to be left with John Higgins ... for him to send to Sarah Fell at Swarthmoor. The black hair for cloth was delivered to Ezekiel Partridge, and he promised to send it by Henry Baker ... to be left with John Higgins in Lancaster to be sent to Sarah Fell at Swarthmoor' (see Cadbury [Ed.], *Narrative Papers of George Fox*, 117).

[194] Norman Penney (Ed.), *The Household Account Book of Sarah Fell of Swarthmoor Hall* (Cambridge: Cambridge University Press, 1920), xii.

[195] *Letter from George Fox to Margaret Fell (April 1678).* (Cadbury [Ed.], *Narrative Papers of George Fox*, 128.)

thou used to do, which caused me to omit it. I perceive thou hast sent things to the children by Leonard; he hath not yet delivered them; but thy company would be more and better to us than all the world or than all the earth can afford.[196]

Funds were sent to Fox while he was away, and he apparently quite frequently bought little 'tokens' for Fell. While Fell and her daughters at home were touched by his gifts, she expressed to Fox a heartfelt desire for him to return to Swarthmoor.

A look through *The Household Account Book of Swarthmoor Hall*, carefully recorded by Fell's daughter Sarah Fell, relates provisions afforded to Fox. The *Account Book* spans almost five years, from September 1673 to August 1678. An entry on 13 August 1674 shows ten pounds being sent to Fox while he was in prison in Worcester, a month after Fell's visit in July.[197] In November the following year, we see payments for 'Letters to father' (payments for the postage of Fox's correspondence are seen repeatedly throughout), and the following month a purchase of '3: Salmons from Lancaster for father'.[198] There is an entry in June 1676 of 'glue and tobacco pipes for father' which may have been either for his use, or to give as gifts.[199] The same year, Sarah had written to Fell during her travels with Fox, asking for Fell to bring back goods to Swarthmoor:

---

[196] Ibid, 128 n 72.

[197] Penney (Ed.), *The Household Account Book of Sarah Fell of Swarthmoor Hall*, 117. Curiously, this is only the second entry of monetary provision for Fox while he was in Worcester gaol, the first being just shortly after he imprisoned in December 1673, the following on 5 January, three pounds 'sent to Worcester to father' from 'Mother's account'. It is also considerably less money than the ten pounds given in August, after Fell visited him in prison.

[198] Penney (Ed.), *The Household Account Book of Sarah Fell of Swarthmoor Hall*, 231, 235. Fox apparently had a penchant for fish, or perhaps it was for good health, as there are several entries of fish 'for father' including salmon, dried salmon and 'Read herrings from Lancaster'. See Penney (Ed.), *The Household Account Book of Sarah Fell of Swarthmoor Hall*, 323, 359, 387.

[199] Ibid, 283. In the Addenda, Penney comments on entries relating to tobacco: 'The references to the use of tobacco for persons and animals are of considerable interest. The purchase of this narcotic for smoking, and of pipes, is noted in general (pp. 71, 253, 291, 371). Pipes were purchased for George Fox (pp. 283, 295, 363) though in his *Journal* he decries smoking by others and states 'tobacco I did not take'. A similar purchase was made for Susannah [Fell] (pp. 491, 501) and may have been used by reason of her ill health ... Mary Lower purchased a quarter pound of tobacco for two pence half penny (p. 403)'. Penney further states there have been mixed opinions regarding smoking tobacco amongst Quakers throughout history, including reference to 'Jane Pierce, a well-known Quakeress, of Philadelphia, [who] continued the habit till the day of her death in 1846 at the age of ninety'. While Fox was at Swarthmoor, he was recovering from illness, perhaps pointing to the use of tobacco for medicinal purposes. Otherwise, it would have been simply for enjoyment or

We desire to know, as soon as thou can, when we may expect you with our dear father, for several reasons as thou may well know. Thou should buy us a cask of wine, of what sort thou judges father likes best, for we have none, only some cider and March beer bottled up; also you should buy us some anchovies, some olives and two larding needles and some oranges and lemons and what else you think fit.[200]

Largely dependent on the land, and the local shops in Ulverston, many things had to be brought in from Lancaster or Kendal.[201] With supplies running low, Sarah anticipated and looked forward to her mother's and Fox's return, and desired that the house be well stocked with food and wine to Fox's liking. In October 1676, an order for 'juniper berries for father' was paid for, as well as a 'whistle for father'.[202] In December and January, there are entries for 'a white horse for father' as well as 'woollen stockens'.[203] In January, 'writeinge paper from Lancaster for father' was purchased, followed by a purchase in March of a 'skin of parchment for father', likely for Fox's voluminous writing and correspondence.[204]

After Fox's departure from Swarthmoor in March, there is an entry in April for 'a coard for one of fathers boxes sent to London', followed by a later payment made to Thomas Curwen of London for 'carrieinge 2 boxes of fathers to Lancaster', both of which indicate many of his effects and provisions were sent to him for his stay in the South of England.[205] In addition to letters, they sent him fish, books and 'some Ireon oare'.[206] There is also evidence of Fox buying items for his wife, including an entry in March 1675: 'To me Received of father that I paid for a pair of Stockens for Mother which hee said hee would buy'.[207] Finally, throughout the *Account Book*, Sarah refers to Fox as 'father' or 'my father', indicating she appreciated Fox as an earthly familiar father, a part of the family in a very real sense, as much as a spiritual father. What are at first seemingly mundane details of a family's day-to-day life actually help to fill out a better picture of the dependence and care taken amongst themselves, and

---

for gifts, the suggested reason for Susannah's purchase (Penney [Ed.], *The Household Account Book of Sarah Fell of Swarthmoor Hall*, 583).

[200] Ibid, xvi. Cited from Maria Lamb Webb (1804–73). *The Fells of Swarthmoor Hall and Their Friends: With an Account of Their Ancestor, Anne Askew, the martyr. A Portraiture of Religious and Family Life in the Seventeenth Century, Compiled Chiefly from Original Letters and other Documents, Never before Published* (London: F.B. Kitto, 1867), 292.

[201] Penney (Ed.), *The Household Account Book of Sarah Fell of Swarthmoor Hall*, xvii.
[202] Ibid, 319, 321.
[203] Ibid, 343, 369.
[204] Ibid, 349, 371.
[205] Ibid, 379, 381.
[206] Ibid, 387, 413.
[207] Ibid, 246.

certainly here illuminate the Fell family's concern and provision for Fox, as father and husband.

After Fox married Fell their exchange of letters shows a change in Fox's salutary address towards Fell. The terms of address and introduction Fox used for Fell in his letters shifted from 'To Margaret Fell' or 'Dear' or 'Dear Sister' to a consistent 'Dear Heart', 'My dear Heart' or 'Dear Love'. Though this was an introduction that was not uncommon in seventeenth-century letters, the change is striking in the correspondence of Fox and Fell. He would also frequently follow this salutation with 'To whom is my love', an addition which again could be considered minor but was an abrupt alteration in salutary remarks after their marriage, which he fairly consistently included. These characteristics in their exchange of letters show a relationship which was affectionate and intimate. Sadly, a number of other letters from Fox to Fell, all beginning with 'Dear Heart', were apparently accidentally destroyed by a fire sometime in the mid-1800s.[208] Other letters referred to in Fox's *Journal* published by Thomas Ellwood, including a letter Fox apparently had written to her from London asking her to meet him in Leicestershire and several written out of Holland in 1677, are no longer extant according to Cadbury.[209] Despite these losses, the letters which are extant provide us with a glimpse into a relationship that resembled a loving and interdependent marital union.

Not long after their marriage, Fell faced a crisis that caused her to rely heavily on Fox for further support and guidance. Upon returning to Swarthmoor, Fell was again taken from her home and imprisoned, this time however at the prompting of her son George Fell.[210] The issue at stake was the control of the estate of Swarthmoor Hall. When Judge Fell died in 1658, he had granted Fell the use of Swarthmoor Hall until her death or remarriage.[211] While Fell was incarcerated at Lancaster prison from 1664 until 1668, George Fell petitioned Charles II in 1664 that the Swarthmoor estate be secured and kept in the family, which was granted. At the time, he, his sisters and mother were on more friendly terms; the sisters remained at Swarthmoor while George Fell, his wife and daughter made their home at Marsh Grange, the childhood home of Margaret Fell near Dalton-in-Furness, then in Lancashire When Fell was freed in 1668, she joined her daughters at Swarthmoor.

However, after Fell's marriage to Fox the following year, Fell's relationship with her son changed for the worse. Likely embarrassed by his mother's

---

[208] Cadbury (Ed.), *Narrative Papers of George Fox*, 95. 'William Fletcher of Cockermouth writing in 1894 reported: "More than a dozen of George Fox's letters to his wife (all beginning with 'Dear Heart') which had been inherited by a relative of mine, were accidentally destroyed by a fire some years ago"'.
[209] Ibid.
[210] Ross, *Margaret Fell*, 222.
[211] Kunze, *Margaret Fell and the Rise of Quakerism*, 51.

associations with Quakerism, and worse, by her marriage to a social inferior, he took advantage of the situation and requested from the local authorities that the stipulations of his father's will be carried out. As she was now remarried, the Hall no longer legally belonged to her, and he moved to take hold of the property as heir, though the property had been granted to the Fell daughters by Judge Fell in his will.[212] Apparently George Fell could not bear to see his father's estate remain a hub and centre for the socially despised Quaker movement, and wanted the estate for himself and his family. While Fox renounced all legal claim to the estate at the time of his marriage to Fell, so too had Fell forfeited any real legal claim to it, due to the stipulations in Judge Fell's will that it remain hers until death or remarriage. But because she was in effect still the one who was in authority over the estate, along with the help of her daughters, the battle was largely between George Fell and his mother, sisters and brothers-in-law, including John Rous the husband of Margaret, Jr, who wrote to Margaret Fell they could not 'prevail anything with him about thy part of Swarthmoor', and Thomas Lower who called his brother-in-law 'barbarous' in his 'unnatural actions'.[213]

Prior to Fell's imprisonment, Fox wrote to her in December 1669 telling her of the rumours he had been hearing regarding George Fell's behaviour, actions and intentions:

> Dear Heart, To whom is my love in the seed of God which is over all, and in that keep, for thou mayest have some trials but in that thou wilt have dominion and wisdom and patience. Here hath been a great noise about thy son George Fell as having orders to send thee to Westchester and me to Jersey ... and I understand his intent is to have Swarthmore ... But in all these things thou may perfectly inform thyself, but in wisdom and patience, that thou may make as little noise of it as may be ... thou may speak to thy brother Richardson about these things (in the seed and life) which are below ... whatever thou dost, keep clear in the power of God to answer that.[214]

After Fell was put in prison, Fox wrote from London:

> My dear Heart ... It was upon me that Mary Lower and Sarah (Fell) should go to the King concerning thy imprisonment, and to (Justice) Kirkby that the power of the Lord might appear over them all in thy deliverance. They went. And then they thought to have come down but it was upon me to stay them a little longer,

---

[212] Ross, *Margaret Fell*, 225.

[213] Kunze, *Margaret Fell and the Rise of Quakerism*, 51–2.

[214] *Letter from George Fox to Margaret Fell from Enfield (December 1669)*. (Cadbury [Ed.], *Narrative Papers of George Fox*, 104–5.) 'Matthew Richardson (d. 1677), J.P., attorney, of Dalton had married Margaret Fell's sister' (Cadbury [Ed.], *Narrative Papers of George Fox*, 105).

that they might follow the business till it was effected which it now is and is here sent down.[215]

Shortly after Fox wrote this letter to Fell from London he became gravely ill in September 1670, and did not recover until the following spring in 1671.[216] Fox stayed with Fell's daughter Margaret who took care of him in London. Nevertheless, he made efforts in London to secure her freedom, as he explained in his *Journal*:

> Upon the notice I received of my wife's being sent to prison again, I sent two of her daughters to the king, and they procured his order to the sheriff of Lancaster for her discharge. But though I expected she would be set at liberty thereby, yet this violent storm of persecution coming suddenly on, the persecutors there found means to hold her still in prison.[217]

At Swarthmoor, the struggle continued, as Fell remained in prison and her daughters and sons-in-law corresponded with her son in an attempt to change his mind. However, the proceedings changed course when George Fell suddenly passed away in October 1670. The following year in April, after efforts from Fox and her daughters, the King granted Fell a pardon and discharge under the Broad Seal, and she was finally released from prison.[218] As Fox explained, after the above attempts to secure Fell's freedom failed, he decided to take further action:

> I was moved to speak to Martha Fisher and another woman Friend, to go to the king about her liberty ... and the Lord gave them favour with the king, so that he granted a discharge under the broad-seal, to clear both her and her estate.[219]

Yet because George Fell had bequeathed to his infant son Charles use of the land and the estate, as well as to his wife Hannah Fell while she remained a widow, Hannah began litigation against her mother-in-law to continue to fight for the property. The Quaker leader Elizabeth Hooton reproached Hannah for her actions:

> It is reported that thou hast gotten a judgment against [Margaret Fox] to sweep away all that she hath, both goods and Lands. What a rebellious daughter-in-law

---

[215] Ibid, 106.
[216] Glines (Ed.), *Undaunted Zeal*, 401.
[217] Fox, *Journal Vol. 2* (1836), 136.
[218] Glines (Ed.), *Undaunted Zeal*, 406.
[219] Fox, *Journal Vol. 2* (1836), 136.

art thou. Was there ever such a wicked thing done in England or in any age before, that thou should ruinate thou husband's mother. The same hand that cut off thy husband will do the same by thee and leave thee neither root nor branch if though do not speedily repent and put off thy wicked invention and let thy mother alone with her estate. The Lord's terrible wrath and plagues will fall upon thee and thine. Therefore fear and dread the living God. While it is time, put by thy wicked intent, lest the same hand that took away thy husband may not take away thee in thy cruelty towards thy husband's mother, who hath not done thee any hurt or hath not wronged thee at all. So the light of Christ in thy conscience return, which will let thee see all thy ways. I am a lover of thy soul, Elizabeth Hooton.[220]

Hannah's relations with her sisters-in-law were unsurprisingly further strained. Nine years later, Hannah began to lock the gate of the one-mile footpath between the Hall and Ulverston in an effort to prevent Quaker meetings. Bitterness apparently remained, as Margaret Fell's legacy to her grandson Charles in her will of 1702 was half the amount that each of the other grandchildren received.[221] Meanwhile, Hannah's litigation failed, with Swarthmoor Hall remaining in the hands of the Quakers who still have it for their use today.

After George Fell's death and Margaret Fell's release from prison in April 1671, Fell returned to London to visit George Fox from May until August of that year. Believing he had been commanded by God to voyage to America, Fox wrote of his desire for Fell 'to hasten to London, as soon as she could conveniently, after she had obtained her liberty, because the ship was then fitting for the voyage'.[222] After Fox and Fell had stayed in London to attend the Yearly Meeting, Fox set sail for America. Fell then returned to Swarthmoor, at which time the Swarthmoor Women's Monthly Meeting was formed, the first continuous Women's Meeting outside of London.[223] Fell and Fox would not see each other again until almost two years later in June 1673, when Fox and Fell met in Bristol on his return from America.

It was shortly after this meeting that Fox was imprisoned again in Worcester. Having spent a year in prison herself just after their marriage, followed by only a couple of shared months with Fox in London, losing him again to prison was likely a strain for Fell. In addition, while in prison Fox became gravely ill as he explained in his *Journal*:

---

[220] Ross, *Margaret Fell*, 226–7.
[221] Kunze, *Margaret Fell and the Rise of Quakerism*, 53. In Fox's *Journal* there is only one mention of George Fell. Fox recalled a time when, in 1652, a young fourteen-year old George Fell had come to him while being beaten by the people of Ulverston: 'And Judge Fell's son running after to see what they would do with me, they threw him into a ditch of water and cried, "Knock out the teeth of his head!"' (see Fox, *Journal* [1952], 127).
[222] Fox, *Journal Vol. 2* (1836), 137.
[223] Kunze, *Margaret Fell and the Rise of Quakerism*, xiv.

> I had a fit of sickness, which brought me very low and weak in my body; and I continued so a pretty while, insomuch that some Friends began to doubt I would recover. I seemed to myself to be amongst the graves and dead corpses.[224]

Fell returned to London in October 1674 to have an interview with the King in an attempt to gain Fox's release. When Fox was discharged from Worcester in February the following year, Fox, Fell and her daughter Susannah would return to Swarthmoor. Fell described this time of respite at Swarthmoor as a period of peace and recovery for Fox, 'We got him home to Swarthmoor where he had a long time of weakness before he recovered'.[225] Fox's stay at Swarthmoor would be his longest, twenty-one months from June 1675 until he returned to London in March 1677.[226] After his departure, she wrote to her daughters:

> Your father is not altogether so weary as he was; but he cannot endure to ride but very little journeys and lights often; but he is pretty well and hearty, praise be to the Lord.[227]

Fox arrived in London on 23 May 1677 and stayed until the following July at which time he travelled to Germany and Holland with Friends, including William Penn and his step-daughter Isabel Yeamans.[228] After these difficult travels, due to his poor health, he returned to Swarthmoor for his last visit from September 1678 until March 1680.[229] In the remaining eleven years of his life Fox would not return to Swarthmoor.[230] Most of his remaining years were spent in or near London, where Fox resided at various places including the home of Fell's daughter Sarah, who was at that time married to William Meade.[231] In 1689, Sarah wrote to her mother:

> Father, I hope, is rather better, though as to his getting strength there is little certainty, for, if he be a little cheery sometimes, then he is presently weak again,

---

[224] Fox, *Journal* (1952), 700.

[225] Ibid, 718. From 'George Fox's Later Years' by Henry Cadbury. Isabel Ross describes Fox's return as 'the first time, since their marriage six years earlier, that husband and wife had been together in their own home' (Ross, *Margaret Fell*, 257).

[226] Fox ends his autobiography here at his stay at Swarthmore with his final recollection, 'And so the meetings have been quiet ever since and have increased' (Fox, *Journal* [1952], 708).

[227] *Letter, 31 March 1677, from Draw-well*, in *The Journal of Friends Historical Society*, 2 no 23. Cited in Braithwaite, *The Second Period of Quakerism*, 429.

[228] Fox, *Journal Vol. 2* (1836), 241.

[229] Ibid, 290. See also Kunze, *Margaret Fell and the Rise of Quakerism*, 122.

[230] Ross, *Margaret Fell*, 312, 411.

[231] Ibid, 313.

for he sleeps but little a-nights which keeps him weak. He was at our meeting last First-day in a coach; he could stay but about three-quarters of an hour in the meeting and was faint and weary when he came home.[232]

Fox clearly began to feel the physical strains of travel and long imprisonments. Fell recollected later that after his last visit to Swarthmoor, Fox 'grew weakly, being troubled with pains and aches, having had many sore and long travels, beatings and hard imprisonments'.[233]

After Fox's last visit to Swarthmoor in 1680, Fox and Fell wrote to each other consistently, while Fox travelled and ministered and Fell continued corresponding with Quakers around the world and holding regular meetings at her home. During their remaining eleven years of marriage, Margaret Fell journeyed to London three times to see Fox, and also to be in touch with the Meetings of the London Quakers.[234] She was apparently aware of external criticisms of their geographic separation, as she explained:

> And if any took occasion, or judged hard of us because of that, the Lord will judge them; for we were innocent. And for my own part, I was willing to make many long journeys for taking away all occasion of evil thoughts.[235]

Fell's three visits were in 1681, the winter of 1684–5 and finally in the spring of 1690.[236] This would be the last time she would see Fox.

> Of all the times that I was at London, this last time was most comfortable, that the Lord was pleased to give me strength and ability to travel that great journey, being seventy six years of age, to see my dear husband ... for he lived about half a year after I left him.[237]

Considering the travelling conditions of the day, Fell's advanced age and Fox's declining health, it is likely that the infrequency of their visits with one another was not due to lack of affection. Their joint decision to live separately, though difficult at times, was done in an effort to unify the movement, a sacrifice they

---

[232] *Letter from Gooses, 6 March 1689* (Spence MSS iii. Fol. 192), cited by Helen G. Crossfield in *Margaret Fox of Swarthmoor Hall* (London: Headley Brothers, 1913), 213. Cited also in Braithwaite, *The Second Period of Quakerism*, 433.

[233] Braithwaite, *The Second Period of Quakerism*, 748.

[234] Ross, *Margaret Fell*, 314, 410–12.

[235] From *The Testimony of Margaret Fox*. Cited in Braithwaite, *The Second Period of Quakerism*, 743.

[236] Ross, *Margaret Fell*, 410–12.

[237] From *The Testimony of Margaret Fox*. Cited in Braithwaite, *The Second Period of Quakerism*, 743.

were apparently willing to make, though both would have preferred the 'comfort' they might have had 'in being together'.[238]

Prior to Fox's death in January 1691, the Toleration Act was passed in 1689, freeing Quakers from fierce consistent persecution, particularly in the courts. Fell largely remained at Swarthmoor, returning to London one last time at the age of eighty-three to settle Fox's will, visit her family, and attend the London Meetings.[239] Fell's influence would remain largely intact in the North, but in London it would wane.[240] After Fox's death, practices such as plainness of dress began to emerge which alarmed and concerned Fell as being contrary to what she and her husband had jointly envisioned for Quakers living in the 'liberty of the Spirit'. In 1700, she wrote her last epistle to her fellow Quakers, a letter against regimentation in which she warned the new generation of Quakers to not fall prey to 'bondage in observing proscriptions, in outward things which will not profit, nor cleanse the inward man'.[241] She concluded her letter stating it was 'not Delightfull' for her to 'have this occasion to write' but that it 'grieved her heart' to see such 'silly outside Imaginary practices'.[242] She warned her fellow Quakers about their misuse of meetings to enforce these rules of dress:

> Our Monthly and Quarterly Meetings, were set up for Reproving, and looking into Superfluous or Disorderly walking, and such to be admonished and instructed in the Truth, And not private persons to take upon them to make orders, and say this must be done, and the other must not be done: And can Friends think, that those who are Taught and Guided of God can be subject and follow such low, mean orders.[243]

In her remaining years she continued correspondence with fellow Quakers, and kept regular Quaker meetings at Swarthmoor. Close to her eighty-eighth birthday, in April 1702, Fell passed away. Her mind was said to be 'clear', as she was surrounded by children and grandchildren.[244] Though ten years Fox's senior, she had survived him by eleven years, remaining active in the leadership of the

---

[238] Ibid.

[239] Bruyneel-Padgett, *The Eschatology of Margaret Fell (1614–1702) and its Place in her Theology and Ministry*, 98.

[240] Ibid. Bruyneel-Padgett writes, 'The great Margaret Fell found herself unwelcome by many Friends in leadership in London, and some in the Yearly Meeting were reported to have made unkind remarks about her with regard to her age'.

[241] Margaret Fell, *To Friends, Brethren, and Sisters* (April 1700). (Glines [Ed.], *Undaunted Zeal*, 470.)

[242] Ibid, 471.

[243] Ibid, 470.

[244] Ibid, 473.

Quaker movement. In an epistle written by Fell in 1698, she reminded her fellow Quakers of the leadership of Fox:

> God the Father or our blessed Lord and Saviour Jesus Christ is a universal God of mercy and love to all people. And in that blessed love he visited us, 'in an acceptable time and in a day of salvation, etc'. And he that early brought unto us the glad-tidings of the gospel of peace [i.e. George Fox], continued in the body amongst God's Plantation up and down forty years; and we had from him certain directions and instructions upon many weighty accounts and occasions. He hath left us several writings and records, to be practised according to the Gospel which he preached amongst us; and we have lived under the teaching of that blessed eternal Spirit of the eternal God, which he directed us to, unto this day. And now it is good for us all to go on and continue hand in hand in the unity and fellowship of this eternal Spirit.[245]

Fell continued to evoke the memory and teachings of Fox in her own leadership. Their interdependence for support and guidance as well as their friendship was strong and consistent through much of the time they were apart.

While their union was considered an apex in the restored marital state, a state to be enjoyed by all Quakers, their marriage was also a very real relationship visited by many trials and separations, and sustained through mutual support. But was it exemplary of the marriage of the Lamb and the New Jerusalem? Certainly over the years the apocalyptic fervour of their marital union subsided. Their marriage was esteemed, both by their contemporaries as well as Quaker scholars throughout subsequent generations, but it has not been understood in light of its initial apocalyptic, highly spiritual context. It can be argued that Fox and Fell's view of their own marriage may have changed, coinciding with the shift in apocalyptic fervour the latter decades of the seventeenth century witnessed. But what is most striking is the greater early preoccupation with the actual marriage approbation process than with the marriage itself. While indeed their marriage was embedded in the framework of the Lamb and the New Jerusalem by themselves and fellow Quakers, a look at their marriage itself shows one which was loving and supportive but was not perfect or without difficulties, ultimately coming up short of the idealistic vision of the restored creation.

---

[245] Barbour and Roberts (Eds), *Early Quaker Writings*, 565.

Conclusion

I have attempted to demonstrate how early Quakers, under the leadership of Fox and Fell, conducted their marriage approbation discipline and why the proper execution of this process was of such great spiritual import. In chapter one, the approbation process, as demonstrated through the early Quaker meeting minutes, exemplified the enormous amount of time devoted to the discipline as well as the many particular difficulties and trials the early Quakers faced while enforcing the correct marriage approbation process. The amount of time they spent points to a religious movement utterly preoccupied with maintaining endogamous marriages – brought together not by human initiative or will, but by God alone. It was a process that took a great deal of time, in an effort to avoid unions which were not representative and indicative of the orderly Quakers. Prior promises to be married to another, disorderly behaviours which would not befit a marriage (such as drunkenness or rudeness), or the failure to provide for the children of a prior marriage (if the future wife was a widow) were just some of the issues the early Friends wanted to avoid. Investigations, if they were required, were carried out to ensure the proper repentance of any wayward behaviour before a marriage took place. Fox and Fell initiated a marriage approbation process that was founded on their belief in direct revelation from God, but which also perpetuated a thorough system of Quaker meetings and a great deal of paperwork, including certificates of clearness and approbation. It was a process thoroughly documented in the meeting minutes, and when all was 'clear' the marriage was then 'published' in the minutes. The form of the wedding itself, conducted in front of witnesses with no relics of the 'false apostate church', differed from many of their contemporaries' weddings and demonstrated their commitment to separate themselves from the 'false church'. Finally, the growing importance of the Women's Meetings and their role in the marriage approbation process demonstrated the desire of the early Quakers to further systematise the marriage approbation discipline.

In chapter two, it was examined how the Quaker marriage approbation system put into practice various aspects of early Quaker theology and spirituality. The marriage approbation discipline was not only shaped by the early Quakers' desire to maintain endogamous marriages, but also to set apart the early Quakers from the 'false church' (e.g. the Catholic Church and the Church of England) as the one and only True Church, and to demonstrate their life in a restored direct relationship with God. It was the critical focal point for the interpretation of their spirituality and theology of restoration out of the wilderness. Fox's understanding of the 'wilderness' as a place of exile set the context for the early Quakers' identity as the True Church. In the True Church, through an encounter with the inward light, all Quakers could call themselves 'Friends' of God as Adam originally did in the Garden of Eden. Their strident approbation procedures show how very seriously they took the endeavour of ensuring and maintaining this identity through a clear marriage discipline in the True Church and illuminate various aspects of their spirituality. The practice of disownment when one married a non-Friend was used in an effort to dissuade marriages 'with the world'. Refusing marriage by a priest in a church, refraining from the use of traditional vows and rings, and abstaining from elaborate wedding celebrations – all were stances against the forms of the 'false church' and an effort to separate themselves from the world. The notion that one had to 'wait' in the 'light' both individually and communally highlighted their belief that in their day and age direct revelation from God was possible. Unity not only with the divine but also with one another was promoted through the communal approbation of marriage. Conforming to unity in the Spirit of God, many faithful Friends consistently relied on hearing the voice of God within their consciences and sought communal approbation for marriage. These practices were intended to foster and demonstrate spiritual unity amongst one another and with the divine. Though exogamy did continue to plague the Quakers, the marriage approbation process remained unchanged for almost two hundred years, based largely on the notion of maintaining the True Church.

Their commitment to exemplify and to embody primitive Christianity also comes to light in Fox's efforts to connect the Quakers' marriage approbation practice directly to the early apostolic church. A marriage approbated communally, conducted in front of witnesses and recorded in a book was, according to Fox, a marriage performed like it was by the first Christians. Marriage conducted in this way connected them to the first generation of Christians who also enjoyed a direct and pure relationship with God, before the 'false church' took power and the True Church 'fled into exile'. In conclusion, the growing importance of marriage as the cornerstone of Gospel Family-Order was considered. The Quakers realised the importance of one's immediate family as an important locus of the instruction and maintenance of Quaker beliefs, as well as the encouragement of endogamous marriages. As prophecy and the apocalyptic fervour abated, the marriage approbation discipline and the adherence to the Gospel Family-Order grew in importance as the markers of the True Church.

Finally, in chapter three, the marriage approbation and marital relationship of Fox and Fell demonstrated a highly apocalyptic event, as their marital union was generally perceived as emblematic of the marriage of the Lamb and the New Jerusalem. As Fox was the forerunning prophet of the True Church emerging from the wilderness, so too was his marriage seen as a sign pointing to the new age at hand. The unity between the divine and the True Church culminated in the marriage of Fox and Fell, an aspired spiritual and physical demonstration of the divine marriage between Christ and the True Church coming up out of the wilderness. The spiritual gravity of their marriage was clearly evident in the testimonies given at their marriage and during their approbation process. Fox and Fell longed for future Quakers to follow in the marriage approbation process and practice, and to see their fellow Quakers' marriages as restored out of the Fall. But the marriage of Fox and Fell was a marriage uniquely esteemed by many in the community, as the great prophet married one of his converts, who would become one of the Quakers' most important leaders. However, a look into their personal correspondence throughout their just over twenty years of marriage betrays a very human relationship, with some disappointment and discord. Within their letters there is little reference to the original apocalyptic fervour of their marriage, but rather remnants of what appears to have been a genuinely affectionate and supportive relationship between two leaders of a movement. Their geographic separation did not necessarily mean there was a lack of affection, but it rather was a pragmatic and strategic way to keep the movement unified in both the North and the South of England. Fell did not revere Fox as the Lamb of God but rather seemed to care for him as a wife would for a husband. She relied on him for guidance and support, as he relied on her for physical and emotional support as well. What is evident is that their utmost, consistent concern was always the unity and propagation of the True Church.

While the early Quaker marriage approbation has been mentioned largely in passing in scholarship, this work has been an attempt to link directly the marriage approbation process with the Quakers' establishment of the True Church. It also sought to more fully explicate the conceptual rationale behind the preoccupation with marriage approbation and exogamy. The Fox and Fell marriage approbation process, likewise not considered at length in the context of the True Church coming up out of the wilderness, was a marriage approbation that in fact demonstrated these beliefs clearly, though in effect the marriage itself did not fully exhibit the original apocalyptic vision of their union. This study focused primarily on the marriage approbation discipline, and did not allow space for the consideration of the actual workings of Quaker marriages. What would be an interesting further study is to explore, beyond marriage approbation, how Quaker marital relationships functioned, and if there was any degree of gender equality demonstrated as compared to their contemporaries. But for the purposes of the task at hand, the link between the early Quaker marriage approbation process and their collective identity as the True Church seems clear.

After 1689, the Toleration Act, which allowed Quakers to meet freely for worship, began a new era for Quakers in which they were no longer heavily persecuted.[1] By the end of the seventeenth century, for the most part, the Quakers

---

[1] Dandelion, *An Introduction to Quakerism*, 54.

were no longer risking their lives by joining a 'despised minority'.[2] The Quakers became increasingly accepted by the state – they were no longer despised, but rather seen as a religious group quietly righteous in their homes and worship, engaging in society through successful (and notoriously fair) business dealings.[3] With the increase of rhetoric on the importance of the gospel-ordering of families it is plausible to argue that while the eschatological urgency faded, the early Quakers were still concerned with instilling and maintaining the identity of the True Church as separate from the world and the 'false church'. However, their strongly held identity as the one and only True Church began to decline in the eighteenth century amidst further internal schisms.[4] Their numbers also began a slow decline in the mid eighteenth century.[5] Some scholars attribute a subsequent gradual decline in numbers to the Quakers' decreasing spiritual fervour and eschatological urgency.[6] At this time, 80–90 per cent of all Quakers were not Friends because of personal conversion, but because they had been children of Quakers.[7] Evidently, Fox and other early Quakers' emphasis on raising children in the Quaker tradition was in part effective, but the slowing growth of membership was due to the lack of personal conversions.

By the mid nineteenth century, the collective Quaker identity as the one and only True Church faded. As membership began to wane and ecumenical perspectives shifted amongst the various schisms, most Friends grew increasingly detached from the notion of being *the* True Church, and saw themselves instead as being *a part of* the True Church. Subsequent generations of Friends were increasingly accepted by other Christians in the world of Protestant Christianity and denominationalism. Quaker scholar Pink Dandelion notes the influence of the Evangelical Revival in the United States, followed by Britain, brought about these theological disputes and resulted in disunity.[8] Interdenominational

---

[2] Vann, 'Nurture and Conversion in the Early Quaker Family', 641.

[3] Davies, *The Quakers in English Society*, 163.

[4] Dandelion, *An Introduction to Quakerism*, 80. See also Hancock, *The Peculium*. 'The primitive Friends said that Quakerism was *the Church*. Modern Friends say it is *a part of the Church* ... In 1658 there was not a Quaker living who did not believe Quakerism to be the one and only true Church of the living God. In 1858 there is not a Quaker living who does believe it' (Hancock, *The Peculium*, 8).

[5] Vann, 'Nurture and Conversion in the Early Quaker Family', 639–43; p. 641.

[6] Pink Dandelion, *The Quakers: A Very Short Introduction* (Oxford: Oxford University Press, 2008), 23–34; Davies, *The Quakers in English Society*, 162–5; Dandelion, *An Introduction to Quakerism*, 47ff. 'Braithwaite, Ingle, Moore, and Reay tend to suggest that Quakerism lost its eschatological edge in the 1660s and adopted a pragmatic approach essential for survival' (Dandelion, *An Introduction to Quakerism*, 47).

[7] Vann, 'Nurture and Conversion in the Early Quaker Family', 639–43; p. 641.

[8] Dandelion, *The Quakers*, 27. The discussion of the various schisms is too broad to be addressed here. Interior spirituality versus stress on scripture was an initial rift. For further

worship began to occur amongst Quakers, as younger Quakers grew interested in the growing field of higher criticism and biblical scholarship, and as the Society of Friends grew increasingly active in interdenominational social justice projects, such as the abolition of slavery and missions to foreign countries.[9]

With this shift from being the one and only True Church to being a part of the True Church, marriage with non-Quakers became accepted by many in the Quaker community as a thoroughgoing commitment to endogamous marriages abated in the meetings.[10] In the year 1860, over two hundred years after Fox, Fell and the early Quakers began preaching about the inward light and instituted the marriage discipline, various schisms within the Society of Friends officially abolished the rule of endogamy.[11] Without the identity as the one and only True Church, endogamous marriages were no longer required.

While Quakers could marry a non-Quaker, they still had to marry within the Meeting House, as well as gain approbation. Though endogamous marriages were no longer required amongst many Quakers, the practice of marriage

---

discussion of this topic, see Dandelion, *The Quakers*, 27ff.

[9] Dandelion, *The Quakers*, 34, 96.

[10] Thomas D. Hamm explains part of the internal debate within the United States Quaker community regarding endogamous marriages, and the eventual breakdown of this doctrine within Quakerism in the mid 1800s: 'The argument against the ban on marriage to non-Quakers was twofold. First, disownment on such grounds resulted in the loss of hundreds of otherwise blameless Friends every year. More seriously, renewal Friends [those seeking reform within Quakerism] argued, the marriage regulations encouraged hypocrisy. Offenders could retain their membership in such cases by an acknowledgment of wrongdoing to their monthly meeting. Reformers argued that the truly conscientious could not see the wrong of such marriages and thus felt that there was no fault for them to acknowledge, while others acknowledged their wrongdoing in an insincere and perfunctory way. Thus the society lost the most valuable members while retaining the least conscientious. During the 1850s Friends began to discuss proposals for change. In 1859, New York became the first yearly meeting to revise its marriage regulations. Under its new system, a Friend who married a non-Quaker had only to indicate that he or she wished to remain a member ... By 1880 the marriage regulations were gone. Not only were Friends free to marry whomever they chose, but also they were free to choose the form, and they flocked to more conventional ceremonies' (Thomas D. Hamm, *The Transformation of American Quakerism: Orthodox Friends, 1800–1907* [Indiana, IN: Indiana University Press, 1992], 51, 91). Many however chose not to return to the Quaker meetings. British Quaker reformer J.S. Rowntree argued in 1859 that disownment of Friends who married contrary to Quaker rule was 'the most influential *proximate* cause of the numerical decline of the Society' (Rowntree, *Quakerism Past and Present*, 153).

[11] Dandelion, *An Introduction to Quakerism*, 112. Most Friends could now marry a non-Friend without fear of disownment. Only a small, conservative remnant maintained the identity as a true church. A study regarding Quaker marriage approbation during this critical time would add further insight to the present study.

without a priest, in the presence of witnesses in a Quaker meeting, along with documentation in the form of a signed certificate remain generally practised within the Friends' tradition.[12] British Friends, as well as other Quakers throughout the world, typically share the following words at their marriage within a meeting for worship: 'Before God and this Meeting, I take thee, –, to be my wife (husband), promising, with God's help, to be unto thee a loving and faithful husband (wife) so long as we both shall live'.[13] The legality of Quaker marriages varies from country to country, but in Britain, following the Hardwicke Act of 1753 (which legalised the Quaker manner of marriage), their marriage form has been accepted as legally binding.[14] The wedding ceremonies vary as well, but many resemble those found in other churches in style, or may be a 'self-designed ritual with the couple choosing their own affirmations'.[15] The marriage discipline as outlined by Fox and Fell also demonstrated their continued earnest desire to avoid disharmonious marital relationships within the Society of Friends. Disharmony led to disunity and discord, characteristics abhorrent to the early Quaker doctrine of unity with the divine and with one another. Fox, Fell and others attempted to prevent difficult marriages from taking place within their communities, an objective that apparently was fairly effective throughout the seventeenth and eighteenth centuries. Disunity in marriage and between one another is still discouraged today amongst most Quaker circles. In the case of divorce, though the Evangelical Friends today allow for it, particularly in cases of 'domestic violence or abuse', they ardently believe 'God hates divorce'.[16]

Amongst the main divisions within modern day Quakerism – Liberal, Evangelical and Conservative Friends – the various groups differ slightly in their understanding of marriage and sexuality. The Evangelical Friends and the Conservative Friends are similar in their interpretations of the meaning of marriage. The Evangelical Friends, in their Yearly Meeting, designate pre-marital sex for example as undesirable, while retaining the 'gift of God' rhetoric of the early Quakers in reference to marriage: 'As a gift of God, a marriage covenant provides the framework for intimate companionship and is the only appropriate content for sexual fulfilment'.[17] In 1992, at their Yearly Meeting, the Conservative Friends of Ohio described marriage in remarkably similar terms to those of Fox and the early Quakers: 'Friends regard marriage as a continuing religious sacrament, not merely a civil contract', and as 'an ordinance of God, appointed for the help and blessing of both partners and for the right upbringing

---

[12] Dandelion, *An Introduction to Quakerism*, 219, 227.
[13] Ibid, 219.
[14] Ibid, 54, 219.
[15] Ibid, 219.
[16] Ibid, 225.
[17] Ibid, 225.

of the next generation'.[18] Interestingly, the majority of Quakers still seek 'the divine will' in regards to sexuality and marriage.[19] Despite the variations that have emerged amongst the current Quaker marital traditions, many of the tenets preached about marriage approbation by Fox, Fell and other early Quakers still remain in the undercurrents of Quaker rhetoric and thought today. The beliefs and practices surrounding marriage approbation of the seventeenth-century Quakers defined and strengthened the early movement, and have had lasting implications regarding marriage amongst the Quakers over four hundred years later, around the world today.[20]

---

[18] Ibid, 227.
[19] Ibid, 230. The Liberal Friends of Philadelphia in their Yearly Meeting asserted, 'Precisely because our sexuality is so powerful, seeking the divine will becomes all important'.
[20] Dandelion, *The Creation of Quaker Theory*, 55; Dandelion, *The Quakers*, 17–18.

Bibliography

Manuscript Sources

'Anna Burden to George Fox' (1663). Swarthmore Manuscripts, 3, no. 102. The Society of Friends Library London.

Burrough, Edward. *A general epistle to all the saints being a visitation of the Fathers love unto the whole flock of God: To be read in all the assemblies, of them, that meet together to worship the Father in spirit and truth*. Henry E. Huntington Library and Art Gallery, Wing B 6005.

Fox, George. *Concerning marriage, 1686*. Swarthmore Manuscripts, portfolio X, folio 66. The Society of Friends Library London.

Fox, George. *A New-England-fire-brand quenched something in answer unto a lying, slanderous book, entituled George Fox digged out of his burrows, &c. printed at Boston in the year 1676, of one Roger Williams of Providence in New-England* (1678). Henry E. Huntington Library and Art Gallery, Wing F 1864.

_____ *Right Marriage, 1679*. Swarthmore Manuscripts, vol. V, folio 44. The Society of Friends Library London.

_____ *Concerning marriage, 1686*. Swarthmore Manuscripts, portfolio X, folio 66. The Society of Friends Library London.

'Richard Sale to George Fox' (26 October 1655). Swarthmore Manuscripts, 4, no. 211. The Society of Friends Library London.

Smith, William. *William Smith to George Fox (April 21, 1664) From Nottingham Country Gaol*. Huntington Library Letters/Manuscripts: SHA 377.

Swarthmore Women's Meeting Minutes of Meetings 1650–1700. Vol. I, folio 44 (1676). The Society of Friends Library London.

Swarthmoor Women's Monthly Meeting Minutes 1671–1700. Reference number 16 b 4. Reduced photocopy. The Society of Friends Library London. Original copy held at Cumbria Record Office, Barrow.

'Thomas Holme to George Fox' (September 1654). Swarthmore Manuscripts, 4, no. 249. The Society of Friends Library London.

'Thomas Lower to George Fox and Margaret Fell' (4 January 1675). Spence Manuscripts, 3, folio 174. The Society of Friends Library London.

Printed Sources

Primary Sources

A copy of a marriage-certificate of the people called Quakers. Importing the method used among them: Humbly presented to the members of Parliament, to manifest the said peoples Christian care, and righteous proceedings, not admitting clandestine or unwarrantable marriages amongst them. And therefore they humbly request that their marriages may not be rendered clandestine or illegal, not they or their children exposed to suffering on that account. London: 1685.

Anonymous. *The Quakers answers, to the Quakers wedding, November 8, 1671.* London: Printed for Dorman Newman in the Kings-Armes in the Poultry, 1671.

Backhouse, James (Ed.) *Memoirs of Francis Howgill, with Extracts from His Writings.* York: W. Alexander and Son, 1828.

Barbour, Hugh and Arthur O. Roberts (Eds) *Early Quaker Writings, 1650–1700.* Wallington, PA: Pendle Hill Publications, 2004.

Bates, Elisha. *An Appeal to the Society of Friends.* London: Hamilton, Adams & Co., Whittaker & Co., and Edmund Fry & Son, 1836.

Baxter, Richard. *Reliquiae Baxterianae, or, Mr. Richard Baxters narrative of the most memorable passages of his life and times faithfully publish'd from his own original manuscript by Matthew Sylvester.* London: T. Parkhurst, I. Robinson, I. Lawrence and I. Dunton, 1696.

Booy, David (Ed.) *Autobiographical Writings by Early Quaker Women.* Farnham: Ashgate Publishing Limited, 2004.

Cadbury, Henry J. (Ed.) *Narrative Papers of George Fox: Unpublished or Uncollected, Edited from the Manuscripts with the Introductions and Notes.* Richmond, IN: Friends United Press, 1972.

Caton, William. *A journal of the life of that faithful servant and minister of the Gospel of Jesus Christ William Caton.* London: Thomas Northcott, 1689.

Cobbett, William and David Jardine. *Cobbett's complete collection of state trials and proceedings for high treason and other crimes and misdemeanors from the earliest period to the present time, Volume 6: Comprising the period from the reign of King Charles the Second, A.D. 1641, to the thirtieth year of the said reign, A.D. 1648.* London: R. Bagshaw, 1810.

Defoe, Daniel. *D'foe's answer to the Quakers catechism: or, a dark lanthorn for a friend of the light.* London, 1706.

Docwra, Anne. *An apostate-conscience exposed, and the miserable consequences thereof disclosed, for information and caution.* London: T. Sowle, 1699.

Ellwood, Thomas. *The History of the life of Thomas Ellwood: written by his own hand.* London: J. Sowle, 1714.

Faldo, John. *Quakerism no christianity, clearly and abundantly proven out of the writings of their chief leaders.* London: Ben Griffin, 1673.

Farnsworth, Richard. *Antichrist's Man of War.* London, 1653.

Fell, Margaret. *False Prophets, Antichrists, Deceivers.* London: Giles Calvert, 1655.

_____ *A testimonie of the touch-stone, for all professions, and all forms, and gathered churches (as they call them), of what sort soever to try their ground and foundation by and a tryal by the Scriptures, who the false prophets are, which are in the world, which John said should be in the last times; also, some of the ranters principles answered.* London: Thomas Simmons, 1656.

_____ *For Manasseth Ben Israel. The Call of the Jewes out of Babylon. Which is good tidings to the meek, liberty to the captives, and the opening of the prison doores.* London: Giles Calvert, 1656.

_____ *A Loving Salutation to the Seed of Abraham among the Jews, wherever they are scattered up and down upon the Face of the Earth.* Holland, 1658.

_____ *Concerning ministers made by the will of man.* London, 1659.

_____ *A call to the universall seed of God throughout the whole world to come up to the place of publick worship, which Christ Jesus the great prophet hath set up, who took not upon Him the nature of Angels, but the Seed of Abraham, whereby he comes to raise up Adams House and fallen State, into an Estate that shall never fall.* London, 1665.

_____ *Womens speaking justified, proved and allowed of by the Scriptures all such as speak by the spirit and power of the Lord Jesus: and how women were the first that preached the tidings of the resurrection of Jesus and were sent by Christ's own command before he ascended to the Father, John 20:17.* London, 1666.

_____ *A touch-stone, or, A perfect tryal by the Scriptures, of all the priests, bishops, and ministers, who have called themselves, the ministers of the Gospel whose time and day hath been in the last ages past, or rather in the night of apostacy: they are tried and weighed by the Scriptures of truth, and are found out of the life and power of the scriptures, and out of the spirit and doctrine of them that gave them forth, and quite contrary to their principle and practice, both Papists and Protestants: unto which is annexed, Womens speaking justified, &c.* London, 1667.

_____ *The daughter of Sion awakened and putting on strength she is arising and shaking her self out of the dust, and putting on beautiful garments.* London, 1677.

_____ *A brief collection of remarkable passages and occurrences relating to the birth, education, life, conversion, travels, services, and deep sufferings of that ancient, eminent, and faithful servant of the Lord Margaret Fell; but by her second marriage, Margaret Fox.* London: J. Sowle, 1710.

Fell Fox, Margaret Askew. *The life of Margaret Fox. Wife of George Fox. Compiled from her own narratives, and other sources; with a selection from her epistles,* etc. Philadelphia, PA: Association of Friends for the Diffusion of Religious and Useful Knowledge, 1859.

Fox, George. *A Warning to all Teachers of Children, Which are called School-Masters and School Mistresses, and To Parents, which doth send their Children to be taught by them; That all School-Masters and School Mistresses may train up Children in the fear of God.* London: Thomas Simmons, 1657.

_____ *The Great Mystery of the Great Whore Unfolded: and Antichrists Kingdom Revealed unto Destruction.* London: Thomas Simmons, 1659.

_____ *The Lamb's Officer is gone forth with the Lamb's Message which is the witness of God in all Consciences, to call them up to the Bar, the Judgment of the Lamb, in his day which is come.* London: Thomas Simmons, 1659.

_____ *Concerning Marriage: How God made them Male and Female in the Beginning, 7th Month 1659.* London: Thomas Simmons, 1661.

_____ *The spirit of envy, lying, and persecution made manifest for the sake of the simple hearted, that they may not be deceived by it: being an answer to a scandalous paper of John Harwoods, who in words professeth God, but in his works doeth deny Him, as may appear by what is herein written.* London, 1663.

_____ *Gospel Family-Order, Being a Short Discourse Concerning the Ordering of Families, both Whites, Blacks, and Indians.* London, 1676.

_____ *The true marriage declared, or, Seven testimoneys from the record of Scripture concerning the true marriages and such as are not according to the truth for Friends and all others concerned to read in the feare of the Lord.* London, 1679.

_____ *A Journal or Historical Account of the Life, Travels, and Sufferings, Christian Experiences and Labour of Love in the Work of the Ministry of that Ancient, Eminent and Faithful Servant of Jesus Christ, George Fox. The Second Part.* London: J. Sowle, 1709.

_____ *A Journal or historical account of the life, travels, sufferings, Christian experiences, and labour of love in the work of the ministry, of that Ancient, Eminent, and Faithful Servant of Jesus Christ. George Fox.* In two volumes. Leeds: Anthony Pickard, Sixth Edition, 1836.

_____ *Journal.* In two volumes. Norman Penney and T.E. Harrey (Eds). Cambridge: Cambridge University Press, 1911.

_____ *The Journal of George Fox: A Revised Edition by John Nickalls.* Cambridge: Cambridge University Press, 1952.

Fox, George and John Burnyeat. *A New-England-fire-brand quenched something in answer unto a lying, slanderous book, entituled George Fox digged out of his burrows, &c. printed at Boston in the year 1676, of one Roger Williams of Providence in New-England.* London, 1678. Henry E. Huntington Library and Art Gallery, Wing F 1864.

Fox, George and Francis Howgill. *Papists strength, principles, and doctrines.* London: Thomas Simmons, 1658.

Garman, Mary (Ed.) *Hidden in Plain Sight: Quaker Women's Writings, 1650–1700*. Wallingford, PA: Pendle Hill Publications, 1996.

Gibson, William. *A General epistle given forth in obedience to the God of peace for the preservation and increase of charity and unity*. London: Printed and sold by John Bringhurst, at the Sign of the Book in Grace-Church Street near Cornhill, 1682.

Gilpin, John. *The Quakers Shaken, or a warning against quaking*. London: Simon Waterson, 1655.

Glines, Elsa F. (Ed.) *Undaunted Zeal: The Letters of Margaret Fell*. Richmond, IN: Friends United Press, 2003.

Gouge, William. *Of Domesticall Duties: Eight Treatises*. London: Printed by John Haviland for William Bladen, 1622.

_____ *A Commentary on the whole Epistle to the Hebrews Vol. III (1655)*. Edinburgh: James Nichol, 1867.

Griffith, Matthew. *Bethel: Or a Forme for Families in which all sorts, of both sexes, are so squared, and framed by the Word of God, as they may best serve in their severall places, for usefull pieces in God's building*. London: Richard Allot, 1633.

Harwood, John. *To All People That profess the Eternal Truth of the Living God This is A True and real demonstration of the cause why I have denied, and do deny the Authority of George Fox, which is the original ground of the difference betwixt us*. London, 1663.

Hendricks, Elizabeth. *An Epistle to Friends in England, To be Read in their Assemblies in the Fear of the Lord*. London: 1672.

Higginson, Francis. *A Brief Relation of the Irreligion of the Northern Quakers wherein their horrid principles and practices, doctrines and manners are plainly exposed to the view of every intelligent reader*. London: H.R., 1653.

Hopper, Isaac (Ed.) *The Works of George Fox: A Collection of Many Select and Christian Epistles, Letters, and Testimonies, written on sundry occasions, by that Ancient, eminent, faithful Friend, and minister of Christ Jesus, George Fox. In Two Volumes*. Philadelphia, PA: Marcus T.C. Gould, 1831.

Keith, George. *The Magick of quakerism, or the Chief mysteries of Quakerism laid open*. London: Printed for Brabazon Aylmer senior and junior, at the Three Pigeons in Cornhill, 1707.

Lawrence, Thomas and George Fox. *Concerning Marriage. A Letter Sent to G.F. And with it, a Copy of an Answer to a Friends Letter Concerning Marriage. And some Queries, and his Reply to the Answer and Queries, and an Additional to G.F.'s Reply, containing 13 Queries concerning Marriage; Also the manner how the parties intending Marriage are to go together*. London: Benjamin Lawrence, 1663.

Loddington, William. *The Good Order of Truth Justified: wherein our womens meetings and order of marriage (by some more especially opposed) are proved agreeable to Scripture and sound reason.* Shoreditch: Andrew Sowle, 1685.

Mather, William. *A Novelty: Or, a Government of Women, Distinct from Men, Erected amongst some of the People, call'd Quakers.* London: Printed for Sarah Howkins, in George-yard, Lumbard-street, 1695.

Morland, Stephen C. (Ed.) *The Somersetshire Quarterly Meeting of the Society of Friends 1668–1699.* Somerset: Somerset Record Society, 1978.

Mortimer, Russell (Ed.) *Minute Book of the Men's Meeting of the Society of Friends in Bristol 1667–1686.* Gateshead: Northumberland Press Limited, 1971.

_____ *Minute Book of the Men's Meeting of the Society of Friends in Bristol 1686–1704.* Gateshead: Northumberland Press Limited, 1977.

Mucklow, William. *The Spirit of the Hat, or, The government of the Quakers among themselves as it hath been exercised of late years by George Fox and other leading-men in their Monday or second-dayes meeting at Devonshire-House.* London: F. Smith, 1673. Penington, Isaac. *Some Principles of the Elect People of God in scorn called Quakers.* London, 1671.

Penn, William. *Quakerism, a new nick-name for old Christianity being an answer to a book entituled Quakerism no Christianity, subscribed by J. Faldo.* s.l., 1672.

_____ *The invalidity of John Faldo's vindication of his book, called Quakerism no Christianity being a rejoinder in defence of the answer, intitled, Quakerism a new nick-name for old Christianity.* s.l., 1673.

_____ *A Collection of the Works of William Penn: In Two Volumes.* London: J. Sowle, 1726.

_____ *William Penn's Journal of his travels in Holland and Germany in 1677, in the service of the Gospel; containing several letters and addresses written while there to persons of eminence and quality.* London: Darton and Harvey, Fourth Edition, 1835.

Penney, Norman (Ed.) *The Household Account Book of Sarah Fell of Swarthmoor Hall.* Cambridge: Cambridge University Press, 1920.

_____ *The Short Journals and Itinerary Journals of George Fox.* Cambridge: Cambridge University Press, 1925.

Rigge, Ambros. *True Christianity Vindicated both in Praeceding, Present, and Succeeding Ages, And the Difference between them who are Christians indeed, and them who are falsly so called Manifested: being a collection of the several testimonies of the antient writers of the doctrine, lives and manners of the primitive Christians many ages ago, which being found coherent with the doctrine, lives and manners of the true Christians, who are nicked named Quakers at this day, are therefore made publick.* London, 1679.

Rogers, Daniel. *Matrimoniall Honour.* s.l., 1642.

Rogers, William. *The Christian-Quaker Distinguished from the Apostate.* London, 1680.

Speizman, Milton D. and Jane C. Kronick (Eds) 'A Seventeenth-Century Quaker Women's Declaration'. *Signs*, 1 no 1 (Autumn 1975).

Stevenson, Matthew. *The Quakers Wedding (October 24, 1671)*. London: Rowland Reynolds, 1671.

The Book of Common Prayer. Available at http://justus.anglican.org/resources/bcp/1559/Marriage_1559.htm (accessed 23 March 2011).

The testimony of William Erbery, left upon records for the saints of succeeding ages. Whereunto is added, The honest heretick being his tryal at Westminster. London: Printed for Giles Calvert, 1658.

Tuke, Samuel. *Selections from The Epistles, &c. of George Fox*. York: Alexander and Son, 1825.

Van Steere, Douglas. *Quaker Spirituality: Selected Writings*. Mahweh, NJ: Paulist Press, 1984.

Waite, Mary. *A Warning to All Friends who Professeth the Everlasting Truth of God*

Whately, William. *A Bride-Bush. Or a Direction for Married Persons Plainely describing the duties common to both, and peculiar to each of them*. London: Benjamin Fisher, 1623.

Whitehead, George. *The accuser of our brethren cast down in righteous judgment against that spirit of hellish jealousie vented in a great confused book, falsly entituled, The Christian-Quaker distinguished form the apostate and innovator, in five parts; the fallacy and force whereof being herein clearly detected & justly repelled*. London: John Bringhurst, 1681.

Whitton, Katherine. *An Epistle to Friends Everywhere*. London: Benjamin Clark, 1681.

Williams, Roger. *George Fox Digged Out of His Burrowes*. Boston: John Foster, 1676.

Winstanley, Gerrard. *The Saints Paradise or, the Fathers teaching the only satisfaction to waiting souls. Wherein many experiences are recorded, for the comfort of such as are under spirituall burning. The inward testimony is the souls strength*. London: Giles Calvert, 1648.

Women's Yearly Meeting at York: A Testimony for the Lord and his Truth (1686). From *The Book of Christian discipline of the Yearly Meeting of the Religious Society of Friends [Quakers] in Britain*, chapter 19, section 56. Available at http://qfp.quakerweb.org.uk/qfp19-56.html.

Secondary Sources

Achinstein, Sharon. 'Romance of the Spirit: Female Sexuality and Religious Desire in Early Modern England'. *English Literary History*, 69 no 2 (Summer 2002).

Adair, Richard. *Courtship, Illegitimacy and Marriage in Early Modern England*. Manchester: Manchester University Press, 1996.

Allen, Richard C. *Quaker Communities in Early Modern Wales: From Resistance to Respectability*. Cardiff: University of Wales Press, 2007.

Almond, Philip C. *Adam and Eve in Seventeenth-Century Thought*. Cambridge: Cambridge University Press, 1999.

Aptheker, Herbert. 'The Quakers and Negro Slavery'. *The Journal of Negro History*, 26 no 3 (July 1940).

Bailey, Joanne. *Unquiet Lives: Marriage and Marriage Breakdown in England, 1660–1800*. Cambridge: Cambridge University Press, 2003.

Bailey, Margaret Lewis. *Milton and Jakob Boehme: A Study of German Mysticism in Seventeenth-Century England*. New York, NY: Oxford University Press, 1914.

Bailey, Richard. *New Light on George Fox and Early Quakerism: The Making and Unmaking of a God*. San Francisco, CA: Mellen Research University Press, 1992.

Barbour, Hugh. *The Quakers in Puritan England*. New Haven, CT: Yale University Press, 1964.

_____ *Margaret Fell Speaking*. Wallingford, PA: Pendle Hill Publications, 1976.

Barbour, Hugh and J. William Frost. *The Quakers*. New York, NY: Greenwood Press, 1988.

Bauman, Richard. *Let Your Words Be Few: Symbolism of Speaking and Silence Among Seventeenth-Century Quakers*. Cambridge: Cambridge University Press, 1983.

Beckles, Hilary McD. *White Servitude and Black Slavery in Barbados, 1627–1715*. Knoxville, TN: The University of Tennessee Press, 1989.

Bickley, A.C. *George Fox and the Early Quakers*. London: Hodder and Stoughton, 1884.

Brailsford, Mabel. *Quaker Women, 1650–1690*. London: Duckworth, 1915.

Braithwaite, William C. *The Second Period of Quakerism*. s.l.: 1919.

_____ *The Beginnings of Quakerism to 1660*. Cambridge: Cambridge University Press, 1955.

_____ *The Second Period of Quakerism*. York: William Sessions Limited, 1979.

Brinton, Howard. *Friends for 300 Years: Beliefs and Practice of the Society of Friends since George Fox started the Quaker Movement*. London: George Allen & Unwin Limited, 1953.

Brown, Elisabeth Potts & Susan Mosher Stuard (Eds) *Witnesses for Change: Quaker Women Over Three Centuries*. New Brunswick: Rutgers University Press, 1989.

Brown, Sylvia (Ed.) *Women, Gender, and Radical Religion in Early Modern Europe*. Leiden: E.J. Brill, 2007.

Bruyneel, Sally. *Margaret Fell and the End of Time: The Theology of the Mother of Quakerism.* Waco, TX: Baylor University Press, 2010.

Bruyneel-Padgett, Sally. *The Eschatology of Margaret Fell (1614–1702) and Its Place in Her Theology and Ministry.* Durham: University of Durham, PhD Thesis, 2003.

Cadbury, Henry J. 'An Obscure Chapter of Quaker History'. *The Journal of Religion*, 24 no 3 (July 1944).

―――― 'Intercepted Correspondence of William Penn'. *Pennsylvania Magazine of History and Biography*, 70 (1946).

Capp, Bernard. *When Gossips Meet: Women, Family, and Neighbourhood in Early Modern England.* Oxford: Oxford University Press, 2003.

Clarkson, Thomas. *A Portraiture of Quakerism, Taken from a view of the moral education, discipline, peculiar customs, religious principles, political and civil economy, and character of the Society of Friends in Three Volumes: Volume II.* London: R. Taylor and Co., 1807.

Corns, Thomas N. and David Loewenstein (Eds) *The Emergence of Quaker Writing: Dissenting Literature in Seventeenth-Century England.* London: Frank Cass, 1995.

Cressy, David. *Birth, Marriage, and Death: Ritual, Religion, and the Life-Cycle in Tudor and Stuart England.* Oxford: Oxford University Press, 1997.

―――― *Travesties and Transgressions in Tudor and Stuart England: Tales of Discord and Dissension.* Oxford: Oxford University Press, 2000.

Cressy, David and Lori Anne Ferrell. *Religion and Society in Early Modern England: A Sourcebook.* New York, NY: Routledge, 2005.

Crossfield, Helen G. *Margaret Fox of Swarthmoor Hall.* London: Headley Brothers, 1913.

Dabhoiwala, Faramerz. 'The Construction of Honour, Reputation and Status in Late Seventeenth- and Early Eighteenth-Century England'. *Transactions of the Royal Historical Society*, 6 no 6 (1996).

Damrosh, Leopold. *The Sorrows of the Quaker Jesus: James Nayler and the Puritan Crackdown on the Free Spirit.* Harvard: Harvard University Press, 1996.

Dandelion, Pink (Ed.) *The Creation of Quaker Theory: Insider Perspectives.* Farnham: Ashgate Publishing Limited, 1994.

―――― *The Liturgies of Quakerism.* Farnham: Ashgate Publishing Limited, 2005.

―――― *An Introduction to Quakerism.* Cambridge: Cambridge University Press, 2007.

―――― *The Quakers: A Very Short Introduction.* Oxford: Oxford University Press, 2008.

Davies, Adrian. *The Quakers in English Society, 1655–1725.* Oxford: Clarendon Press, 2000.

Eales, Jacqueline. *Women in Early Modern England 1500–1700*. London: UCL Press Limited, 1998.

Erb, Peter. *Pietists, Protestants, and Mysticism: The Use of Late Medieval Scriptural Texts in the Work of Gottfried Arnold (1666–1714)*. London: The Scarecrow Press, Inc., 1989.

Fletcher, Anthony. *Gender, Sex, and Subordination in England 1500–1800*. Yale: Yale University Press, 1999.

Fraser, Antonia. *The Weaker Vessel: Woman's Lot in Seventeenth-Century England*. London: Methuen, 1984.

Frost, J. William. *The Quaker Family in Colonial America*. New York, NY: St. Martin's Press, 1973.

———— 'George Fox's Ambiguous Anti-slavery Legacy'. In Michael Mullett (Ed.) *New Light on George Fox (1624–1691): A Collection of Essays*. York: William Sessions Limited, 1991.

Gardiner, Judith. 'Margaret Fell Fox and Feminist Literary History: A "Mother in Israel" Calls to the Jews'. *Prose Studies*, 17 no 3 (1994).

Gibbons, B.J. *Gender in Mystical and Occult Thought: Behmenism and Its Development in England*. Cambridge: Cambridge University Press, 1996.

Gill, Catie. 'Identities in Quaker Women's Writing'. *Women's Writing*, 9 no 2 (2002).

———— *Women in the Seventeenth-Century Quaker Community: A Literary Study of Political Identities, 1650–1700*. Farnham: Ashgate Publishing Limited, 2005.

Gillis, John R. *For Better, For Worse: British Marriages, 1600 to the Present*. New York, NY: Oxford University Press, 1985.

Gowing, Laura. 'Women, Status and the Popular Culture of Dishonour'. *Transactions of the Royal Historical Society*, 6 no 6 (1996).

Gragg, Larry Dale. *The Quaker Community on Barbados: Challenging the Culture of the Planter Class*. Columbia, MO: University of Missouri Press, 2009.

Graves, M.P. 'Functions of Key Metaphors in Early Quaker Sermons, 1671–1700'. *Quarterly Journal of Speech*, 69 no 4 (1983): 364–78.

Greaves, Richard L. (Ed) *Triumph over Silence: Women in Protestant History*. London: Greenwood Press, 1985.

———— *God's Other Children: Protestant Nonconformists and the Emergence of Denominational Churches in Ireland, 1660–1700*. Stanford, CA: Stanford University Press, 1997.

Gucer, Kathryn. '"Not Heretofore Extant in Print": Where the Mad Ranters Are'. *Journal of the History of Ideas*, 61 no 1 (Jan 2000): 75–95.

Gwyn, D. *Apocalypse of the Word: The Life and Message of George Fox, 1624–1691*. Richmond, IN: Friends United Press, 1986.

Hamm, Thomas D. *The Transformation of American Quakerism: Orthodox Friends, 1800–1907*. Indiana, IN: Indiana University Press, 1992.

_____ *The Quakers in America*. New York, NY: Columbia University Press, 2003.

Hancock, Thomas. *The Peculium: An Endeavor to Throw Light on Some of the Causes of the Decline of the Society of Friends*. London: Smith, Elder and Co., 1859.

Hayden, Judith. *In Search of Margaret Fell*. London: Quaker Books, 2002.

Hill, Christopher. 'The Religion of Gerrard Winstanley'. *Past and Present: Supplement 5*. Oxford: The Past and Present Society, 1978.

_____ *The World Turned Upside Down*. London: Penguin Books, 1988.

_____ "Till the Conversion of the Jews'. In Richard H. Popkin (Ed.) *Millenarianism and Messianism in English Literature and Thought, 1650–1800*. Leiden: E.J. Brill, 1988.

_____ 'Quakers and the English Revolution'. In Michael Mullett (Ed.) *New Light on George Fox (1624–1691): A Collection of Essays*. York: William Sessions Limited, 1991.

_____ *The English Bible and the Seventeenth-Century Revolution*. London: Penguin Books, 1993.

Hinds, Hilary. *George Fox and Early Quaker Culture*. Manchester: Manchester University Press, 2011.

Horle, Craig. *The Quakers and the English Legal System 1660–1688*. Philadelphia, PA: The University of Pennsylvania Press, 1988.

Hudson, Winthrop S. 'Gerrard Winstanley and the Early Quakers'. *Church History*, 12 no 3 (September 1943).

_____ 'A Suppressed Chapter in Quaker History'. *The Journal of Religion*, 2 no 2 (April 1944).

Ingle, H. Larry. 'A Quaker Woman on Women's Roles: Mary Penington to Friends, 1678'. *Signs*, 16 no 3 (Spring 1991): 587–96.

_____ 'Unravelling George Fox: The Real Person'. In Michael Mullett (Ed.) *New Light on George Fox (1624–1691): A Collection of Essays*. York: William Sessions Limited, 1991.

_____ 'George Fox, Millenarian'. *Albion: A Quarterly Journal Concerned with British Studies: Published by The North American Conference on British Studies*, 24 no 2 (1992): 261–78.

_____ *First Among Friends: George Fox and the Creation of Quakerism*. New York, NY: Oxford University Press, 1994.

Ingram, Martin. *Church Courts, Sex and Marriage in England, 1570–1640*. Cambridge: Cambridge University Press, 1994.

Jacob, Margaret and James R. Jacob (Eds) *The Origins of Anglo-American Radicalism*. London: Allen & Unwin, 1984.

Jantzen, Grace M. 'Before the Rooster Crows: The Betrayal of Knowledge in Modernity'. *Literature and Theology*, 15 no 1 (March 2001): 1–24.

Jones, Rufus Matthew. *The Quakers in the American Colonies*. London: Macmillan, 1911.

_____ *Spiritual Reformers in the 16th and 17th Centuries*. London: Macmillan, 1914.

_____ *The Life and Message of George Fox 1624–1924*. New York, NY: Macmillan, 1924.

_____ *Studies in Mystical Religion*. London: Macmillan, 1936.

_____ *Faith and Practice of the Quakers*. Richmond, IN: Friends United, 1997.

Koyré, Alexandre. *Mystiques, Spirituels, Alchimistes du XVIe Siècle Allemand*. Paris: Gallimard, 1971.

Kunze, Bonnelyn Young. *The Family, Social and Religious Life of Margaret Fell*. Rochester: University of Rochester, PhD Thesis, 1986.

_____ 'An Unpublished Work by Margaret Fell'. *Proceedings of the American Philosophical Society*, 130 no 4 (Dec 1986): 424–52.

_____ 'Margaret Fell versus Thomas Rawlinson'. *Quaker History*, 77 (Spring 1988): 52–4.

_____ 'Religious Authority and Social Status in Seventeenth-Century England: The Friendship of Margaret Fell, George Fox, and William Penn'. *Church History*, 57 (June 1988): 170–86.

_____ *Margaret Fell and the Rise of Quakerism*. Stanford, CA: Stanford University Press, 1994.

Levy, Barry. *Quakers and the American Family: British Settlement in the Delaware Valley*. Oxford: Oxford University Press, 1988.

Lindberg, Carter. *The Pietist Theologians: An Introduction to Theology in the Seventeenth and Eighteenth Centuries*. Oxford: Blackwell, 2005.

Lloyd, Arnold. *Quaker Social History: 1669–1738*. London: Green and Co., 1950.

Louth, Andrew. *The Wilderness of God*. London: Darton, Longman & Todd, 2003.

Mack, Phyllis. 'Feminine Behavior and Radical Action: Franciscans, Quakers, and the Followers of Gandhi'. *Signs*, 11 no 3 (Spring 1986): 457–77.

_____ *Visionary Women: Ecstatic Prophecy in Seventeenth-Century England*. Berkeley, CA: University of California Press, 1994.

Macfarlane, Alan. *Marriage and Love in England: Modes of Reproduction 1300–1840*. Oxford: Basil Blackwell Limited, 1986.

Mahl, Mary R. (Ed.) *The Female Spectator: English Women Writers Before 1800*. Bloomington, IN: Indiana University Press, 1977.

Marietta, J.D. *The Reformation of American Quakerism, 1748–83*. Philadelphia, PA: University of Pennsylvania Press, 1984.

Marshall, Peter and Alec Ryrie (Eds) *The Beginnings of English Protestantism*. Cambridge: Cambridge University Press, 2002.

Matchinske, Megan. *Writing, Gender and State in Early-Modern England: Identity Formation and the Female Subject.* Cambridge: Cambridge University Press, 1998.

McGregor, J.F. and Barry Reay (Eds) *Radical Religion in the English Revolution.* New York, NY: Oxford University Press, 1984.

Mendelson, Sara H. 'The Weightiest Business: Marriage in an Upper-Gentry Family in 17th Century England'. *Past and Present,* 85 (1979): 126–35.

Mendelson, Sara Heller and Patricia Crawford. *Women in Early Modern England, 1550–1720.* Oxford: Clarendon Press, 1998.

Mentzer, Raymond A. and Andrew Spicer (Eds) *Society and Culture in the Huguenot World 1559–1685.* Cambridge: Cambridge University Press, 2002.

Midgley, James Herbert. *Margaret Fell (afterwards Margaret Fox): The Mother of the Early Quaker Church.* London: Headley Brothers, 1908.

Miller, Shannon. *Engendering the Fall: John Milton and the Seventeenth-Century Women Writers.* Philadelphia, PA: University of Pennsylvania Press, 2008.

Moore, Rosemary. 'Leaders of the Primitive Quaker Movement'. *Quaker History,* 85 (Spring 1996): 29–44.

―――― *The Light in Their Consciences: Early Quakers in Britain, 1646–1666.* University Park, PA: Pennsylvania State University Press, 2000.

Mortimer, Russell. 'Marriage Discipline in Early Friends: A Study in Church Administration Illustrated from the Bristol Records'. *Journal of Friends Historical Society,* 48 no 4 (Autumn 1957).

Mullett, Michael. *Radical Religious Movements in Early Modern Europe.* London: Allen & Unwin, 1980.

―――― (Ed.) *New Light on George Fox (1624–1691): A Collection of Essays.* York: William Sessions Limited, 1991.

Ng, Su Fang. *Literature and the Politics of Family in Seventeenth-Century England.* Cambridge: Cambridge University Press, 2007.

Nickalls, John. 'George Fox's Library'. *Journal of the Friends Historical Society,* 28 (1931).

Nuttall, Geoffrey F. *The Holy Spirit in Puritan Faith and Experience.* Oxford: B. Blackwell, 1947.

Osherow, Michele. *Biblical Women's Voices in Early Modern England.* Farnham: Ashgate Publishing Limited, 2009.

Outhwaite, R.B. *Clandestine Marriage in England: 1500–1850.* Cambridge: Cambridge University Press, 1995.

Popkin, Richard H. (Ed.) *Millenarianism and Messianism in English Literature and Thought, 1650–1800.* Leiden: E.J. Brill, 1988.

Popkin, Richard H. and Michael A. Singer (Eds) *Spinoza's Earliest Publication? The Hebrew translation of Margaret Fell's 'A Loving Salutation to the Seed of*

Abraham among the Jews, wherever they are scattered up and down upon the Face of the Earth'. Assen-Maastricht: Van Gorcum & Co., 1987.

Prior, Mary. *Women in English Society, 1500–1800*. London: Methuen, 1985.

Reay, Barry. 'The Social Origins of Early Quakerism'. *Journal of Interdisciplinary History*, 11 no 1 (1980): 55–72.

_____ 'Popular hostility towards Quakers in mid-seventeenth century England'. *Social History*, 5 no 3 (October 1980).

_____ *The Quakers and the English Revolution*. New York, NY: St. Martins, 1985.

_____ *Popular Cultures in England, 1550–1750*. London: Longman, 1998.

Rickman, Johanna. *Love, Lust, and License in Early Modern England: Illicit Sex and Nobility*. Farnham: Ashgate Publishing Limited, 2008.

Ross, Isabel. *Margaret Fell: Mother of Quakerism*. York: William Sessions Book Trust, 1996 (first published 1949).

Rowntree, John Stephenson. *Quakerism Past and Present: Being an Inquiry into the Causes Of Its Decline in Great Britain and Ireland*. London: Smith, Elder and Co., 1859.

Rules of Discipline of the Religious Society of Friends, with Advices: Being Extracts from the Minutes and Epistles of Their Yearly Meeting, Held in London, From its First Institution. London: Darton and Harvey, Third Edition, 1834.

Ruether, Rosemary Radford. *Introducing Redemption in Christian Feminism*. Sheffield: Sheffield Academic Press, 1998.

Sagafi-Nejad, Nancy Black. *Friends at the Bar: A Quaker View of Law, Conflict Resolution, and Legal Reform*. Albany, NY: State University of New York Press, 2011.

Scully, Jackie Leach and Pink Dandelion (Eds). *Good and Evil: Quaker Perspectives*. Farnham: Ashgate Publishing Limited, 2007.

Smith, Hilda L. *Reason's Disciples: Seventeenth-Century English Feminists*. Chicago, IL: University of Illinois Press, 1982.

_____ (Ed.) *Women Writers and the Early-Modern British Political Tradition*. Cambridge: Cambridge University Press, 1998.

_____ *All Men and Both Sexes: Gender, Politics, and the False Universal in England, 1640–1832*. University Park, PA: Pennsylvania State University Press, 2002.

Smith, Nigel. *Perfection Proclaimed: Language and Literature in English Radical Religion, 1640–1660*. Oxford: Oxford University Press, 1989.

_____ *Literature and Revolution in England, 1640–1660*. New Haven, CT: Yale University Press, 1994.

Spargo, Tamsin. 'The Fathers' Seductions: Improper Relations of Desire in Seventeenth-Century Nonconformist Communities'. *Tulsa Studies in Women's Literature*, 17 no 2 (Autumn 1998): 255–68.

Stone, Lawrence. *The Family, Sex, and Marriage in England 1500–1800*. London: Weidenfeld and Nicolson, 1977.

_____ *Uncertain Unions: Marriage in England, 1660–1753*. Oxford: Oxford University Press, 2001.

Sugar, Max. *Religious Identity and Behavior*. New York, NY: Plenum Publishers, 2002.

Tabbernee, William. *Montanist Inscriptions and Testimonia: Epigraphic Sources Illustrating the History of Montanism*. Macon, GA: Mercer University Press, 1997.

Tarter, Michele Lise. 'George Fox and Christian Gnosis'. In Pink Dandelion (Ed.) *The Creation of Quaker Theory: Insider Perspectives*. Farnham: Ashgate Publishing Limited, 1994.

Thickstun, Margaret Olofson. 'Writing the Spirit: Margaret Fell's Feminist Critique of Pauline Theology'. *Journal of the American Academy of Religion*, 63 (1995).

Thomas, Kathleen H. *The History and Significance of Quaker Symbols in Sect Formation*. Lewiston, NY: The Edwin Mellen Press, 2002.

Thomas, Keith. 'Women and the Civil War Sects'. *Past and Present* 13 (1958); reprinted in Trevor Aston (Ed.) *Crisis in Europe, 1560–1660*. London: Routledge & Kegan Paul, 1965.

_____ 'The Double Standard'. *Journal of History of Ideas*, 20 (1959).

Trevett, Christine (Ed.) *Women's Speaking Justified and Other 17th Century Quaker Writings about Women*. London: Quaker Home Service, 1989.

_____ *Women and Quakerism in the 17th Century*. York: Sessions Book Trust, 1991.

_____ *Quaker Women Prophets in England and Wales, 1650–1700*. Lewiston, NY: Edwin Mellen, 2000.

_____ '"Not Fit to be Printed": The Welsh, the Women and the Second Day's Morning Meeting'. *Journal of the Friends Historical Society*, 59 (2001).

Tual, Jacques. 'Sexual Equality and Conjugal Harmony: The Way to Celestial Bliss. A View of Early Quaker Matrimony'. *Journal of the Friends Historical Society*, 55 no 6 (1988).

Underhill, Evelyn. *Mysticism: A Study in the Nature and Development of Spiritual Consciousness*. Mineola, NY: Dover Publications, 2002.

Underwood, T.L. *Primitivism, Radicalism, and the Lamb's War: The Baptist-Quaker Conflict in Seventeenth-Century England*. Oxford: Oxford University Press, 1997.

Vann, Richard T. *The Social Development of English Quakerism, 1655–1755*. Cambridge, MA: Harvard University Press, 1969.

_____ 'Nurture and Conversion in the Early Quaker Family'. *Journal of Marriage and Family*, 31 (November 1969).

Vann, Richard T. and David Eversley. *Friends in Life and Death: The British and Irish Quakers in the Demographic Transition, 1650–1900*. Cambridge: Cambridge University Press, 1992.

Wagstaff, William R. *A History of the Society of Friends, compiled from its standard records and other authentic sources: Part I*. London: Wiley and Putnam, 1845.

Wallace, Terry H.S. *A Sincere and Constant Love: An Introduction to the Work of Margaret Fell*. Richmond, IN: Friends United Press, 1992.

Webb, Maria Lamb (1804–73). *The Fells of Swarthmoor Hall and Their Friends: with An Account of their Ancestor, Anne Askew, the Martyr. A Portraiture of Religious and Family Life in the Seventeenth Century, Compiled Chiefly from Original Letters and Other Documents, Never Before Published*. London: F.B. Kitto, 1867.

Weddle, Meredith Baldwin. *Walking in the Way of Peace: Quaker Pacifism in the Seventeenth Century*. Oxford: Oxford University Press, 2001.

Wells, Robert V. and Michael Zuckerman. 'Quaker Marriage Patterns in a Colonial Perspective'. *The William and Mary Quarterly: Third Series*, 29 no 3 (July 1972): 415–42.

Whitbeck, Caroline. 'Friends Historical Testimony on the Marriage Relationship'. *Friends Journal: Quaker Thought and Life Today*, 35 no 6 (June 1989).

Wiesner, Merry E. *Women and Gender in Early-Modern Europe*. Cambridge: Cambridge University Press, Second Edition, 2000.

Wiesner-Hanks, Merry E. *Christianity and Sexuality in the Early Modern World*. London: Routledge, 1999.

Wilcox, Catherine. *Theology and Women's Ministry in Seventeenth-Century English Quakerism: Handmaids of the Lord*. Lewiston, NY: Edwin Mellen, 1995.

Willen, Diane. 'Women and Religion in Early-Modern England'. In Sherrin Marshall (Ed.) *Women in Reformation and Counter-Reformation Europe*. Indianapolis, IN: Indiana University Press, 1989: 140–65.

Williams, David Ross. *Wilderness Lost: the Religious Origins of the American Mind*. London: Associated University Presses, Inc., 1989.

Williams, E.M. 'Women Preachers in the Civil War'. *Journal of Modern History*, 1 (1929): 561–9.

Wiltenburg, Joy. *Disorderly Women and Female Power in the Street Literature of Early Modern England and Germany*. Charlottesville, VA: University Press of Virginia, 1992.

Index

Barbados 30, 36, 62–5, 77–8, 101, 185, 189–96; *see also* slavery
Barclay, Robert 90, 125, 144–6, 148
Bugg, Francis 231, 234, 250–1

Caton, William 56–9, 170
celibacy 23, 164–5, 177, 179, 181 n.263, 229 n.109, 248–9, 251–3
certificates
    certificates of contrition 51, 66, 82 n.210, 106–108, 112, 146; *see also* letters of contrition; papers of contrition
    marriage certificates 23, 31–2, 46–9, 65, 67–8, 84–7, 91, 98, 112, 146–8, 154, 178, 272
    parental consent, of 51, 62–3, 66–7
Charles II 122, 210, 211 n.38, 258
children
    childbearing 179
    child rearing 118, 180–88, 270
    gospel family order 94, 97, 196
    illegitimacy concerns 7, 34–5, 45–7, 49–50, 75, 86 n.225
    provision for 45, 47, 75–6, 86 n.225, 110, 118, 213
    sanctification of 176–7
Church of England, the 3–7, 25, 27, 40–41, 43, 77, 124, 134–5, 136 n.92, 151, 163, 164–5 n.194, 166, 267
Cromwell, Oliver 1, 3 n.16, 122, 129, 131, 235
courtship 31–2, 38–9, 42, 53–62, 90–91
    Fell and Fox, of 208–14; *see also* marriage process of Fell and Fox

Dewsbury, William 4, 123, 126–7, 141, 142

Diggers, the 1, 4, 5 n.26
disownment of Quaker identity 70–73, 106, 112, 178–9 n.253, 209, 240, 268, 271 n.10
divorce 69 n.164, 108, 158 n.173, 174, 272

Ellwood, Thomas 14–16, 53–5, 153, 159 n.177, 215–16 n.57, 238, 241 n.147, 258
endogamy 7, 9, 31, 64–5, 69, 118, 143–4, 154, 183, 267,–8, 271
English Civil War, the 1–2, 32, 38, 62 n.137, 121–2, 126, 177–8 n.250
exogamy 31 n.1, 51, 63, 68–9, 71–2, 84, 107, 117, 154–61, 268–9

Faldo, John 167 n.201, 184
Family of Love 134 n.81, 136, 143
Fell, Charles 260–61
Fell, George 211 n.38, 258–61
Fell, Margaret
    Judaism and 20
    marriage approbation, role in constructing 7, 9, 31–3, 37, 43–5
    marriage to Fox *see* marital relationship of Fell and Fox; marriage process of Fell and Fox
    marriage to Thomas Fell 5, 47, 69 n.164; *see also* Thomas Fell
    mother in Israel 207, 225–6, 233, 238
    mother of Quakerism 4, 16–7
    nursing mother persona 19, 26–7, 225, 237–8
    origins of Quakerism and 4–5, 10, 16–21
    pregnancy, possibility of 249–51, 252 n.180

women's preaching, advocacy of 18–19, 211
Fell, Margaret (the younger) 155–61, 173
Fell, Rachel 211, 213–14, 219
Fell, Sarah 102, 107, 255 n.193, 256, 257, 262–3
Fell, Thomas 69 n.164, 158–61, 173
Fox, George
  childhood 11–12
  marriage approbation, role in constructing 7–8, 31–3, 37, 43–5
  marriage to Fell *see* marriage process of Fell and Fox; marital relationship of Fell and Fox
  nursing father persona 236
  opposition 218 n.63, 231, 234, 250–2
  perception of marriage to Fell *see* marriage process of Fell and Fox
  Quaker origins and 4–6, 13, 15–16
  self-perception 11–14, 26; *see also* Second Adam
Franck, Sebastian 134–5

Garden of Eden, the 8, 120, 127, 140–2, 161, 165–6, 173, 268; *see also* Paradise
Gibson, William 89–90, 146–8, 246–7
Gospel Family–Order 17, 118, 142 n.111, 180, 185–96, 265, 268, 270; *see also* motherhood
Gospel Order 9, 100, 118–19, 144, 147–9, 188
Gouge, William 38, 165–6, 171–3, 176, 182

Harwood, John 209–10, 240–42
Hendricks, Elizabeth 141–2
Hooton, Elizabeth 3, 15 n.59, 90, 260–61
Howgill, Francis 4, 52, 127 n.53, 236–7

Inward Light 3, 5, 6, 18, 59, 87, 108, 116, 127–8, 130, 132, 138–42, 153–4, 161–3, 167, 170–71, 187, 203 n.10, 234, 240, 242 n.149, 246, 253, 268, 271

Israelites *see* Judaism

Jones, Charles 76, 80, 82, 83 n.216
Judaism (or Jews) 90, 119–20, 137 n.93, 150 n144, 157, 160, 182, 231
  Fell, writings on 19–20, 129–30,
  Fox, writings on 19–20, 80, 115, 140, 147–8, 154–5, 169 n.209, 185–7, 195–6, 229
  mothers in Israel 182, 187, 199; *see also* Margaret Fell, mother in Israel

Keith, George 35–6

letters of contrition 106–108; *see also* certificates, certificates of contrition; papers of contrition
Loddington, William 64, 103
Love, John 62, 71, 75–6, 83
Lower (neé Fell), Mary 211, 219, 236, 256 n.199, 259
Lower, Thomas 211–14, 219–20, 236

marital relationship of Fell and Fox 19 n.82, 21–5, 253–66
  criticisms of 230–31, 234, 250–52
  Fell's perception of 8, 22, 27, 153, 227–8, 233–6
  Fox's perception of 8, 25, 27, 117, 153, 228–34
  pregnancy, possibility of *see* Margaret Fell
  undefiled bed 229, 247–9, 252
marriage certificates *see* certificates
marriage process of Fell and Fox; *see also* marital relationship of Fell and Fox
  approbation of 8, 9, 22, 30, 153, 199, 202, 204, 208–15, 217–26, 230 n.113, 268
  criticisms of 230–31, 234, 250–52
  secondary literature and 21–5
  testimonies 8, 215–24, 228, 234
    Fell, of 225–6, 236
    Fox, of 226–7

Marriage Act (1653) 41, 42–4, 62 n.137
Mather, William 97–9
Mollineux, Mary Southworth 161
motherhood 17, 26, 45, 55, 63, 70, 89, 94–5, 111, 149, 158, 165 n.195, 169
   gospel family order and 180–89
   Jerusalem as mother 232–3
   nursing mother *see* Margaret Fell, nursing mother persona
   sanctification and 179–80
Mucklow, William 231, 234

Nayler, James 3–4, 37, 133 n.73, 235, 238
Nicholas, Henry 134, 135 n.85, 136

papers of condemnation 66–7, 72–3, 107, 146
papers of contrition 71–4, 106–108, 146; *see also* certificates; certificates of contrition; letters of contrition
Paradise 59, 119–22, 129, 133, 138–42, 147, 165–7, 171, 199–202, 224, 230, 232, 246–7, 251
Penn, William 12 n.47, 19, 48 n.81, 56, 87, 90, 94, 117 n.8, 126, 134 n.78, 163, 167 n.201, 177–8, 184, 208, 216–17, 221–2, 237, 249–51, 262
Penington, Isaac 51–3, 58 n.124, 138
Penington, Mary 55–6, 59, 90, 95
Perrot, John 36–7

Ranters, the 2, 5 n.26, 18 n.76, 33, 121, 123, 125 n.42, 145 n.119, 148 n.39, 177 n.250, 252
Rigge, Ambros 92, 125–6

Salthouse, Thomas 216, 221
Second Adam 26, 139, 142–4, 173–4, 206, 231–3, 247
sexuality 33–6, 38, 84, 159 n.177, 161–79, 248 n.166, 273; *see also* celibacy; undefiled bed
slavery 120, 129, 130, 271
   marriage between slaves 189–96

Story, John 95, 99, 243
Swarthmoor Hall 17, 19 n.82, 57 n.113, 59, 100, 147, 207, 210, 211 n.38, 221, 264
   Fox and 251, 254–63
   Women's Meetings and *see* Women's Meetings

testimonies 6, 37, 152, 253; *see also* marriage process of Fell and Fox, testimonies
Toleration Act (1689) 264, 269–70
True Church, the 3, 5–9, 13, 26, 28, 115–30, 132, 135–9, 142–4, 147–66, 174–6, 179–80, 186, 189–93, 196, 201–202, 206, 230, 232, 234, 241, 253, 267–71

undefiled bed 9, 23, 117, 119, 161–2, 171–9, 193–4; *see also* marital relationship of Fell and Fox

weddings
   ceremonies 9, 32, 40–43, 44 n.58, 48 n.80, 83, 85–93, 127–8, 147–8, 164–5 n.194, 166
   Fell and Fox, of 214–15, 225–7; *see also* marriage process of Fell and Fox
   marriage by a priest 7, 25, 31, 34–5, 39–40, 43–8, 65–6, 69, 72–3, 84–90, 94, 105–108, 117, 121 n.26, 127, 156–7, 167, 170, 227, 268, 272
   vows 39–40, 86–8, 199, 216, 268
   wedding rings 41 n.45, 88–90, 127, 146 n.129, 268
West, William 155–61, 173, 235, 245
Whitehead, George 216, 220–21, 231–2, 238, 243
Whitton, Katherine 196–7
Wilkinson, John 95, 99, 243
Williams, Roger 137
Winstanley, Gerrard 121, 133–4, 136 n.86, 202 n.6

Women's Meetings 23, 32, 50, 64, 73,
　　93–112, 118, 182–3, 187 n.295,
　　191–2, 211, 217–18, 227–8, 261,
　　267
　Fox and 93–7, 101–103
　marriage approbation and 63 n.144,
　　103–4, 108–11

　opposition against 95–9
　Swarthmoor Hall, of 100–11, 261

Yeamans (neé Fell), Isabel 188, 213–4, 219,
　　223, 262

CPSIA information can be obtained
at www.ICGtesting.com
Printed in the USA
JSHW021511221219
3113JS00001BA/59